COMPUTERS
AND
SOCIAL
CHANGE

COMPUTERS AND SOCIAL CHANGE

INFORMATION, PROPERTY, AND POWER

JUDITH A. PERROLLE

Northeastern University

WADSWORTH PUBLISHING COMPANY
Belmont, California
A Division of Wadsworth, Inc.

Sociology Editor: Sheryl Fullerton
Production Editors: Leland Moss and Debbie McDaniel
Assistant Editor: Elizabeth Clayton
Managing Designers: MaryEllen Podgorski and Julia Scannell
Designer: Vargas/Williams/Design
Print Buyer: Barbara Britton
Copy Editor: Sylvia Stein
Compositor: Kachina
Cover: Vargas/Williams/Design
Illustrator: Susan Breitbard

Printed in the United States of America   **30**

1 2 3 4 5 6 7 8 9 10—91 90 89 88 87

ISBN 0-534-07464-2

Library of Congress Cataloging-in-Publication Data

Perrolle, Judith A.
   Computers and social change.

   Bibliography: p.
   Includes index
   1. Computers—Social aspects.   I. Title.
QA76.9.C66P47   1987   303.4'834   86-18979
ISBN 0-534-07464-2

for Jeanette
and her generation

they seize the instruments of harmony; they throw away
The spear, the bow, the gun . . .

—William Blake

CONTENTS

LIST OF FIGURES

LIST OF TABLES

LIST OF BOXES

PREFACE

Most texts about the computer and society introduce students to programming or to the way computers work. This book does something different. It provides a framework for understanding the social context and consequences of information technology, including the role of information in human history. Because the computer is a general-purpose tool for communication and control, it affects how people interact with one another, significantly changing what we know and how we behave. By altering the ways we create and use information, computers are contributing to changes in the ways property and power are distributed in society. The effects of computers on individual health and psychology, changing social relationships and workplaces, the protection of electronic information, the preservation of privacy, and the political and military uses of information technology have all become controversial public issues.

This book was "field tested" in university classes attended by a mix of liberal arts, computer science, engineering, and business students. Through their participation in Northeastern University's Cooperative Education Program, most of my students have been actively involved in the computer revolution, and their contributions helped shape what is intended as a text for future classes. Although I assume that the reader is already somewhat familiar with computers (the majority of students entering American colleges in 1985 had already written a computer program), computer terminology has been kept to a minimum. Technical terms that appear without explanation are included in a glossary. Because student backgrounds in the liberal arts are more diverse, introductory-level social science material has been included. Less experienced students have found this material a helpful introduction to the study of society; those with previous coursework have found that it links the humanistic and technological dimensions of their education.

To social scientists, the computer is both a technological product of a society's shared way of life and a source of social change. C. Wright Mills describes the perspective from which many sociologists approach the world as the ability to imagine "the intersection of biography and history" and the ability to see "private troubles" as "public issues." The social significance of the computer lies not only in the personal experiences of the people who interact with it as part of their individual biographies, but also as part of broad historical changes in societies. Problems such as "computer phobia" or "computer illiteracy" are more than the private troubles of some individuals; they are part of public issues of economic transformation and cultural change.

My own biography intersects with the history of computers at several points. In the 1950s I was an enthusiastic young observer of Sputnik and the first UNIVAC computers. Somewhere in my parents' attic is a cardboard "teaching machine" planned for a junior high school science fair project. As a humanities and electrical engineering student at MIT, I was introduced to the challenge of artificial intelligence and to the ethical role of professionals in social change by two excellent professors, Marvin Minsky and Noam Chomsky. In the late 1960s and early 1970s I worked in the computer software industry, first in Boston's Route 128 area and later in Asia, where I was faced with cultural and political issues that dwarfed the technical problems of transferring computers to developing countries. Returning to graduate school in sociology, I have since studied and taught about technology and social change. What began for me as an uncritical enthusiasm for computers became a set of "private troubles" coping with the human factors in computing and eventually a professional specialization.

Computer technology is sometimes viewed as a phenomenon to be promoted or opposed. A positive or optimistic approach to the benefits of computers is contrasted with the "other side"—a negative or pessimistic view. However, this perspective is often fatalistic, based on the belief that social change just "happens" to people and that nothing can be done about it. In this view, the only choice is whether the inevitable future is "good" or "bad." However, the purpose of the social sciences is not to judge the goodness or badness of phenomena but to describe them in ways that add to our understanding of the world and our ability to predict and influence change. Social science can also provide a basis for democratic policy, by clarifying the consequences of technological choices.

When the computer is viewed as part of large-scale social change, some of its effects may seem beyond our influence. Yet people's choices do make a difference. Studying the social impact of the computer can have practical consequences for our decisions about how computers will be used. As individuals, computer specialists and other professionals are often in a position to choose the direction of technological development. For example, a programmer coding a piece of medical records software may make a minor modification to improve accuracy and reduce human misery. An office manager may choose between two data display screens and save employees from eyestrain. Organized groups of people can affect larger public issues. Parents, through their local PTA and school board, may have a direct say about computer use in their children's schools. Voters, through their elected representatives, can influence local, state, and national legislation. Business and employee organizations can negotiate issues of computers in the workplace.

Considering the current popular enthusiasm for computers, much of this book may seem critical. Yet, if we allow our enthusiasm for technology to obscure our judgment of its consequences, we will restrict our capacity to make informed choices about the use of that technology. If we look only at social benefits, we will fail to assess social costs.

THE PLAN OF THE BOOK

The book is organized into four parts. The first examines the social context of information technology, providing a conceptual framework for understanding the computer as an information-processing tool capable of producing enormous changes in human life far beyond the immediate purposes for which it was designed. Chapter 1 introduces the basic concepts of information, society, and technology. A theoretical background to the study of social change is provided in Chapter 2. In Chapter 3, the role of information, property, and power in human history furnishes a perspective from which to assess the significance of the new information age.

The second part of the book considers immediate effects of computers by examining the subject of ergonomics—the human/technology interface. The individual's experience with computers is the subject of Chapter 4. The physiology of computer use is presented as a discussion of ergonomic research aimed at improving both health and productivity. Design criteria for computer equipment and systems that improve human well-being are considered, with a focus on aids for the handicapped. The topic of the psychology of the human/computer interaction is organized around the issue of self-esteem and includes computer phobia, the fascinations and hazards of hacking, sex differences in computer use, and the question of what "user-friendly" actually means in terms of human satisfaction. In Chapter 5, a review of recent research on social interaction among computer users connects the individual's experiences to broader public issues of family change, education, and new forms of recreation.

The third part of the book analyzes the computer transformation of work. Chapter 6 presents the computer's impact on work as part of a major industrial transformation of the economy accompanied by job dislocations as well as enhanced productivity. Chapter 7 considers microlevel issues of computers in the workplace, with emphasis on changing conditions of work in blue-collar, clerical, and professional occupations.

The fourth section of the book deals with the computer's effects on information, property, and power in democratic institutions. In Chapter 8, legal consequences of information as a form of property are examined. The transformation of legal institutions involves changes in copyright and patent protection for computer software and data bases. It also affects law enforcement and the definition of white-collar crime. The tension among legal guarantees of individual privacy, public "right to know," and emerging property rights in information are analyzed in terms of information's role in social control. Chapter 9 looks at the role of computers in society's decision-making processes. Ethical and professional issues are examined in a discussion of computer use in business, government, and military decisions.

ACKNOWLEDGMENTS

As participant observers in workplaces undergoing rapid technological change, my students informed and educated me. I gratefully acknowledge their contribution to this work, though any errors of interpretation and synthesis are my own. I thank them for their patience with experimental electronic manuscript drafts and with ideas in progress. Special thanks to Mike Gunderloy, Margery Rossi, William Swanson, and Cathy Swindlehurst for help with the tedious chores of proofreading and typing.

I am indebted to many colleagues for comments and criticisms at all stages of the work. Conversations with Joseph Weizenbaum clarified the moral and ethical framework of the project. The late Lila Leibowitz contributed to the anthropological perspective in Part One. For Part Two I am grateful for Sherry Turkle's psychological insights. Journal and conference panel reviewers' suggestions improved the theoretical argument about computers and capitalism, especially as it was applied to the transformation of work in Part Three. Members of the Harvard/MIT faculty study group on technology and civil liberties provided useful advice for Chapter 8; material prepared by the Computer Professionals for Social Responsibility was invaluable for completing Chapter 9. I am also indebted to the following reviewers for their valuable suggestions: Professors Harold Borko, U.C.L.A.; Gary Marx, M.I.T.; Bernard Phillips, Boston University; Charles Van Loan, Cornell University; John Williamson, Boston College; and Vance Wisenbaker, Eastern Kentucky University.

The people at Wadsworth Publishing have been enormously helpful, from the initial encouragement of John Moroney through the capable editorship of Sheryl Fullerton. The fact that I have never met face-to-face with Leland Moss or the other members of the production staff confirms my belief that cooperative projects with geographically dispersed participants can be an effective way to organize work in the information age.

Finally, to Gwendolyn Bikis, whose assistance with research, rough draft editing, word processing, and proofreading kept the manuscript going through hectic schedules and numerous revision, thanks are insufficient. She was a partner in producing the book and will be a partner in sharing the royalties.

Judith A. Perrolle
Boston, Massachusetts
August, 1986

COMPUTERS
AND
SOCIAL
CHANGE

THE
SOCIAL
CONTEXT
OF
INFORMATION
TECHNOLOGY

1

INFORMATION, SOCIETY, AND TECHNOLOGY

Have you ever found out how a machine works by reading the instructions or watching someone else use it? Have you ever wondered how that was possible? We take the familiar, like reading or observing human action, for granted. Something new is strange and challenging. Yet when we think about it, the familiar world of human society is just as intriguing as technological innovation. To understand the social consequences of computers, we will have to begin with a closer look at information, society, and technology.

THE NATURE OF INFORMATION

The computer is an information-processing tool, but what is information? In a book comparing many scientific disciplines' approaches to the study of information, Fritz Machlup observed:

> Information is not just one thing. It means different things to those who expound its characteristics, properties, elements, techniques, functions, dimensions, and connections. Evidently, there should be *something* that all the things called information have in common, but it is not easy to find out whether it is much more than the name. If we have failed and are still at sea, it may be our fault: Explorers do not always succeed in learning the language of the natives and their habits of thought. (Machlup, 1983:4–5)

In the following discussion that "something" called information is defined in ways useful to understanding the social consequences of computer technology.

It is important to keep in mind that each of the information sciences has its own definitions for its own particular purposes.

Data, Information, and Knowledge

The term *information* means many things in ordinary language. We may mean facts about the world represented by numbers, words, or pictures (for example, the word *trees*, a photograph of trees, or the phrase "four trees"). We also say "information" when we mean relationships among facts—for example, the sentences "There are more trees in Idaho than in Rhode Island" or "The maple is a common urban tree." Finally, in our evaluation or understanding of the world, we speak of information like "Oak makes better furniture than pine" and "Trees help maintain humidity and prevent erosion on hillsides." To distinguish among these meanings, we can use the words *data, information,* and *knowledge.*

DATA   **Data** are specific numerical or symbolic representations of "facts" about the world. Data are the elements to be input, stored, and manipulated by the computer. During data processing, computers are simply used to transform facts from one medium to another, for example, printing a payroll check from a list of employee salaries. **Validity** refers to the question of whether or not our data adequately describe the reality they were meant to. Invalid data can be due either to a correctable error (as when we type the wrong number at our terminal) or to a conceptual mistake (as, for example, if we used people's voter registration as Democrats or Republicans to represent which party they voted for in the 1984 election).

INFORMATION   **Information** is a useful organization and selection of facts, not the number of facts available. Information is a structural characteristic of data because it involves relationships among the represented facts. Computers process information when they store, retrieve, or rearrange relationships among data. For example, a telephone book contains data representing the names, addresses, and telephone numbers of people in a city. The information in the phone book is the relationship between name and phone number and the alphabetical order of the names. If you know someone's name, you can use that information to find his or her phone number. There is less information to help you find the name of someone whose phone number you have—you might have to look at each item of numerical data before you could use the information relating name to number. A phone book for the whole world would contain more data than a city directory, but it would not necessarily have more information unless it were organized by region or in other useful ways. Indeed, it might contain too much data for you to find the information you want. If you are trying to reach the only Mr. Ohara in your town, it would not be helpful to see how many Japanese or Irish men with that name have telephones.

A computerized phone book (such as those used by directory assistance operators) displays a page when a person's last name is typed in. When the operator selects the desired number, the computer plays a recording of the digits. Information is transmitted to the caller, but no new information is produced. In order to "make" information, new connections must be made between data. This can be done by physically rearranging the data, as when a person or a computer sorts records into some kind of meaningful order. As another example, if we put data on people's smoking habits together with data on lung cancer, we can produce information about the risks of smoking.

KNOWLEDGE   **Knowledge** involves evaluating and understanding information. It refers to the meaning of information with respect to human interests and purposes. You could have a great deal of information available to you, as for example in an encyclopedia, without understanding what it means or how to apply it to your own situation. In the telephone book example, your knowledge includes an understanding that the names refer to people and the number is a code enabling you to operate a machine to speak with them. Your understanding of how to use a telephone is a form of knowledge; so is an understanding of how it operates or knowing that you should call your mother on Mother's Day.

The expression "garbage in, garbage out" applies to computerized information in several ways. If the data are not valid, no amount of careful organization can make them represent reality. If the data are valid but our arrangement is at fault, then we will not have accurate information. Finally, if we have valid data organized to provide excellent information about things of no interest or value to us, we have not contributed to our knowledge.

INFORMATION HIERARCHIES   Sometimes information is treated as data, for example, each item in a library catalog might be a whole book of information on some subject. A library's data-retrieval system actually contains "information about information." **Higher-level information,** as information about information is called, is a way of structuring data. Humans understand and interact with the world using hierarchies of concepts that are also structured in this way. In this case "higher" means "more abstract," as in the following sequence of concepts:

this dog	a particular object
all dogs	a class of all similar objects
the word *dog*	a symbol representing a set of properties that defines a class of objects
concrete nouns	a set of words defining properties of classes of objects

High-level computer languages allow programmers to refer to complex sequences of machine instructions or arrangements of data with commands that "make sense" in human conceptual terms. Advanced information-processing systems allow users to create useful structures of relationships

FIGURE 1

RELATIONAL DATA BASE: AN EXAMPLE OF HIERARCHICALLY ORGANIZED INFORMATION

The physical structure of a relational data base is invisible to the user. Storage is handled conveniently for computer hardware:

LOCATION 1	LOCATION 2	LOCATION 3
data for green apples	data for red roses	data for yellow bananas
LOCATION 4	LOCATION 5	LOCATION 6
data for yellow roses	data for yellow apples	
LOCATION 7	LOCATION 8	LOCATION 9
	data for red apples	

The logical structure of a relational data base defines relationships among data entities. The user sees information arranged conveniently in tables. The user does not see any physical connections among the stored data. In other words, the order of items in rows and columns is not related to the position in storage:

SENTENCES

COLOR	THING	TEXT
RED	APPLES	ARE MOST POPULAR...
RED	ROSES	ARE SYMBOLS OF...
YELLOW	APPLES	INCLUDE THE GOLDEN...
GREEN	APPLES	ARE UNRIPE UNLESS...
YELLOW	BANANAS	ARE NOT RIPE UNTIL...
YELLOW	ROSES	GROW IN TEXAS AND...

TYPES

OBJECT	TYPE
APPLES	FRUIT
BANANAS	FRUIT
ROSES	FLOWER

among different levels of information. At higher levels of abstraction, much of the detail of data is lost, but important information is preserved. A road map, for example, preserves relationships among routes and distances between towns. It does not contain all the detail of an aerial photograph, but it is much easier to read.

When computer users complain that they cannot get the information they need from their data bases, it is often because their information-retrieval system is little better than a data-retrieval system. It does not let them select the relevant and avoid the unwanted detail. Relational data base architecture,

FIGURE 1
(continued)

A relational data base inquiry defines the relationship sought, using a high-level language. If the user types:

```
SELECT    COLOR, THING, TEXT
FROM      SENTENCES, TYPES
WHERE     COLOR = YELLOW
          AND THING = OBJECT
          AND TYPE = FRUIT
```

The computer will display information about yellow fruit. The user does not have to understand where or how the actual data is stored and can use a higher-level concept, fruit, instead of a list of all the kinds of fruit in the data base:

COLOR	THING	TEXT
YELLOW	BANANAS	ARE NOT RIPE UNTIL THEY HAVE SMALL, BROWN SPOTS.
YELLOW	APPLES	INCLUDE THE GOLDEN DELICIOUS VARIETY.

Source: E. F. Codd. "Relational Data Base: A Practical Foundation for Productivity," ACM Turing Award Lecture. *Communications of the ACM* 25(1982):109–17; C. J. Date. *An Introduction to Database Systems.* Reading, MA: Addison-Wesley, 1982.

shown in Figure 1, is one solution to the problem of how to match computer data structures to hierarchies of human concepts.

Cultural Information

Unlike that of many other animals, most human knowledge is learned, not genetically built in. As members of society, individuals do not carry all necessary information in our brains. Instead, we rely on the external storage of information in the form of culture. Though the word is popularly used to describe classical music and great literature, **culture** is a broad term defining the entire way of life shared by a people. Thus, the English language, several religions, a two-party political system, soap operas, computers, fast-food restaurants, and garbage cans are all part of U.S. culture. Although it includes our tools and artifacts, much of human culture consists of information. Language, ideas, beliefs about the meaning of life, and information representing our shared impressions of the physical world are all part of our culture.

SYMBOLS Symbols are the units of cultural information. A **symbol** is a meaningful representation of some object or abstract concept. Cultural knowledge is expressed and shared through our linguistic and nonverbal communications. Although we appear to have the genetic capacity to use symbols, we must be taught their meanings. Symbols can represent human emotion, as when we draw a heart to stand for love. Mathematical symbols, like the unknown x of algebra, represent abstract quantitative relationships. A crucifix and the American flag are examples of religious and political symbols. Money is used as a symbol for the economic value of goods and services. Words, which are themselves symbols, can be used to express visual and emotional concepts, as in poetry:

> For all the history of grief
> An empty doorway and a maple leaf
> *MacLeish, 1962:51*

In his capacity as Librarian of Congress, Archibald MacLeish expanded its collections to include film records of the Great Depression. These photographs of impoverished farm families, some of which can be seen in James Agee and Walker Evans' *Let Us Now Praise Famous Men* (1960), are powerful examples of visual symbols.

Although computers can "see" through video cameras and can "recognize" letters and numbers, they have not been very successful at handling abstract symbols, especially those referring to the emotional qualities of human experience.

SACRED AND SECULAR KNOWLEDGE   Historically, our culture has conceptually divided reality into the realms of the secular and the sacred. The **secular** is the ordinary reality of science and everyday life; the **sacred** is the realm of religion, magic, and the supernatural. As scientific understanding developed, the domain of the secular expanded to include first astronomy and physics, then chemistry and medicine. With each expansion, there was a social struggle to replace "mysterious" explanations with rational ones.

The secular and the sacred have not always been so differentiated. **Myths** traditionally explained human beings' relationships to time, life, death, and the sacred. According to Giorgio de Santillana and Hertha von Dechend (1969), myths are the form in which our earliest scientific knowledge was passed from generation to generation. Although a myth has the form of a story, it is a high-level symbolic expression of the workings of the universe.

Myths today still have the power to explain the human condition in symbolic terms. An example is the Greek myth of Prometheus, who was punished for bringing technology to humanity. Although we do not believe the story to be true in the scientific sense, scholars have used the Promethean theme to symbolize the unforeseen consequences of technological change. In applying it to computers, Patricia Warrick (1980) argues that the myth is a warning that nature has placed limits on humanity's ability to create and control.

THE TWO CULTURES   C. P. Snow (1963) introduced the term *the two cultures* to describe the twentieth-century split between seeking knowledge through scientific inquiry and through religion, the arts, and the humanities. Although cultural information is not neatly divided between the two, there can be misunderstanding between technically and humanistically oriented people, as if they came from different societies rather than sharing the same culture. Humanistic knowledge is a way of understanding what the world means. It is a source of wisdom based on our society's whole range of experience. Scientific knowledge is an understanding of how the world works, validated through a careful process of experimentation. We expect it to change over time. Although cultural symbols also change, we tend to experience meaning as absolute truth validated by inner faith.

Although no one can know his or her entire culture, people who learn only one way of understanding are ignoring an entire dimension of the world. If they knew only *how* things worked, their lives would be without meaning. If they were entirely ignorant of technological culture, they would find modern society full of mysterious phenomena and incomprehensible machines. When the two cultures merge, we find people who are intrigued by both the how and the why of the universe. Today in the computer field there are philosophers, musicians, and historians. There is also a growing number of applications of computers to the work of writers, artists, and performers. Computer science, by adding a new dimension to the question "What does it mean to think?" is making a new contribution to an age-old philosophical question as well as expanding the realm of rational scientific knowledge.

COMPUTERS AND CULTURAL VALUES   The selection criteria that define what information is relevant to human purposes are part of our culture's values. Values are the "oughts" and "shoulds" of society. American values include respect for individuals, freedom of speech, property rights, and equal opportunity for all. We also value things like automobiles, health, money, and fresh air. Sometimes, as in the case that we ought to be able to drive automobiles and we ought to be able to breathe unpolluted air, cultural values are contradictory.

Cultural analysts agree that computers themselves are highly valued in American society and that this evaluation will have consequences for the rest of culture. Sherry Turkle (1984) predicts that the experience of using computers will cause us to devalue calculation and logical reasoning. In other words, the ability to calculate and reason logically will become less important for people as it is done more and more by machines. Instead, she finds computer users placing higher value on emotion and feelings to define what it means to be human. Daniel Bell (1980b) believes that information will become more highly valued, with the ability to use it becoming our most important skill. Joseph Weizenbaum (1976) suggests that computer-based data will become so important that we will neglect our cultural traditions and fail to explore new nontechnological areas of human experience. Echoing the theme of the Promethean myth, he fears that our fascination with the power of the computer to let us design and control imaginary worlds will lead us to tragedy in the real world of social cooperation and conflict.

The Scientific Study of Information

Traditional Western culture distinguishes between ideas and material objects. The notion that an idea or other intangible form of information can be studied scientifically is still at odds with cultural beliefs about the difference between "real" objects and "unreal" abstractions. For people who believe that information is ideas and that scientists study things, measuring information seems impossible. However, to the physicist, our familiar world of solid objects is a representation of a complex universe consisting of energy and empty space. Since Einstein, we have known that matter itself is a form of energy. Yet scientists are like everyone else when it comes to treating tables or trucks as solid objects. At one level of understanding, they know that a truck isn't "really" solid. At another, they understand how to avoid them when crossing streets. Information, although it is abstract, is "real." It can be studied and measured.

MEASURING INFORMATION   Some people object to measuring information because they do not want to reduce symbolic expression of human relationships to mere data. The philosophical concept of **reification** describes such situations. For example, if I treat relationships (such as my friend's affection for me) as if they were merely things (the box of chocolates my friend gave me), I have lost something important about human love. If I evaluate a book by counting its pages, I will be mistaking data for knowledge. Because human understanding has many levels, a computer analysis of dancers' motions does not reduce the symbolic meaning of a ballet to numeric data. Instead, it offers an additional way to understand dance. The scientific study of information becomes reductionistic only if we mistake one approach to knowledge for the only way to understand.

Information measurement in the computer field owes a great deal to Norbert Wiener (1948) and Claude Shannon (1948). They define the quantity of information in a system as a statistical measure of its organization. Shannon defines information as the *probability* of a message being transmitted. In an electronic transmission system, *noise* is the highly probable, randomly generated part of the transmission (for example, the static during a telephone conversation). The *signal* is the nonrandom, information-bearing part of the transmission (for example, the voice you are listening to in a noisy room). Low-probability signals contain more information than highly probable ones. For example, if someone tells you something you've heard many times before (and that you expect to hear again and again), there's not much information in the message. A letter from my bank saying they made a $1000 mistake in my favor has more information than one saying I bounced another check.

Shannon's approach to measuring information is now most commonly used in the fields of telecommunications and electronics. In studies of information transmission, the focus is on the speed and accuracy with which data can be communicated through a variety of electronic media. This approach is invaluable for the development of computer hardware and communications software. It does not, however, really consider the meaning of information to humans. Thus, linguists have criticized Shannon's definition by pointing out that a sentence like "Fred is a dog" contains more information than the less probable sentence "Fred is a mammal," although Shannon's theory predicts it should contain less information. However, his theory was intended to deal with message transmission, not with symbolic meaning. Nor does Shannon's theory suggest that more data transmission through computer networks will automatically add to our cultural knowledge.

CYBERNETICS   From Wiener's perspective, information is the key to the way machines or living organisms modify their behavior to take into account the outcome of their previous actions. He defines the field of cybernetics as the study of communication and control mechanisms. **Feedback** is the information process that allows an organism or a machine to be self-regulating, as in the way a thermostat works to maintain room temperature. Information about how hot the room is causes the thermostat to turn the furnace on or off, changing room temperature in the desired direction. Another example is when you reach for a moving object. You see where your hand is in relation to the object, then use that information to correct the motion of your hand. This sort of feedback is an essential part of the way humans survive in their environments. The application of the feedback principle to computers allows us to build robots that can correct their own behavior. It also allows us to design "self-regulating" computer-controlled machinery.

ENTROPY   **Entropy** is a measure of the natural tendency of physical systems to become disordered. For example, most of us comb our hair every morning; by afternoon it has become disordered "all by itself." Throughout our lives we put energy into activities like combing hair or straightening up our rooms. By random processes of the wind blowing and our putting things down anywhere, our hair and our rooms get messy. Of all the possible ways our heads and houses could be arranged in space, only a few are "neat"; the vast majority is not. Thus, the untidy state is much more probable than the neat state. Wiener related information to negative entropy by showing that it had the same mathematical properties. Information is analogous to negative entropy because we use it to create improbable, organized systems.

When we pick up a room, we scan the situation, locating objects in space and comparing their distribution to our mental pattern for "clean room." We select each object that is out of place and put it where it belongs. As we identify, select, and relocate objects, we are using information to identify objects and feedback to observe and control our cleaning activity. As we work, the arrangement of objects in the room gets closer to our mental goal. To appreciate how you use information to create order, try cleaning a room in the dark. Unless you are blind and used to identifying objects by touch and sound, you may find cleaning difficult in the absence of visual information.

Computer novices often have a similar problem keeping track of their files. Without the visual feedback they are used to from books and papers, they have trouble imagining "where things are" in the computer. The fact that even experienced programmers find it helpful to draw "pictures" of their data structures illustrates the indispensability of mental concepts. We cannot create order unless we have in our minds a set of criteria for selecting and arranging the objects we are trying to organize. These nonrandom mental criteria for identification, selection, and action are themselves a form of information stored in the biochemical processes of our brains. In the computer they can be made part of information-processing software or hardware. In writing software or building hardware, they are an essential element of design. The entropy concept also underlies the need for computer hardware and software maintenance. Computer systems will become disorganized unless we continue to use energy and information to keep them functioning properly. Although maintenance jobs are sometimes viewed as unexciting, they are a large part of computer system costs and an essential ingredient in their success (Couger, 1985).

INFORMATION AND SOCIAL SCIENCE   Social scientists can measure cultural information by asking people what they believe or observing how they communicate. Historical research gives us information about past cultures. Studies of cognition and education provide us with knowledge of how people learn. Like cybernetics, sociology is concerned with how information affects behavior; the difference is that sociologists study social facts rather than physical phenomena.

A **social fact** is a cultural belief that has consequences for human behavior. Cultural values, for example, are social facts, as is the commonsense wisdom of "what everybody knows." Social facts may be true in the scientific sense (for example, if students major in computer science rather than history because they believe that starting salaries are lower for historians). Often, however, social facts are not true. As an example, so many people believe that AIDS can be spread by casual contact that individuals with the disease have been fired, evicted, and expelled from school. Our scientific information indicates that AIDS is spread only through sexual or direct blood product contact; yet the social fact of erroneous medical knowledge produces very real patterns of fear and discrimination. Among the social facts about computers are the following:

1. Computers never make mistakes.
2. If something went wrong, it was a computer error.

Like cultural values, social facts are sometimes contradictory.

MEASURING THE VALUE OF INFORMATION PRODUCTS   In order to make and sell such information products as computer software and data bases, businesses must be able to measure the costs of producing them and their value to consumers. We often think of an amount of information in terms of its physical form—a book of 354 pages or a disk file of twelve tracks. The cost of producing information, however, is often not directly related to its physical size. For example, if your job were to make a mailing list of parents who might be interested in buying ACME Baby Toys, you could start by computerizing records of recent births in your sales region. It would be expensive to travel to your state's department of vital statistics, select the appropriate birth certificates, and enter the data into your computer. Your final product, although large, would contain many names of people not interested in your line of toys. A potentially cheaper way to acquire a better list might be to hold a contest with ACME Baby Toys as prizes. The list of contestants would be your information product. In this case much of the work of identifying who might be interested in baby toys would be done by the prospective customers, not by ACME clerical employees. Even cheaper might be to sort and copy part of the National Toy Company's computerized records of who recently ordered baby toys. If National were unwilling to let ACME access the data, a bribe to one of their employees or an attempt to break into National's computer might obtain the list.

Besides the ethical and legal problems involved in this example, it should be clear that the cost of making an information product is not proportional to its size, but depends upon how much effort and expense is involved in locating, selecting, and arranging the data. Once made, an information product can be copied at little cost. Size is often exponentially related to the time it takes to search for information in a library or data base. It is not, however, a good measure of the original cost of making the product.

The value of information products to consumers depends upon what they want to know and how difficult it would be for them to get the information elsewhere. Because people expect some kinds of information to be freely available, they may resist having to pay for it. If the costs of information products are high, people will be tempted to copy them, feeling that "stealing" information doesn't really harm the original. As we will see in Chapter 8, the difficulties of protecting information property present a new challenge to our legal system.

IV   The Data Explosion and the Information Lag

The growth in the production of information (as estimated by the number of periodicals or books published each year or by the approximate number of words communicated by electronic media) has been called "the information explosion." As shown in Figure 2, the volume of printed media has grown quite slowly since the 1960s while electronic media (including television) have expanded rapidly. However, the information explosion should probably be called the "data explosion" because we are being confronted with facts faster than we are able to integrate them into useful information.

INFORMATION OVERLOAD   The human capacity to read or hear this increased volume of words has not expanded appreciably; nor is it clear that all

FIGURE 2

THE CHANGING PRODUCTION AND CONSUMPTION OF MEDIA

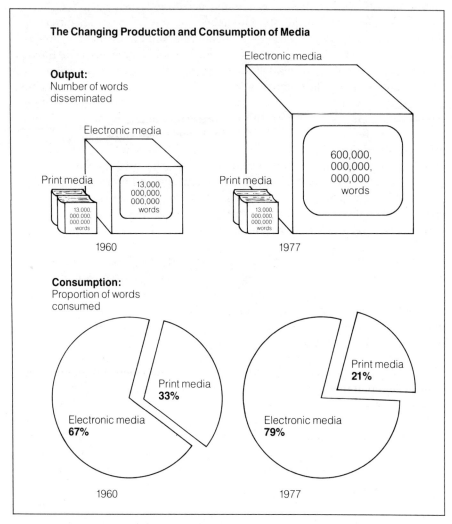

(From *The Boston Globe*, October 17, 1983, p. 44. Reprinted by permission.)

the words being produced are particularly relevant to us. According to many analysts, we are facing an information glut that threatens to overwhelm us. Results from a research project on how Americans process the news indicate that people have several effective strategies for handling too much information. According to Doris Graber (1984), we pay full attention to only about 20 percent of news we read and less than 10 percent of TV news. Our selection schemes ignore redundant information, accepting what is important to our own schema of thinking. Although we remember details haphazardly, our fund of general knowledge grows. By organizing data into information and information into knowledge, we are able to reduce the volume of facts with which we are confronted.

THE CRISIS IN DATA PROCESSING   According to James Martin (1984), the computer industry is facing its own information overload. We are often unable to get the information we need from our computerized data. There is an information lag between our relatively slow progress in information reorganization capability and our rapid progress in data base capacity. The information lag is a common experience of managers and others who want information relevant to their decision-making processes. A student might experience the information lag by locating 483 publications with a computerized library search—on the topic of a paper due the following week. The problem of how to select the "best" references is beyond the capacity of most automated library systems. A trip to a bookstore in search of an introduction to programming a home computer provides a similar experience. One computer professional suggests the following solution to dealing with the estimated 75 technical and 175 popular computer magazines: when the pile of unread publications gets two feet high, throw them all away because the technology they describe will be obsolete (Turner, 1984). More seriously, Hiltz and Turnoff (1985) point out that computer systems can be designed to reduce information overload by automatically filtering unwanted input. For instance, if you received your mail through a computer, you could program it to throw away junk mail (assuming you can clearly define what messages are to be considered junk).

INTELLIGENT INFORMATION PROCESSING   Computer science is grappling with how to get computers to apply human selection criteria to data. Many experts believe that if the information lag is to be overcome, we must develop software that can help us reorganize data and information. One solution is to find better ways to computerize graphs and pictures organized so that the observer can easily grasp the general concept displayed. Visual displays of quantitative information have a long history (Tufte, 1984) and are often preferred for business or educational data presentation.

The field of computer science known as **artificial intelligence,** or AI, involves the design of computer programs and automated equipment, such as industrial robots, with a limited capacity to behave in ways that at least resemble human thought processes. (For a technical survey see Barr and Feigenbaum, 1982; Hayes-Roth, 1983; Coombs, 1984. For a sympathetic popular history see McCorduck, 1979.) Information from the outside world can be sought, interpreted, and used as the basis for "heuristic" decisions, which in humans would be called "best guesses." The programs can, within the narrow range of the world to which they are applied, draw inferences, suggest solutions to previously unsolved problems, select relevant information according to their own internal criteria, and modify their own behavior as a result of the outcomes of their previous actions.

Automated programming, industrial planning by machine, and mechanization of the professions were topics on the agenda of a 1958 international conference on the emerging field of artificial intelligence (National Physical Laboratory, 1959). In addition to saving labor, managerial control and profitability were among the reasons advanced for supporting AI. During the next twenty-five years, artificial intelligence was transformed from academic research projects to widely publicized commercial applications (Feigenbaum and McCorduck, 1983; Hayes-Roth, 1984).

KNOWLEDGE ENGINEERING   Expert systems are a type of AI software developed by knowledge engineers. They promise that their software will "capture" experts' knowledge in programs that enable a less-skilled person to achieve expert results:

> Knowledge is a scarce resource whose refinement and reproduction creates wealth. Traditionally the transmission of knowledge from human expert to trainee has required education and internship years long. Extracting knowledge from humans and putting it in compatible forms can greatly reduce the costs of knowledge reproduction and exploitation . . . skill means having the right knowledge and using it effectively. Knowledge engineering addresses the problem of building skilled computer systems, aimed first at extracting the expert's knowledge and then at organizing it in an effective implementation. (Hayes-Roth, Waterman, and Lenat, 1983:5,13)

The theoretical possibility of representing human knowledge and decision-making processes in computer programs has been fiercely debated on both scientific and moral grounds, with the strongest objections coming from the philosopher Hubert Dreyfus in *What Computers Can't Do* (1972) and the artificial intelligence expert Joseph Weizenbaum in *Computer Power and Human Reason* (1976). One important issue is the degree to which human decision making is believed to be rational and logical. Intelligent software has been most successful in those applications in which the knowledge of human experts is very well understood and rather routine. Critics of knowledge engineering doubt that computers can actually be designed to handle any but the simplest symbolic meanings.

While the debate between those who argue that machines can think and those who argue that they can't continues (Boden, 1977; Haugeland, 1981), the practical success of "intelligent" programs that play chess, infer chemical structures from molecular data, and diagnose illnesses clearly indicates that artificial intelligence is being put to work at industrial and professional tasks, despite the reservations of many theorists.

The most ambitious practical proposals involving expert systems are those for the new fifth-generation "supercomputers" (Feigenbaum and McCorduck, 1983). Promising higher industrial productivity and greater national security, the proposals call for many areas of military and civilian expert decision making to be turned over to the faster, soon-to-be-smarter machines. In his critique of the fifth-generation idea, Weizenbaum (1983a) questions

Feigenbaum's assertion that computers will *produce* the future knowledge of the world, asking how we are to understand just what information the computer produces and how. But if information itself is seen as a product made for profit by efficiently organized employees, then information can be produced by the computer in the same way that products were made by the factory machinery of the first industrial revolution.

 ## SOCIETY

In order to understand social change, we must have a conceptual model of society. In other words we have to understand the "something" that is changing. Throughout history, models have been proposed as convenient ways of thinking about society. Society as a family with ruling "parents" or society as a self-contained city are two traditional models. During the past few centuries, models of society as an evolving biological organism or as a machine became popular with theorists. Today the model of society as a system is attractive to many social scientists.

System Characteristics

A **system** is a model of specific *components* interconnected by well-defined *relationships*. A system has a *boundary* that separates what is being analyzed from the rest of the world. **Input/output characteristics** describe the way the system interacts with its environment. An example of a simple system is a light bulb, a switch, and a battery connected by wires. The bulb, switch, and battery are components; the wires form the interconnections between them; everything else is considered outside the system. Light is a possible output; the hand that moves the switch can be considered an input.

Matter, energy, or information may flow through a system. **System processes** describe the way components act on one another and on the material flowing through. In this example energy flows through the system; the bulb processes electricity to produce light. The **function** of a system is a description of what it does; our example provides light. The function of a component is what it does within the system; the switch controls the flow of electricity and "remembers" if the light is on or off.

The **state** of a system is one possible arrangement of parts, with each part in a particular condition. For example, the bulb, switch, and battery system has six states:

1. bulb burning, switch on, battery supplying electricity
2. bulb not burning, switch off, battery not supplying electricity
3. bulb not burning, switch on, battery supplying electricity
4. bulb not burning, switch on, battery not supplying electricity

5. bulb burning, switch off, battery supplying electricity
6. bulb not burning, switch off, battery supplying electricity

When the system is functioning as intended, there are only two states, on and off, associated with whether or not the light is burning and the switch is set to accomplish that purpose. If we have a defective switch, a loose connection, a short circuit, a dead battery, or a burned-out light bulb, other states occur. An investigation of the way a system changes from one state to another can often help us understand how it functions (or doesn't). In investigating the relationship between the battery and the bulb, we would have discovered that electric current must flow through the system if the bulb is to burn and would have made an empirical generalization about the little world of our circuit.

Once we understand the functions of a system, we can begin to predict its behavior, such as expecting the bulb to light when we close the switch. However, even in the simplest of systems, we cannot predict all behavior (such as the conditions under which we can expect short circuits and burned-out bulbs). This is because our conceptual model oversimplifies the system we are observing and fails to take "everything" into account. This is especially so when we have ignored inputs to our system from the "outside" (How did the battery get charged?) or failed to understand lower-level processes (How does the electricity come from the battery and move in the wires?). Dead batteries and short circuits are understandable only if we know more about the situation than I have modeled here.

In large systems there are so many possible states and transitions between them that we cannot predict the system's behavior, except in probabilistic terms. For some large systems that can be formulated mathematically, we may build computer simulations or solve mathematical equations to make predictions. For less well defined systems, like weather patterns or societies, the mathematics of systems analysis is not usually applicable. For these the concept of a system remains a useful aid to thinking, but does not often provide a method of quantitative analysis.

Social Interaction

As part of identifying a shared way of life, cultural information defines appropriate behavior that individuals are expected to engage in. These behaviors occur as informal social interactions. A **social interaction** is a situation in which two or more persons communicate and modify each other's actions. Social interaction is the fundamental process in a social system. Conflict and cooperation are two of its forms.

INFORMATION AND POWER IN SOCIAL INTERACTIONS   From the individual's perspective, power is both the ability to affect the physical environment and the ability to make other people do what he or she wants them to do, even against their will. From a social perspective power is the ability of groups to interact successfully with one another and the physical world. The capacity to motivate individuals for cooperative purposes is an essential part of a society's ability to survive. Although we may think of our power in terms of military strength or superior technology, our abilities to investigate problems and negotiate solutions are just as important. Power is more than the ability to control others; it is also the capacity to organize effective action.

The exercise of power requires information. We cannot influence people unless we can communicate with them. We cannot offer them material rewards to do our bidding unless we can come to an understanding about the exchange. We cannot even forcibly move people or objects without knowledge of where they are vulnerable to our efforts. Planning long-term actions requires procedures to gather new information, evaluate it in terms of shared goals, and use it in choosing a course of action.

Although **coercive power,** or force, occurs in social interactions where the will of one person or group is imposed on the unwilling, most power in interactions is of other sorts. We may be influenced by others because we like or respect them. Or we may do what they ask because we think it is *legitimate* (right or legal) for them to give us orders. This is called **normative power,** named after **norms** (the unwritten—often even unspoken—rules for how to behave in specific situations). Wearing clothes in public, pausing in a conversation so that someone else may speak, and not eating one another are all examples of norms. We tend to think of norms as human nature, but children have to be taught to dress, not to interrupt, and not to bite. Norms are based on the more general moral and ethical principles, cultural values.

COMPUTERS AND SOCIAL INTERACTION   Because the meaning communicated through information exchange is the basis of social interaction, one important impact of computer technology is the way it changes the process of interpersonal communication. For example, microcomputer users are beginning to form electronically based communities organized around the exchange of information about common interests. However, in some computerized workplaces employees report increased isolation and a lack of human contact on the job. At present the computer's effects upon human social interaction appear contradictory, as will be explored in Part Two of this book.

Computers are sources of power for those who use them to manage information. In some cases individuals or groups can use computers to increase their power at the expense of others. In other cases the use of computers can make it easier for people to negotiate and reach decisions. The uses to which computer power can be put is the subject of the remaining sections of this book, especially in the concluding chapter, where their effect on social decision making is explored.

Social Structure

Repeated social interactions help define social groups such as families, teams, or networks of friends. Relatively stable patterns of interaction among components form the **social structure** of a group. When social scientists speak about the structure of a society (or smaller social group), they refer abstractly to the concept of relationships among people performing particular activities. For example, the structure of a softball team involves nine positions to be filled by real human beings, as well as a set of expected behaviors associated with each position. Because some social positions are similar, we can group them into such categories as infielders or outfielders to make a simpler model of social structure.

SOCIAL ROLES   Positions in society, along with their associated norms of expected behavior, are called **social roles.** Roles often occur in pairs— doctor and patient, parent and child, teacher and student, pitcher and batter. **Socialization** is the process through which we learn roles, norms, and values. From a systems perspective, socialization produces new components whose properties fit into the existing social structure. From an individual's perspective, socialization is the process of learning how to behave from families, schools, friends, and co-workers.

Some norms for roles are formal rules (in the baseball example, "Third basemen may not pitch to the batter"). Others (such as "Shortstops cover second base when the second baseman goes after an infield ground ball") are informal rules. In the case of formal rules, special social positions often exist (for example, baseball umpires) to make judgments and enforce expectations. In the case of informal rules, people apply social pressures (for example, dirty looks, praise, or a shove) to keep others behaving properly. Norms are essential to cooperative human activity. Social interactions to enforce norms are one part of the process of **social control.** Cooperative forms of social control (such as making sure a church congregation behaves reverently) are generally based on symbolic communication more than on force or economic power.

STATUS   Occupational roles—programmer, engineer, administrator, data-entry clerk, and so on—are an important part of how people define their "place" in an industrial society. When some of these roles are believed to be more honorable, powerful, or important than others, sociologists describe them as being ranked by **status.** For example, softball players will be evaluated by their teammates not only according to how well they can play, but also according to the status of their positions. Although players bring personal characteristics to their positions, right fielders are presumed to be less able than center fielders. Sometimes characteristics people are born with and cannot change (like sex or race) are used to assign them to positions or to make judgments about their expected performance. For example, when a female comes up to bat, many male outfielders move in on the assumption that she is a poor hitter. In professional baseball, black men were presumed unqualified until Jackie Robinson began his career. Part Three of this book examines the changing status of jobs in the computer field and looks at whether or not they are open to everyone on the basis of merit.

Institutions

The larger elements of social structure are fairly durable arrangements of social roles called **social institutions.** Schools, churches, and the family are all social institutions. These involve complex patterns of expected behavior on the part of people in such roles as student or professor, minister or member of the congregation, parent or child. The impact of computers on social institutions occurs as the technology changes how people are expected to behave. The use of computer-aided instruction, for example, can radically alter the mutual expectations of student and teacher.

Institutions like business, government, and the military make up the economic and political structure of society. Law, government, and the other institutions supporting a democratic political process in society perform several functions. They are the way we make decisions affecting all of us, the way we allocate our public resources, and the way we establish official agents of social control. As discussed in Part Four of this book, these institutions are changing as we introduce new information technologies.

Economic institutions produce and distribute society's material goods and services. As discussed in Part Three of this book, computer technology is being used to redefine the tasks expected of employees. Computer applications have begun to alter business management, product design and marketing, and financial record keeping. Computer technology is also being used to alter the basis of our economy—property.

PROPERTY   Property appears to be a relationship between people and things. For example, if you own land, a car, or a dog, you may think you have absolute control over what happens to it. However, social custom and law limit your rights to use and dispose of property. You can't plant marijuana or block public access to a beach without penalty. What you can do with (or in) your car is limited by regulations and standards of acceptable public behavior. Surveillance by your neighbors and the Society for the Prevention of Cruelty to Animals discourage you from beating your dog. Thus, property is also a relationship between people. Cultural information defines social controls over property as well as ownership rights.

Computers affect property relationships in two ways. First, information production is changing the kind of industries we have and the sorts of jobs that are available. Because some individuals and companies are better able to take advantage of these new economic opportunities, there will be some changes in society's distribution of wealth. The issue of how information is to be used is a second way computers affect property relationships. The democratic social values of privacy and freedom of information are often in direct conflict with our concepts of personal and corporate intellectual property.

STRATIFICATION   **Stratification** is an institution based upon the inheritance of unequally distributed property, power, and status. As with other systems, stratification is defined by specifying the relationships between components. Here the relationships are rankings based on resources, power, and influence. Individuals, families, or large groups with the same economic status (called **social classes**) are the components of a stratification system. When studying stratification, sociologists usually look at occupational roles or at classes. Processes within the stratification system include social interactions involving the exercise of influence and economic or political power, especially those that pass on advantages to our children.

In societies where individuals can choose their jobs and their religious and other group memberships and can raise or lower their social rank through education and effort, a person's place in the stratification system is only partly inherited. During the **social mobility** process, people rise or fall from the status they received at birth. Where mobility is possible, the institutions of family and education are where people acquire the skill and training to be "successful" or are judged "failures."

The computerization of work will probably be the major mechanism by which the computer alters social stratification. Because so much of a person's social status in modern societies depends upon his or her occupation, changes in the types of work people do (especially if there are corresponding changes in wages and salaries) can drastically alter the stratification system. If many new jobs are created at the "top" of the social structure, more individuals will have opportunities for success and status. If new jobs are created at the low-wage "bottom," gaining social status will be more difficult for individuals. If computers are seen as appropriate for use mainly by men, status opportunities for women could be restricted. If educational institutions provide computer science education mostly to middle-class children, poor and minority children could experience even greater barriers to occupational success.

TECHNOLOGY

Computer technology represents the introduction of new tools for communication, information processing, and remote control. Technology, however, is more than tools. It involves the social processes that produce tools, the social behaviors involved in using tools, and the socially defined meanings of tools. Information about tools, whether their designs or the techniques for using them, is an essential component of technology.

The Computer as a Tool

In its most general sense, a **tool** can be defined as an object or agent through which human activity is directed toward some goal. Thus, I can speak of my computer as a tool for writing this book. Calling my research assistant a tool for writing this book would be insulting as well as inaccurate. She has her own goals and is self-directing; tools are only instruments. In social relationships involving power *over* others, people are used as tools for someone else's purposes. In cooperative social interactions, people use the power of influence to arrive at common purposes.

The purpose of tools can be as specific as the zax (used for punching holes in slate roof tiles) or as general as a rope (with thousands of uses, from walking a dog to putting up a flag). Tools are often used as extensions of the human body to gather information about and to manipulate the physical world. Microscopes and telescopes extend our vision; hammers and space probes extend the reach of our hands. Cameras or tape recorders store sensory information; implements for writing and painting allow us to make a durable record of our ideas and visions that can be shared with others. Information-storage media, from stone carvings to data bases, facilitate the communication from person to person and from generation to generation.

Computers can be very specific tools (to play Pacman or to regulate a single engine's performance) or very general-purpose tools such as the programmable digital computer. Although many people consider the computer useful only for computation, it is a tool for *communication and control* of all types of information. Analog computers handle nondigital processes (like monitoring an electric current or room temperature); graphics capabilities enable us to process visual images and create pictures or charts; peripheral devices such as remote sensors can process sound, pressure, and a host of other data.

As an information-processing tool, the computer's major characteristic is the speed with which it processes extremely large quantities of data organized in complex ways. Although computers are popularly noted for their perfect accuracy, all large and interesting computer systems are prone to error. Hardware and software bugs, human errors in data entry, and the built-in possibilities for less than perfect performance (such as the ability to "guess" or "forget" that is a feature of the heuristic programs used in artificial intelligence) mean that computer technology is not the way to perfection. For many applications, however, computers offer more efficient means of performing tasks than previous methods.

The control over geographically dispersed information is an extremely important feature in business and military applications, as well as in the communications industry. Computer technology provides us with remote-controlled extensions of our bodies. Remote sensors used in satellites and space probes extend our ability to gather information on subjects as diverse as the vegetation of Africa or the rocks of Mars. With telecommunications equipment we can hear from any part of the earth and far into space. Via robotics we can work from a safe distance on the ocean floor or with hazardous chemicals. Also, and more dangerously, computerized weapons have vastly extended our ability to throw deadly objects at one another.

Computer-based decision making is at the heart of the integrated software systems now being designed for industrial and military uses. These systems coordinate decisions from the purchase of raw materials through automated plant operation to customer billing. Although the expression "com-

Hacker: A highly skilled person who is fascinated by the process of computer programming and motivated by the feeling that system resources ought to be available to anyone who can find clever ways to acquire, use, and redistribute them.

p... ...ome almost a folk saying,
d... ...singly sophisticated.
... ...ind, enhancing both our
... ...ganize information. Edward
... ...to a "partnership" in which
... ...ions while we exercise their
... ...ed by Joseph Weizenbaum
... ...an judgment and reason that
... ...w doors opened by computer
... ...important doors of human

Techniques

In order for any tool to be used successfully, ... technique for using it must be understood. A **technique** can be thought of as a method for performing a task without necessarily including a full scientific or social explanation of what is being done. The technique for driving a car can be learned without understanding how an internal combustion or diesel engine works. No knowledge of traffic rules or the consequences of driving head-on into a truck is necessary to put in the key, start the engine, put the car in gear, and go. The techniques of safe driving include a broader understanding of the social consequences of making a car run. The techniques of automotive design include a much fuller scientific knowledge of the principles behind the car's motion. The techniques of social impact assessment include understanding the consequences of the automobile for such phenomena as the patterns of urban residence, air pollution, energy resource use, and the industrial structure of the economy.

COMPUTER LITERACY AS A TECHNIQUE   The techniques for using the computer can be as simple as a set of instructions for turning on a machine and entering data into a packaged program or as complex as knowing how to design hardware or software. Most computer users, even those within the profession, know how to use the computer in a limited fashion. Very few of us could build one, especially if we had to create our own chips from materials we dug out of the earth, because contemporary industrial society depends upon an enormously complicated and interrelated set of techniques for making and using tools. Social theorists like Jacques Ellul (1964) have even suggested that our techniques are so complex that individuals can understand modern technology only in fragments.

Despite a great deal of recent discussion about "computer literacy," most individuals, even in the most computerized of futures, will need little knowledge about computers to go about their daily lives. Like driver's education for motorists, computer literacy can be the teaching of simple techniques. As automobile technology became more complicated, fewer drivers knew how to repair their own machines; fewer still could design and build them. Automobiles became, with the introduction of automatic transmission, more "user-friendly."

Hacker:

A highly skilled person who is fascinated by the process of computer programming and motivated by the feeling that system resources ought to be available to anyone who can find clever ways to acquire, use, and redistribute them.

p ... ome almost a folk saying,
d ... singly sophisticated.
... ...ind, enhancing both our
... ...ganize information. Edward
... to a "partnership" in which
... ions while we exercise their
... ...ed by Joseph Weizenbaum
... an judgment and reason that
... w doors opened by computer
... important doors of human

In order for any tool to be used successfully, ... technique for using it must be understood. A **technique** can be thought of as a method for performing a task without necessarily including a full scientific or social explanation of what is being done. The technique for driving a car can be learned without understanding how an internal combustion or diesel engine works. No knowledge of traffic rules or the consequences of driving head-on into a truck is necessary to put in the key, start the engine, put the car in gear, and go. The techniques of safe driving include a broader understanding of the social consequences of making a car run. The techniques of automotive design include a much fuller scientific knowledge of the principles behind the car's motion. The techniques of social impact assessment include understanding the consequences of the automobile for such phenomena as the patterns of urban residence, air pollution, energy resource use, and the industrial structure of the economy.

COMPUTER LITERACY AS A TECHNIQUE   The techniques for using the computer can be as simple as a set of instructions for turning on a machine and entering data into a packaged program or as complex as knowing how to design hardware or software. Most computer users, even those within the profession, know how to use the computer in a limited fashion. Very few of us could build one, especially if we had to create our own chips from materials we dug out of the earth, because contemporary industrial society depends upon an enormously complicated and interrelated set of techniques for making and using tools. Social theorists like Jacques Ellul (1964) have even suggested that our techniques are so complex that individuals can understand modern technology only in fragments.

Despite a great deal of recent discussion about "computer literacy," most individuals, even in the most computerized of futures, will need little knowledge about computers to go about their daily lives. Like driver's education for motorists, computer literacy can be the teaching of simple techniques. As automobile technology became more complicated, fewer drivers knew how to repair their own machines; fewer still could design and build them. Automobiles became, with the introduction of automatic transmission, more "user-friendly."

involving power *over* others, people are used as tools for someone else's purposes. In cooperative social interactions, people use the power of influence to arrive at common purposes.

The purpose of tools can be as specific as the zax (used for punching holes in slate roof tiles) or as general as a rope (with thousands of uses, from walking a dog to putting up a flag). Tools are often used as extensions of the human body to gather information about and to manipulate the physical world. Microscopes and telescopes extend our vision; hammers and space probes extend the reach of our hands. Cameras or tape recorders store sensory information; implements for writing and painting allow us to make a durable record of our ideas and visions that can be shared with others. Information-storage media, from stone carvings to data bases, facilitate the communication from person to person and from generation to generation.

Computers can be very specific tools (to play Pacman or to regulate a single engine's performance) or very general-purpose tools such as the programmable digital computer. Although many people consider the computer useful only for computation, it is a tool for *communication and control* of all types of information. Analog computers handle nondigital processes (like monitoring an electric current or room temperature); graphics capabilities enable us to process visual images and create pictures or charts; peripheral devices such as remote sensors can process sound, pressure, and a host of other data.

As an information-processing tool, the computer's major characteristic is the speed with which it processes extremely large quantities of data organized in complex ways. Although computers are popularly noted for their perfect accuracy, all large and interesting computer systems are prone to error. Hardware and software bugs, human errors in data entry, and the built-in possibilities for less than perfect performance (such as the ability to "guess" or "forget" that is a feature of the heuristic programs used in artificial intelligence) mean that computer technology is not the way to perfection. For many applications, however, computers offer more efficient means of performing tasks than previous methods.

The control over geographically dispersed information is an extremely important feature in business and military applications, as well as in the communications industry. Computer technology provides us with remote-controlled extensions of our bodies. Remote sensors used in satellites and space probes extend our ability to gather information on subjects as diverse as the vegetation of Africa or the rocks of Mars. With telecommunications equipment we can hear from any part of the earth and far into space. Via robotics we can work from a safe distance on the ocean floor or with hazardous chemicals. Also, and more dangerously, computerized weapons have vastly extended our ability to throw deadly objects at one another.

Computer-based decision making is at the heart of the integrated software systems now being designed for industrial and military uses. These systems coordinate decisions from the purchase of raw materials through automated plant operation to customer billing. Although the expression "com-

If we are to understand computers better than we do automobiles, we will have to look beyond the techniques for operating them. In the meantime many Americans are struggling to learn computer techniques. Because there are relatively few skilled individuals to help them, many people learn through a frustrating process of trial and error. Although part of the fascination of hacking is to discover some new (and usually unintended) way of using a computer system, most new users like to be shown. One of the major frustrations of computer use is when poor documentation makes a simple technique seem mysterious. Even for experienced users, a face-to-face human demonstration communicates technique more effectively than an instruction manual.

TECHNIQUE AND RITUAL   **Rituals,** group activities in which people act out symbolic meanings, are a very old form of transmitting cultural techniques. Although today we think of rituals as religious activity, in many nonindustrial societies there was no clear-cut separation between the sacred and the ordinary. For example, in one Southeast Asian society, agricultural rituals taught techniques of planting and harvesting as well as the sacred meaning of agriculture. Even when participants fail to grasp the meaning of what they do, the habit of ritual ensures that people will continue to behave in symbolically appropriate ways.

Some people learn to use computers in ritual ways. Without necessarily understanding what they are doing, they go through a sequence of steps to make a computer "magically" respond. Computer technology appears to them as one of the mysterious forces of the universe. Although it is still possible to transmit technique through ritual, there are more effective ways to learn to use a computer. Also, these private computer user rituals lack the social dimension of shared meaning that make public ritual a continuing element of human culture.

Ⅲ   Design

Whether by accident, through casual play, or on purpose according to an imagined mental plan, humans invent tools and develop the techniques to use them. In the case of the programmable digital computer, the original design (by Charles Babbage in the 1830s) preceded practical implementation by many decades. Babbage's design was itself inspired by earlier tools for operating looms and for aiding mathematical computations. Today computer scientists and engineers typically develop designs based upon mathematical principles and plan techniques well in advance of the actual construction of hardware or software.

CREATIVITY AND DESIGN   Industrial and artistic design can be considered two different processes (Jervis, 1984), but both are part of a creative process that connects imagination to rational judgment. Whether for a computer program, for a building, or for a painting, a design is an imaginative vision connected to a practical implementation plan. Design involves more than rational calculation of known facts. Creative people report that unconscious mental processes and play are important elements in the ability to reach past the boundaries of conventional knowledge and integrate formerly disparate information (Ghiselen, 1952).

Popular explanations of creativity often equate it with the free expression of unconscious impulses, with mysticism, or even with insanity (Becker, 1978). Misunderstandings of brain function lead some people to assume erroneously that creative people use the right half of their brains (the part that usually controls the left side of the body), and analytic people are "left-brained" (Calvin, 1983). Instead, creative people seem to be able to use their whole brains effectively. Creative designers imagine gestalts—whole, complex patterns—that can be translated into real-world materials and shared cultural symbols. The artist Michelangelo wrote that he "saw" his sculptures in the stone and had only to take away the extra material around them. Karl Marx said that the difference between an architect's building and a bee's hive is this human ability to build in the imagination.

COMPUTER-AIDED DESIGN   Computer-aided design (CAD) has been described as a partnership between human and tool in which the computer performs the drudgery and the person provides the creativity (Teicholtz, 1985). In programming, techniques like CAD are called "software tools." Although a tool is usually thought of as a material object and a technique as an abstract method for using tools, programs to help us design, write, and test other programs are tools. If the "things" with which we work are plans, designs, concepts, and data—in other words, if we are doing mental work—then some information products serve us as logical tools. We use them to create other information products, like programs or data bases.

The effects of computer-aided design are controversial. Proponents argue that CAD frees designers from time-consuming drafting and calculating chores, enabling them to try out more imaginative designs. CAD critics question whether such programs really encourage human creativity or, like Lego sets and coloring books, limit the range of possible plans. The effects of CAD on software design are similar to the use of standard parts for craftsmen. If a cabinetmaker's standard parts include screws and nails of certain sizes and boards of different thicknesses, there may be no negative impact on his or her ability to design furniture (and it saves the tedious labor of cutting trees and forming metal parts). If the cabinetmaker's standard parts are preformed cabinet pieces that merely have to be assembled, however, little original design is possible.

Ⅳ   Technology and Reification

By building tools and developing techniques, we make our imagined designs real. But sometimes as we embody our ideas in machines, we reify social relationships as well. In other words, we imagine that our relationships to one another are "in" the technology. An example of this is lie detection technology—polygraphs or the newer computerized voice stress analyzers.

Lying is a very human phenomenon. We often present ourselves to others as nicer, smarter, more attractive, or more competent than we secretly feel. People deliberately distort information for their own advantage or to try to avoid hurting others' feelings. Although we have strong norms against lying to gain power over others, we expect "white lies" in polite conversation. We often say, "I'm fine, thanks. How are you?" when we feel terrible.

Lie detectors, according to a review by the Office of Technology Assessment (Saxe, 1985), do not detect lies. They detect the physiological changes that occur when we are emotionally stressed. There are many sources of such stress besides guilt or fear of being caught at lying. If someone lies without guilt or fear, the technology detects nothing. An honest answer to an embarrassing or disturbing question will show evidence of stress. Yet some people treat lie detectors as if they were a technology to reveal the "truth" in others' minds without our having to go through the social interaction processes that establish trust in one another. For them, trust based on social interaction has been replaced by trust in technology.

At its best the use of computer technology will give us new power to cooperate and realize common purposes. At its worst the relationships between people and computers will be substituted for social ones. But before going on to examine in detail the effects of the human/computer interface, we must take a closer look at the process of social change and the question of why people began to use computers at all.

Treating a Social relationship or an Abstract concept as if it were an object

CHAPTER

2

SOCIAL CHANGE

How is the world today different from that of your childhood? As you think back over your biography, you probably remember historical events as small, personal experiences. I was a baby when the first atomic bomb exploded; my own baby watched television as men walked on the moon. As a child, I was impressed when my relatives replaced their farm horses with a tractor. I knew nothing about the transformation of American agriculture, but I did miss the animals. As we grow older, we learn to place the things that happen to us in a broader context. We also learn to act in order to bring about changes we believe are good. By the time I heard Martin Luther King speaking on the steps of the Lincoln Memorial, I was already a participant in the civil rights movement.

To understand social change, we need more than a sense of history as it happens to us; we need a conceptual framework in which to organize our experience. We also need theory to explain why change occurs and to give us some ability to predict our future. Only by anticipating the future can we make choices about social change.

A CONCEPTUAL MODELS OF SOCIAL CHANGE

The study of social change is almost as diverse as the study of society because any pattern of social life that can be identified can be examined over time. New symbols for the meaning of life in religion, art, literature, or music would be examples of cultural change. Changes in family, in the economy, or in the stratification system are structural changes and are the subject of large-scale or **macrotheory.** Changes in the way individuals interact with one another or in small group processes are the subject of small-scale or **microtheories.**

29

⅑   Theories and Paradigms

Theories are logically interconnected statements about the world that describe, explain, and predict the occurrence of phenomena. They are based on **empirical generalizations** about the world, which are in turn based upon analysis of our direct observations. Theories are made by the logical process of **induction,** reasoning from a set of cases to a general principle. We observe regularities in the world and identify a general pattern. We then systematically organize these patterns into an explanatory theory. According to Karl Popper (1968), science is the activity of validating theories. By the logical process of **deduction** (reasoning from general principles to expected outcomes), we develop specific hypotheses based on our theory. **Hypotheses** are statements about events expected to occur in particular circumstances. We **operationalize** hypotheses by specifying how we will go about measuring the phenomena of interest and interpreting the results. These results allow us to support our theory (it seemed correct in this particular case) or reject it (it failed in this case). The results of our tests can then be used to make new generalizations and construct new versions of our theory.

From a sociological viewpoint the process shown in Figure 3 is an oversimplification. Scientists, like other human beings, do not look for new explanations for what they already know. When a theory is widely believed, few scientists test its basic assumptions. Even when scientists themselves discover unexpected evidence, they can find it difficult to believe. A biologist who discovered a fish that was believed extinct for more than 50 million years wrote:

> I was irrationally quite fearful, because although my intellect was completely satisfied with the irrefutable evidence my eyes had seen, completely satisfied that the fish was indeed a true Coelacanth, it seemed too impossible, too fantastic, that this could have happened. A Coelacanth. Alive! (Westrum, 1985:51)

Although successful revolutionary thinkers might be rewarded by Nobel Prizes, they may be considered deviant for many years by their peers and have trouble publishing and financing their work (Keller, 1983). However, the strongest social controls in the scientific community are applied to those who break the methodological rules for "how to do science." For example, fraudulent presentation of data is considered a serious offense against the integrity of science itself.

PARADIGMS   According to Thomas Kuhn (1970), most scientists spend their time working out the details of existing theory. Inconsistencies are puzzles to be worked out within the accepted framework. Kuhn called these shared conceptual frameworks **paradigms** (general models of the way the world works). Unlike theories, they do not have well-operationalized propositions. For example, the concept that microorganisms cause disease is a paradigm.

FIGURE 3
THE RELATIONSHIP BETWEEN THEORIES AND "REALITY"

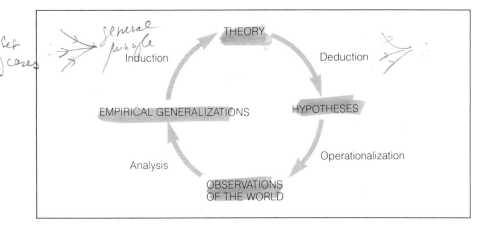

Early theories within the paradigm explained how particular bacteria caused specific diseases. The discovery of viruses resolved many puzzling inconsistencies. Today cancer researchers studying viruses are more likely to be funded than those studying some other factors, like diet, that lie outside the dominant paradigm.

Kuhn argued that a scientific revolution must occur before a new model of the world can replace an older paradigm. Although a new paradigm often leads to more adequate theories, a struggle in the scientific community can occur between supporters of the new and old concepts. Albert Einstein, whose concept of relativity created one scientific revolution, resisted quantum mechanics, with its disturbing vision of a probabilistic universe (Kevles, 1978:162–163).

PARADIGMS FOR SOCIETY   In social science there is more than one paradigm for society. Three of the major ones are functionalism, symbolic interactionism, and the conflict perspective. Functionalism and the conflict perspective are macrolevel; they are views of large-scale social structures and processes. The major difference between them is that functionalist theories tend to stress processes of social stability and gradual change; conflict theories tend to be about power, social disruptions, and relatively rapid transformations. Symbolic interactionism is a microlevel perspective; it is a conceptual model of social interaction between individuals and in groups.

The concept of society as a system was historically associated with functionalism. In recent years, however, conflict theories have appeared from a systems perspective, and interactionists have taken up the study of social networks (which implies a systems model of society). Because any collection of interconnected parts can be considered a system, such a model does not automatically provide us with an idea of how "the social system" works. That depends upon what kind of a system we conceive society to be.

Boundaries, Dynamics, and the Origins of Change

By selecting a boundary for their models of a social system, theorists define the domain of their study. Microtheorists might look at a small group, at families, or at a community. Many macrotheorists select a nation or a large cultural group (for example, Latin Americans). A few macrotheorists have begun to analyze what they call the **world-system,** an economically and politically interconnected system that covers almost the entire globe. Environmental sociologists even include other species and mineral resources in their model of the social system. If boundaries are drawn large, most social change occurs from within society; if boundaries are narrowly drawn, then external sources of social change become more probable. An economist studying U.S. production will have to consider imports, exports, or foreign investment as inputs or outputs of the system. To an economist looking at the global market, these phenomena appear as internal processes.

The question of where change comes from, however, involves more than drawing conceptual boundaries. It also involves the theorist's assessment of how the internal dynamics of a social system work and the extent to which external forces or internal processes determine the state changes of the system. Here there is a major difference between the functionalist and conflict paradigms in social science. External forces supplied by different cultures and the internal tensions between competing groups within a single culture are the agents of change for the conflict theorist. Internal processes of growth, evolution, and cyclical change are the sources of change for the functionalists.

Macrotheories

STRUCTURAL CHANGE   When some social positions, like particular occupations, are being eliminated or when new kinds of roles are being created, the process of **structural change** is occurring. Social scientists refer to structural change when the number of positions in a social structure is changing or when the roles for various positions are being redefined. A structure "grows" as new positions are added; it "shrinks" when positions are eliminated. The structure of the softball team can be changed by adding a short fielder (raising the number of players to ten) or by having the team at bat catch for themselves while the pitcher covers home plate (thus reducing the number of players to eight and changing the role of the pitcher).

Structural differentiation is one kind of structural change during which new, specialized roles develop. An informal game of "catch" turning into a more formal game with players each taking on a specific position instead of just throwing the ball around would be an example of structural differentiation. Modern industrial societies have a higher degree of structural differentiation than societies of the past. The use of computers contributes to structural differentiation in the economy by creating new specialized jobs.

Structural differentiation creates new roles, institutions, and other components of social structure; **social integration** connects new elements and coordinates their functions. In many theories of large-scale social change, integration takes place after a period of structural differentiation, making the new roles part of a common culture. Small-scale social integration can be seen when strangers are thrown together in social settings like sports training and emerge a team.

DYNAMIC STABILITY   Stability is important in all cultures, even in one that values progress and growth as much as does America. Models of society are usually relatively stable systems, with institutional structures that function to preserve order and maintain the pattern of culture. But in social theory, stability is not the same as no change at all. Instead, it refers to slow changes during which the important processes and structures of society are preserved. Even the most traditional societies of the past did change over time; the changes, however, were very slow compared to contemporary experiences.

Models of society with a tendency to "grow" and evolve have been popular since the nineteenth century. The systems on which they are based are found in biology and are examples of *dynamic stability*. Feedback mechanisms to restore system equilibrium following disruptions or changes are common features of these models. They imply a belief that societies have a "natural" tendency to preserve themselves.

PROGRESS   The choice of systems with dynamic stability as models for society is based on the historical experience of the contemporary industrial societies. But by ignoring the history of some other cultures that "failed," in the sense of being absorbed into another or extinguished by the death of all their members, these models also express our hopes for the continuation of our own way of life. The idea of social change as a form of progress is a thread that runs through the history of our social theory. *Progress* is a gradual transition from one system state to a "better" one. Although a desirable form of social change, it is by no means the only kind.

REVOLUTIONARY CHANGE   Models of revolutionary social change are not paradigms of endless social chaos. Instead, they are models of rapid, disruptive, and often violent state changes from one relatively stable form of society to another. In revolutionary theory, social tensions and conflict can be viewed as leading to improved social arrangements, making revolutions a form of evolution or progress. The difference between gradual and revolutionary social change is the degree to which existing social processes and structures are replaced.

Figure 4 illustrates stability and change in a simple system consisting of a marble in a cup inside a bowl. If you push on the marble gently, it will roll back down the cup, an example of dynamic stability. The relationship "marble in cup" is maintained. If you hit the marble harder, it will roll completely out of the cup into the bowl, an example of revolutionary change. There was a transformation from "marble in cup" to "marble in bowl." If you hit it harder still, the marble will roll out of the bowl and across the floor, an example of catastrophe.

FIGURE 4
STABILITY AND CHANGE IN A VERY SIMPLE SYSTEM

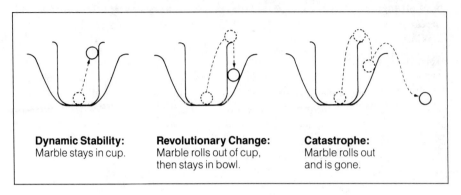

Dynamic Stability:
Marble stays in cup.

Revolutionary Change:
Marble rolls out of cup,
then stays in bowl.

Catastrophe:
Marble rolls out
and is gone.

CATASTROPHIC CHANGE   Dynamic stability and revolutionary change are not the only ways that systems behave. Readers familiar with computer time-sharing systems have probably experienced a kind of system degradation as response time gets longer and longer until we declare the system "down." Another kind of degradation occurs when the system cannot perform one or more of its functions. Sometimes a social organization (perhaps a bureaucratic office) stops "working" in this way.

Another type of system failure is probably also familiar—suddenly, and without much warning, the system "crashes" (perhaps losing our disk files in the process). Catastrophe theorists are beginning to apply these models to the social system, especially at the small-scale level of studying how companies or communities can cope with disaster (an earthquake, a power failure that destroys company data bases, or the accidental release of poison gas or radioactivity). Two interesting treatments of this type of system occurrence are Kai Erikson's (1976) sociological study of community relationships following a disastrous flood and Chinua Achebe's novel, *Things Fall Apart* (1959), about disruptive social change in an African village after the arrival of European colonists. What distinguishes catastrophic changes from gradual or revolutionary ones is that the society, community, or company, does not survive.

A Model of Information and Tools in Social Change

Information and tools play a role in social change because they modify how society interacts with its environment. Information is the way we interpret the world; tools are means of acting in it. Figure 5 illustrates these interrelationships.

THE SOCIAL INTERPRETATION OF REALITY   Besides our own *perceptions*, socially shared experiences and preconceived *cultural conceptions* contribute to our understanding of the world. Individuals grow up learning what to expect

FIGURE 5

INFORMATION AND TOOLS MODIFY THE RELATIONSHIPS BETWEEN THE SOCIAL SYSTEM AND THE PHYSICAL ENVIRONMENT

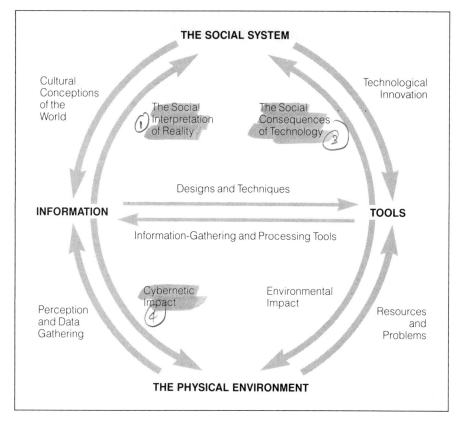

from their environment. In psychological experiments, individuals have been found to deny the evidence of their senses when confronted with the unexpected, especially when other human observers agree among themselves that the phenomenon isn't really occurring. The reverse process also seems to occur in some cases of mass hallucination, in which a group of people observes phenomena that are not present according to scientific instruments. This tendency of human groups to share a systematic pattern of information selection is essential to such recreations as watching cloud pictures with a friend or enjoying a magician's performance. It is also an essential part of the way humans develop and share a common culture.

Our sensory system is a biologically based data-gathering and processing system. However, the meaning of this "direct" experience is provided by our culture. Although many animal species have preprogrammed responses to environmental stimuli as a part of their genetic "hardware," humans base most of their actions on cultural "software." Each culture, through its language, beliefs, and habits, encourages individuals to select information from the world in socially appropriate ways and provides interpretations of the meaning of the information selected. An example of this is the differences among the ways skiers, Eskimos, and others experience snow. Eskimos and skiers have large vocabularies to describe snow according to its properties. Their activities, such as traveling downhill or building an igloo, depend upon their ability to distinguish different kinds of snow and to understand the meaning of those differences. For most of the rest of us, snow is not important enough to be perceived in such detail. Even the sensory data we do pay attention to is modified by our perceptual mechanisms for sight, hearing, touch, taste, and smell (Wallach, 1985). We receive input from the world only after it has been filtered through our nervous systems and our cultures.

With computer technology we can gather new kinds of information. New information sources will in turn alter our ability to predict and control physical and social events. As we change our ability to predict and act in the world, our cultural concepts of the world will change as well. For example, in computer modeling, we create abstract mathematical representations of our environments and even our internal biology. By using these models, we are able to make predictions or gain new insight into how the world "behaves." Sometimes these models become metaphors for features of society, the physical world, or the human nervous system, which are spoken of "as if" they were computers or computer programs. In fields such as neurophysiology, the computer has become so popular a metaphor that critics have to remind us that brains are not actually computers (Gregory, 1981; Calvin, 1983). One positive consequence of computer system metaphors for the world has been to improve our ability to conceive of complex "wholes" and to see ourselves as part of a single environmental and social system (Perrolle, 1985b). For many people this sense of being part of something much larger and more important than themselves is an experience of the sacred quality of human life.

INTERACTIONS WITH THE ENVIRONMENT THROUGH TOOLS   The environment can be thought of as presenting us with a set of problems of subsistence and survival and providing us with materials to solve those problems. Another way to put it is that the physical world contains resources that we use to satisfy biologically and socially defined needs. Through the process of *technological innovation*, societies have developed new tools to deal with the physical world as they perceive and interpret it. Some of these problems, like food and shelter, are basic to our species' biology. Other problems, like war and peace or economic production and distribution, are central to human interaction within a society and to the way societies interrelate. Historically, agricultural technology has provided food, weapons have been the means for aggression and defense, and craft and manufacturing tools have supplied products defined as socially desirable or necessary. Theories of technological innovation do not assume that an environmental problem, such as food shortages, will automatically produce a technical solution, like improved agriculture. Instead, these problems provide societies with a strong incentive to innovate.

Once developed, tools have an environmental impact on the world. The environmental effects of new technology have often been unexpected and undesirable. Our use of tools to solve one set of survival problems, for example, generating energy, can create another set of problems, such as environmental pollution. For this reason, gathering information about the consequences of technology and trying to anticipate potential new problems are important for our survival.

The conventional wisdom a few years ago was that the ecological movement and the computer revolution were in "fundamental harmony" (Hyman, 1980:126). Unlike our older "smokestack" industries, high technology was viewed as "environmentally sound, non-polluting, and non-destructive of the ecology of an overcrowded planet" (Martin, 1978:4). Recent experience has drastically altered our understanding. Serious air and groundwater pollution have been reported in California's Silicon Valley (LaDou, 1984; "Toxic World," 1984:3). The California Department of Health Services found miscarriages 2.4 times the normal rate and birth defects 2.5 times the normal rate in Silicon Valley communities whose water supplies were contaminated by high-tech manufacturing (Burton, 1985). Toxic exposures in the workplace have also been reported in the Massachusetts Route 128 area (Chinlund, 1984). The computer has a great potential as a tool for solving environmental problems, but its own environmental impact must be carefully assessed (Perrolle, 1984a).

THE SOCIAL CONSEQUENCES OF TECHNOLOGY   Tools affect the social system out of which they were developed. Although we are used to computers doing what we tell them to, computers and other tools also "tell" people what to do. Once we have told a computer what to do, we have created an environment that may define our pattern of activity. For example, once we have designed a computer's data base architecture and specified data-entry formats for a particular application, we often find ourselves limited to defining tasks and problems according to the computer system's capabilities and requirements. If it's easy to do on the computer, we do it. If it's difficult or impossible, we don't. For example, if a library has a computerized keyword index of journals going back to 1980, researchers might not take the time to look at older references. Also, if a particular topic is not covered by a keyword, fewer people will have the persistence to research it anyway.

The effects of a new tool can change individual social interactions. The use of a two-person saw requires a particular working relationship between a pair of people. If they are then put to work using new single-person power saws, the social relationship of the sawing team will be "broken." Many of the problems associated with introducing new computer systems are caused by this sort of alteration in people's social interactions. Although computer professionals have grown used to considering how user friendly an interactive program is to a single user, it is also important to consider how computer systems change people's interactions with one another. Even people who respond enthusiastically to computer networks report a reduction in social contact with co-workers (Diebold, 1984).

Technology also has consequences for larger patterns of human activity. For example, the widespread use of data-processing systems can radically change the number and kinds of jobs available to members of a society. This sort of feedback from tool use to the social pattern that produced the tool in the first place makes technological innovation a major source of social change. Often tools have a social impact far beyond their intended purpose, as illustrated in Box 1. To understand the consequences of a tool, one must understand the context in which it is used and something of how it came to be

BOX 1
THE SOCIAL CONSEQUENCES OF A TOOL

The ani-ani is a small knife held in the palm of the hand. It was used for centuries on the Indonesian island of Java to harvest rice. When ani-ani knives were replaced by longer-bladed sickles, observers predicted that this "progress" would lead to more efficient food production in the villages and a higher standard of nutrition. Although rice production did increase, so did poverty and malnutrition, especially among women and children. These undesirable consequences resulted because the ani-ani was more than a tool for cutting rice; it was also a tool for dividing up shares of the harvest. Because the ani-ani was inefficient, wealthy farmers with large fields had to call upon friends, relatives, and landless villagers to help them harvest. The landless poor (who were often divorced women with small children) thus had a means of livelihood and a share of the food.

When the sickles were introduced, the wealthier farmers began to hire work teams from outside the village at harvest time. This was partly to avoid the embarrassment of selecting only a few of the many people who had formerly helped them and partly because the entrepreneurial work teams went from village to village offering to do the harvest work for a smaller share of the rice than the poor villagers' traditional portion. The loss of jobs and the flow of food out of the village in the form of work team wages was blamed on the inevitability of modern "progress." The wealthy farmers grew wealthier because they now got their harvesting done more cheaply. Formerly cordial social relationships between rich and poor villagers were strained, and political unrest grew. Even the villagers' religion (in which the ani-ani played an important part) began to change.

Surely, the technological differences between the small knife and the large knife did not cause all this change. What did cause the change was the rearrangement of social relationships "needed" in order to use the sickles. Although there is an enormous difference between harvesting knives and computers, the use of computers, like that of all tools, can have unexpected consequences in the context of a complex pattern of social relationships.

Source: William L. Collier, Gunawan Wiradi, and Soentoro. "Recent Changes in Rice Harvesting Methods." *Bulletin of Indonesian Economic Studies* 9 (1973): pp. 36–45; Masao Kikuchi, Anwar Hafid, Chaerul Saleh, Sri Hartoyo, and Yujiro Hayami. "Class Differentiation, Labor Employment and Income Distribution in a West Java Village." *Rural Dynamics Series* No. 7 (1979). Bogor, Indonesia: Agro-Economic Survey.

developed. This entails examining the tool's unintended social and psychological effects as well as its intended purpose.

Once we understand the consequences of our tools, we can choose to use
or not to use them. Our choices, however, are severely limited by what is
available, what is considered socially appropriate, what we can afford, and
whether we are influenced or threatened. If computers are expensive and we
have little money, we cannot easily choose to own one. If the company we
work for installs a computer system, our choice to use it or not is usually the
choice of keeping our job or not. Because technology is a social product, it is
often developed or financed by individuals and groups who have a particular
interest in replacing older ways of doing things. Because new tools are rarely
of equal interest to everyone in a society, a considerable amount of conflict
can occur during the innovation process. For this reason we must also
understand society's economic and political processes in order to understand
technological change.

THE CYBERNETIC IMPACT   Cybernetics provides a useful conceptual model of
one-way information functions in the social system. It assumes that human
groups develop new behaviors based on feedback about the results of their
past actions. Many theories of how human society works involve an implicit
assumption of some sort of cybernetic steering mechanism (the "invisible
hand" of Adam Smith's free market theory is one example), but the relationship between cultural ideas and historical experiences in the material world
remains highly controversial in theories of social change. The term **cybernetic impact** is used here to refer to the way the informational content of culture
affects the physical world. It is not ideas by themselves, nor the physical
forms in which the ideas are expressed, but the way in which these ideas guide
human behavior that creates change.

Although we may think that technology alone has an environmental
impact, beach visitors walking barefoot can disturb the fragile ecology of a
sand dune. The intrusions of our very observations can alter physical phenomena. Our mental models, the way we organize information and apply it to
activity, are part of cybernetic impact. Research into how we create and use
mental models has been spurred by the fields of artificial intelligence and
expert systems, with many computer scientists and engineers hoping to create
"intelligent" problem-solving tools. However, no matter how intelligent our
tools, we must still choose what to apply them to. Our cultural values and the
choices we base on them are as significant as our technology.

THEORIES OF SOCIAL CHANGE

Because conceptual models serve only to guide our thinking about the general
shape of society, we need more specific theories in order to describe, predict,
and explain social change. However, unlike scientific fields, which have a

generally agreed upon theory, in the social sciences there is a great diversity. Two theories compete when they offer different interpretations and predictions for the same phenomenon. If both theories make predictions, research can be designed to compare them. Often, however, when social theories disagree on what the most important aspects of social change are, they cannot be compared easily, because they are really about different things. Because experiments can rarely be carried out to test social change theories (especially macrolevel ones), long periods of time must pass before the adequacy of competing theories can be compared.

Some theories of social change emphasize how societies confront external circumstances, for example, by arguing that such environmental problems as food shortages alter food production. Other theories focus on the historical relationships between societies or on the internal dynamics of a particular society. They identify external sources of change (like trade and warfare between cultures) and internal ones (like class struggles or the rise of new religions). The internal changes are often viewed as the result of internal dynamics and strains within society. In some of these theories, individuals play an important role in causing social change. In others, natural occurrences or historical circumstances are viewed as more important than the ideas or actions of any single person. In some of our oldest theories of social change, religious or mystical ideas caused change. In later ones, the "idealists" and the "materialists" debated over whether abstract concepts or physical conditions caused change. Contemporary perspectives tend to avoid single-cause explanations in favor of an analysis of the complex processes of social change in which ideas, material factors, and social relationships are intertwined.

The Classical Insights: Smith, Malthus, and Darwin

Modern theories of social system change owe a great deal to three thinkers of the late 1700s and early 1800s. Adam Smith, whose *Wealth of Nations* was published in 1776, was an economist who viewed markets as self-regulating systems. His term *the invisible hand* describes the principle of feedback in economic systems. He argued that this invisible force provides stability in an ideal "free market." Smith's theory asserts that supply and demand are interconnected in ways that automatically regulate prices and production. Smith's work affected the thinking of all later economic thinkers and is still considered valid by conservative economists. Later theorists did not dispute Smith's finding that supply and demand are interconnected, but argued that the relationship is not sufficient to provide social stability, especially when low production and high prices affect the poor. Neoclassical economists are often concerned with the effects of government and business efforts to modify supply and demand. Later social theorists were concerned about the effects of economic system fluctuations on social welfare.

Thomas Malthus (1766–1834) was an English parson who believed in the moral inferiority of the poor. His *Essay on the Principle of Population* (1798) warned of the dangers of overpopulation caused by the failure of moral restraint on the reproductive urge. He predicted that without abstinence from sexual relationships, positive checks (war, famine, and disease) or the preventive checks of vice (contraception and abortion) would act to halt unrestrained population growth. Malthus is theoretically important not for his views of the moral depravity of the lower classes but for his insight into the dynamics of population growth and the importance of the material conditions (especially food supplies) of social life. Changes in food production technology (like the Green Revolution of the 1960s), changes in the distribution of food (as in revolutions that overthrow a landowning aristocracy), or changes in reproductive behavior (the demographic transition) have often been used as evidence that Malthus's theory was wrong. Modern limits-to-growth theorists, however, argue that, for any particular patterns of human reproduction, food production, and economic distribution, the Malthusian checks to population growth are constraints on a social system.

Charles Darwin (1804–1882) was a naturalist whose 1859 publication of *The Origin of Species by Means of Natural Selection* created an intellectual furor by arguing that species had evolved from primitive ancestors. Darwin proposed a mechanism for change—the principle of natural selection—by which individuals possessing traits that give them an advantage in their environment are the most likely to survive long enough to reproduce and pass genes for those traits on to their offspring. Darwin's evolutionary model was applied to social systems by many nineteenth-century thinkers. Karl Marx offered to dedicate *Capital* to Darwin, and some version of the idea of evolution was part of nearly all of the next century's theories of social change. Pre-eighteenth-century ideas of progress were concepts of a developing morality or civilization; nineteenth-century progress became focused on material conditions.

Later theorists (especially Herbert Spencer) applied Darwin's principle of natural selection to social characteristics, arguing that "survival of the fittest" is the mechanism by which cultural traits evolve. Some Social Darwinists tried to link social traits to genetic characteristics, arguing that poverty, crime, or the lower social status of women and minorities are inherited. Draconian social policies based on Social Darwinist principles include the Nazi genocide program that exterminated millions of people and an early twentieth-century U.S. immigration policy that excluded southern European, Asian, Latin American, and African immigrants (Chorover, 1980). These oppressive policies were justified with the belief that whole racial or cultural groups could be physically superior to others. Before the eighteenth century (and equally at odds with contemporary beliefs) people were enslaved in the name of superior cultural or religious ideas (Davis, 1985). Both phenomena illustrate the tendency of human groups to use a scientific or philosophical theory to legitimate their own social structures and practices. When this occurs, the beliefs become part of ideology and are no longer subjected to scientific or philosophical inquiry.

Today sociobiology has taken up the question of how genetics and human behavior are related on a more scientific basis than its Social Darwinist predecessors. Many of sociobiology's critics (Barash, 1979; Lewontin, Rose, and Kamin, 1985), however, are wary of the ideological and social policy implications of a theory that social behavior is determined at birth by genetic traits. Theories of technology and social change also have ideological consequences if they are widely believed to be truths that require no scientific testing.

The theories of Smith, Malthus, and Darwin are widely used today in ideological arguments about free markets, population problems, and evolution. What they have in common as theories is insight into the systems characteristics of human society. Mechanisms of stability, self-regulation, structural evolution, and limiting external conditions are all features of social systems under certain conditions that can be investigated. Questions facing later theorists include the following: Under what conditions does self-regulation provide stability or failure? How do evolutionary processes occur? Under what conditions is change gradual or abrupt? Can social change lead to extinction? What are the external limitations on social systems?

The Internal Dynamics of Capitalism: Marx, Durkheim, and Weber

Social change theories of all sorts are to some degree theories about history. The computer did not appear automatically or inevitably, but was one product of several hundred years of social change known as the industrial revolution. The most important structural feature of the industrial revolution was the emergence of the worldwide capitalist economic system. Growing out of changes in sixteenth-century European agriculture, mining, commerce, and beliefs, the industrial revolution was accompanied by massive political and social upheaval in Europe and a wave of colonial expansion to other parts of the world. By the twentieth-century this "world-economy" had expanded to include most of the globe. Former European colonies, like the United States, had established their political independence but remained linked into a single economic system (which includes relationships between capitalist and socialist nations).

Three of the most important theorists of the late nineteenth and early twentieth centuries grappled with the problem of how to explain the rise of capitalism and the industrial revolution. Karl Marx (1818–1883), Emile Durkheim (1858–1917), and Max Weber (1864–1920) developed different models of the internal dynamics of society. Because these models do not focus on the same structural features of the social system, these theorists are not competing in the sense that only one of them can be "right." Instead, they are competing in that each identifies a different set of characteristics as "most important" to understanding social change.

MARX: A MODEL OF SOCIAL TRANSFORMATION   In a three-volume book, *Capital* (1867), Karl Marx argued that social change proceeds through what he called "internal contradictions" of the social system. The *mode of production* (which includes the social relationships of economic activity and productive forces like technology or natural resources) is the starting point for Marx's theory. Other cultural features, such as beliefs and political arrangements, are part of a *superstructure*, which is shaped by the economic *base*. When Marx argued that capitalism contains "the seeds of its own destruction," he was referring to the internally generated social conflicts he saw occurring as a result of structural tensions in the dynamic relationship between base and superstructure. Marx's model is called a materialist one by those who think he argued that changes in natural resources, technology, and the production of material products cause social change. However, Marx was a social theorist and considered these material forces of production only part of the source of social change. The *social relations of production* (how work and property ownership are socially arranged) were equally important to him.

Capitalism arose, according to Marx, out of conflicts between merchants and manufacturers and the feudal property relationships that hindered them. The early industrialists formed a social class (the *bourgeoisie*) whose economic interests were in opposition to the political and cultural arrangements of the traditional society. As they grew in wealth and power from their economic activities, the bourgeoisie was able to make revolutionary changes in society—in 1776 in the United States and in 1789 in France. In the process the beliefs and social structures of traditional culture were transformed.

An internal contradiction in capitalist society occurs between the successful bourgeoisie and the wage workers they employ. Marx, observing the dismal factory conditions of the early industrial revolution, argued that the workers (who formed a class called the *proletariat*) were alienated from their own economic activity and oppressed by the capitalist mode of production. Marx predicted a proletarian revolution that would be violent (because the workers had no other sources of power) and would replace capitalism with a socialist mode of production in which private property would become collectivized. Because Marx believed that the government was an instrument of the ruling class and that under communism there would be no rulers, he predicted that socialist revolution would lead to a "withering away of the state" and a transition to a stable communist social system.

History has shown that Marx failed to predict the rise of labor unions and a middle class of managerial, technical, and professional employees in the bourgeois democracies. Also, his predictions of societal dynamics after a socialist revolution have not proved correct. Contemporary socialist states show no signs of withering away and tend to have a managerial ruling class. Marx's analysis of the dynamics of class conflict, however, have had such a major impact that all of modern social theory has been called a "debate with Marx's ghost." A diverse group of contemporary conflict theories continue to address Marx's central question of how the economic structure of society produces class conflict and social change.

DURKHEIM: SOCIAL DIFFERENTIATION AND INTEGRATION   In *The Division of Labor in Society* (1893), Emile Durkheim analyzed the forms of solidarity in traditional and modern societies. The strong group identifications by members of traditional societies occurred, he argued, because people shared similar patterns of work and experience. They felt connected to one another because they thought and acted in the same ways. Durkheim called this **mechanical solidarity.**

The industrial revolution broke down mechanical solidarity by creating different specialized jobs. This structural differentiation of society meant that people no longer lived in the same pattern as their neighbors. However, according to Durkheim, people in industrial society become increasingly dependent on one another's work, creating a new form of **organic solidarity** because no one is able to survive without the specialized skills of others. People are joined by their common need for one another's differences. Thus, for Durkheim structural differentiation provides a new way to integrate industrial people into a common culture.

In choosing the terms *mechanical solidarity* for traditional societies and *organic solidarity* for modern ones, Durkheim was replacing an older system model of society as a clockwork mechanism with a model based on the way the specialized parts of a biological organism are integrated into a single entity. What is also significant about Durkheim's model is that culture plays a major role in providing stability. Social norms and values, especially those of religion, are the "glue" that holds his model together. Social conflict is a form of pathology (again a model borrowed from biology). Contemporary functionalist theorists are still concerned with Durkheim's question of how societies maintain their cultural patterns from generation to generation and with how a cooperative division of labor produces social integration. Empirical social science research is also indebted to Durkheim for pioneering (in his study of the causes of suicide) the use of statistical data to develop information about society.

WEBER: RATIONALITY AND POWER   Max Weber's unfinished *Economy and Society* and his comparative history of the world's religions (*The Protestant Ethic and the Spirit of Capitalism* is one of the series) attempted to link cultural ideas and social structure. He believed that changes in power, religious beliefs, and economic activities are joined by the common thread of rationalization. *Rationalization* refers to the process by which social institutions become organized, using formal rules and specialized roles to achieve specific purposes. In rational organizations work roles are clearly defined, assigned according to technical merit, and separated from people's personal lives. Rational social relationships apply the same rules of conduct to everyone without favoritism. Record keeping becomes more important as organizations seek the most efficient means to carry out their goals. Power plays an important role in Weber's theories, but it is not (as in Marx) entirely based on economic arrangements. Weber argued that ideas can have unanticipated economic consequences and that sometimes ideas (like the religious beliefs of the fundamentalist Protestants) contribute to new social structures (in this case industrial enterprises).

In his studies of the evolution of rational bureaucratic organizations and modern legal and governmental institutions, Weber argued that the exercise of power was becoming more rational in modern society. Although his analysis shows that bureaucracy developed as a rational and efficient means to administer businesses and political units, Weber feared that what he called the "iron cage" of impersonal bureaucratic structures would come to dominate society. Despite his personal dislike for bureaucracies, his analysis of them has become the basis of most of our contemporary theories of industrial and business organizations. His inquiry into why people accept the legitimacy of political power and why then political regimes can change provides contemporary sociology with some of its central problems.

Weber's theory seems most like a systems model when he talks about cause and effect. It is very difficult to specify causal relations in systems. (For example, if you and several friends are bouncing on a trampoline, who is making whom move?) Weber used the concept **elective affinity** to describe an interconnected relationship where it is hard to determine which is the cause of the other. He also used the concept of **ideal type** to represent his conceptual models of social phenomena. These concepts have had an important impact on the conduct of social research that compares different social systems and on theoretical models of the "shape" of society.

The Individual Component: Freud and the Classical Theorists

In *Civilization and Its Discontents* (1922) Sigmund Freud argued that the human instincts toward pleasure are repressed so that the needs of society can be met. **Repression** is a psychological phenomenon; it involves individuals forgetting or ignoring their physiological urges. In Freud's analysis people are not naturally inclined to labor and must be forced to work. To accomplish this, society must create in its members personalities that are able to postpone immediate physical gratification in order to seek socially useful goals. Agricultural civilization, for example, requires people who will do the work of planting and harvesting without an immediate result of food. Even the work of preparing a family meal requires a cook who can wait to eat until the food is ready and the relatives are assembled. From a Freudian perspective, human needs to achieve satisfaction through work are culturally created. Society would be impossible without social constraints on human instincts; the feeling of guilt for enjoying yourself when you should be working is the price of civilization.

In contrast Karl Marx believed that work is basic to the human species. He describes labor as a process "in which man of his own accord starts, regulates, and controls the material re-actions between himself and nature" (1967:177). For Marx human nature is expressed through people's relationships to the products of their work, to the activity of work itself, to their human potential, and to one another. Where Freud saw a socially necessary repression of human instincts, Marx saw an oppression of human creative instincts by capitalist society. With industrialization, work became *alienated labor.* In other words, people were separated from the voluntary process of work, from control over the products of their labor, from their creative potential, and from other people. According to Marx workers in capitalist society are not free to choose what they will do and how they will dispose of the results. The constraints of private property and the capitalist mode of production also interfere with "natural" social relationships and with individuals' expressions of their own creative powers (Marx, 1964:106–19).

For Durkheim the individual is also connected to society through work, but work is regulated by norms. Society for Durkheim is primarily a sacred moral order. An individual's identification with a profession and its ethical values is a source of social solidarity. **Anomie,** or normlessness, is a problem of rapid social change if the old mechanical solidarity breaks down before the new division of labor integrates people into organic solidarity. Individuals suffering from anomie lack a "place" in society and are prone to deviance and suicide. Where Freud saw repression and Marx saw alienation, Durkheim saw a failure of social norms.

Weber looked at individuals as social actors who calculate their interests and estimate how others will evaluate their behavior. He argued that individuals' status in industrial society depends on their *life chances* (what they are able to sell their labor for), but Weber's contribution to the role of individuals in social change is his analysis of *charisma.* Charismatic leaders are people like Jesus, Hitler, Gandhi, or Martin Luther King, who can move their religious or political followers to make extraordinary changes. Weber argued that the charismatic people have a special relationship with whatever their followers hold sacred and are able to give them new moral values and norms. Weber thought individuals accept even the exploitative social relationships of capitalism because they believe them to be legal and legitimate. Ultimately, for Weber, the institutions of law and bureaucratic organizations bind individuals to industrial society.

Contemporary Perspectives on Computers and Social Change

Like other technological innovations of the industrial revolution, the computer has consequences for the patterns of human activity. Unlike many other innovations, the social impact of the computer appears to many contemporary macrotheorists so great that its introduction following World War II represents the beginning of a radically new period of social change. Some microtheorists believe that the experience of using computers will dramatically alter the

social relationships that form the basis of larger social structures. For many people the new technology offers the possibility of novel solutions to world problems of hunger, poverty, and conflict. However, the introduction of modern technology will not automatically solve social problems without a corresponding change in social life and social structure.

TECHNOLOGICAL DETERMINISM AND THE DIFFUSION MODEL   Technological determinism sees technology as the major cause of social change; most other perspectives view technology as the product of social change, as well as one of many causes. The theory was developed by William Ogburn (1932:200–13) as the cultural lag hypothesis. He argued that societies are evolving to a technologically superior form and that technical progress occurs naturally. Although most contemporary theorists reject his argument, Ogburn's statement: "Forces that produce changes are the discovery of new cultural elements that have superior utility, in which case the old utilities tend to be replaced by the new. The slowness of culture to change lies in the difficulties of creativity and adopting new ideas" (Nisbet, 1972:71) is compatible with popular conceptions of technological progress.

The **diffusion model** of social change is related to technological determinism in its assumptions about the natural spread of superior technique. Individual choice is the driving force behind this model, which emphasizes the role of individuals in spreading new ideas and tools. A diffusion approach to the new information age would explain how the use of computers spread from the *innovators* who developed them to other people and cultures. The **demonstration effect** is an important part of the diffusion model. It predicts that, as people see demonstrations of the computer, they will evaluate its applicability to their own needs and make a decision to adopt the new technology.

Research on the institutional contexts of technical innovation supports the idea that individuals play a major role in developing technology (Calder, 1970; Tornatzky et al., 1983), but the diffusion model does not provide a very good explanation for involuntary changes experienced by employees or colonized nations. It has been useful in describing how innovations spread among members of a society who are in a position to make choices. Companies' marketing strategies are often based on a diffusion model, as they arrange demonstrations or attempt to place equipment in universities or with the "leaders" of a particular industry. Diffusion studies are often able to identify factors associated with acceptance or rejection of new equipment. The adoption of computers among farmers, for instance, is associated with youth, large farm size, and high income (Yarbrough, 1984).

THE FUNCTIONS OF TECHNOLOGY   Functionalist theories of social change argue that societies evolve in their ability to deal with the world in which they exist. This **adaptive capacity** is enhanced by new technologies and new social arrangements that help large human groups survive and prosper. Four system processes, shown in Table 1, are identified as common to all societies.

TABLE 1

NECESSARY FUNCTIONS FOR ALL SOCIAL SYSTEMS

Structure	Function It Performs
Community	Integration: maintains relationships among components and provides social control
Culture	Pattern Maintenance: socialization of people to fit into the system and manage tensions
Politics	Goal Attainment: sets goals, establishes priorities, and uses resources to achieve goals
Economy	Adaptation: seeks resources from the environment, converts them to usable form, and distributes them to rest of system.

Source: Adapted from Talcott Parsons. *The System of Modern Societies.* Englewood Cliffs, NJ: Prentice-Hall, 1971, pp. 4–11; Jonathan H. Turner and Alexandra Maryanski. *Functionalism.* Reading, MA: Benjamin/Cummings, 1979, p. 75.

A common criticism of functionalist reasoning is that it tends to overestimate the stability of societies and is much better as a method of describing societies than as a theory of social change (Turner and Maryanski, 1979). This is because the idea that certain arrangements *must* exist in societies tends to lead to the assumption that what does exist should continue to exist in order for society to continue functioning. For example, if society has a king, by some methods of functionalist reasoning, society wouldn't work without one. Functionalists argue that such innovations as the division of labor in industrial societies or the capitalist economic system represent a form of social progress by making societies more fit to survive in the competition for world resources. Functionalists would tend to view computers as a technology that increases the adaptive capacity of a society by enhancing its ability to gather information about the world and make vital decisions about itself and its environment. They would also be concerned with the effects of computers on social relationships and the processes of socialization, social control, and politics.

CONFLICT THEORIES   The term **conflict theory** describes a collection of very different theories that share a common focus on conflict as a source of social change. Although it is often contrasted with functionalist theories, the two can be combined, as in Lewis Coser's work on the functions of social conflict (1956). Conflict theories are also often socially devalued in American sociology by associating them with contemporary Marxist revolutionary beliefs. Conflict theorists would try to understand the computer in terms of power, social classes, and intergroup conflict rather than by focusing only on what it is "good for." Analysts like Cooley (1980) or Shaiken (1984) study the technology in the context of struggles between labor and management. Perrolle (1985a) examines the computer revolution from the perspective of classical Marxist theory. Conflict theorists following in the tradition of C. Wright Mills (1956) would study the effects of computer technology on the distribution of power among elite decision makers. Theorists working in the Weberian tradition would look at the computer's effects on the patterns of political power in societies and in bureaucratic organizations. Even microlevel theories could be considered conflict theories if they analyze the effects of computer-based interactions in terms of the relative power obtained by the individuals involved.

THE SYMBOLIC INTERACTIONIST PERSPECTIVE   Although theorists working in the interactionist perspective would differ widely among themselves over how to study computers and social change, they would all be interested in the meaning of computers. The psychological responses of individuals to computers and the effects of computers on our symbolic interpretation of reality are studied by Turkle (1984) and other social psychologists. The human/computer interface has been the focus of research in education, psychology, and communications (reviewed in Chapters 4 and 5). Philosophical questions about the meaning of artificial intelligence are raised by both philosophers (Haugeland, 1981; Dreyfus, 1972) and computer scientists (Weizenbaum, 1976). Since most interactionist theories are microlevel, they are usually about how individuals and small groups experience social change.

COMPARATIVE HISTORICAL THEORY   Comparative historical theories are made by observing past events and comparing the circumstances in which different social changes occur (Skocpol, 1983). Following the traditions of Weber and Marx, and often combining functionalist and conflict approaches, comparative historical theorists try to explain contemporary events as variations in more general principles of social structure and process. They may apply a general model to explain historical change, may seek to clarify our understanding of a contemporary concept, or may test hypotheses about historical problems. The next chapter examines changes in information, property, and power through history to identify useful elements for a theory of computers and social change.

CHAPTER
3

INFORMATION, PROPERTY, AND POWER IN HISTORY

Why study history, especially in a book about computers and social change? History is the closest thing social scientists have to a laboratory for investigating large-scale social change. Only by observing the past can we make empirical generalizations about the process of change. To understand a revolution in information, we will have to begin even before recorded history, for the relationship between information and social change began long before we were able to make written records of our experience.

EVOLUTION AND REVOLUTION

Most theories of change in the earliest forms of human society are about *evolution*. They attempt to explain how human beings, with their characteristic patterns of group life, slowly evolved from prehuman species. The appearance of agriculture at about 30,000 B.C. and the industrial revolution of the eighteenth century were, in contrast, marked by such rapid changes in social structure that they have been termed *revolutions*. The introduction of computers is, to many theorists, simply an evolution of the industrial revolution. To others, computers represent a new, major period of revolutionary change. The choice of whether a social change is to be called an evolution or a revolution is rather arbitrary. Revolutions are relatively rapid and disruptive; evolutions maintain continuity and are gradual.

51

Tools, Information, and Human Evolution

One source of continuity between the computer revolution and much earlier forms of social change is the human use of information. From the genetically encoded information in the brains of prehuman species to the scientific knowledge of modern industrial societies, information has been an integral part of human evolution and revolution. Tools, especially tools for gathering and recording information, have also played an important role. There have been revolutions when new means of information processing have appeared suddenly, but much of the human history of information processing is an evolutionary one.

THE ORIGIN OF THE SPECIES   With the general acceptance of Darwin's theory of evolution in the late nineteenth century, scientists and educated laymen began to investigate the evolution of the human species from its more primitive ancestors. Theories in the fields of paleontology, archaeology, social anthropology, and sociobiology have been formulated and revised as new scientific evidence has been discovered. For scientists, the topic remains exciting and controversial.

The first theories of human origin emphasized the information-processing capacity of the brain, which, it was speculated, led to the invention of tools by the intellectually advanced *Homo sapiens*—the first true human. More recent evidence indicates that tool use by small-brained prehuman species predated the evolution of the human species. Thus, the use of tools apparently began before we were mentally capable of planning designs for them. Darwin suggested that tool use was both the cause *and* the effect of the natural selection process that produced an intelligent species walking on two legs. Freedom of the hands to carry sticks or stones may have led, accidentally, to tool use by erect but small-brained ancestors. Those who were more inclined to walk on two legs had a survival advantage in the use of tools and were thus more likely to reproduce.

The evolution of humans as an intelligent tool-using species involved more than genetic selection, however. Human culture, including techniques that can be taught to each new generation, made the species unique. It is extremely difficult to study early patterns of social interaction, but scholars have proposed that the earliest information transmission was probably visual, with one person showing another what he or she had learned to do. A computer program has recently been used to argue, by analogy, that cooperation is the best survival technique for interacting organisms (Axelrod, 1984). TIT-FOR-TAT, as the program is called, first cooperates with new "individuals" it meets, remembers how they acted toward it, and on the next encounter behaves in the same way. Although it retaliates against uncooperative behavior, the program is quick to "forgive."

Evidence from tool use in some modern primates (our closest genetic relations) is also used to draw plausible inferences about the behavior of our ancestors. Chimpanzees, especially the females, use rocks to crack the nuts they have gathered. The use of tools to crack nuts is in turn taught to the young. Young monkeys have been observed inventing and teaching to others new food-gathering techniques. There are thus two important points about primitive tool use. First, use involves techniques, or information about using the tool, that can be learned and adopted through demonstration. The second is the role of innovation. Experimental activity is adopted and develops into regular patterns, with adults demonstrating to their offspring methods of gathering food, using tools, and avoiding environmental hazards. This kind of evidence fits a diffusion model of early technical innovation.

LANGUAGE AND ART For a period of several million years, most communication was probably nonverbal. Nonverbal communication is still an essential ingredient of social interaction. (Indeed, one of the technical difficulties of "natural language" software is the fact that humans rely on body posture, eye contact, and gesture to communicate meaning.) The first two innovations in information processing were spoken language and art. The paleontological evidence indicates that visual representations of objects had begun by the time humans were hunters of large animals. By then, people had learned to represent information as carvings and pictures. They had also begun to bury their dead with flowers, suggesting that they had begun to ponder the symbolic meaning of their existence.

Although there is no "hard" scientific evidence that dates our first use of language, some of our oldest myths and religious traditions refer to the long food-gathering part of our past, when we lived in a "garden" and began to give names to animals and things. In an ancient Chinese poem, the sacred spirits object strenuously when people begin to speak. One explanation for the cultural theme that symbolic representation through art and words was somehow sacrilegious (as in the Judeo-Christian prohibition against graven images) is that face-to-face, emotional communication is an important source of group solidarity. In many religious traditions, such as the Greek mysteries or some modern forms of group prayer, a sacred silence helps produce feelings of connection among humans and between humans and the sacred.

The linguistic distinctions among specific ideas that may bring dissent into human communication also facilitate greater coordination of human activity. Unlike the genetically encoded communication systems of insects and other animals, human language allows the formation of an infinite number of thoughts. This is because language contains recursive grammar, which can generate an infinite number of sentences with a finite vocabulary. An example of an infinitely long sentence is "The integers are one and two and three and four. . . ." An example of a recursive sentence is "I know that you know that I know that you know that I know that."

The advantages of the spoken word for early humans were great. With only gestures, it would be difficult to communicate the suggestion "You people go around behind that mammoth and chase it toward the cliff while we come in from the side" unless group hunting of large animals were already built into the genetic heritage. (American Sign Language and other contemporary gesture-based communication systems have the grammatical structure of a verbal language and are not like the preverbal gesture systems.) Words are also useful for communicating in the dark, at a distance, or to someone behind a tree. More important, as cave drawings represent an animal not immediately present, so words allowed humans to refer to the past, the future, and the hypothetical. With the evolution of language, the human species was able to deal with information beyond its immediate experiences.

Symbolic communication contributed to more complex forms of social and economic life. Songs, stories, art, and myth communicated to each new generation the wisdom of the past. This process of cultural information accumulation contributed much more to our evolution than the slower processes of genetic selection.

THE DIVISION OF LABOR   As human culture evolved, it reflected the history of human interactions within the environment. Projectile weapons appeared with the hunting of large game; previously, we were hunters of frogs and rabbits and may even have been scavengers. Many scholars believe that, with the advent of big-game hunting, a **division of labor** developed, with adult males ranging farther from home while females, older males, and the young continued to gather food. With this specialization of activity, **status** distinctions based upon age and sex appeared. Certain forms of information became associated with particular statuses. For example, spear use might be restricted to adult males; firewood gathering could be defined as children's work. From observations of contemporary gathering and hunting societies, anthropologists theorize that the process of transmitting information was also defined and divided. Transmission might occur through the ritual initiation of boys into sacred knowledge about animal habits or the initiation of girls into knowledge of the locations and healing properties of plants. Such technical skills as tool making might become specialties passed down from craftsman to apprentice.

A new problem for hunting societies was how to divide the food surplus from a successful hunt. In gathering societies there is no surplus. Food is usually shared among the group members as it is collected. Hunter societies, however, have social "rules" about who gets what shares of the game, often distributed by "leaders" according to the local concept of fairness. Leaders were sometimes chosen on the basis of personal attributes like wisdom or hunting ability or might be the oldest members of the society. Often, however, the leadership was religious in nature, involving people called shamans, who were believed to have magical power over the environment. These influential men and women could interpret and explain events and the world. In their minds, and in their art and myth, cultural information was stored, added to, then passed on. For most of our history on earth, memory was the storage medium for information; the sudden death of a shaman or elder might "erase" a good portion of a group's knowledge.

The Agricultural Revolution: New Techniques and Social Structures

Sometime during the last twenty thousand to thirty thousand years, communities of people scattered across the globe learned to raise plants and animals for food. Although evidence indicates that some of the tools and techniques of herding and early agriculture diffused from group to group, others seem to have been discovered, independently, on several continents. Because this does not fit a diffusion model, one theory suggests that population growth placed pressure on the food supplies of hunting-and-gathering societies, giving them a powerful incentive to seek alternative food sources. Our earliest agriculture was seminomadic, similar in many ways to gathering wild plants.

More rapid population growth and the low productivity of early agriculture pressured human groups to improve their food-producing technology. Archaeological evidence suggests that by at least 10,000 B.C. people had begun to settle in villages organized around permanent farming plots. Compared to previous cultural developments, information, tools, and social organization evolved rapidly. During the next few thousand years, humans developed a variety of extraordinarily complex cultural forms.

CHANGES IN CULTURAL INFORMATION   From a functionalist perspective, the growth of agriculture posed a new set of survival problems and information "needs." The reproductive habits of plants and animals were learned and formalized as a set of myths and customs, as part of the new techniques of food production. Knowledge of animal reproduction increased the amount of information about human biological relationships, and fertility took on a central role in religion. Weather deities, especially those in charge of rainfall, were worshiped.

As early as 30,000 B.C. (which is as far back as carbon 14 dating can reliably be done), the inventory of tools included calendars that could predict the annual agricultural cycles. These were analog rather than digital devices, dependent on the relative positions of sun, moon, and stars to "compute" the changing seasons. Because we have no similar evidence (like counting sticks or the sand table abacus) for any development of mathematics that early, it appears that our first computers were developed *before* computation. Our earliest calculators expressed relationships in terms of visual sacred symbols, such as the signs of the zodiac or the image of the sun god being pulled across the sky by horses. A contemporary version of ancient analog computational techniques is the elegant and efficient navigation system of the Micronesian islanders. Without modern calculations or instruments, they are able to follow their traditional star paths for long distances across the Pacific with remarkable accuracy (Huchins, 1983).

THE DIVISION OF LABOR IN AGRICULTURAL SOCIETIES   Symbolic evidence for an early sexual division of labor in agriculture comes from the fact that earth and fertility deities were usually female, but the principal gods of nomadic herding cultures tended to be male. This suggests to some scholars that gardening began as women's activity, and animal husbandry grew out of men's hunting activities. In many contemporary agrarian societies agriculture was traditionally women's work, although this sort of evidence must be used cautiously when making arguments about prehistorical cultures.

Besides apparently furthering the sexual division of labor, early agriculture created new food surpluses, in the form of animals and grains, that could be stored for long periods of time. The wide variety of social solutions to the problem of surplus distribution included the establishment of early forms of private property and inheritance. Information about both kinship and property became an important part of culture. Genealogies, often in the form of song or ritual, were memorized and played an important part in disputes over rights and shares of social resources. Even today much data processing involves the maintenance of ownership records.

THE ORIGIN OF THE FAMILY   The prehistoric origins of the family cannot be known for certain because social relationships do not usually leave archaeological evidence. Research on primates and contemporary preindustrial cultures, however, strongly suggests that:

> The family is a human institution, not found in its totality in any prehuman species. It required language, planning, cooperation, self-control, foresight, and cultural learning and probably developed along with these. The family was made desirable by the early human combination of prolonged child care with the need for hunting with weapons over large terrains. The sexual division of labor on which it was based grew out of a rudimentary prehuman division between male defense and female child care. But among humans this sexual division of functions for the first time became crucial for food production and so laid the basis for future economic specialization and cooperation. (Gough, 1980:38)

NEW RELATIONSHIPS OF PROPERTY AND POWER   New social arrangements were based on food surpluses that freed some individuals from the tasks of tilling the land. Men and women could specialize in their economic roles, exchanging baskets, jewelry, tools, cloth, or beer for food. Leaders assumed more important roles in society, interpreting both social rules and religious traditions. At times the leadership divided, with different tasks and statuses for the sacred and the secular. From the secular evolved early forms of government and politics; from the sacred developed magic and ritual in astronomy and agriculture. Hereditary rule often evolved, and leaders were entitled at birth to large shares of social resources. Military activity, important for the protection of many village settlements, became a specialty. Groups conquered one another and established patterns of slavery and enforced rule.

Over time, those in power defined cultural meanings and remembered and explained the "official" history and religious tradition. The **state** thus appeared in human society. Defined by Weber as a territorially based institution with a monopoly on the legitimate use of force, the state provided military protection, enforced social order, and regulated the exchange and distribution of economic surplus. Because state rulers appropriated much of the surplus to support their own activities, they often became an upper class, passing their wealth and privileges on to their children. A few agricultural societies developed the most unequal stratification systems ever observed, with people's occupations rigidly defined at birth. As early forms of agriculture established the division of labor by age and sex, so settled agriculture divided labor by social class as the ideal of personal property in the form of food, tools, or ornaments that could be used was transformed into the idea of private wealth that could be amassed by a privileged group.

Information gathering and processing became increasingly important for the functioning of the state. Agricultural surplus, in the form of taxes, had to be extracted from villagers. Property ownership had to be established, and specialized staffs of warriors, priests, craftsmen, artisans, and slaves had to be supervised. China, the oldest of the agrarian empires, was the origin of major innovations in information technology to support the activities of the state.

INNOVATIONS IN INFORMATION PROCESSING   As the three-thousand-year-old oracle bones of China indicate, early writing developed from pictures and was part of a religious information system. The important advantages of writing, as opposed to oral or nonverbal communication, as a method of information transmission is that information is stored outside the human mind and is less subject to memory loss or idiosyncratic changes as it is passed from person to person. Even nonverbal information lasts longer in a permanent storage medium. For example, a written Chinese musical score discovered by archaeologists was recently played for the first time in eighteen hundred years.

Along with the earlier invention of the abacus, writing provided the Chinese state with the means to build and administer an empire, based on irrigated rice cultivation, that lasted several thousand years. Taxes were raised to construct cities, waterworks, and defensive fortifications like the Great Wall. Censuses were taken and armies drafted. A strict class division between the educated elite and the common people appeared. For the elite, the arts flourished. Progress in mathematics was made as part of administrative and ritual calculations; paper, invented as a wrapping material, became the medium for producing and storing written records.

Agricultural civilizations also developed in other parts of the world. Although they shared with China some of the patterns of extreme class inequality, there were some important differences in their cultures' use of information. Languages like Egyptian evolved away from pictographs, toward the representation of sounds by individual symbols. The invention of phonetic alphabets greatly simplified written language, with the result that lower-class people, and even some slaves, could become literate. The alphabetic languages lowered the barriers between social classes because much less leisure time was required for mastery of them. Chinese is a difficult written language even for native speakers. It remains a major challenge to word-processing and data communication designers because there are thirty-five thousand individual characters that can be pronounced a maximum of sixteen hundred ways; this makes phonetic transcription impractical due to an excessive number of homonyms (like "here" and "hear"). The most promising approach appears to be the use of computer graphics ("Chinese/Kanji . . .," 1985; "Hunan Research Institute . . .," 1985).

Alphabetic languages facilitated information processing for encyclopedias, libraries, and other early data bases. The burning of the Great Library at Alexandria, Egypt, destroyed a major part of the Mediterranean world's knowledge and demonstrates the vulnerability of early information storage. Although several methods of storage were used, all were expensive and time-consuming. Literacy was rare. Manuscripts had to be copied by hand (with the inevitable addition of errors) or printed the way artists make woodblock prints. Not until the widespread use of paper and Gutenberg's invention of the modern movable-type printing press did written materials become widely available in Europe. By then, in the middle of the fifteenth century, Europe was on the threshold of the industrial revolution. (See Table 2 for a concise history of information technology.)

THE INDUSTRIAL REVOLUTION

The industrial revolution was the greatest period of social change in history, culminating in an international capitalist economic system. It began in England, occurred mainly from the mid-eighteenth to mid-nineteenth centuries, and had its origins in sixteenth- and seventeenth-century European culture. The details of why and how it occurred are still being debated by social theorists and historians. By any theory, however, the industrial revolution marked the transformation of the world's economic and social life.

The Great Transformation

Innovations in sixteenth-century English agriculture included new tools and soil preparation techniques. These raised food productivity and supported a population growth in the seventeenth century. Trade in agricultural products among European countries created an international division of labor that expanded with European colonization. For example, English colonial expansion into India provided a new raw material, cotton, suitable for the textile industry that had begun with wool. Lower labor requirements in English agriculture displaced rural workers, who found their way to cities like Manchester, where they were organized to weave cloth.

The rational organization of workers in a single building was found efficient in the manufacture of other products besides textiles. Technological innovations in power generation and machinery were adopted, and the factory

TABLE 2

EVOLUTION AND REVOLUTION IN INFORMATION TECHNOLOGY

Time	Events
By 30,000 B.C.	Calendars, cave paintings, sculpture
By 1500 B.C.	Pictographic writing
1500 B.C.– beginning of common era	Libraries, sand table abacus, Hindu-Arabic number system, clay tablets
Beginning of common era to 10th century	Paper, first printed book, mechanical clock, water-powered mills
11th century	Movable type, modern decimal system
12th century	Modern abacus
14th century	Division of hours and minutes into 60's, European clock
15th century	First book in movable type (Korea), scientific mapmaking, Gutenberg's printing press
16th century	Taxi meters, algebraic symbols, camera with lens and stop, first scientific society, lead pencil, automatic ribbon loom, Gregorian calendar revision, European decimal system
17th century	Research on electricity and magnetism, logarithms, first log tables, slide rule, adding machine, calculating machine capable of multiplication and division (lost in a fire), first patent law, patent for steam engine, calculus, fountain pen, Pascal's calculating machine, probability, probability applied to insurance calculations, steam automobile model, Leibnitz's multiplication machine, first determination of the speed of light
18th century	Typewriter, three-color printing, paper-tape controlled loom, photographic plates, Watt's steam engine, spinning machinery, interchangeable parts for muskets, power loom, telegraph, industrial revolution begins

system was created. Between 1780 and 1840, steam engines were introduced into textile, coal, and iron works, and the modern factory came to dominate the English industrial towns.

By 1776 (at the beginning of industrialization), Adam Smith could describe the ideal economy as a "free market" in which people could sell land, labor, and manufactured products without constraint. Although many people believe that this is the "natural" way for human beings to arrange their economic activities, it is important to realize that this is a culturally defined pattern of behavior of fairly recent origin. Impersonal market forces only gradually replaced traditional social regulation of economic activity. To Marx (who lived through the worst social disruptions of the industrial revolution), the social relationships inherent in human work became culturally redefined as impersonal relationships among things, with workers transformed to sellers of labor and alienated from the products of their own work. Theorists writing after the industrial revolution emphasized other features of social change: Durkheim argued that the more complex division of labor in production would make people more dependent upon one another and increase social solidarity. He also saw a transitional period in industrial societies during which property rights would be unregulated by social norms (1957:207–15). Weber saw the rise of law and administrative bureaucracies taking over the function of regulating economic activity and property rights. In one of the more interesting contemporary analyses, Karl Polanyi (1944) describes the industrial revolution in Britain as a "great transformation" in which an economy embedded in a society became a society embedded in an economy. What he refers to is economic forces controlling the pattern of social life instead of the other way around.

The Transformation of Property

The concept of property involves more than possession. It also includes the socially defined ways in which possessions can be "owned" and disposed of. Gifts, inheritance, barter, and sale are all ways of exchanging possessions. In each society, some things are defined as "not for sale." In modern societies, you can sell your land but not your children. In many earlier ones, land could not be owned by individuals, but was instead the collective property of a kinship group. People could inherit the right to use a share but not to sell or give it to strangers. Some of these societies did permit the sale of human beings, in a few cases even people's own children.

THE CONCEPT OF COMMODITY PROPERTY   The rise of capitalism altered social restrictions on property. A particular form of property, the **commodity,** became more prevalent. Unlike most earlier products, which were made to be used or exchanged in the context of a social relationship between producer and consumer, commodities were made to be sold for profit using rationally organized wage labor. The value of a commodity is measured by a universal medium of exchange, money. The price of a commodity represents its value and includes the cost of materials, wages, other production expenses, and profit. When it is sold, the exchange is based upon the price of the product, not upon the social positions of the buyer and seller. A set of impersonal market relationships reduces direct social contact between the maker and the consumer, who may be strangers to each other.

   To understand the difference between commodities and older forms of property, consider all the things you own. If you have something made for you, for example, a sweater made by a friend or relative, it is *not* a commodity. The handmade sweater is more than a sweater; it is a gift expressing your relationship to the giver. That particular sweater has a social meaning knit into it; you could never buy another one just like it. A sweater bought in a department store was made to be sold; the other sweater was made for you. But what about the gift that someone bought for you? To the extent that the gift has sentimental value, you are preserving some of the traditional meanings of property exchange. To the extent that the value of the gift is measured only by its price, you are treating it as a commodity. However, the purchased gift is a commodity, even though it has sentimental value, because your sentiment is not toward the people who work in the sweater factory. To both you and the person who gave you the gift, the labor that went into it is an impersonal part of the economic system appearing only as part of the cost of the sweater.

COMMODITIES AND CAPITALISM   When commodity production began, it was hindered by traditional social obligations that prevented people from selling their labor, by customary prices and land use rights, and by cultural beliefs that interest and profit were immoral. During the rise of capitalism, land and human labor were socially redefined as being "for sale." Although they did not become commodities by most strict definitions of the term (because they are not "made"), they did become private rather than social.

In the case of land, the transformation from collective to private property began hundreds of years before the industrial revolution. Beginning in the twelfth century in England, the feudal nobility began to use its power to redefine traditional land use rights. First they restricted the commoners' use of forests for hunting and foraging. The social conflict of England's "Robin Hood" period was one result. Later, village pastures and common lands (examples of which can still be found in the older towns of New England) were declared private and enclosed by hedges and fences. A poem attributed to that period indicates both popular objection to the change and an explanation for why it was possible:

> The law locks up the man or woman
> Who steals the goose from off the common
> But lets the greater felon loose
> Who steals the common from the goose.

The nobility had much more influence upon the social interpretation of law than did their villagers.

The conflict over changing cultural definitions of property was not simply one of rulers versus peasants. As demands for wool from the weaving industry caused many landlords to evict villagers entirely in order to raise sheep, displaced peasants created an enormous crisis of social welfare in the English countryside. Until the middle 1600s, supporters of traditional society (including many religious leaders and the Tudor and early Stuart monarchs) tried to halt the enclosures. Yet by the beginning of the industrial revolution, land had been firmly established as the private property of individual landowners. In the process, the nobility and the citizens of the towns had won a degree of political independence from the monarchy (Tierney, 1983:273–82). In doing so, they established the foundations of English parliamentary law, which became the basis of the U.S. Constitution. The legal and political institutions that arose during the industrial revolution guaranteed citizens both democratic and property rights.

The Transformation of Labor

In nonindustrial societies, work is intertwined with the other pursuits of life. Most people did not work for wages, but out of social obligations to friends and relatives. People exchanged the products of their work as gifts or through barter. People in the lowest positions of society might be slaves or serfs, with the entire pattern of their lives tied to obligations to their master or feudal lord. More fortunate members of society, however, tended to find their work filled with meaning and purpose. As they farmed or made objects, they also expressed themselves as human beings in a complex network of kinship and community. Their patterns of work were part of the broader patterns of their culture. As Nash (1966:47) reports of a New Guinea culture:

> Why the Siane work is fairly obvious. First, they must work to eat; but need alone does not call forth the effort, for in theory a man may eat even if he does little or no work. Clan status entitles a person to subsistence, but an obligation to work is vested in clan status. Within the clan all men are considered brothers, and brothers are obliged to help each other and share work loads.

During the industrial revolution, human labor was freed from the social restrictions of feudalism (including requirements that villagers work a certain number of days each year for their lord and obtain permission to travel). Instead, villagers were free to travel in search of work for wages. As capitalism released people from the social obligations of feudal society, work for wages became a social and economic necessity because traditional obligations for employers to provide housing and other social services were reduced, and greater geographical mobility removed people from the supports of kinship and community. Great poverty and social unrest were created by changes in the pattern of social relationships that had supported people in sickness or old age. Unemployment, almost unthinkable in preindustrial society, where economic activity was embedded in social life, became possible on a large scale.

The resulting social welfare crisis was debated fiercely in the British parliament during the early years of the industrial revolution. Adam Smith (1966:164) recommended higher wages and education, fearing that "too much division of labor would reduce the worker to a remarkable degree of stupidity in which he is not able to exercise his civic duties." The wretched condition of the English lower class is vividly described in the novels of Charles Dickens, although he did not write about the industrial towns. Observations of factory conditions led Marx to write the *Communist Manifesto* and predict a proletarian revolution.

A group called Luddites smashed machinery in a futile attempt to halt industrialization. According to the judge who sentenced seventeen of them to hang, their intention was:

> . . .the destruction of machinery invented for the purpose of saving manual labor in manufactures: a notion, probably suggested by evil designing persons, to captivate the working manufacturer, and engage him in tumult and crimes, by persuading him that the use of machinery occasions a decrease in the demand for personal labor, and a consequent decrease of wages, or total want of work. (Burke, 1966:5)

Today the term *Luddite* is used to refer to senseless violence against technology, but the original Luddites attacked machines only in the factories where they were being put out of work. As the industrial revolution continued, the English working class turned its political attention away from attacking machinery toward organizing labor unions and struggling for better working conditions (Thompson, 1968).

The Rationalization of Culture

Although the industrial revolution is often considered a revolution based on tools—Jacquard's 1801 loom with its punch card controls being particularly important for later data-processing technology—it was also a revolution in cultural conceptions of the world. The rationalization of economic activity was only part of a new cultural conception of a rational universe. The Reformation's challenges to religious authorities and the rise of rational scientific inquiry were precursors to the industrial revolution.

THE ECONOMIC CONSEQUENCES OF RELIGIOUS IDEAS   Capitalist ideas of property were part of a transformation of European religious beliefs. For example, the medieval view that usury (making interest on a loan) was a violation of Christian doctrine inhibited investments in manufacturing. John Calvin's mid-sixteenth-century theological argument that usury was immoral only if it created social inequity helped make investment more socially acceptable (Nelson, 1969:79). Max Weber suggests that other ideas of the Protestant Reformation had unanticipated consequences and that the Protestant ethic provided ideological justification for new forms of industrial organization. In the area of technology the desire of medieval monks to make their monasteries self-sufficient and isolated from worldly influences led them to make innovations in water mills. Water power, used in Europe from the ninth century on, provided Europeans with considerable experience in machinery long before the industrial revolution (Reynolds, 1984).

THE AGE OF SCIENTIFIC REASON   The scientific revolution that contributed so much to the techniques of manufacturing began as a challenge to established religious views of the nature of the physical world. During the sixteenth century, the "mechanical arts" flourished, setting the stage for the machines of the industrial revolution. A fascination with clocks and the laws of motion led to the invention of all sorts of mechanical devices. A systematic study of astronomy and physics began as such observers of the heavens as Johannes Kepler looked for mathematical, instead of mystical, regularities. Similarly, alchemists became chemists (Vickers, 1984). The age of scientific reason created a view of the world as a rationally organized mechanism that could be understood, predicted, and controlled.

TEMPORAL RATIONALIZATION   The appearance of public clocks marked a new temporal rationalization of society. Beginning in the monasteries and moving into the early factories, clocks organized people to pray and work in unison. In earlier epochs, time was socially measured by events, like the cycles of light and dark or the passage of seasons. Ritual, song, and dance were activities where groups kept the same time, but the idea of a universal, regular time pattern seemed wrong. (If it is hard to believe people rioted over clocks and calendar reforms, consider the reasons why today there are objections to daylight savings time.)

As work in Western Europe and the United States moved out of the homes and villages into urban factories, there appeared a cultural separation of work time and leisure time that we now regard as a normal part of human life. The organization of people to work at the same pace became part of the industrial revolution because the new machinery worked with clocklike precision. In studies of industrialization in contemporary societies, the acceptance of a Western industrial concept of time and labor discipline (measured in surveys by the ownership of a clock or watch and an understanding of the concept of being "on time" for work) is considered an important variable in the creation of a modern labor force. To Americans, there is nothing unusual about scheduling our days in hours and minutes.

THE RATIONALIZATION OF SOCIAL INTERACTION   A **particularistic social relationship** is one based on emotional evaluations of "who a person is." Race, sex, kinship, and other characteristics acquired at birth are used to determine how to act toward another person. Clear distinctions are made between behavior appropriate toward strangers and behavior appropriate to one's own group. **Universalistic social relationships** are based on general principles for acting toward other human beings. Rational judgments of how a person is acting are more important than "who" he or she is. The industrial revolution transformed particularistic social relationships into universalistic ones (Parsons and Shils, 1951:76–84). The positive contribution of universalism to human interaction was a greater willingness to cooperate with people outside one's own family, village, or region. This made possible an expansion of the international division of labor, involving the coordination of many strangers into new production processes and social structures. The negative aspect of universalism has been a loss of social solidarity in family and community and a lack of consensus in values (Berger, Berger, and Kellner, 1973).

Information and the Rise of Capitalism

Secrets are not new. Throughout history, both individuals and groups have guarded particular forms of information. The best location for fishing or finding flint for arrowheads, the techniques for working metals, magical hunting or healing techniques—all of these have been made secret. Egyptian priests kept knowledge of land surveying to themselves. Each year following the Nile floods, they ritually recalculated property boundaries, with the result that their own lands tended to get larger. Some of the first makers of iron weapons tried to prevent the diffusion of metallurgy technology, hoping to gain military superiority. Medieval European guilds used the secrets of their crafts to gain some independence for their cities against the political rule of feudal landowners. At the beginning of the industrial revolution, England prohibited the export of weaving technology; the first textile machinery in the United States was smuggled to Rhode Island piece by piece. Once assembled and copied, this illegal technology became the basis of New England's cotton industry—a major competitor for England. Yet most of this secret information was not property in the modern sense.

In nonindustrial societies, information was rarely for sale. Cultural tradition defined who was allowed to know what. In India, occupational techniques could be used only by persons of the same caste. Similarly, in many societies (including the American South), it was forbidden to teach slaves to read. Because information about supply and demand is essential to the operation of a free market, early capitalist manufacturing and trading organizations pressured their governments to provide more information about resource availability and prices. With equal fervor, however, they tried to protect information about their own activities from their competitors and their governments. Information was not transformed into commodity property in the way that land and labor had been. However, we can find the origins of information products in the printed maps and travel records of the fifteenth and sixteenth centuries. Although guarded by nations and individual navigators, the widespread copying of such documents helped broaden Europe's knowledge of geography and trade routes (Mukerji, 1983:ch.3). Innovations in accounting and bookkeeping also contributed to the rise of capitalism, but the market for the business information services we take for granted today developed very slowly. We can find its origins in railway schedules and shipping announcements of the 1800s and in the growth of banking and mail service.

The most important changes in social views of information during the rise of capitalism occurred in the political and religious spheres to challenge traditional beliefs about who should know what. The ideas of political democracy put into practice by the American and French Revolutions included the belief (expressed in the First Amendment of the U.S. Constitution) that citizens should be able to exchange information freely. With the spread of literacy, newspapers, and other publishing, freedom of information became one of the cornerstones of democracy in industrial societies. This linkage between the origins of political democracy and the industrial revolution does not imply that capitalism and democracy will necessarily continue to coexist or that industrialization is automatically the route to democracy in the developing countries of the world (de Schweinitz, 1964). The historical link between democracy and the industrial revolution was a common cultural value for free inquiry and innovative ideas.

Archibald Cox (chief Watergate prosecutor) described how the freedom to communicate information is linked in the U.S. Constitution to religious and political freedom:

> The authors of the First Amendment moved from religious liberty through the freedoms of speech and the press to political rights to assemble peaceably and to petition the government for the redress of grievances. Thus, as the freedoms of speech and of the press are linked to spiritual liberty on the one side, so they are tied to and find justification in political liberty and democracy on the other. (Cox, 1981:2)

Although information, like land and labor, was gradually freed from traditional social constraints during the rise of capitalism, it did not generally become private property. Instead, through the spread of literacy and scientific knowledge, modern information became a new collective property. Education became a major way for individuals to acquire personal knowledge from the expanding cultural storehouse. Although many people today think of education as an investment that increases the value of their labor, our public schools, libraries, and support for scientific research are indicators of the extent to which information is still defined as social property. A large-scale redefinition of information as a commodity would have a sweeping effect upon these institutions as well as upon our democratic political institutions.

 # COMPUTERS AND CAPITALISM

Marx is often misquoted as having said that the hand mill produced feudalism and the steam mill produced modern capitalist society, but his theory was not one of simple technological determinism. Before new machinery could be introduced, he argued, work must be reorganized to accommodate the equipment by those who have the power to redefine tasks and products. It was from this reorganization of work in the factory that the social and political consequences of the industrial revolution emerged. A theory of computers and social change based on the historical experiences of the rise of capitalism begins by considering computer technology as an instrument of production and information as a form of commodity property. By examining the consequences of a new division of labor made possible by computerized manufacturing and information production, we can predict the social effects of the computer revolution.

I   The Industrial Origins of the Modern Digital Computer

The modern computer has its origins in both the machinery of the early factories and the seventeenth-century mathematicians' and astronomers' fascination with computational and timing devices. For both industrialists and inventors, the rational organization of human activity was the means toward the desired goal of "progress." As the seventeenth-century mathematician Liebnitz wrote: "it is unworthy of excellent men to lose hours like slaves in the labor of calculation which could be safely relegated to anyone else if machines were used" (Smith, 1959:156–64). The "anyone else" was the person who operated the machine.

Charles Babbage, whose 1833 design for the "analytical engine" was the prototype of the modern computer, owned factories organized around the principle that "human labor is similar to capital, raw materials, etc. It is therefore subject, or ought to be subject, to similar input/output analyses, measurement, standards and controls" (Babbage, 1982:2).

The substitution of machinery for labor was an early part of the industrialization process. Marx (1973:110–26) agreed with Babbage's definition of a machine as a division of labor in which a single engine links particular operations performed by a single instrument. In this process, factory workers became components of the machine as their work is first rationally divided into coordinated tasks. Later they were replaced by machines designed to do their specialized part of the operation.

The techniques that led to the eventual development of robots and other automated equipment appeared first on factory assembly lines with manual workers serving as semiautomatic components. In fact, the word *computer* was first used to describe the jobs of women who performed calculations and wired hardware for the pioneering ENIAC. It only later meant the machine that replaced them. Such changes were not "because of" computers or any other technology; they occurred because those who had the power to decide how technology would be used reorganized the division of labor to accommodate the computer in ways they believed to be economically rational.

II   A New Division of Labor

Computer technology makes possible an extension of industrialization that Norbert Wiener (1967:208) called a "second industrial revolution," in which "the sporadic design of individual automatic mechanisms" is replaced by "communication between machine and machine." Robots based on cybernetic principles are able to do the factory work of even highly skilled workers. Their introduction extends the industrial revolution's factory automation and allows greater coordination of differentiated tasks. But, because the computer is a general purpose tool for communication and control, a radically new division of labor is now possible.

THE TRANSFORMATION OF INDUSTRIAL TIME AND SPACE   In industrial revolution factories, people worked at a pace set by machinery and enforced by supervisors. Although the temporal logic of factory machinery required a temporal discipline on the part of workers, in some new computer systems, the machine can accommodate multiple tasks occurring at different tempos and in different sequences. The new technologies speed up the production process, shortening the time between design and product. They can also be used to coordinate work performed by individuals acting at their own pace and under their own direction. Communications and control technology also makes it possible to coordinate the work of people in different cities and countries. Work has been freed from the spatial requirement of the industrial revolution that people work together in the same factory or office building. The workplace can be anywhere.

Just because the computer makes it technically possible to free people from the time and space constraints of the industrial revolution doesn't mean that work will necessarily become freer in a social sense. The division of labor in the industrial revolution was *designed* to treat people as parts of assembly lines—that was not the only way economic activity could have been arranged. The working conditions of the industrial revolution will be carried over into the information age if we design our computer systems to imitate factories.

THE INDUSTRIALIZATION OF MENTAL LABOR   After the industrial revolution, the work of clerical and technical people supported the productive work of factories. Now, with a growing market for information products, many mental laborers are directly involved in commodity production. Intellectual labor can be subjected to the same processes of rationalization and control that affected manual labor during the industrial revolution. Word processors and other automated office technologies make it possible to organize rather routine mental work into small tasks coordinated by computers. Applications like computer-aided design offer the same possibilities for some kinds of technical work.

Knowledge engineering promises the capacity to rationalize professional and managerial work as well. An enormous gap exists between the actual performance of intelligent software and knowledge engineering's claim that computers can perform as technical experts. But there are enough successes in the two hundred or so commercial expert systems to demonstrate that machines can perform a few of what were previously human mental activities (Pylyshyn, 1980; Frenkel, 1985). Growing business and military support for the "fifth generation" of intelligent computers indicates that the mechanization of thought is becoming a social fact despite theoretical reservations of philosophers and cognitive scientists.

The Social Consequences

The transformation of industrial time and space will shift attention from the social conditions of work to the physiological and psychological conditions of the human/computer interface, as more work is controlled remotely by computer systems instead of directly by managers. Response time in "conversations" with computers will replace machine pacing as a source of stress. Subjective feelings of control, mastery, and self-esteem will be sources of job satisfaction as social relationships of power and control are embodied in technology rather than experienced directly.

The production of information commodities will have an impact on the institutions that socialize people for work, for consumption, and for decision making. Although homes may become workplaces, the family is not likely to recapture its preindustrial social functions. Leisure and mass communication media will become more important socializing agents, with some of the functions of educational institutions transferred to the private sector. The forms of mental work that machines can do will be devalued as sources of self-esteem and occupational status.

Although many of our computer systems are being designed to look like factories, there will be a gradual transformation from the workplace to the work space. In the process much of the unionized industrial labor force and routine clerical work will be automated.

New jobs in the information society will be in what is now the service sector of the economy. According to one line of reasoning, these will be more creative and satisfying than those of the industrial revolution. According to an alternative argument, there will be a restratification of society marked by a declining middle class, a sharper distinction between a knowledge elite and information workers, and the growth of an impoverished underclass.

Democratic institutions will be challenged by changing definitions of property and by new means of exerting power. Conflicting demands will be placed upon the law to protect information both as property and as personal privacy. New technologies of social control will be possible in law enforcement, in government, in the military, and in business. Alternative designs are available to provide technologies of social integration that support a widespread participatory democratic process and facilitate international cooperation. The institutions of public decision making are confronted with choices that will determine the future distribution of information, property, and power.

The computer is a means to produce and distribute information, a tool both for making new forms of property and for exercising power. How computers affect individuals and society depends on the choices made in applying them to work and social life. But before discussing our choices, we should examine how computers appear to the people who are already using them. In the next two chapters we will begin the study of computers in modern society at the microlevel of analysis with the subject of *ergonomics*, the human/technology interface.

FURTHER READING FOR PART ONE

Bendix, Reinhard. 1977. *Max Weber: An Intellectual Portrait*. Berkeley: University of California Press.

Bic, Lubomir, and Jonathan P. Gilbert. 1986. "Learning from AI: New Trends in Database Technology," *IEEE Computer* (March):44–53.

Bottomore, T. B., ed. 1964. *Karl Marx: Selected Readings in Sociology and Social Philosophy*. New York: McGraw-Hill.

Boulding, Kenneth E. 1981. "Commodities as an Evolutionary System," chapter 2 in *Evolutionary Economics*. Beverly Hills, CA: Sage.

Buckley, Walter. 1967. *Sociology and Modern Systems Theory*. Englewood Cliffs, NJ: Prentice-Hall.

Calvin, William H. 1983. *The Throwing Madonna: Essays on the Brain*. New York: McGraw-Hill.

Chirot, Daniel. 1977. *Social Change in the Twentieth Century*. New York: Harcourt Brace Jovanovich.

Collins, Randall. 1985. *Three Sociological Traditions*. New York: Oxford University Press.

Fromkin, Victoria, and Roberta Rodman. 1983. *An Introduction to Language*. New York: Holt, Rinehart and Winston.

Giddens, Anthony. 1971. *Capitalism and Modern Social Theory*. Cambridge: Cambridge University Press.

Hall, Edward. 1977. *Beyond Culture*. New York: Doubleday Anchor.

Hampson, Norman. 1968. *The Enlightenment*. Harmondsworth, Middlesex, England: Penguin Books.

Hobsbawn, E. J. 1968. "The Origins of the Industrial Revolution," in *Industry and Empire*. London: Pelican.

Kling, Rob. 1980. "Social Analyses of Computing: Theoretical Perspectives in Recent Empirical Studies," *Computing Surveys* (March):61–110.

Landes, David S. 1983. *Revolution and Time: Clocks and the Making of the Modern World*. Cambridge, MA: Harvard University Press.

———. 1972. *The Unbound Prometheus*. Cambridge: Cambridge University Press.

Lukes, Steven. 1973. *Emile Durkheim: His Life and Work*. London: Penguin Books.

Machlup, Fritz, and Una Mansfield, eds. 1983. *The Study of Information*. New York: Wiley.

Mandrou, Robert. 1973. *From Humanism to Science: 1480–1700*. Harmondsworth, Middlesex, England: Penguin Books.

Menninger, Karl W. 1969. *Number Words and Number Symbols: A Cultural History of Numbers*. Cambridge, MA: MIT Press.

Merton, Robert K. 1968. *Social Theory and Social Structure*. New York: Free Press.

Mills, C. Wright. 1967. *The Sociological Imagination*. New York: Oxford University Press.

Moore, Wilbert E. 1963. *Social Change*. Englewood Cliffs, NJ: Prentice-Hall.

Mumford, Lewis. 1963. *Technics and Civilization*. New York: Harcourt, Brace.

Nash, Manning. 1966. *Primitive and Peasant Economic Systems*. San Francisco: Chandler.

Nisbet, Robert A. 1969. *Social Change and History*. London: Oxford University Press.

Plumb, J. H. 1950. *England in the Eighteenth Century*. Harmondsworth, Middlesex, England: Penguin Books.

Polanyi, Karl. 1944. *The Great Transformation*. Boston: Beacon Press.

Postan, M. M. 1975. *Medieval Economy and Society*. Harmondsworth, Middlesex, England: Penguin Books.

Skocpol, Theda, and Kay Trimberger. 1986. "Revolutions: A Structural Analysis," pages 58–65 in Jack A. Goldstone, ed. *Revolutions: Theoretical, Comparative, and Historical Studies*. New York: Harcourt Brace Jovanovich.

Smelser, Neil J., ed. 1973. *Karl Marx on Society and Social Change*. Chicago: University of Chicago Press.

von Bertalanffy, Ludwig. 1968. *General Systems Theory*. New York: George Braziller.

Wallerstein, Immanuel. 1974. *The Modern World-System*. New York: Academic Press.

Weber, Max. 1958. *The Protestant Ethic and the Spirit of Capitalism*. New York: Scribner's.

PART TWO

ERGONOMICS: THE HUMAN/TECHNOLOGY INTERFACE

CHAPTER

4

MICROERGONOMICS: PHYSIOLOGY AND PSYCHOLOGY

Is using a computer sometimes, literally, a pain in the neck? Do your eyes have trouble focusing on the screen? I know mine do as I write this sentence. Physical stress is one of the physiological problems with the video display terminal operation. Ignoring my own advice to you in this chapter, I've been sitting here five hours.

Are computers fun? Are they convenient? Does using one make you feel competent and in control? These are some of the psychological satisfactions of a "user friendly" tool. At the moment, my answers are no, yes, and yes.

But how friendly can a computer be when "friend" is a social relationship? Are you talking more to computers and less to people? Or are you using the computer as a way to communicate, perhaps the way I'm talking to you? These are some of the social issues of ergonomics, the study of the human/ technology interface. Most computer ergonomic research is microlevel. It studies the physiology and psychology of the immediate connection between computers and people.

TECHNOLOGY AND HUMAN NEEDS

The effect of the computer on the individual is often considered a technical issue involving user friendly interfaces between the person and the machine. Human factors research (as ergonomics is also called) is a relatively new field that looks at the match between the machine and the human being as a biological organism (Helander, Billingsey, and Schurick, 1984). Cognitive factors of perception and learning are also taken into account in order to create interfaces that accommodate the user. A "good" interface is *user friendly*; it meets human needs. But to understand the human/computer interaction, we must consider what human beings need.

A Functionalist Model of Human Needs

The model of human needs developed by A. H. Maslow is one of several psychological approaches to the growth of human personalities. As shown in Figure 6, it represents an overlapping set of needs whose relative strengths vary according to individual situations and personalities. Basic biological needs are strongest determinants of our actions when we are children. As our personalities develop, the "higher" cognitive and psychological needs become more important. For example, we may ignore our hunger in order to finish a computer program before dinner. Maslow's theory assumes a moral progression from personalities organized to satisfy immediate wants to those oriented toward acting responsibly in the social world.

Using Maslow's model, we could ask how computer use satisfies or frustrates individual need. The physiological requirements of human beings— food, shelter, and air are some of these—are not usually directly met by computers. However, computers indirectly contribute to the production and distribution of clothing and food. Computers may also be used to regulate furnaces and thermostats to provide a tolerable temperature. Sensory input can also be considered a physiological need because the human organism cannot interact with its environment without information. Research on cognitive factors in computing addresses the issues of how computer-generated information can be matched to human perceptual characteristics.

The next two levels of need refer to peoples' social needs. Society provides for the safety and security of its members and gives them a sense of group membership. Social institutions like the family and social relationships like friendship provide a sense of love and belonging. Although a person can survive physically without others, that person's self-identification as a member of a social group is a basic part of his or her social nature. Computers act on this level of need through their effects on institutions and relationships.

The higher needs Maslow defined are the individual psychological ones. Self-esteem is social insofar as the approval of others is a contributing factor, but self-esteem can also be personal. Self-actualization is the need to act on the basis of one's sense of self and to feel that one's activities are successful in whatever terms one values. In a study of self-actualizing persons, Maslow found them

> more efficient in perceiving reality, more accepting of themselves and others, more spontaneous in their relationships, with a tendency to center on problems and their solution; to have a quality of privacy and detachment, and autonomy from cultural influences, a freshness of appreciation, a capacity for transcendence and oceanic feelings, a deep identification with humanity, more profound

FIGURE 6
MASLOW'S MODEL OF HUMAN NEEDS

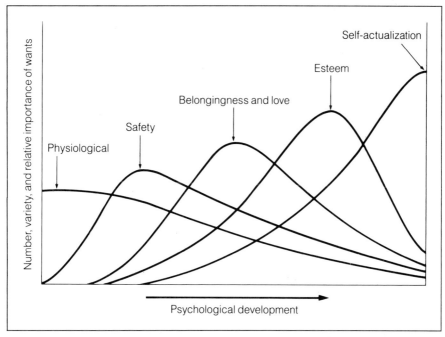

Source: David Kretch, Richard S. Crutchfield, and Egerton L. Ballachey. *Individual in Society.* New York: McGraw-Hill, 1962, p. 77. Used by permission of McGraw-Hill Book Co.

human attachments, a humorous and democratic character structure, and a rare capacity to resolve moral dichotomies and dilemmas. (Hampden-Turner, 1982:118)

Although all social theorists would agree with Maslow that individuals have biological, social, and psychological needs, not all would agree with his selection or his priorities. There is great disagreement over what peoples' biological requirements are and where biology gives way to culture in defining them. Some theorists would add competition or territoriality to the list; others would argue about whether self-esteem is based on social status or on private, internal feelings of satisfaction. Others would question whether the needs for personal identity are "higher" than the social needs to fulfill the obligations and gain the benefits of group membership. Environmentalists would argue that there is a higher need to preserve and protect the earth for future generations; philosophers and theologians would make a case for an even higher level of spiritual need.

Ⅴ Capitalism and Human Needs

Critical social psychology argues that "as society becomes increasingly commodified, social interaction and the conditions which make it possible disappear" (Wexler, 1983:97). Advertising creates artificial social needs and develops personalities whose self-satisfaction is derived from consumption (Ewen, 1976). As the market for commodity production expands, it replaces social relationships in providing material security and supplying recreational and even emotional needs (Braverman, 1974:276–77). From this perspective, computer-mediated social interactions represent an additional intrusion of the commodity market into social life.

According to this viewpoint, the goal of ergonomics research is not to meet any individual needs, but to match humans with computers in ways that raise productivity. Improved comfort or user satisfaction are most important in cases where improved satisfaction leads to productivity increases. Where there is a conflict between productivity and comfort, design choices will be made for productivity.

THE PHYSIOLOGY OF THE HUMAN/COMPUTER INTERACTION

Computer use is a physical activity involving hands, eyes, ears, and body. The goals of improving the health and safety of computer users is usually compatible with the goal of higher productivity. This is because the factors causing physical stress or damage also tend to make people less productive.

Physical Stress

Computer users frequently report muscular and skeletal stress. Like any other job requiring long periods of sitting at attention, using a terminal can be uncomfortable. With properly designed furniture, much of this stress can be alleviated. The chair should be at a height to prevent leg strain; the keyboard should be at a height to prevent tension buildup in the back of the neck caused by holding the arms in an awkward position. Wrist rests, advocated by some designers, have been found by researchers to be unnecessary or even a hindrance to someone constantly using the keyboard.

Unless a workstation is to be used by only one person, furniture must be adjustable (as shown in Figure 7). Designs for the average man or woman are usually unsuitable for just about everybody except those few whose body proportions happen to be exactly average. For example, I am of average height for a woman when sitting down and of average height for a man when standing up. Before adjustable workstations were common, my legs were "too long" and my body was "too short" for on-the-job comfort. From the perspective of ergonomics, variations in human proportions are a "given"; the designer's task is to make a machine that accommodates the variety in human form.

No amount of design, however, can change the fact that the human body did not evolve the ability to remain motionless for long periods of time. Frequent changes in position and physical exercise are both essential for

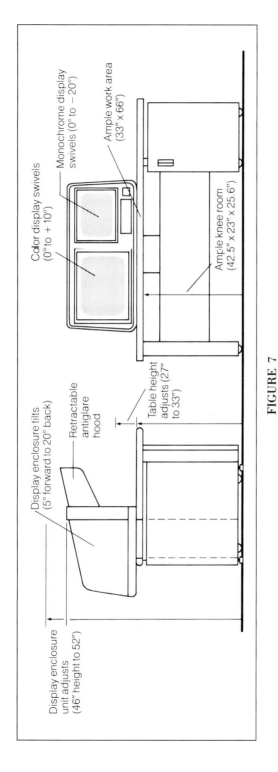

FIGURE 7

ERGONOMIC WORKSTATION PARAMETERS

The range of adjustment for ergonomic features is shown in this figure, reprinted by permission of Control Data Corporation.

maintaining muscle tone and avoiding stress and fatigue. Improvements in voice-operated computers may be the best way to match active humans to immobile machines. In the meantime, computer users and workstation designers are developing more awareness of the physical consequences of their work. "User friendly" hardware shouldn't give the user a pain in the neck. When you have the choice, you should plan your own work to avoid long sessions seated at a computer terminal. I find short walks and long backrubs ideal.

Vision

The human eye is a rather delicate optical system. The most well documented health problems associated with computer use have been eyestrain, with sometimes permanent damage. Eyestrain can result both from poor lighting (Sliney, 1985) and from poor resolution of displayed characters. Glare can be reduced by keeping a screen away from windows and ensuring that no light fixtures shine directly on the screen. Overhead lighting for workstations is less effective than indirect lights on the material being typed in an otherwise dim room. Fluorescent lighting creates a special visual problem because the cathode ray tube in the terminal and the fluorescent bulb both fluctuate rapidly. This may cause a flicker effect that is very stressful to the eyes. Incandescent light (the ordinary light bulb) is recommended. Eye specialist Lowell Glatt (*VDT News*, May/June 1985:5) recommends that people with any visual problems should not work at video display terminals.

The productivity factor of most concern to designers of screen displays is the eye's ability to distinguish shapes. In addition to causing eyestrain, failure to make visual discriminations can result in higher error rates for whatever type of work is being done. Character fonts (the shape of letters and numbers) can be designed to improve people's recognition of individual characters. When characters are displayed as a pattern of small dots on the screen, the greater the number of dots used, the greater the character's readability. In character fonts made in a 7 × 9 matrix (the smallest number of dots for legible characters), the following letters are most often confused (Ericsson, 1984:8–9):

- O and Q
- T and Y
- S and 5
- I and L
- I and 1

In addition, some one-way confusion occurs:

- C read as G
- D read as B
- H read as M or N
- J or T read as I

- K read as R
- 2 read as Z
- B read as R, S, or 8

Improvements in font design include using more dots per character and designing the shapes of commonly confused letters so that they appear quite distinct.

Proper contrast between character and background is an important lighting factor. Sharp edges between a character and its background improve our ability to see it. Many personal computer screens are quite fuzzy. Although light characters on dark backgrounds are most common, glare and user error rates are reportedly lower for dark characters on light backgrounds. Improvements in display resolution include the use of color combinations (like the popular amber on black) that are easier on the eyes.

Although the use of color in screen displays can reduce fatigue and be psychologically more interesting, about 8 percent of all males (and about 0.5 percent of females) are colorblind to some extent, most commonly to red, green, or both (Birren, 1978). Color vision involves high-level processes of the brain and can affect people's moods as well as their perceptions of objects. Blues and greens tend to be soothing and make objects appear more distant; reds and yellows are more exciting and near (Gregory, 1981:125; Radl, 1985:26). What is important about color vision for computer designers is that people do not all see color in the same way. In applying research findings to the art of making computer displays, Gerald Murch (1984:49–54) offers several suggestions:

- Avoid the simultaneous display of highly saturated, spectrally extreme colors.
- Pure blues should be avoided for text, thin lines, and small shapes.
- Avoid adjacent colors that differ only in the amount of blue.
- Older operators need higher brightness levels to distinguish colors.
- Colors change in appearance as the ambient light level changes.
- The magnitude of a detectable change in color varies across the spectrum.
- It is difficult to focus upon edges created by color alone.
- Avoid red and green in the periphery of large-scale displays.
- Red and green or yellow and blue make better combinations than red and yellow or blue and green for images.
- For color-deficient observers, avoid single-color distinctions.

Ergonomic factors in screen design include information about how people read. In English and other left-to-right languages, screens that present material from left to right are more successful than top-to-bottom ones. This applies as well to the number pad found on many terminals and calculators. When the numbers 7, 8, and 9 are on the top row, users make more errors than when the top row is 1, 2, and 3. Although many of our designs are "traditional," even experienced users adjust easily to a new layout and quickly improve their performance.

A final example of a visual discrimination problem built into a traditional design is the data-entry form with little boxes for each letter. Filling in the boxes by hand takes 16 percent longer than writing the material on a straight line. Reading the boxes takes 28 percent longer than reading material written on a line. The boxes also result in a higher error rate when someone types from them onto a computer keyboard (Wright, 1984). The people who first designed forms with boxes probably thought they were matching human data-recording techniques with the requirements of efficient keypunch machine operation. But microergonomic research showed us that an interface that doesn't match human perceptual requirements is less efficient for data processing.

Based on its best available information, the Human Factors Society (1985) proposed an American National Standard for Human Factors Engineering of Visual Display Terminal Workstations. For information on the current status of ergonomic recommendations, consult the current version of the standard.

VDT Radiation

Radiation is an emotionally charged topic, more likely to be associated with nuclear explosions than with familiar objects like microwave ovens or color television sets. Video display terminals (VDTs) can emit electromagnetic radiation from extremely low frequencies (ELF) to the low end of X rays, as shown in Figure 8. So do other electrical and electronic appliances. Almost all of this radiation is low-frequency, nonionizing. The dangerous ionizing radiation associated with nuclear reactions is in a much higher frequency range. Medical X rays, not computers, account for over 95 percent of our exposure to ionizing radiation (Grundy, 1978).

According to recent research, VDT terminals meet the guidelines established by the American National Standards Institute for safe levels of exposure to both ionizing and low-frequency radiation (Murray, 1984). However, because it is difficult to measure extremely low frequency electromagnetic fields, and because human neurological and cell processes occur in that range, scientists do not have enough evidence on the biological effects of VDT radiation in this range to conclude that it is harmless (Harvey, 1984).

STATIC ELECTRICITY   If your computer terminal gives you small electric shocks, especially after you walk across a wool rug, it's not radiating—it's building up an electrostatic charge. Just as socks cling together when they come out of the dryer, this can attract dust to the screen, interfering with your vision. Some research suggests that particles can also be attracted to the VDT operator, causing in rare cases a skin rash (Tjønn, 1984). Companies make antistatic features (including floor coverings and deionizing devices) to protect floppy diskettes and other magnetically encoded data from being accidentally erased by static electric discharge.

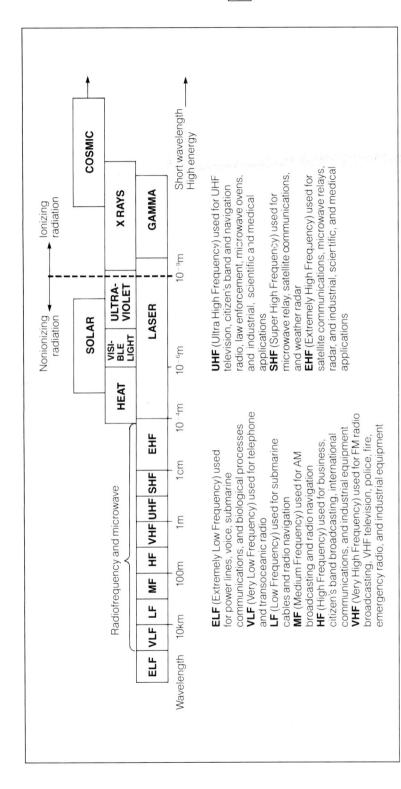

FIGURE 8

THE ELECTROMAGNETIC RADIATION SPECTRUM

Used by permission of the Radiation Protection Bureau, National Health and Welfare, Canada.

Static buildup may also affect your mood. An imbalance of positively charged ions in the air can cause irritability and fatigue. A balance of negatively charged ions (as often found in mountaintop areas) is reportedly invigorating. Some research has found that negative ion generators reduce the frequency of headaches and make employees feel more comfortable and alert (Hawkins, 1984).

THE RISKS OF EXCESSIVE MICROWAVE EXPOSURE   A long-term study of career officers in the Polish military has found a positive correlation between cancer and long, job-related exposures to high levels of microwave and radiofrequency radiation (Dolnick, 1985). Microwaves can cause cataracts, according to studies by ophthalmologists. In the United States, a lawsuit for cataract damage believed to be caused by VDT radiation was settled out of court, awarding $10,000 to a woman who was unable to read for more than ten minutes or to tolerate bright light. The New York Workman's Compensation Board ruled that there was a "recognizable link" between VDT work and a claimant's eye damage (*VDT News*, Jan./Feb. 1985:8). However, microwave ovens and color televisions are more common sources of microwave exposure than are VDT terminals. When appliances and terminals are functioning properly, they do not "leak" dangerous levels of microwave radiation.

Terminals can be shielded to prevent emissions. Although the Computer and Business Equipment Manufacturers Association called the announcement of a VDT radiation shield an "irresponsible" appeal to the fears of people who know little about radiation (CBEMA, 1985), an IBM report recommended shielding older terminals. It concluded that the newer ones are better designed and represent no hazard (*VDT News*, March/April 1985:4–7). People who are worried about the possible effects of display terminal radiation should also be concerned about their TV set. Doubling the distance between yourself and the screen will reduce your exposure to any possible emissions by 75 percent.

POSSIBLE REPRODUCTIVE HAZARDS   The possibility of a connection between VDTs and reproductive hazards is an issue characterized by few facts and much controversy (Foster, 1986). One study reported that continuous exposure to an extremely low frequency field over several months reduced the sperm viability of male rats; another reported an increased rate of birth defects in the children of fathers working at high-voltage electric power plants (Nordstrom, Birke, and Gustavsson, 1983). This possible damage to male reproductive cells is believed to be because some sperm cells become heated, the way a microwave oven heats food (Jensh, Weinberg, and Brent, 1982).

Women, whose reproductive organs are better protected by layers of body tissue, have also been studied for possible reproductive damage. Although clusters of problem pregnancies have been reported among VDT operators, the evidence has been insufficient to establish any radiation hazard. Physical stress, for example, might be a contributing factor in miscarriages. Several major international studies are under way to evaluate any potential problems (*VDT News*, July/August 1985:4–6). A large Finnish study of birth defects found no evidence that they were related to VDT use by the mothers (*VDT News*, Jan./Feb. 1985:12); one Swedish study linked VDT radiation to fetal malformations in mice (*VDT News*, March/April 1986:4–7). A United States National Institute for Occupational Safety and Health (NIOSH) study, held up by the administration since 1982, began looking at the potential reproductive hazards among American women who use VDTs in the fall of 1986 (Sun, 1986).

DEFINING VDT HEALTH RISKS   Defining health risks is more than a scientific question of what radiation is produced by computers and what effects electromagnetic fields have on biological organisms. It is also a social issue, defined by the concerns of employees and their unions, the interests of manufacturers and businesses, and the policy-making institutions of government and law. My own research on reproductive protection policy for industry makes me appreciate how difficult it is to make decisions in the absence of good information.

The possible health effect of VDT radiation remains an unresolved issue in ergonomic research, in public policy, and in computer design. Should the hazards finally be assessed as serious, shielding users from extremely low frequency emissions would become a social priority in computer technology. Although the U.S. Congressional Office of Technology Assessment (1985a, 1985c) concluded that there is insufficient evidence of risk to establish VDT regulations, it recommended continuing research. Many states and countries have passed laws regulating VDTs, and the World Health Organization (1986) has begun a working group to evaluate reproductive, visual, musculoskeletal, and skin disorders that may be associated with VDT use. While the health effects of computers are as yet uncertain, they have already become a subject for the political process through which we define and develop remedies for social problems.

Computers for the Handicapped

Although most microergonomics research focuses on the industrial applications of computer technology, another important area that studies the match between humans and machines is bioengineering. There the focus is on medical procedures, artificial limbs, and computer aids for the blind, deaf, or physically immobilized. In the functionalist model of the human/computer interface, computer aids for the handicapped are a clear example of meeting the most basic sort of human need. From a critical perspective, these would be viewed as contributing new products to the market for medical commodities and as making handicapped people better able to do productive work.

COMMUNICATION FOR THE DEAF   One of the earliest telecommunication networks, the TELEX system, supported a class of specially designed terminals (TDDs) for the deaf. Intended to replace the telephone, they allowed subscribers to transmit written messages to one another. Today, any personal computer with communication capability can be used to transmit written text, and the five-bit code for the TDDs can be easily translated to and from the standard ASCII communication code. A recent innovation is a computerized pair of eyeglasses that displays a visual signal generated by a small voice analyzer. Designed as an aid to lip readers, the display distinguishes sounds that look deceptively alike. Implanted electronic ears have been in use since the 1960s. Researchers now plan to develop a microchip version that will provide voice recognition signals (Zoler, 1983).

DATA ACCESS FOR THE BLIND   Specially equipped terminals are used by the blind, who may also expect to benefit from improvements in voice-activated systems. The Kurzweil reading machine was an early practical result of voice analysis research. It uses an optical scanner and sound synthesizer to "read" printed text aloud. Although it is expensive (about $30,000) and limited in capability, it is part of what may be a major new area of computer applications for sighted as well as blind users. New technologies for braille writing and reading are being developed, but better technology to convert visual images to three-dimensional representations is still needed. A recent innovation is a computerized tactile grid that allows the blind to "see" graphics output. Even more exciting are the experiments in transmitting computer-generated visual signals that bypass the eyes. Although this is not expected to restore sight, it is hoped that it will enable some blind people to distinguish shapes.

ROBOTICS FOR THE PHYSICALLY IMPAIRED   Robots are tools for manipulating objects by remote control. Although most current developments in the field are aimed at military and industrial interests, the same technology can be applied to preserve the health of people working with hazardous chemicals and to provide hands and arms for people whose mobility is limited. At the University of Utah, researchers use advanced robotics and computer graphics to design artificial arms that can be controlled by the amputee's nervous system. Similar graphical techniques are coming into use to analyze body motion in sport and dance (Deken, 1983:137–43; Voy, 1984). Voice recognition and other nonkeyboard data-entry systems, although still in the experimental stages, should benefit individuals who have physical trouble handling books, telephones, and other information equipment. Also in the experimental stages is a computer-controlled device to transmit nerve impulses to the legs of people paralyzed by spinal cord injuries.

MEETING HUMAN NEEDS?   Like the Kurzweil reading machine, many of the new computer applications for the handicapped are prohibitively expensive. A voice synthesizer for a mute child can cost $100,000 (*Newsweek*, Nov. 4, 1985:65–66). Even the relatively inexpensive lip-reading glasses are expected to cost about $4000. Other products are announced with great enthusiasm while they are still experimental. Bioengineer Howard Chizeck (1985) criticizes commercial promises of electronic devices to let the paralyzed walk again, arguing that they hold out false hopes for a product that is really years away. There is a gap between what a computer professional knows the technology can do, if resources are available to develop an application, and what is practically feasible for the majority of handicapped people. Chizeck asks "Who will pay?" and concludes that computer applications that save health care costs and make people employable will be paid for by insurers. Those that only improve the quality of life, like being able to walk when you can already get to work in a wheelchair, may not be. Although the technology is available, it may not be affordable.

THE PSYCHOLOGY OF HUMAN/COMPUTER INTERACTION

Psychology is the study of human beings as they relate to the world, to one another, and to themselves. Although the sociologist takes the relationships among people in larger groups as a starting point for study, the psychologist focuses on the individual. In a review of the literature on self-concept, Louis Zurcher (1977) identifies four rather distinct ways in which individuals think of themselves. If you would like to try Zurcher's model on some actual data, write the phrase "I am _____" twenty times. Fill in the blanks before reading the next paragraph.

The *physical self* is your experience of yourself as a biological organism. If you wrote "I am six feet tall" or "I am hungry," you were describing yourself in this way. The human/computer interface influences this dimension of self-concept by changing our physical activities and physiological experiences. If your statements included a description of your roles ("a student," "a parent," "a vice-president"), your particular social relationships ("Mary's best friend"), or your group identifications ("an American"), you were thinking of your *social self*. This dimension of the self is of most interest to sociologists. The feeling of self-esteem is part of the social self-concept.

In religious or mystical experiences, people report an *oceanic self* that is part of the whole universe. If your sentences described your relationship to the sacred, you were describing this dimension of self-concept. Many cultures encourage people to think of themselves in this way; ours tends to view mysticism outside of conventional religious institutions as a form of deviance. An oceanic sense of oneself as having special insight into or power over the universe can medically be considered a symptom of mental illness. It can also be considered sacrilegious by people who believe in God. Because the computer interface can heighten our feelings of connectedness and our feelings of power, some observers think the technology will encourage the oceanic self-concept.

There is also a dimension of the self that thinks about its own existence. If you wrote a sentence like "I am someone who thinks about who I am," you were experiencing your *reflexive self*. Self-actualizing people are reflexive. They not only act in satisfying ways; they comprehend the meanings and consequences of their actions. Some psychologists think that, by reflecting on our experience of the human/computer interface, we will change our understanding of what it means to be human.

The Psychology of Stress

The stresses computer users experience are psychological as well as physical. One theory proposes that stress has two components: the physical effects of the human/machine interface on the body and the degree of control people have over their activities (Karasek et al., 1981). For example, secretaries report more signs of stress (headaches, eyestrain, and back problems) than do their bosses (*Chronicle of Higher Education*, November 28, 1984:5). High-stress jobs are those with some physical strain and very little autonomy.

Jobs like air traffic controller are reportedly high-stress occupations, but studies have shown air traffic controllers to suffer few physiological symptoms. They seem to enjoy the pace, responsibilities, and status of their jobs. However, they have little voice in decision making or advancement into management, which is quite authoritarian (Landsbergis, 1985). A study of Silicon Valley found electronics assembly work one of the five most stressful occupations in the region, along with air traffic controller, intensive care nurse, police officer, and teacher (*Global Electronics Information Newsletter* January 1981:4). Most of these are not physically stressing jobs so much as positions of great responsibility with very little discretion.

Managers and individuals can use research findings about stress when they plan work activities. As shown in Figure 9, the way that work itself is organized can affect physical strain. Workers with more control over their activities at the terminal report less physical stress. Stress can be reduced by an organization of tasks that do not require continuous keyboard operation. Long sessions at the keyboard can be broken up. Activities that require standing or walking can be interspersed with those that require sitting. In addition to improving productivity, such arrangements can help prevent chronic and permanent muscular and skeletal damage.

Stress also seems to have a temporal dimension. Research on assembly line workers has shown that people do not like to work with perfectly regular, clock-tick motions. Instead, people like to be able to control the tempo of their own work. When they are able, assembly line workers prefer to alternate speeding up and slowing down the line. It gives them a feeling of control over their work and breaks the monotony.

Response Time

Although human reactions to computer response times are partly psychological, there is some evidence that human beings have a limited range of rhythms to which they can physically adjust. According to Edward Hall

FIGURE 9
EFFECT OF JOB DESIGN ON STRAIN

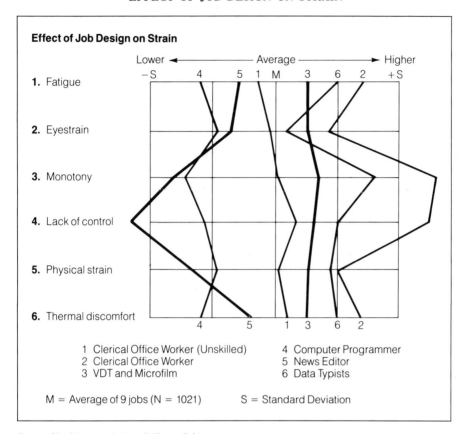

Effect of Job Design on Strain

1 Clerical Office Worker (Unskilled)   4 Computer Programmer
2 Clerical Office Worker   5 News Editor
3 VDT and Microfilm   6 Data Typists

M = Average of 9 jobs (N = 1021)   S = Standard Deviation

Source: Used by permission of Ahmet Cakir.

(1983), **entrainment** occurs when people interact with one another. During this process, all participants begin to synchronize their speech and motions. Sea chanteys and other work songs are some of the cultural aids to entrainment; music and dance are expressions of this social process. If you have ever found yourself getting "into the swing" of some activity, you are probably experiencing entrainment.

Programs that pace the user at a fixed speed have the same effects as assembly lines; they have been most successful in software designed to help people increase their typing speeds by "driving" them to type faster. Because people have chosen the typing software to improve their own skills, the response time demands are a challenge—not an imposition. When response time was increased in an on-line computer system at work, employees initially reported higher levels of stress (Turner, 1984).

Although much of the research on computer response time is concerned with speeding up data processing, it seems possible that some patterns of human/machine interaction do not suit human beings. In a study at Ogden,

Utah, medical researcher Charles Seizler found rotating shift work associated with cardiovascular, sleep, and digestive disorders. As with jet lag, the people in his study had trouble moving their internal clocks forward. In other words, you have more trouble changing your schedule to get up several hours earlier than usual than you do staying up several hours later.

RESPONSE TIME AND CONVERSATIONAL TIMING   Because interaction with the computer is often interpreted by the user as "conversation," a slow computer can have a psychological effect similar to waiting for a particularly slow speaker to finish a sentence. As an experiment, try talking to someone with long pauses between all your words and watch his or her reaction.

Table 3 lists response times found acceptable to computer users. Notice that acceptable response times for actions that are analogous to manipulating objects are shorter than those for conversationlike interactions (for example, waiting for the computer to answer your question). Recent research by IBM has found user productivity increased by as much as 100 percent when "conversational" response times are decreased from two seconds to a few tenths of a second (Brady, 1986). Such findings have been criticized by analysts, who warn that we need more and better ergonomic research before we rush out to buy expensive new equipment for the sake of a fractional increase in response time (Lyman, Anderson, and Plewa, 1985).

We also need to understand what faster response time means to users. We could, for example, interpret the study as showing that higher productivity can be obtained by pushing people to work faster. But faster response time may instead represent a change in the way the user thinks about the human/ machine interface. Higher productivity may be obtained by thinking of the computer as a tool that does not require the human conversational tempo. If we think of a computer as a device for turning pages or moving data rather than as a conversational partner from which we expect appropriate pauses, we may handle information much more quickly. Because a few tenths of a second is a reasonable time to wait before the "thing" we push moves, perhaps the shorter interaction times represent an end to thinking of computer interaction as "conversation" and the beginning of thinking about it as a tool.

AGE AND RESPONSE TIME   As we age, the speed of our mental processes slows. Designing computer interfaces with extremely short response times may create stress for older users; although some people view any signs of confusion in the elderly as signs of impending senility, all of us become disoriented in interactions that move faster than we can. As an example, I have enjoyed playing cards with (and losing to) my mother for many years. Lately I have begun to win when the game moves too quickly for her. However, when we play at a slightly slower pace she still beats me regularly. Unfortunately for me, rapid response time is not a measure of knowledge or wisdom. When designing computer interfaces we should realize that people have a wide range of normal response times. A user friendly interface should let us age gracefully by slowing down as we do.

TABLE 3
ACCEPTABLE RESPONSE TIMES

Time from key depression to display of character	0.2 secs
Time from issuing a command to response	2.0 secs
Response time for simple query	2.0 secs
Response time for complex query	5.0 secs
Display new page	1.0 secs
Scrolling	0.5 secs
Time between entry of error and error message	2.0 secs

Source: Ericsson Information Systems. *Proceedings of the World Conference on Ergonomics in Computer Systems.* Garden Grove, CA: (September 1984), pp. 8 9.

Conversations with a Computer

Can you really have a conversation with a computer? Or is it a reification of human social relationships to imagine ourselves communicating with a machine instead of with its programmer? People sometimes treat computers, automobiles, teddy bears, and other objects as if they were living beings with wills of their own. Software for children often encourages this with error messages like "I DON'T KNOW HOW TO ————." Even adults can relate to software as if it were a person.

COMPUTER PROGRAMS AS COUNSELORS   The ELIZA program simulates a Rogerian psychotherapist, chosen because Rogerians try to have the patient take all the initiative in conversation. Using a keyword-driven sentence generator, ELIZA produces sentences like "TELL ME MORE ABOUT YOUR MOTHER" in response to a user's sentence containing the word *mother.* If you typed "My mother country is Czechoslovakia," ELIZA would "ask" for more information about your mother. If you typed "I dreamed about matricide," the version of ELIZA I have wouldn't "know" you dreamed of killing your mother because *matricide* isn't in its keyword dictionary. Joseph Weizenbaum, who created ELIZA as a simple demonstration of an artificial intelligence technique, was appalled by the degree to which people derived "interpersonal" satisfaction by "conversing" with his program. To social psychologist Sherry Turkle (1983), these conversations provide "the illusion of companionship without the demands of friendship."

THE FUTURE OF THE CONVERSATIONAL INTERFACE   Artificial intelligence researcher Richard Bolt (1984) believes that computer interfaces of the future should become even more conversational. He thinks that computers should "know" where users are looking and accept speech and gestures as input, responding to the presence and normal behavior of the human. But Bolt's experimental interfaces that respond when you point or look at them are not conversations in the social sense. Instead, they are projections of one of our deepest fantasies—to have our wishes become deeds without effort on our part. The idea that a glance or a gesture could have a physical impact on the world satisfies a powerful desire for mastery and control that some people bring to the human/computer interface.

Commercial software companies have begun to take advantage of our willingness to talk to computers by selling counseling software on topics ranging from sexual impotence to how to make a better sales pitch (Murray, 1983; Rogers, 1984b; Rice, 1986). In advertising, the promise that a new computer system "lets you be the master of your universe" appeals to oceanic fantasies of power.

Children's Ideas and Adult Attitudes

Computer users report a range of attitudes, from excitement and satisfaction to fear or boredom. "Computer phobia," the irrational fear of using computers, can be a rational response to individual experiences with computer use. Attitude differences with regard to age and sex have been found, and some observers suggest that an obsessive fascination with the computer is a new form of neurotic behavior. From studies of children relating to computers, some researchers have predicted that the computer will radically change our views of ourselves and our world.

MASTERING THE MACHINE   Seymour Papert (1980) argues that the computer is an ideal tool for teaching children abstract mathematical and spatial relationships. Papert and his MIT colleagues developed the LOGO language and with it taught children geometry and programming as a form of play. With a terminal, children directed the activities of a robot "turtle" and easily learned to draw by writing turtle programs. The children eagerly taught one another techniques they had discovered and proceeded on their own to learn more about what the turtle could do; in addition, they invented programs for themselves. The lesson—that computers are controlled by humans (rather than vice versa)—was clear.

Even for adults, LOGO is a rewarding introduction to computer programming. It is as simple as the elementary BASIC language yet contains the recursive procedures and list-processing features of higher-level languages like LISP. New users get the immediate satisfaction of seeing the turtle (usually a small triangle on the screen) do just what they told it to do. More important, after playing with LOGO, beginners have a fairly broad sense of what a computer can do.

For children, LOGO is an introduction to computers that bestows a sense of mastery over the machine. For them, the computer is a fascinating toy that does all kinds of things after you give it orders. They learn that they can use a computer to act out an imagined design. The experience also teaches them the value of making mistakes. Many of their favorite discoveries are made after giving the turtle a "wrong" command.

THE SECOND SELF   To better understand how children think about themselves in relation to computers, Sherry Turkle observed a children's play group for five years. During that time she recorded their conversations, their interactions with electronic toys, and their interactions with one another. She compared her findings with Piaget's earlier work on how children develop reasoning and moral judgment. In looking at how children understand what it means to be alive and human, Turkle found some interesting differences from Piaget's findings of the 1940s. Children who played with computer toys put more emphasis on feelings and emotions as defining characteristics of human beings and less stress on reason and calculation. Her findings, reported in *The Second Self: Computers and the Human Spirit*, suggest that computer use does not, as many observers had feared, make people less sensitive to the emotional and interpersonal aspects of being human. If anything, it appears that instrumental rationality (or goal-oriented logical reasoning) may become less important in our culture's definition of "being human."

COMPUTER PHOBIA AND SELF-ESTEEM   *Computer phobia* is a popular term for an irrational fear of using the computer. To a psychologist, phobia is more than fear. For instance, my reluctance to go to the dentist is rational if I am afraid of the pain of having my teeth drilled; it is a phobia if the very thought of seeing a dentist makes me tremble, and I can't make myself drive down the street his office is on. From a sociological viewpoint, computer phobia is often a case of "blaming the victim" (Ryan, 1971). This occurs when any possible problems with hardware reliability, software design, user interface, documentation, and real threats to the user's economic status and self-esteem are ignored. Instead, the reluctant user is blamed for being irrational. When the computer is perceived as a hostile object threatening human control over situations and interactions, the solution is not to focus on the irrationality of the reluctant user, but to analyze the basis of his or her fears.

A person's experience with a computer can affect self-esteem in positive ways (for example, a person can be proud of being a good programmer). Computers can also contribute to self-actualization (for example, through the satisfaction a programmer gets from making a program work). Or computer use can have a negative effect on self-worth if the experience makes a person feel incompetent or unfulfilled. For example, people who feel competent and skillful because they are expert typists may feel less satisfied when first learning to use a word processor. Initially, they will be less able to apply their skills to turning out high-quality finished text.

If a person is highly skilled and performs well within an existing organization, computers may render his or her skills obsolete. This is a threat to job status, individual pride, and satisfaction. It can also raise real barriers to the successful implementation of computer technology in organizations (Warner, 1984c). If the computer is introduced in ways that allow people to preserve their positions and enhance their skills, less "phobia" will result.

USER FRIENDLY FOR WHOM?   In some cases, the basis of reluctance to use computers is that they are difficult to learn, and people are afraid of looking foolish. The situation calls for good documentation, nonthreatening training, and the opportunity for users to see for themselves that the new way is "better." This assumes, of course, that the new way *is* better. In some cases, in our enthusiasm to computerize our activities, we embark on the process with equipment and procedures that are in some ways *less* effective. Word processors, for example, are ideal tools for text that must be revised, corrected, and reprinted. They are often not as quick as a typewriter or a pen for a short memo or note. Sometimes the new equipment breaks frequently and cannot be easily fixed, causing very real frustrations. Figure 10 shows the printout from a computerized taxi meter. Although management might dismiss the driver's complaints as computer phobia, the driver maintained that no matter how often the computers were repaired, they did not stand up to potholes.

User friendly software can be as much of an affront to human self-esteem as systems that are frustratingly difficult. If "designing for idiots is the highest expression of the engineering art" (Noble, 1980:xvi), then how are the operators of that machine to feel a sense of status and accomplishment? One solution is to design "natural" user interfaces in which the machine matches the habits of the people. One example of this is an experimental electronic mail system. Its command language was constructed based upon the words chosen by naive users to accomplish mail searching, reading, and deleting (Good et al., 1984). Another solution is to provide "training wheels" to make software extremely friendly for new users yet allow experienced users to avoid annoying prompts and menus (Carroll and Carrithers, 1984). New multimedia interfaces are being designed for users at different levels of skill and for those who prefer visual explanations (Mozeico, 1982; "Multimedia Communications," 1985; Thomas et al., 1985). In the experimental APEX system, documentation is by demonstration—the user is shown techniques through computer-generated motion pictures (Feiner, 1985). Bolt's conversational interfaces are extremely user friendly.

Sex and the Compulsive Programmer

The sense of mastery, identified by psychologists as an important part of positive attitudes toward computers, has become for some people an obsession. Among many of the adults interviewed by Turkle (1984), a feeling of empowerment contributed positively toward self-esteem. Computer users report feeling satisfaction and a sense of accomplishment from getting the machines to carry out their commands. But Joseph Weizenbaum (1976) finds that among computer hackers, elaborate fantasies of computer mastery are unrelated to real-world events or issues.

THE COMPULSIVE PROGRAMMER   The compulsive programmer described by Weizenbaum is caught up in the process of programming and views it as an unending contest between hacker and computer. Working programs are not the goal—compulsive programmers rarely finish programs. Nor is the goal to realize a mental design—hackers' code is marked by patches, poor documentation, and bugs, and is rarely planned in advance. The main goal for the

FIGURE 10
COMPUTERIZED TAXICAB PRINTOUT

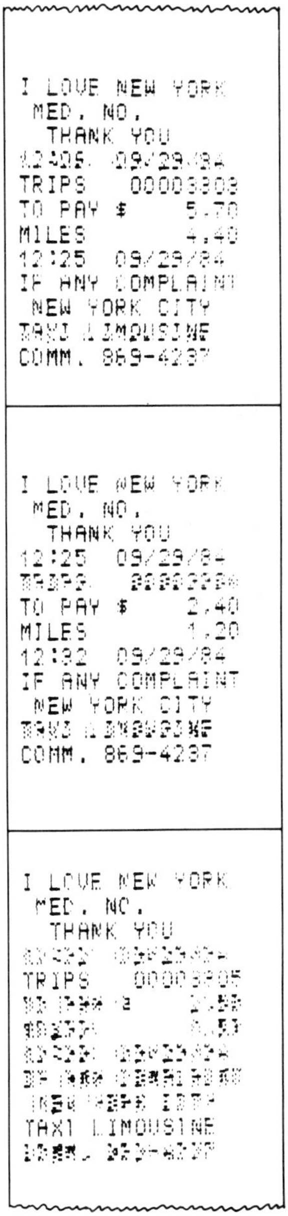

```
I LOVE NEW YORK
 MED. NO.
   THANK YOU
12505  09/29/84
TRIPS   0000330B
TO PAY $    5.70
MILES       4.40
12:25  09/29/84
IF ANY COMPLAINT
 NEW YORK CITY
TAXI LIMOUSINE
COMM. 869-4237
```

```
I LOVE NEW YORK
 MED. NO.
   THANK YOU
12:25  09/29/84
TRIPS   0000330B
TO PAY $    2.40
MILES       1.20
12:32  09/29/84
IF ANY COMPLAINT
 NEW YORK CITY
TAXI LIMOUSINE
COMM. 869-4237
```

```
I LOVE NEW YORK
 MED. NO.
   THANK YOU
       09/29/84
TRIPS   00003305
TO PAY $
MILES
       09/29/84
IF ANY COMPLAINT
 NEW YORK CITY
TAXI LIMOUSINE
COMM. 869-4237
```

compulsive programmer seems to be control over the computer. Not only does programming interfere with social relationships; compulsive programmers seem to find it a substitute for them.

The successful programmer usually does like to finish projects and see a program actually working. Although creative professionals may put in long hours and spend the last weeks of a project ignoring everything else, they live in a real world with other humans and company deadlines. Their goal is to accomplish something in the world rather than to live out a fantasy of the grandiose but never-finished computer program. Professional programmers are part of a division of labor. Norms for their roles include communication and cooperation with others (including producing good documentation). Although the professional programmer often gets psychological satisfaction from programming, the process itself is not a substitute for living in the social world.

Many adults view computer hackers as young geniuses, but more experienced computer professionals recognize that, as employees, they are disorganized, difficult to manage, and often incapable of designing or adequately documenting software. When the software industry was beginning, compulsive programmers were often tolerated by companies suffering a shortage of skilled labor. Today compulsive programmers are less employable. Most companies want reliable men and women who do the work that the company wants done. For even the most creative work, companies have a tendency to insist on real-world relevance. When compulsive programmer tendencies do crop up in professionals, management often handles them as a problem. Some psychologists, like Dr. Steven Berglas, argue that the computer profession does tend to attract rigid, control-oriented personalities. Psychotherapist Craig Brod argues that such "techno-centered" people represent a new type of problem personality. However, psychological tests of programmers found their personalities far from neurotic (Guster, 1985).

THE HACKER AS ROBIN HOOD   In a time when the English nobility was converting public forests to private property, Robin Hood became a folk hero for asserting the commoners' right to poach royal deer. His descendants, if he had any, most likely worked in the factories of the industrial revolution and struggled for better working conditions. Hackers poaching information in the private data bases of the computer revolution insist that information is free. Like the Luddites, some turn to sabotage, as if crashing individual computer systems could halt a social change they find offensive.

The original computer hackers, described as "heroes of the computer revolution" by Steven Levy (1984), were MIT students of the 1950s and 60s dedicated to the ethic that technology and information should be freely available to anyone who could make good use of it. Hacking was a part of the general student culture when I was at MIT in the mid-1960s. Not only computers, but buildings, telephones, newspapers, and dormitory rooms were considered the proper subject matter for technically elaborate pranks. Most serious hackers were anarchists; they disliked bureaucracy and administration of any sort. As the computer industry developed, hackers appeared in Silicon Valley and became embroiled in conflicts over who should have access to computer technology. They were directly involved in developing the personal computer, recreational software, and decentralized bulletin boards. They have seen a new generation of younger hackers who do not share the belief that the purpose of stealing computer resources is to make good use of them. And they have seen the computer industry become businesslike and rational to the point of having little use for hackers or their ethic.

Some older programmers see the shrinking opportunities for hackers as one sign that programming as a craft is becoming programming as a set of tasks. Many programmers found in the early home computers a satisfying hobby that compensated them for the progressive fragmentation of their work. Later, when home computers became more common, the attractions for buyers were this challenge of craftsmanship, the sense of mastery over technology, and the hacker's escapism. Today compulsive programming often takes the form of recreation. In leisure activities, escapism and fantasy do not meet with social disapproval, though complaints from families of compulsive home computer owners and from friends of compulsive computer game players indicate that "computer addiction" is still considered antisocial by many people.

Occasionally, hacking becomes a more serious form of social protest. A U.S. government employee who was officially reprimanded for making what he considered a legitimate complaint changed the password on a federal data base and then "forgot" it. It had, he said, something to do with the Declaration of Independence. If they would reread that document, they might figure it out (*New York Times*, Feb. 13, 1986:A14). For the most part, however, hackers are no longer viewed as heroes, but as outlaws.

SEX DIFFERENCES IN COMPUTER USE   Curiously, most compulsive programmers are male. One way to understand why some young men, and an occasional young woman, become so engrossed with the computer that they neglect their appearance, social relationships, schoolwork, and even physical needs for food and sleep is to consider the process of sex role socialization. **Socialization** is the process by which children are taught their culture and their place in society. **Gender** is the term sociologists use for the culturally defined roles appropriate to each sex. **Sex role socialization** is the process through which boys and girls (biological categories) learn to be masculine or feminine (cultural categories).

Great controversy exists over the extent to which our culturally defined categories are based on real biological differences between men and women. Although most people assume that the differing behaviors of men and women are innate, there is actually very little biological basis for many of these differences. In rare cases, children whose sex was misidentified at birth have been raised to have the traits of the opposite gender. At puberty, with the emergence of physical differences, their status was changed, though their personalities remained more appropriate for the gender in which they were raised. Whatever the real differences are, however, the combination of biology and culture produces divergent behavior patterns between boys and girls. Among these are two directly related to computer use: mathematical competence and desire to achieve mastery.

The facts that few girls become hackers and most girls seem less interested in computers than boys do not indicate biologically based differences in ability. Perhaps most, or even all, of boys' higher scores on tests of mathematical reasoning and higher achievements in engineering, sports, and other fields emphasizing competition and domination are due to the differences in the ways children are raised and social expectations about their behaviors. Also, because many girls have exceptional talents along these lines, the findings do not apply to individuals—they are differences in the average performance of the two groups. The percentages of women who enter mathematically related occupations (12 percent of U.S. scientists and engineers) or computer science (30 percent of 1983 bachelor's degrees) are much smaller than can be accounted for by lower test scores. Sociologists point to a complicated combination of subtle social pressures and outright discrimination. For example, female computer science majors are more likely than their male counterparts to drop out of school (Campbell and McCabe, 1984). Some researchers have suggested that this is because adolescent girls are taught to avoid demanding situations, and boys are encouraged to deal with them (Fox, 1977; Wolleat et al., 1980). Also, defining women's personalities as cooperative rather than competitive, verbal rather than mathematical, and interested in relating to people rather than to objects tends to discourage their interest in programming.

Women are not encouraged to develop control over objects or engage in fantasies of power. Men tend to dominate conversations; women are expected to respond supportively and tolerate interruptions (Kollock, Blumstein, and Schwartz, 1985; Molm, 1986; Pearson, 1985). Even in preschool children, psychologist Malcolm Watson finds differing fantasy patterns. Boys tend to imagine fanciful adventures, and girls, more realistic and domestic dramas (Muro, 1984). Within the computer industry women are found, in disproportionate numbers, in jobs like documentation (using verbal skills) or technical support (involving personal interactions with customers). Whether because of discrimination ("women's jobs" in the computer industry are lower paid) or women's preferences for these types of work, the pattern of female computer use is different from that of males. In both the compulsive world of hackers and the more ordinary world of industry, computer power is more often sought and obtained by men.

As computerization expands, such differences may decrease. There has been a trend toward less sex role stereotyping in U.S. children's books (*Chronicle of Higher Education*, July 31, 1985:11). There is also a national trend toward more egalitarian views of women's roles (Thornton, Alwin, and Camburn, 1983). If the computer comes to be viewed as a general-purpose tool applicable to a wide variety of tasks, instead of a mysterious piece of "high technology" over which to obtain mastery, the psychological attitudes that link computers to the male sphere of activity may diminish. Already office automation is producing computer systems designed specifically for a female clerical staff. Microcomputer manufacturers are trying to sell the idea of the computer as a household appliance. Also, women with mathematical talent and an interest in technology are increasingly ignoring traditional social definitions of what they are "supposed to" want to do. A 1985 study of California high school students found no differences in male and female attitudes toward computers (Fisher and Pulos, 1985).

The Reflexive User

Reflexive, a scientific word meaning action based on automatic reflex, is also a philosophical term meaning reflective or meditative. The term **reflexive user** is intended to describe a computer user who develops automatic habits but keeps the ability to think about what it all means. Despite children's enthusiasm and adults' fears about the effects of computers on the job and in the video arcade, most computer users settle into a routine and cease to think about why they are using a computer or what the interaction is doing to them. For most of us, the psychological effects of computer use are unconscious. Once the computer's workings are mastered, the machine becomes an ordinary part of life. As in the case of higher productivity through shorter response times, using a computer by automatic reflex can make us more efficient. Acquiring those habits, however, can interfere with our awareness of the social consequences of computers. The reflexive user acquires the reflexes to use computers as tools but does not lose the capacity to reflect on the social meaning of the human/computer interface.

When I first used an automatic teller machine, I thought about the jobs of tellers. I wondered if anyone had been put out of work by my actions and in what ways the work would change. My brother-in-law had eventually married the teller who cashed his paycheck every Friday—the opportunities for that sort of social interaction might be reduced. Yet I had observed bank customers arguing with tellers and being generally unpleasant, so maybe the loss of social interaction on the job would bring improvements as well as lost opportunities. Then there was the awkward business of following the simple instructions for entering my card and code numbers while people waited in line, and I felt slow and incompetent. Was this really a better way to get money out of a bank? Today the card goes in the slot and I punch the numbers without conscious thought. I use the teller machine by reflex; jobs for bank tellers are predicted to decline by up to 30 percent. The small nagging guilt at having contributed to the loss of someone's job is part of why I wrote this book.

Individuals experience the computer revolution as a series of minor changes in the world. We confront each small change as a temporary disruption in our comfortable patterns. Unless we reflect on our negative experiences with technology, we soon forget or rationalize them as part of our inevitably changing society. We adapt to change, alter our habits, and carry on. Unless we are caught up in the popular enthusiasm for the computer (or unless our jobs are eliminated or altered), most of us will notice very little change from day to day. Only when we pause to think over the experiences of our lifetimes, or when we listen to the accounts of older acquaintances, do we see the intersection of biography and history and realize that we and our culture are changing.

5

MACROERGONOMICS: THE CONSEQUENCES FOR RELATIONSHIPS, PROCESSES, AND STRUCTURES

Does your family have a computer? Were they used in your schools? Do you play with them? If so, what have you learned from using computers? How have they changed your social relationships? **Macroergonomics,** the study of the technology/society interface, looks beyond the immediate connection between person and machine to the consequences for social institutions in which the technology is used. The effect of the computer in these institutions depends on more than the interface between individual and machine. It depends on the way computers are linked together into communication networks and how computer-based communication alters social interaction among people.

The family and the school are the two most important socializing institutions. Within them, children are introduced to the intricacies of their culture. For older children and for adults, social networks and economic institutions are important agents of socialization, providing opportunities to learn new social roles and behaviors. As the commercial production of information expands, some of the socializing functions of family and school have been taken over by leisure activities and mass entertainment. In place of public interactions among communities of people, we often find private interactions between people and machines. But in the social interactions among people using computer networks, we find new evidence of social integration and community formation.

SOCIAL INTERACTION AMONG COMPUTER USERS

For some philosophers, the dilemma of modern humanity has been the development of instrumental rationality in science, technology, and business at the expense of the human need for meaning, continuity, and belonging derived from direct, face-to-face interaction with one's particular group. The advantage of the rationalization of culture has been the development of universalistic social relationships. We are able to form larger communities and treat strangers with less suspicion. The disadvantages have been individual isolation, reification of social relationships, and a weakening of shared norms and values. Computer-based communication shows evidence of being a continuation of the trend toward universalism in social interaction. It also offers some new possibilities for enhancing social integration in organizations and communities.

Loss of Face-to-Face Contact

Loss of face-to-face communication is reported in many studies of computerized homes and offices. About 20 percent of the secretaries surveyed by the Diebold Group (1984:16,18) reported less face-to-face contact with their peers. Twenty-two percent of the managers and professionals also reported a decrease in face-to-face contact. A study of women working with computers in their homes found social contact between them and their friends to be reduced, although interaction with their children and spouses increased (McClintock, 1984). Even when face-to-face contact is replaced by more contact via telephone and electronic messages, the *quality* of interaction changes. In other words, people report that talking through a computer network is "just not the same" as talking face to face.

Consider, for example, the difference between a proposal of marriage by computer mail and a proposal in person. Even when two users of an electronic bulletin board fell in love via network, the marriage proposal was made face to face ("Love, Computer Style," 1983). The emotional overtones of social interaction are expressed through gestures, tone of voice, and even smell (with chemicals called pheromones). Just as the telephone removed vision and physical presence from human conversations (giving us in return the ability to communicate over vast distances), so most computer message systems remove the perception of sound and sight from interaction.

THE ABSENCE OF VISION   In a review of the effects of the withdrawal of visual contact on conversational outcomes, Reid (1977) concluded that there is no measurable impact on people's abilities to exchange factual information and cooperate in problem-solving tasks. These results suggest that we may expect interactions via computer network to be as effective for communicating technical information as direct contact. Although experiments found people able to form accurate impressions of others' traits, they tended to rate others less favorably when they couldn't see them. In the absence of vision, they were also less confident in their judgments of personal characteristics. This means that, even in the absence of visual clues, we get accurate information about people from what they say but are less able to make positive, emotionally based evaluations of them. This can mean the loss of emotional solidarity in computer network communication because feelings contribute to the strength of group ties.

The absence of vision is an advantage for people who "look" low status or unattractive. Attractive people are perceived as more competent, and "ugly" people tend to be devalued (with the exception of attractive women—who are often perceived as less competent). The telephone removed visual clues to a person's age, sex, race, ethnicity, and social status. Computer networks remove many of the verbal clues (for example, accent and pitch of voice) to status as well. If everyone has equal access to computer networks, we may find ourselves paying more attention to what they are saying than to how important they look and whether they appeal to us emotionally. Another alternative is that we will find ways to indicate emotion in printed communications. One of my students, who operates a bulletin board, reports the evolution of "colon critters" to represent the facial expressions:

Smile   :-)   or <^-^>
Frown   :-(or <'.'>
Wink   ;-)   or <^-*>

Also, a message surrounded by <FLAME ON> and <FLAME OFF> is commonly understood to be an emotional tirade.

MULTIMEDIA INTERFACES AND EMOTIONAL COMMUNICATION   Multimedia interfaces that let you hear the person you are exchanging information with and let you see him or her on television offer us the possibility of adding emotional communication to computer networks. This could restore some of the social control that now appears to be missing from computer conversations. But this technological innovation will not necessarily strengthen our perception that we are speaking to another human being. What is most important in face-to-face contact is our ability to imagine ourselves in the presence of another self. Because this is an emotional response to another person, the addition of nonverbal elements to computer messages can make it easier to perceive another's humanity. However, if our emotional response to someone's accent, color, sex, or status makes it more difficult to imagine them as like ourselves, the quality of our interaction will not be improved by multimedia interfaces. Multimedia interfaces will certainly increase the distance over which we can present ourselves to others; but they will not automatically supply us with the cultural value that we should communicate with them.

Computer-Aided Conversation and the Problem of Trust

In a collection of essays on communication and social evolution, Jurgen Habermas (1979) points out that communication involves claims on the part of participants about the following:

- the nature of external reality
- the internal reality of the speaker's intentions
- the shared reality of the social norms governing conversation

In conversation we evaluate the truth of what is being said, the motives of the speaker, and the social appropriateness of the communication. We can predict that the use of computer-mediated conversation will increase our attention to validity claims about the world—in other words, claims that the messages are "true." As it becomes more difficult for us to tell who is speaking, we may have trouble evaluating the speaker's intentions. We may expand our willingness to trust the unseen stranger whose words we read, or we may place our trust in the computer itself as provider of messages. In the latter case, we may think of ourselves as engaged in conversation with an anonymous network and lose sight of the humans whose programs and messages we are using.

TRUST AND THE NATURE OF EXTERNAL REALITY   Part of the problem of trust is a question of validity. Is what is being said true? Is the information in our computer data base accurate? In the past, we have arranged an elaborate set of social conventions about authorship, official editions, authoritative versions, and so on in order to define which information is reliable (Foucault, 1984). Until we have developed a new set of social norms for validating computer information, there will be some uneasiness about how much we can trust computer networks (Thompson, 1984). For example, new users of an electronic mail system go through a period in which they read everything because they haven't learned to trust its reliability (Hiltz and Turnoff, 1985). A survey of data-processing managers found only 10 percent completely trusted their computer filing system (*Computerworld*, Dec. 2, 1985:2). In both social interactions and interactions with computers, trust is based on experience. Our experience teaches us that our friend's loyalty can be counted on; we trust that the sun will rise tomorrow because it always has. When I worked on the first time-sharing systems of the 1960s, our experience taught us not to trust computers very much. Crashes and catastrophic data losses were chronic. One company I consulted for had lost $1 million worth of accounts receivable records. Today, although a computer is much more likely to work as it was designed to, there is still an enormous problem with data base validity. Our computerized information can at best approximately reflect external reality.

Computer graphics raise a new problem of trust. Research has shown that people trust pictures more than they do printed words and that they are more likely to trust a television image than a newspaper article (Graber, 1984). Thus, we could predict that computer graphics will increase our trust in computer-based information. But computer graphics allow us to manipulate images in realistic looking ways. As it becomes harder to tell "real" pictures from "retouched" ones, we may be reluctant to accept pictures as evidence of external reality (Brand, Kelly, and Kinney, 1985). For example, one bank distributed a picture of its building in downtown Columbus, Ohio. A rival bank's sign had been deleted from the image, and a parking lot had been filled with grass (*Wall Street Journal*, March 27, 1984:37).

INTENTIONS IN CONVERSATIONS WITH A COMPUTER   ANIMALS is a program distributed with the Apple IIe computer. A version of the game Twenty Questions, ANIMALS builds a data base as you play with it. As you converse with ANIMALS, the program begins by trying to "guess" the animal you are thinking of with the question "DOES IT LIVE IN THE WATER?" If you type "yes," you are asked if you are thinking of a frog. If you type "no," you are asked if you are thinking of a moose. If you weren't thinking of a frog or a moose, the program "says," "ALL RIGHT, I GIVE UP. WHAT ANIMAL WERE YOU THINKING OF?" When you type in the name of a new animal (for instance "goat"), the program asks, "WHAT QUESTION WOULD HAVE THE ANSWER YES FOR GOAT AND NO FOR A MOOSE?" If you supply the question "Is it a small ruminant?" the information that goats are small ruminants will go into ANIMALS' data base. In the sense that artificial intelligence researchers use the word *know*, the ANIMALS program now knows the difference between goats and moose. If you used ANIMALS long enough, it would have all the information about animal names and characteristics that you do. You would have made ANIMALS into a very simple expert system for guessing animals according to their traits. The educational function of the game (and presumably the intention of the programmer) is to teach you that you can have fun while putting data and relationships of your choice into a computer.

An interesting article in *The Humanist Sociologist* (Brownstein, 1984) provided an entirely different interpretation of the conversational intentions of the ANIMALS program. The author is a novice computer user who assumed he was having a conversation with the programmer who wrote ANIMALS. Understanding the verb "to know" from a humanistic perspective, the author knew that a computer program can't really know anything. Not being able to know anything, it couldn't guess. So the author guessed that the programmer was making a joke. He missed the programmer's lesson about computer data bases but raised a fundamental philosophical problem: to whom are we speaking when we converse with a computer?

The answer from artificial intelligence researcher Richard Bolt (1984: 87) is that we are engaged in a process of mutual self-disclosure: "The information base discloses itself to you as you disclose yourself to it." If this is the case, conversational interfaces are not social activity. In place of the intentions of another speaker, we have the external "reality" of the data base. This is an example of a reified social relationship. The relationship between the programmer and the program's user appears to be a relationship between the user and the program. As Kiesler reports from her study of social interactions in electronic mail systems, the user's attention gets focused on the message rather than on the people (Fersko-Weiss, 1985).

COMPUTERS AND CONVERSATIONAL NORMS   Studies of interruption patterns in conversations show that, in America, women are interrupted by men over 80 percent of the time. Women, who make less than 20 percent of conversational interruptions, are expected to allow themselves to be interrupted (Zimmerman and West, 1975). There are similar conversational norms allowing high-status people to interrupt low-status ones (Molotch and Boden, 1985). By interfering with our ability to tell if we are conversing with a man or a woman, the computer interface could change the social norm of interruption of women by men. An alternative less favorable to women and low-status people would be the establishment of social hierarchies in the access and priority designs of computer networks. Status differences can be preserved if our computer message systems tell us who is more important than whom. For example, the system on which this book was typed has several communication privilege levels. Faculty members can send files across the system; students are restricted to a subset of resources. The social history of the telephone gives reason for optimism in the prospects for equality in computerized communication. Early advertisements for the telephone depicted it as a device for giving orders to employees or servants; it became a means for two-way conversations between equals instead (Cherry, 1977).

There is also reason for optimism in Reid's (1977) review of conflict and decision making in the absence of vision. Although some studies report a reduction in cooperation and a lengthening of decision-making time, others report an increase in participants' willingness to change their opinions. Emotionally based arguments, which often sway opinions in face-to-face situations, are less likely to influence the outcomes of computer-based discussions. Kiesler has found the negative effect of removing emotion from discussion (Fersko-Weiss, 1985). Participants in her study were "out of control" and violated the rules of polite conversation. We use emotional expressions of approval or disapproval to exert normative power. With these ordinary mechanisms of social control missing, participants in computer-based discussions are free to develop new conversational rules and arrive at unconventional decisions.

These findings for telephone and computer network decision making suggest that computer-aided decision making will be more rational in terms of the information available to participants but less strongly controlled by shared (or conflicting) emotional evaluations. For low-status participants, and in technical decisions where shared emotions are less relevant to the outcome than questions of fact, this should be an improvement. For decision making about human goals, however, the absence of face-to-face contact can be a problem. The same nonverbal processes that reinforce feelings of interpersonal solidarity or antagonism also act to affirm shared values or to arrive at new ones. Therefore, it is possible that computer-aided conversation will loosen the "glue" among groups of friends but also facilitate conversations among strangers.

Social Integration in Electronic Networks

The negative effects of computer-based communication—loss of face-to-face contact, strains on trust, and a reduction in normative social control—are balanced by the possibilities for social integration in communities formed around electronic networks.

ORGANIZATIONAL INTERFACES   Thomas Malone (1985) defines an organizational interface as the parts of a computer system that connect human users to one another. A text-sharing system, for example, is an organizational interface. The computer system I use in teaching has common storage areas for each class, so students can use the same files. Assignments and exam questions are "read-only" to discourage unauthorized modifications by class members. An announcements and current events file is available for everyone to write in. For hackers there is a protected file called GRAFFITI. At the start of every academic term, it contains the single line: "Students may read this, but they cannot write in it."

Other kinds of organizational interfaces are management tools for keeping track of resources and tasks (Kedzierski, 1982; Fox et al., 1983; Sluizer and Cashman, 1985). The design choices for such interfaces are an important macroergonomic issue. If, like telephone conference calls, they are made for cooperative interaction, the organizational interfaces will integrate individual activities and facilitate the development of group goals. If organizational interfaces are designed to monitor activities and allocate tasks to people, they become the instruments of managerial control. They will supervise and coordinate individual activities without providing the social interactions that produce group solidarity.

In a review of organizational interfaces allowing many-to-many communication, Chandler Stevens (1981) identifies several attitudes that inhibit people from using computer networks in social ways:

- feelings of isolation and powerlessness
- inability to understand the information available on the network
- the belief that important decisions should be left to expert decision makers
- the expectation that information comes in premade packages, rather than being exchanged through social interaction
- the belief that competition is more advantageous than cooperation

These attitudes are relevant to organizational interface design. If users are restricted to small subsets of system resources and given few choices, they will be isolated and powerless. If the interface is not user friendly, people will have difficulty understanding what is available to them from other people on the network. If the designer assumes that only experts should make decisions, it may not be technically possible to use the system for any other form of decision making. If information comes in packages supplied by the system, the "nature of external reality" cannot be negotiated by those using it. Finally, if those who build organizational interfaces do not believe that cooperation is worthwhile, it may be difficult to use the interface for cooperative purposes.

COMMUNITY INTERFACES   Our traditional concept of a community has a geographical base, with people in regular face-to-face contact with one another. Yet widely scattered people have maintained their social ties through letters, phone calls, and periodic gatherings. My family of several dozen aunts, uncles, and cousins has an annual reunion; the professional community of American sociologists gathers at the end of every summer to go through the ritual of delivering papers and talking to colleagues.

One kind of computer network that facilitates solidarity within groups is the electronic bulletin board. Community bulletin boards like Berkeley, California's Community Memory Project are experiments in social integration and democratic participation. Terminals in public places provide access for individuals who do not have computer terminals at home or work. Commercial information utilities like the Source or CompuServe offer bulletin board services to a variety of special interest groups (Glossbrenner, 1984). Churches and informal religious groups—from born-again Christians to mystic pagans—hold study classes, communicate with parishioners, and exchange information over computer networks ("Churches Move into the Computer Age," 1984).

But computer-based social networks, like other communities, can generate conflict between groups. From the Aryan National Liberty Net, identified by the FBI as sponsored by a right-wing terrorist group believed responsible for several murders, you can get a list of America's enemies (*New York Times*, February 15, 1985:11). Hacker bulletin boards are the target of U.S. software and credit companies, who blame them for promoting credit card fraud and software piracy (*Newsweek*, April 15, 1985:17). In their enthusiasm to do away with software pirates, some companies have suggested outlawing all noncommercial bulletin boards. In their defense, many of the bulletin board operators point out that they are encouraging free speech and social interaction, not theft.

THE SOCIAL USE OF PUBLIC SPACE   Even the best interface design for an organizational or community interface has its limitations. As Scragg (1985) points out by comparing his company's electronic mail system to Post-It notes, sometimes we want to put a message in a place, not send it to a person. If the message shown in Figure 11 were put in everyone's electronic mailbox, it would not be as effective for group communication as a note on the door. The door is a public place; comments on it are group property. In most interface

FIGURE 11
EXAMPLE OF A PUBLIC MESSAGE

PERSON who drinks coffee

WOULD THE LAST ~~MAN~~ OUT PLEASE TURN OFF THE COFFEEPOT?

Why doesn't Nancy have to turn off the coffeepot if she's the last one?

OK. BUT WOULD THE LAST PERSON OUT PLEASE MAKE SURE THE LAST COFFEE DRINKER TURNED OFF THE POT SO we won't have a fire?

Because I don't drink coffee! Nancy

designs, there is no provision for public places or public commentary. And without public social interaction, we cannot have communities (Sennett, 1974).

It is not enough to have public places where common information is stored and retrieved. As Jane Jacobs points out in *The Death and Life of the Great American Cities* (1961), social interaction in public spaces provides social control over what goes on in them. Without norms for public conversation, public messages collect graffiti—individual expressions of art, obscenity, philosophy, or protest. The message about the coffeepot is not just information to be stored and retrieved. It is a public discussion about organizational behavior and responsibility. It is this sort of discussion that distinguishes a social interface from an interface that only coordinates individual human/computer connections.

COMPUTER-AIDED SOCIALIZATION

Through **socialization,** individuals acquire the information and techniques needed to function in society, and society maintains its culture and social structure from generation to generation. Socialization teaches people their roles and places them in a social class. It provides them with norms of behavior, values to live by, and beliefs to explain how and why they "fit" in a society. The family and the school are the two most important socializing institutions; within them, children are introduced to the intricacies of their culture. For older children and for adults, social networks and economic institutions are important agents of socialization, providing opportunities to learn new social roles and behaviors. Experiences in the workplace, as Adam Smith pointed out in 1776, are how "the understandings of the greater part of men are necessarily formed."

Social change limits the effectiveness of socializing institutions; when society changes, the preparation people have received through socialization may be irrelevant. Because schools and families prepare individuals for occupational roles and teach them to understand their culture, an institutional "crisis" can occur during periods of rapid change. From a functionalist perspective, such a crisis poses a challenge to the adaptive capacity of an institution because it is forced to reorganize to accommodate to a changing environment. Today both the family and the school are widely believed to be in crisis.

Home Computers and Family Change

The availability of inexpensive personal computers is expanding the potential, begun by the introduction of the telephone, for people to shop, obtain information, transact business, and communicate with others without ever leaving the home. Whether this will mainly reduce the amount of time spent on travel and errands or will have a major impact on social relationships is still unclear. We have only begun to study computers in the home. To some observers, home computers represent a new form of social integration, mending the separation of work and personal life that occurred during the industrial revolution. Alvin Toffler (1980:194–207) and Joseph Deken (1981:340–43) argue that personal computers will make work at home more common, giving us "electronic cottages." They predict that "telecommuting" instead of driving to work will strengthen the bonds of family and community, provide employees with greater control over their work, and benefit the environment by reducing gasoline consumption and air pollution.

Despite the speculations of observers, it is not yet clear if the home computer will reintegrate family and economic institutions. Many owners have not yet decided what to do with their computers; others oppose the idea that more activity should take place in the home at all (Bombeck, 1982). The home computer may integrate telephones, stereos, cameras, and televisions into home entertainment centers, rather than integrate work and family life. Even if home computers do put work and family life in the same place, it is highly unlikely that large corporations will distribute their considerable economic power to new home-based industries. Those who view the electronic cottage as a return to the good old days before the industrial revolution when families were economic units and divorce rates were low have an idealized view of traditional families and of modern economies.

THE NOT-SO-TRADITIONAL FAMILY   A culture's assumptions that its own particular social arrangements are human universals are especially strong when it comes to families. Less than one-fifth of U.S. households are of the "traditional" form of working husband, housewife, and children. And the "tradition" was a radical concept during the industrial revolution. We often imagine families of other cultures, or our own past, as having many children, many generations living together, early marriage, and infrequent divorce. This was hardly universal. High death rates and low life expectancy made multiple generation households rare even in cultures that valued them. High infant mortality, occasional infanticide, and restrictions on marriage kept families smaller than would otherwise be expected from their high birth rates. During one period of English history, when the land and other resources needed to set up a new family were scarce, the average woman didn't marry until she was twenty-eight years old. In rural Indonesia, divorce rates have been higher than our own.

Preindustrial families of Western Europe and nonindustrial families in other regions of the world were (and still are) remarkably varied in structure. Families of multiple husbands are occasionally found; multiple wives are more common. By one anthropological estimate, 80 percent of the world's cultures have a nonmonogamous ideal family form. First cousin marriages are forbidden in some places but the ideal form of marriage in others. Even socially approved brother-sister marriage has been found among the ancient Egyptian upper class (Middleton, 1962) and the Hawaiian royalty. If we look to biological examples as evidence of a "natural" family structure, we find among primates the tamarins, where one female breeds with a group of males, and the males take an active part in caring for her young (Abrahamson, 1985).

CAPITALISM AND FAMILY CHANGE   William J. Goode (1970) argues that our "ideal" family structure—wife, husband, and children living without other relatives—developed as the dominant form because it "fit" the requirements of the industrial revolution. This argument about parallel changes in the economy and the family is based on the fact that the preindustrial family *was* an economic institution. In other words, there was a lack of differentiation between economic and household roles because household tasks were part of a production process. When the industrial revolution began, work moved out of the home. As families migrated from farms to cities, they were physically separated from kin and community relationships. Because families that were smaller and less burdened with kinship obligations could migrate easily, they were "ideal" for the labor demands of the industrial revolution.

Whole families worked in the early factories. Legislation protecting children from dangerous factory conditions (and getting them out of jobs that could be filled by unemployed men) redefined work as a paid, adult activity. This new definition of work contributed to the creation of "the child" as a distinct family role. Also, with the need for someone to watch children away from the places where work was done, the role of the modern housewife was focused on child care. In urban areas, mass-produced commodities were substituted for formerly homegrown or homemade products. Economically productive household tasks like gardening, raising poultry, or making clothes were gradually replaced by "housework." By the end of the industrial revolution, "work" meant paid tasks performed in a specific place; the ideal housewife no longer worked. In fact, housewives during the industrial revolution often engaged in paid work—perhaps sewing at home or peddling. Women also continued to be factory workers, especially in the garment industry. The new sexual division of labor in the industrial revolution did not move women away from economic activity so much as it redefined their expected roles. Work for wages became a primary role for men; it became secondary for women. Housework contributed less and less to the direct production of goods and more to providing unpaid services for working men.

A rising standard of living encouraged the domesticity of women because more families could be supported by a single wage earner. Removed from direct participation, the ideal woman contributed to the economy by socializing her children for the world of work. Before the invention of the child as a social status, European children were considered small people who could learn how to work by working and by watching others. As "the family began to hold society at a distance, to push it back beyond a steadily extending zone of private life" (Aries, 1962:398), women were expected to replace the emotional supports once provided by community and kin. In its ideal form, the modern family became a "haven in a heartless world: a refuge from the highly competitive and often brutal world of industry and commerce. Husband and wife, according to this ideology, were to find solace and spiritual renewal in each other's company" (Lasch, 1980:80).

Subjected to enormous external pressures and often lacking the supports of strong social relationships with kin, neighbors, and friends, the modern family rarely matches its ideal. The crisis of the modern family is, to some observers, largely a problem of the intrusion of external circumstances into this private haven. Health, education, and welfare services formerly provided by family networks have been steadily replaced by impersonal state bureaucracies (Peden and Glahe, 1986). Other observers locate the crisis in the internal tensions of the family itself. In Philippe Aries's (1977:234–35) analysis of the crisis in the contemporary family:

> We are witnessing the inability of the family to fulfill all the many functions with which it has been invested, no doubt temporarily, during the past half-century. The twentieth-century post-industrial world has been unable, so far, either to sustain the forms of social intercourse of the nineteenth century or to offer something in their place.

THE ELECTRONIC COTTAGE FAMILY   Telecommuting (discussed further in Chapter 7) gives people the possibility of locating their work and their family in the same place by using computer terminals and communications systems. Some proponents of telecommuting believe that it will replace the lost social solidarity of the preindustrial world. Others believe that it will make it possible for working mothers to live up to their ideal role by combining work and child care in the home. A forum sponsored by the Moral Majority embraced the idea of women returning to working in the home; Islamic nations are investigating the arrangements as a way to keep women in seclusion while allowing them to participate in modern economic activities.

Such visions assume that it is possible to care for children while working at a computer terminal. Although preindustrial work was often organized so that social interaction and child care could be done along with the task, computer use demands an exclusive attention. Studies show that home computers take time and attention away from interpersonal interactions (Brod, 1984). When home computers are compared to television, we find that television is more social. In most homes, television forms a background to social relationships rather than a focus of attention ("When the TV Is On," 1982). When people buy home computers, they cut down on the time spent watching television, doing hobbies, sleeping, and engaging in outdoor recreation. They also spend more time by themselves and less in activities with family members (Vitalari, Venkatesch, and Gronhaug, 1985).

A study of people who use home computers for working found that telecommuters experience increased communication and conflict but also a better *quality* of relations with children and spouses (McClintock, 1984). Women, especially those with children, experience more change and more conflict. The conflicts McClintock found focus on the use of time and space. Where conflict was satisfactorily resolved, a new pattern of behavior often resulted. This is an example of a positive function of conflict. It can be an important mechanism for working out new ways of cooperating. A closer look at household conflict indicates how home computer users can spend less time together but still experience more communication.

As a personal example, I found that my computer and assorted peripheral equipment have grown to the point where they take up a whole room that used to be shared. When I'm telecommuting, I close the door and make it clear that I don't want to be disturbed. Nobody else can use the phone. If they "forget" and pick up the phone anyway, I get disconnected and lose part of my work. When I telecommuted at night (to take advantage of better response time), my printer seemed to bother people at 3 A.M. My roommate and I, who used to spend a lot of time in each other's company watching television or reading, now spend much less time but do more talking. We've negotiated solutions to the space, phone, and printer problems. It's now my room, but I bought a hard disk and am switching from nighttime telecommuting to doing the work on my own computer at reasonable hours. Before using the phone for data transfer, I ask if anyone wants to make a phone call first. And there's a note for the hall phone saying "In use." The quality of our less frequent household interactions now seems better than before our home became an electronic cottage. We used to take each other more for granted. Now we've gotten the habit of paying more attention to each other when we're together.

The possibility that telecommuting could bring women back to the home from the office to take up the combined role of home worker dismays many American women who have struggled for decades to get out of the home and

into the labor force on equal terms with men. Yet a home-centered environment, in which husbands and wives work and raise children, is attractive to
those fathers who see it as an opportunity for a new parental role. In the
future, debate over the desirability of telecommuting will, no doubt, center on
how family roles *ought* to be arranged. Theorists with traditional (or at least
recent traditional) beliefs may turn to sociobiology for evidence that women
should maintain their industrial revolution family role (see, for example,
Tomkins, 1965). Feminist theorists like Nancy Chodorow (1978:219) argue
for new roles:

> We live in a period when the demands of the roles defined by the sex-gender
> system have created widespread discomfort and resistance. Aspects of this
> system are in crisis internally and conflict with economic tendencies. Change
> will occur, but the outcome is far from certain. The elimination of the present
> organization of parenting in favor of a system of parenting in which both men
> and women are responsible would be a tremendous social advance.

Whatever the directions in home computing, it seems unlikely that they
will in themselves relieve the interpersonal tensions to which the family
is subject. Although personal computers can bring enormous amounts of
information and new activities into private life, sustainable family roles
will not be created by the technology. Instead, they will develop out of
negotiations among family members over time, space, and expectations
of one another.

Computers and the Changing Schools

The ideal function of education in an industrial democracy is to provide equal
opportunity for all to develop their talents and prepare for occupational
success. For society, the school's function is to develop its human resources
and place people in appropriate jobs and roles. In the words of Horace Mann
(1842:164), a leader in developing public education during the American
industrial revolution, "Education is not only a moral renovator and a multi-
plier of intellectual power, but also the most prolific parent of material riches.
It is not only the most honest and honorable, but the surest means of amassing
property."

Critics of this view argue that education has another, less obvious
function for society. They believe that a major function of education is to
maintain the existing stratification system by convincing unsuccessful individuals that they have "failed." If there are more talented individuals than
there are high-status job opportunities, then those who do not find rewarding
jobs might see their position in society as a social rather than a personal
problem. From this perspective, one purpose of education is to convince
individuals to accept the status quo as a "given" and to define their success or
failure in personal terms. Education in this way serves as an agent of social
control, teaching students to conform to existing social structures. From either

perspective, educational institutions experience a crisis when other social institutions are going through a period of rapid change.

THE CRISIS IN AMERICAN EDUCATION   The report of the National Commission on Excellence in Education (1983) presents an overwhelming indictment of U.S. public education and calls for sweeping reforms. It found that nearly 40 percent of seventeen-year-olds cannot draw inferences from written material and that only one-third can solve a math problem of several steps. Among the commission's recommendations is a required three years of science, three years of mathematics, and one-half year of computer science in the high schools. Unfortunately, there was already a great shortage of math and science teachers in 1983, and 50 percent of those teaching then were rated as "unqualified" by their principals.

One proposed solution to the shortage of science and math teachers is to retrain mid-career high-tech professionals (Everett, 1983; Frederick, 1983). Yet teaching pays poorly compared to technical and professional work. With a 1982 national average salary of $17,000 for twelve-year veterans of teaching and entry-level salaries as low as Mississippi's $11,275 (Williams and Smith, 1982), very few mid-career high-tech professionals are likely to volunteer to help save America's schools. Although President Reagan interpreted the commission report as calling for "an end to federal intrusion" ("Report on Excellence . . .," 1983), the commission assigns the federal government "the primary responsibility for identifying, funding and supporting the national interest in education." This view is reaffirmed in the Twentieth Century Fund Task Force on Federal Elementary and Secondary Education Policy ("America's Competitive Challenge . . .," 1983). Yet it is not clear how education is to be funded, especially since budget plans have included cutting federal support for education.

COMPUTER LITERACY AS A TECHNOLOGICAL FIX   The term *computer literacy* encompasses a vague concept of something our schools are failing to provide for the future citizens of the information age. Joseph Weizenbaum (1983b) considers public concern with computer literacy another instance of the American habit of searching for a simple "technological fix" for complex and fundamental problems. Weizenbaum argues that the ability to work with a computer will be like the ability to read and write, do arithmetic, or drive a motor vehicle. Although these were once rare skills that assured placement in a job, they are now expected of most adults in industrial countries. Although computer literacy may, like driver education, be taught in the schools, a rudimentary understanding of computers is no solution at all to our basic educational shortcomings. Indeed, if we fail to

> require literacy in communication, sciences, and mathematics before applying computers to the tasks at hand, we may find that we have developed individuals who may be proficient in coding programs, who may even write some simple ones, but individuals who cannot do much more than rely on pre-packaged

subroutines to accomplish anything technical or scientific of any significance. (Zelby, 1983:34)

The College Board's definition of *computer competency* considerably broadens the concept of computer literacy. It includes basic knowledge of the workings and use of computers, including how to develop programs, how to evaluate computer results through "mental calculation and estimation," the knowledge of when and how computers can be used, and "some understanding of the problems and issues confronting individuals—and society generally— in the use of computers, including the social and economic effects of computers and the ethics involved in their use" ("Text of the College . . .," 1983:14–15). University innovations are integrating the use of computers with more general education, as in new programs at MIT, Carnegie-Mellon University (Williams and Allan, 1982), Harvard Medical School (Culliton, 1985b), and Oberlin (Williams and Young, 1983). Even in professional computer science programs, the goal is "not to generate technicians" but to graduate "educated experts" with substantive areas of noncomputer skills and a base in the humanities and social sciences (Kalaghan, 1983).

The outlook in high school and secondary school curricula is less promising. Most teachers do not understand computer science, and existing in-service training programs provide only rudimentary skills (Coons, 1983; Smith, 1983; Watt, 1983b). Most new lesson plans are little more than computerized versions of study guides and rote teaching (Aeppel, 1983:B2; Bonham, 1983). Some notable exceptions are LOGO (Papert, 1980; Watt, 1983a), Sesame Street instruction systems for children, and PLATO computer-based science courses (Bonham, 1983). In short, computer-aided instruction is a long way from being a solution to the crisis in American education.

Prescriptions for improvements in education generally assume that we know what learning and teaching are about. Many theorists believe that education involves human elements that cannot be programmed. Social interactions among students and teachers, facilities of intuition and imagery, and shared biologically and culturally based "nature" are all part of the traditional teaching process (Bruner, 1962, 1966; Galyean, 1983). They would dispute the claim by artificial intelligence expert Patrick Winston (1977:11) that "the methodology involved in making smart programs transfers to making smart people." Also, at an estimated 1983 cost of $125 per pupil per year, many school administrators are unable to afford a technological solution for their problems even if they believe it would improve the quality of education (Pogrow, 1983).

In the 1983 *World Yearbook of Education*, devoted to an examination of computers and education, editor Jacquetta Megarry argues, "the explosive growth of knowledge and the spectacular advances in microtechnology have underlined the importance of teaching students *how* to learn and *how* to retrieve information, rather than facts and even skills which may become rapidly obsolescent" (Megarry et al., 1983:23). This is a call for a return to basics in education—not better techniques for transmitting basic facts to students, but a better teaching of basic reasoning from information. If the wisdom of the past is presented to students as just more data, it is not likely to be of much help to them in the future.

THE EMERGING ROLE OF THE PRIVATE SECTOR   From a conflict perspective, schools are one of the arenas in which the battles of social change are waged. During the industrial revolution, manufacturers organized institutes to train craftsmen in science and technical skills. It took a hundred years before the English state came around to their point of view and began to support government-financed education for the industrial working class (Wrigley, 1982). Behind the furor over the current state of American education are strong pressures from industry and business, as spelled out quite clearly in the 1983 report of the Business–Higher Education Forum (" 'America's Competitive Challenge' . . .," 1983). The decline of American industrial preeminence in the world is, in this view, a business problem to be solved by restructuring education to serve corporate needs. Elizabeth Useem (1986:235) concludes that there is a need for corporate involvement in education, but indicates that conflicts exist between the goals of businesses and educational institutions, and "despite the calls for reform that dominate the political airwaves, cutbacks and decline still haunt the hallways of American schools."

Reductions in student loans and federal assistance to universities may be offset by new private sector educational activities. In areas of particularly rapid technological change, businesses complain that students are inappropriately prepared by the schools. They often sponsor on-the-job training programs for workers in new technologies and professional education and reeducation programs. Some industries are trying to improve the situation by supporting universities with gifts of equipment, the loan of employees for university teaching, and cooperative work-study programs for students (Desruisseaux, 1984). Corporations have also begun to compete with universities in providing technical education (Abelson, 1985). By 1985, corporate enrollments and expenditures were almost as large as those of American colleges and universities (Frank, 1985).

There is also a growing number of small-scale entrepreneurs interested in educating others with the aid of information technology. Some of these companies design professional training programs modeled after academic conferences, but sometimes they look like little more than sales pitches for new hardware or software. Other companies provide training in programming and home computer usage in order to solve part of the "computer literacy" problem. These new private sector efforts appear to be concentrated in the marketing of new techniques rather than in the general transmission of cultural information. Although they are certainly a part of an information production and distribution economy, most have not yet tried to compete with public and nonprofit schools as socializing agents.

One limit on the expansion of education for profit is the society's need for educated citizens. Most businesses want more than technical specialization, especially in their upper-level employees. Companies seek general skills in planning, defining and solving problems, and communicating ideas. Interaction skills and general cultural knowledge are more important to career success than many preprofessional students realize. To the extent that this is the case, we should expect strong business support for what Education Secretary William Bennett calls the university's function of "preparation for life," even as the private sector takes over the function of preparing people for work.

Yet there is disagreement over what preparing people for work means. As will be discussed in Chapter 7, experts who predict that new computer technology will enhance employee skills assume the existence of a highly competent work force. Likewise, predictions that the technology will be used to routinize work and control labor assume a strong management interest in taking decisions out of employee hands. Unless education provides graduates with decision-making competence and employment skills, it is not likely that management will seek technological innovations that give employees greater autonomy. But unless business management believes that employees should be well educated for their new jobs, it is likely that they will confine their efforts to job training rather than improving the quality of general education.

EDUCATION AND SOCIAL EQUITY   Efforts to solve the crisis in American education with technological fixes and private sector job training may be threatening the access of minorities and the poor to education. Corporations need more than one kind of employee. The well-educated college graduates who would supply companies with competent managers and researchers form only part of the work force. Some jobs require minimal training and labor discipline, not education (Fruchter, 1983; "High Tech and the Schools," 1983). These can be obtained from a poorly financed public educational system that teaches "computer literacy" in the narrowest sense of being able to use a computer terminal without understanding or thinking about it. A student who is "computer literate" in the sense that he or she can push buttons in response to machine cues (perhaps selecting a picture of a hamburger on a fast-food sales terminal) can also operate a complex computer system capable of handling sales, orders, delivery, and inventory.

From a functionalist perspective, universal educational opportunity is essential for maintaining social equity. The uneducated represent a waste of human resources and a potential source of social unrest. If, as conflict theorists argue, education perpetuates social inequality by discriminating against the disadvantaged, new patterns of discrimination can be expected from shifts in the educational system. The emergence of a two-class educational system, with high-quality instruction for the elite and narrow vocational training for the rest, would make the main task of the schools to select elite students for separate education and to convince those left in deteriorating educational institutions that it is their own fault. And, because business's needs for labor are global rather than national, reforms in education for the underdeveloped world may increasingly take the form of training inexpensive workers rather than providing the human capital needed for economic development.

THE FUTURE OF EDUCATION   It is impossible to predict the future of educational institutions with any accuracy, but computers probably will not solve their problems. A gradual improvement in educational software should make computer-aided instruction a more useful educational tool than it is at present. The capacity of computer networks to support communication at a distance may be used to replace many teachers, through the development of centralized electronic instruction that resembles television studios more than traditional classrooms (McDonell, 1984; Turner, 1984). Or computer-aided instruction may be used by students for information and practice and by teachers in their interactions with students. The outcome is not a technological issue. It depends on how we understand education and its purposes. As private sector education expands, bringing the cultural transmission of knowledge more into the marketplace, we will have to make some political choices about how much we want education and socialization to remain public processes.

The Changing Functions of Leisure

In ancient Greek culture an elite of citizens dominated a society of slaves and noncitizen craftsmen and merchants. This elite valued leisure as a hallmark of their culture. Although the classical social theorists considered work the source of civilization and society, some contemporary theorists have taken up the Greek theme that leisure is the highest expression of human creativity. Huizinga (1980) argues that play satisfies the human need of expression in a wholly voluntary activity. During play, people express themselves as individuals by engaging in a pleasurable process of mutual interaction. Friedmann (1961) argues that self-actualization can best be achieved through new opportunities for meaningful leisure. He sees the separation of work and leisure as a positive contribution to the human condition.

LEISURE TIME   Separate analyses of computers as tools for work and as toys for play obscure the relationships between work and leisure and make it difficult to understand debates about computerized work. Work and leisure are social conceptions that divide human activity rather arbitrarily. We tend to think of **work** as time spent on activities we are paid for. Yet sometimes activities like taking out the garbage are considered work even though we don't get paid for them. In such cases, we are working to fulfill some necessary social obligation. Work often means time spent in unpleasant or difficult tasks performed in order to achieve some goal.

   Leisure is usually thought of as "free" time during which we voluntarily choose enjoyable activity. Leisure is activity for its own sake, rather than for some future outcome. In practice, however, it is difficult to distinguish the two. We often "work" toward some goal but enjoy the process; recreation can involve strenuous mental or physical effort to achieve a desired result—

solving a puzzle or getting to the top of a mountain. For example, writing a computer program is work if you are being paid for it or if it is a class assignment. If you wrote the same program in the same room on the same computer for "fun," it would be a leisure activity.

In a contemporary theory of the relationship between work and leisure, Stanley Parker (1983) presents the concepts in terms of constraints in the two dimensions of time and activity, as shown in Table 4. Parker's table reflects the temporal arrangements of modern society by dividing time into work time and nonwork time. Constraints on our activity are shown ranging from the immediate demands of employers and our own bodies to completely free choice.

COMPUTERIZED LEISURE   Computerized recreation to most people is video games or home computers as a hobby. Yet leisure activities in the United States are the focus of a major service industry that produces recreational equipment, entertainment products, and leisure services. Brutzkus (1980) characterizes the leisure sector of the economy as being aimed at the quality of human life. In sports we have computerized baseball statistics (*Sport*, June 1986:72), computerized ocean racing (Chamberlain, 1983), and even an athletic shoe with a built-in chip to keep track of joggers' strides (Marbach, 1985). One effect of computerized sports has been to increase our fascination with data—more sports statistics are being produced than ever before. Computer-based information is also leading to changes in the management of professional sports. New York Yankees ex-manager Billy Martin points to a change in baseball trading: "With all the data available in the computers, everything is done by the statistics, and there is no way anybody can hide the dogs" (*Fortune*, Jan. 7, 1985:11).

In the theatre, computer-controlled lighting systems make possible effects that are too fast for the human hand (such as the cats' eye sequence in *Cats*) (Van Gelder, 1984). In music, we have software to record compositions from a keyboard and new languages for printing musical scores (Gourlay, 1986). There is also a new instrument, the Kurzweil 250, that can emulate the sound of human voices and forty-five musical instruments (D. Russell, 1985). Although computer aids to musicians have been criticized as inadequate (Gaus, 1984), improvements in sound reproduction technology have made greater resources available to serious musicians and listeners (McLaughlin, 1984). John Glasel (*In These Times*, April 24–30, 1986:21), president of the 17,000-member New York City musicians' union, sees sound synthesizers making music more of a solo activity (and reducing the number of jobs for orchestra performers).

In art, as Negroponte (1980) predicted in the 1970s, developments in computer graphics have opened new vistas for "Sunday painters." Although he also predicted that computer graphics would not be taken seriously as "real" art, the evolution of computer graphics (shown in Figure 12) has begun to capture the imagination of contemporary artists ("Art and Animation," 1985; Chandler, 1985). Some see the possibility of reintegrating work and culture in their own activity (Palyka, 1985). But most of us find that computers in the arts have provided more to watch and to buy than to do.

TABLE 4
A TIME AND CONSTRAINT MODEL OF LEISURE

Time	Activity		
	Constraint		Freedom
Work time	Work (employment)	Work obligations (connected with employment)	"Leisure in work"
Nonwork time	Physiological needs	Nonwork obligations	Leisure

Source: Stanley Parker. *Leisure and Work.* London: George Allen and Unwin, 1983, p. 10. Reprinted by permission of the publisher.

FIGURE 12
THE EVOLUTION OF COMPUTER GRAPHICS

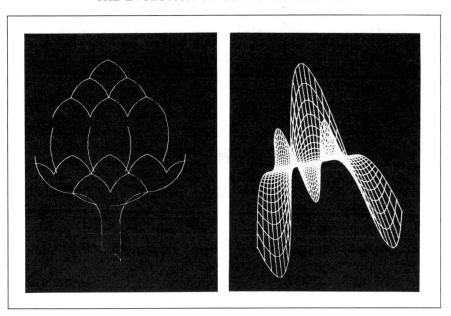

During the past fifteen years the techniques of computer graphics have evolved from primitive two-dimensional figures and simple rotations of three-dimensional objects to strikingly realistic images produced using fractal geometry. Fractal-surface generation is a shortcut method for creating an image of irregular terrain. It involves subdividing a simple triangular mesh into a large number of irregular facets. At each step the sides of all triangles are broken at a point displaced from the middle by a random amount. The new points are then linked to form four triangles from each preexisting triangle. This process continues until the individual triangles are so small that their edges can no longer be distinguished.

Fractile-surface generation.

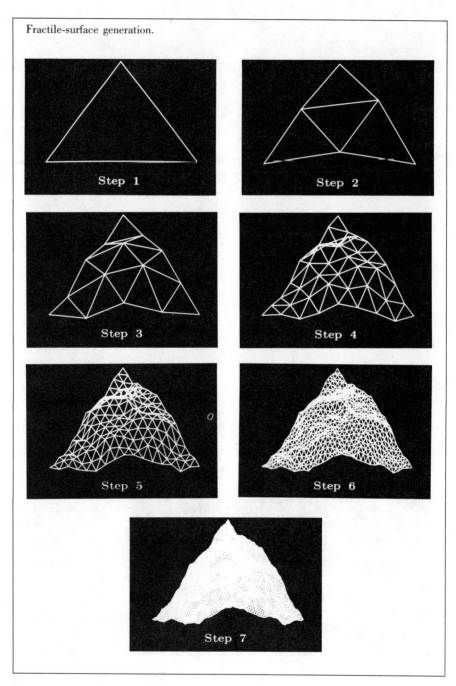

Sequence courtesy of Alvy Ray Smith, image by Loren Carpenter, both of Lucasfilm, Ltd. Used by permission.

Road to Point Reyes

This landscape was defined using patches, polygons, fractals, particle systems, and a variety of procedural models. The various elements were rendered separately and later composited. Rob Cook designed the picture and did the texturing and shading, including the road, hills, fence, rainbow, shadows, and reflections. Loren Carpenter used fractals for the mountains, rock, and lake, and a special atmosphere program for the sky and haze. Tom Porter provided the procedurally drawn texture for the hills and wrote the compositing software. Bill Reeves used his particle systems for the grass and wrote the modeling software. David Salesin put the ripples in the puddles. Alvy Ray Smith rendered the forsythia plants using a procedural model. The visible surface software was written by Loren Carpenter, and the antialiasing software by Rob Cook. The picture was rendered using an Ikonas graphics processor and frame buffers, and was scanned on FIRE 240, courtesy of MacDonald Dettwiler & Associates Ltd. The resolution is 4K×4K, 24 bits/pixel.

Source: Courtesy of Robert L. Cook. Used by permission of Lucasfilm, Ltd.

THE FUTURE OF LEISURE   Although analysts since Bernal (1939) have predicted a technological enhancement of leisure, Stanley Parker (1983:104) argues that "technology as applied to leisure is more sophisticated—but not noticeably more likely to enhance sociability or personal development." Computers have not substantially altered the passive quality of most of our recreations. There is more mental activity in interactive programming or computer games than in watching television, but most of these activities involve little social interaction. As Ellul (1964:400–402) wrote: "Leisure time is a mechanized time and is exploited by techniques which, although different from those of man's ordinary work, are as invasive, exacting, and leave man no more free time than Labour itself."

Debates about the future of leisure involve changing conceptions of what work and leisure mean. Art critic Clement Greenberg (1961), commenting on the difficulty of carrying out a leisure-oriented tradition in a work-oriented society, suggests we should shift the center of gravity away from leisure and into work. From Ellul's perspective, computerized leisure becomes more like work in the sense of being more goal oriented and governed more by external obligations than by "free" choice. Also, with the computer, the techniques of work and leisure may become increasingly similar. As we will see in Chapter 7, some analysts believe computers will bring more "leisure in work" by giving us more creative choices in our paid activities. Others suggest that we will continue to seek our gratifications from leisure as computers give us less control over work.

Video Games as Socializing Agents

Children learn about social expectations through play and can often be found "practicing" for adult roles. Some analysts see video games, which may appear as simply another expensive fad, as part of a new pattern of life. Many parents and communities are concerned about the time and money their children spend on machines, often voicing fears of an association between video arcades and drugs or crime. One of my favorite cartoons is of a video game called "Gimme Your Quarter." In the country of Malaysia, arcade video games have been banned altogether on the grounds that the money spent on them interferes with the nutrition of poor children, provides an immoral influence conducive to theft and violence, and represents a cultural intrusion ("Video Games Under Fire," 1982). Like the controversy over TV violence, the question of the impact of computer games on children continues.

Psychologist Robert S. Gable argues that the video games are teaching young people technical skills in a way more suitable to a computer-based society ("A Generation . . .," 1981:50–60). Patricia Greenfield (1983) finds video games contributing to children's spatial skills and ability to do dynamic parallel processing—keeping track of many changing events at the same time. Because the pace of many games is set by the machine, some analysts see them as socializing children into labor discipline—learning to enjoy "work" at controlled paces in fixed environments defined by computers. But, compared to television, video games do give the player some control over the situation, even though the rules are set by the machine. Social psychologists worry about the possibility that video games reduce children's opportunities to engage in social interactions with their peers.

Although the characteristics of computer games that allow players to interact quickly with complex arrangements of information certainly introduce children to the human/computer interface, the crucial issue is the degree to which computerized recreation distances human players from experiencing physical and social interactions. Against the positive effects of children exercising imagination and control via the computer must be balanced the dangers of substituting mastery over unreal computer environments for games that involve "real-world" interactions. It is through social interactions with one another that children are first socialized for decision making in a democratic society.

PLAY AND POLITICAL SOCIALIZATION   Few elements of society seem as far apart as recreation and politics. Our culture defines leisure as a part of private life given over to enjoyable processes and social interactions. By politics we generally mean the formal institutions of government. Yet when politics is understood as a general process by which human groups arrive at collective decisions and go about implementing them, there is politics in all of social life. **Political socialization** is the way we learn the process of group decision making and our roles (like citizen or elected official) in political institutions. To a sociologist, even the leisure activity of going out for a pizza with friends involves political processes. The question of what goes on the pizza, for instance, often requires discussion and debate. And, as is the case in formal political institutions, those who supply the transportation or the money often have a disproportionate influence on the decision.

Authoritarian values include the belief that one ought to give unquestioning obedience to persons in social positions of authority, without any critical thought about the moral, ethical, or social consequences. Authoritarian beliefs are at odds with many of the political values of American society. Democratic beliefs require citizens to question authority and maintain an independent moral and ethical viewpoint. Rules that are considered wrong can be opposed and changed by a majority. In much of a child's socialization, authority figures—parents and teachers—establish rules of conduct and enforce orderly behavior. As a child grows older, however, the process of **internalization** occurs. During this process, the norms, values, and roles of adult society are incorporated into the child's personality. The child develops a conscience and begins to act in ways that are morally right rather than out of fear of punishment. Democratic decision making requires a high degree of internalized rules and depends less upon the formal institutions of social control than do authoritarian forms of decision making.

Jean Piaget (1948) analyzed the cooperative forms of rule making in children's games. These, he argued, were important in teaching nonauthoritarian forms of justice and law. As he watched children playing marbles, Piaget saw them learning to interpret and enforce rules by interacting with one another. In later research on children's conflicts, Douglas Maynard (1985) argued that they were acquiring political skills and learning to make social structures in their small groups. Based on these observations, we might expect that children who play video games would have reduced opportunities to learn that rules in democratic society are arrived at by mutual agreement rather than handed down by outside authorities.

IN DEFENSE OF COMPUTER GAMES   When asked to comment on the hypothesis that computer games teach authoritarian values, students in my college class defended them, arguing that playing against machines reduced their competitiveness against one another. "Do you really think that the game of Monopoly would make us more cooperative than Pac-Man?" asked one. Another pointed to the new trends in fantasy games in which players actively cooperate to alter the course of events. In these games, the rules of play are not always fixed by the machine, but can be determined by the players. Even more impressive in defense of computer games are examples like Tom Snyder's The Other Side. In it, teams of players try to build a bridge between two potentially hostile nations without blowing up the world. In the course of the game, children are actively involved in the social interactions that teach conflict resolution.

Researchers studying what adolescents like in their activities found that they most enjoy "flow experiences" (Csikszentmihalyi and Larson, 1984). These are activities involving high levels of concentration, rules of interaction, feedback, suspension of self-consciousness, and a sense of belonging to something larger than oneself. These activities also involve being with family and friends. As we saw in Chapter 4, younger children learn to value human feelings by playing with computer toys. Changes in toy industry sales show a new interest in "huggable" toys. Electronic toy sales dropped 50 percent between 1983 and 1984, although robots and fantasy toy sales rose. What was "in" were dolls and bears (R. Miller, 1985). There is no evidence that interaction with computer toys is alienating our children from social relationships. In the player/game interface, as with other forms of computer interface, we can design for individual isolation or we can design for sociability.

FURTHER READING FOR PART TWO

Bolt, Richard A. 1984. *The Human Interface: Where People and Computers Meet*. Belmont, CA: Lifetime Learning Publications.

Bowles, Samuel, and Herbert Gintis. 1976. *Schooling in Capitalist America: Educational Reforms and the Contradictions of Economic Life*. New York: Basic Books.

Burch, John L., ed. 1984. *Computers: The Non-Technological (Human) Factors: A Recommended Reading List on Computer Ergonomics and User-Friendly Design*. Lawrence, KS: The Report Store.

Cakir, A., D. J. Hart, and T. F. M. Stewart. 1980. *Video Display Terminals: A Manual Covering Ergonomics, Workplace Design, Health and Safety, Task Organization*. New York: Interscience.

CBEMA (Computer and Business Equipment Manufacturers Association). 1985. "Guide to the Draft American National Standard for Human Factors Engineering of Visual Display Terminals." CBEMA, 311 First St., NW, Washington, DC 20001.

Eimbinder, Jerry, and Eric Eimbinder. 1982. "Videogame History," *Radio-Electronics* (July):50–54.

Erikson, Erik. 1964. *Childhood and Society*. New York: Norton.

Jencks, Christopher, et al. 1972. *Inequality: A Reassessment of the Effect of Family and Schooling in America*. New York: Basic Books.

Kegan, Robert. 1982. *The Evolving Self*. Cambridge, MA: Harvard University Press.

Lowe, Marian. 1983. "Sex Differences, Science, and Society," pages 7–17 in Jan Zimmerman, ed. *The Technological Woman: Interfacing with Tomorrow*. New York: Praeger.

Milgram, Stanley, 1969. *Obedience to Authority*. New York: Harper and Row.

Pearce, Brian, ed. 1984. *Health Hazards of VDT's?* New York: Wiley.

Population Reference Bureau. 1983. "The Changing American Family," *Population Bulletin* 38, 4 (October).

Shorter, Edward. 1975. *The Making of the Modern Family*. New York: Basic Books.

SIGCHI Bulletin. Publication of the ACM Special Interest Group on Computers and Human Interaction.

Skolnick, Arlene. 1978. *The Intimate Environment: Exploring Marriage and the Family*. Boston: Little, Brown.

Skolnick, Arlene, and Jerome Skolnick, eds. 1980. *Family in Transition*. Boston: Little, Brown.

Useem, Elizabeth L. 1986. *Low Tech Education in a High Tech World*. New York: Free Press.

VDT News: The VDT Health and Safety Report. Bimonthly. New York.

Video Games and Human Development: Research Agenda for the '80s. 1983. Cambridge, MA: Harvard Graduate School of Education.

THE
COMPUTER
TRANSFORMATION
OF
WORK

6

THE INFORMATION ECONOMY: FROM MANUFACTURING TO KNOWLEDGE PRODUCTION

What jobs did your parents have? Your grandparents? When we reach your great, great grandparents' generation, the chances are very good that you will say farmer. Today there are few farmers; structural change during the industrial revolution eliminated them. What jobs will people have four generations from now? That may be as difficult for us to imagine as it would have been for farmers of the early 1800s to imagine the economic institutions of today. In the short run, however, we can observe changes taking place in the structure of work.

THE STRUCTURE OF WORK

When we analyze work in terms of the actual people performing jobs, we use the concept of a **labor force**—all the people who work for wages. When we are interested in the jobs themselves, rather than the individuals in them, we use the concepts of occupation and industry. **Occupation** refers to the tasks performed by a person, such as computer programming. **Industry** refers to what is produced by the company employing the person. For instance, a programmer could be working for a bank, a manufacturing firm, or an educational institution. His or her occupation would be the same in each case, but the industry would be different. The computer transformation of work involves different issues, depending on whether we are analyzing the effects on the labor force or the effects on occupation and industry.

The Labor Force

In terms of social norms, the labor force is all the people who are or "should be" working. Popularly, this includes all able-bodied adults, with some debate over whether those responsible for small children "should" or "shouldn't" work. Everyone who either has a job or is looking for a job is "in" the labor force. But the way we officially measure the labor force is more restrictive; it leaves many people uncounted. The United States labor force is defined by the Bureau of Labor Statistics as all the people over the age of sixteen who are employed, unemployed, or in the military. This may sound like everybody, but the way employment and unemployment are measured creates a conceptual gap between our social and our statistical understandings of work.

You are officially *employed* if you did any work at all for pay (or worked at least fifteen hours unpaid for a family business) during the week that the monthly Current Population Survey is taken. You are also employed if you are away from your job on unpaid vacation, on strike, sick, or stranded by a snowstorm. In the extreme case, a person who worked for one hour a month at minimum wage could be counted as employed. Almost a fifth of the U.S. labor force is now employed part-time (Nardone, 1986:16). People who have a full-time job but want longer hours or more suitable work at higher pay make up another substantial portion of the employed.

If you are out of work, you still won't be counted as unemployed unless you were available for work (not seriously ill, not enrolled full-time in school, and not waiting to start a new job you've already been hired for). Also, unless you made a serious effort to find work (job applications, not just reading the want ads), you are not unemployed—you're "out" of the labor force. This leaves out students, full-time housewives, and people in hospitals or jails, as well as those who don't have jobs but who have given up looking (the "discouraged workers"). The official unemployment rate thus understates the number of people who are without regular work in a social sense.

Occupation

The occupational structure of a society consists of all available jobs, filled or not. Because occupational structures contain thousands of different positions, descriptions of job categories are more convenient than long lists. Several different classification schemes have been developed; Table 5 shows some

TABLE 5
UNITED NATIONS INTERNATIONAL STANDARD OCCUPATIONAL CLASSIFICATIONS

Occupation
0.   Professional, technical, and related workers
1.   Administrative, executive, and managerial workers
2.   Clerical workers
3.   Sales workers
4.   Farmers, fishermen, hunters, loggers, and related workers
5.   Miners, quarrymen, and related workers
6.   Workers in transport and communication occupations
7/8.   Craftsmen, production-process workers, and laborers not elsewhere classified
9.   Service, sport, and recreation workers
X.   Workers not classifiable by occupation
Armed forces

common occupational categories. "Blue-collar" and "white-collar" categories describe the social distinction between clean and dirty work. White-collar managerial, professional, technical, clerical, and sales employees could wear white shirts to work without getting them filthy. Sometimes the lower-status ranks of clerical and sales occupations are called "pink-collar" work, describing the fact that the people in them are overwhelmingly female.

Occupational and labor force categories were created to provide useful statistical descriptions of society. In a study of the rural Philippine economy, I used many categories of agricultural occupations—like coconut tree climber—and the category nonagricultural occupations for everyone else. The categories chosen by governments and international agencies are important because they define the data base that future researchers will have to use. Economic activities not reported to statistical agencies are especially difficult to study. Mowing someone's lawn, selling illegal drugs, fixing dinner for your family, or writing a computer program for someone who fixes your car in return are all examples of informal economic activities. One of the reasons researchers don't have good information on the spread of small-scale computer-based entrepreneurial activity is that people don't report it.

Industry

Table 6 shows some of the commonly used industrial categories. Industries are usually divided into sectors, but different analyses use slightly different definitions of which products belong to which sector. The primary (also called extractive) sector includes agriculture, forestry, hunting, and fishing. It also often includes mining. The concept behind the primary sector is the extraction

TABLE 6
UNITED NATIONS INTERNATIONAL STANDARD INDUSTRIAL CLASSIFICATION OF ALL OCCUPATIONS
(first digit of a three-digit code)

0 Agriculture, forestry, hunting, and fishing	Primary (Extractive) Sector ISIC 0&1	Primary (Agricultural) Sector ISIC 0
1 Mining and quarrying		
2 and 3 Manufacturing	Secondary (Transformative) Sector ISIC 2-5	Secondary (Mining and Manufacturing) Sector ISIC 1-5 plus 7 [includes transportation, storage, and communications]
4 Construction		
5 Electricity, gas, water, and sanitary services		
6 Commerce	Tertiary (Service) Sector ISIC 6-8	Tertiary (Service) Sector ISIC 6 and 8 [does not include transportation, storage, and communication]
7 Transportation, storage, and communications		
8 Services		
9 Activity not adequately described		

of raw materials from the environment. The secondary sector of the economy is the one that transforms raw materials into manufactured products. This includes construction and the public utilities (gas, electricity, water, and sanitation). Sometimes it also includes transportation, storage, and communications industries. When studying computer technology and industrial sector change, it is hard to compare data that count the communications industry in different sectors. The service sector includes the rest of the economy—all those industries that produce services rather than goods.

"High-Tech" Industry

High tech is a popular rather than a technical term. In the labor analyst's terms, high-tech industry is mainly located in the communications industry and in the manufacture of electrical machinery, appliances, and supplies. Some labor force analysis has been done with high tech defined as a new industrial sector (Burgan, 1985), but, because no standard definition has been made, we don't have good data that can be compared from one study to another.

The term *high tech* is sometimes used by people to mean a particular form of professional occupation. Although the occupations in the computer industry include managers, engineers, hardware and software specialists, sales and documentation personnel, and equipment operators, it is important to note that many high-tech jobs are for janitors, receptionists, electronic component assemblers, and other rather poorly paid personnel. In Silicon Valley less than 40 percent of high-tech workers are professional, technical, or managerial (Eisenscher, 1984:7).

INDUSTRIAL CHANGE IN THE INFORMATION SOCIETY

When new products are produced or the number of people involved in making an old product decreases, structural change in industry occurs. During the industrial revolution, there was a structural change from agricultural industries to manufacturing ones. At present we are experiencing a shift from manufacturing jobs to service sector jobs. Besides changing available jobs, industrial change redistributes economic power among corporations. In competitive industries, many small firms compete to sell their products. When industrial concentration occurs, large firms buy up or force their competitors out of business. Since the industrial revolution, competition has also occurred among nations marketing their products in the world economy.

As we enter what Daniel Bell (1980b) has called the "information society," industries and occupations that produce and distribute information are becoming central to the economy. In an analysis of the U.S. economy, Marc Porat (1978) argues that the production and distribution of information accounts for about half of the U.S. gross national product and more than half of all salaries. Sixteen years before Porat published his analysis, the information industries were estimated at only half of that (Machlup, 1962). As more information products are made, analysts are finding the three-sector model of industry less useful. Figure 13 shows Daniel Bell's four-sector breakdown of the U.S. economy over the past century. A reanalysis of old industry data made it possible to estimate the growth of the information sector. In Table 7 (pp. 138–139), Bell compares the characteristics of the information society with those of industrial and preindustrial societies.

The industries that produce and distribute the most information products are the media. These include the traditional media of publishing, motion pictures, radio, television, telephone, telegraph, and the mail service. They also include new media such as cable TV and new forms of voice, image, and text transmission. The technological and organizational base of these new information industries is the manufacture and distribution of computers, electronic components, and the equipment for printing, image creation, and transmission.

FIGURE 13

FOUR-SECTOR AGGREGATION OF THE U.S. WORK FORCE, 1860–1980
(using median estimates of information workers)

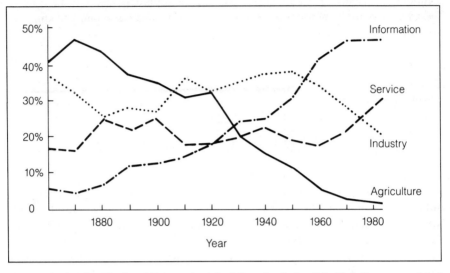

Source: Daniel Bell, "The Social Framework of the Information Society," in M. J. Dertouzos and Joel Moses, eds. *The Computer Age: A Twenty-Year View.* © 1979 by the Massachusetts Institute of Technology. Published by M.I.T. Press. Used by permission.

Publishing

The publishing industry produces books, newspapers, magazines, and government documents. The U.S. Government Printing Office and the Library of Congress are the major public producers and distributors of printed media. In the private sector, the centralization of newspaper publishing into fewer large firms has occurred in the U.S. despite laws against multiple ownership of local papers (Branscomb, 1983). In France and other European countries, there has been a similar concentration of press ownership since World War II (Freiberg, 1981). Book publishing, however, has long been one of the most open and competitive of U.S. industries (Coser, Kadushin, and Powell, 1982).

COMPUTERS IN PUBLISHING   The introduction of computer technology into publishing appears likely to revolutionize the industry. This is not because of books and magazines about computers, though they were the fastest growing area of publishing in 1982 and 1983 (*Newsweek*, October 4, 1982:75; *Wall Street Journal*, April 14, 1983:1). Instead, it is because computer technology is being used to change the way printed materials are made. Computer systems already available from Xerox and Hewlett-Packard allow text, graphics, and data to be integrated and printed (Douglas, 1983). The Association of American Publishers has begun a project to develop standards for the preparation of electronic manuscripts that would allow them to be transmitted directly from authors to publishers. At present, most books produced on a word processor (like the one you are reading now) must be converted to hard copy and typeset before publishing. This creates a delay of several months between manuscript completion and publication. The Library of Congress is conducting a study for the U.S. Senate on the future of the book in the age of electronic publishing and has a pilot project on the use of optical disk technology (*Computerworld,* April 14, 1986:13). Since books published after the nineteenth century are usually printed on wood-pulp paper and disintegrate within one hundred years, electronic storage media offer a way to preserve our government and library archives.

One of the advantages of automated publishing is that it makes the rapid production of small quantities of books economically feasible. The economics of the factory assembly line made mass production of large quantities of identical products most profitable. Applying factory organizational logic to book production, some publishers have been concentrating on the high-volume market for textbooks and best-sellers, making it more difficult for authors and readers with more specialized interests. With computerized publishing, the work of setting up a printing run can be automated. No major changes in machinery are required to switch production to the next book. For example, one small company offers hardcover reprints of out-of-print books, conference proceedings, and books too specialized for noncomputerized publishers. They promise delivery within three weeks at competitive prices. "In-house" corporate publishing has boomed as low-cost equipment makes it possible to integrate word-processing and printing equipment. A computer manufacturer, Digital Equipment Corporation, is now New England's largest publisher. Nationwide in 1985, there were about a hundred firms specializing in computer-aided publishing (Bushnell, 1985).

Another advantage of electronic publishing is its ability to keep information up-to-date. The authoritative Oxford English Dictionary is being put "on-line" in a computer data base. Although we may think of words in a dictionary as defining a language once and for all, language is constantly evolving. In a televised interview the OED editor, Robert Burchfield, said he plans to have frequent updating of the computerized version, reducing the time lag between the appearance of new words and their inclusion in the dictionary (Boston Channel 2, May 27, 1986, 6:50 P.M.).

The effects of this revolution on labor in the publishing industry are mixed (Blauner, 1964: Chap. 3; Wallace, 1985). In Sweden, the printer's labor union is actively involved in planning the future of electronic publishing. They anticipate skill enhancement and new responsibility (Howard, 1985). In other places, labor unions have been wiped out by the new technologies. British newspaper publisher Robert Murdoch fired his printers, replacing them with electronic publishing (*Fortune,* March 3, 1986:8).

PAPERLESS SOCIETY? Although some analysts envision our reading books directly from our home computer screens (Moses, 1980), students who read this book when it was only a file on their university computer unanimously chose to make hard copy versions. "It is difficult," said one, "to use a yellow

TABLE 7
THE INFORMATION SOCIETY

	Preindustrial
Mode of Production	Extractive
Economic sector	**Primary** Agriculture Mining Fishing Timber Oil and gas
Transforming resource	**Natural power** Wind, water, draft animal, human muscle
Strategic resource	Raw materials
Technology	Craft
Skill base	Artisan, manual worker, farmer
Methodology	Commonsense, trial and error; experience
Time perspective	Orientation to the past
Design	Game against nature
Axial principle	Traditionalism

Source: Daniel Bell, "The Social Framework of the Information Society," in M. J. Dertouzos and Joel Moses, eds. *The Computer Age: A Twenty-Year View.* © 1979 by the Massachusetts Institute of Technology. Published by M.I.T. Press. Used by permission.

Industrial	Postindustrial
Fabrication	Processing: Recycling

Secondary	Services	
Goods-producing		
Manufacturing	**Tertiary**	**Quarternary**
Durables	Transportation	Trade
Nondurables	Utilities	Finance
Heavy construction		Insurance
	Quinary	Real estate
	Health, education	
	Research, government	
	Recreation	

Created energy	**Information**
Electricity—oil, gas, coal, nuclear power	Computer and data-transmission systems
Financial capital	Knowledge
Machine technology	Intellectual technology
Engineer, semiskilled worker	Scientist, technical and professional occupations
Empiricism, experimentation	Abstract theory, models, simulations, decision theory, systems analysis
Ad hoc adaptiveness, experimentation	Future orientation; forecasting and planning
Game against fabricated future	Game between persons
Economic growth	Codification of theoretical knowledge

hi-liter on your terminal screen." "Besides," said another, "I like to read under a tree or in the bathtub." They also complained of headaches and blurred vision. Among the advantages of electronic books are the ability to add interactive graphics, film, and sound to the text (Yankelovich, Meyrowitz, and van Dam, 1985). As an electronic book, this one had all the disadvantages and few of the advantages. It did allow multiple readers to access it and was interactive in the sense that students could get me to change the text. But that feature caused problems for students who wanted to know which version of a chapter was the "right" one. And the whole experiment in "paperless" books used up a lot of computer paper.

Although the advent of electronic print media is sometimes predicted to give us a "paperless" society (Vyssotsky, 1980:131), other observers see *more* paper being used as the ease of making copies increases (Strassmann, 1985:ID19). An analyst of electronic funds transfer systems for banking observed: "It is ironic that a system designed to eliminate the need for paper has so many paper requirements" (Zaki, 1983:114). One humorist added up all the paper that went into publicizing and providing background material for a lecture on the paperless office, asking the speaker to explain why he used so much paper to argue that we would use less.

The Xerox Corporation (which has a stake in the fate of paper copies) explains the changing uses of paper by comparing early presses and modern computers: "Before Gutenberg, paper was used mainly for information storage; the printing press helped transform it into an information transmission medium. Now, computerization of information is emphasizing the importance of paper as a medium of action" ("Surviving the Paper Tide," Xerox Corporation advertising supplement, 1984). According to them, computers will replace paper for the storage of information, but paper will continue to be used for working with information. Indeed, as paper becomes a temporary working medium, we may use even more of it than before. In writing this book, I collected two filing cabinets and several bookcases full of notes and copies of articles. The computer printouts for early drafts of the manuscript are stacked all over my home and university offices. I estimate the volume of paper to be about ten times as great as for an earlier book written without a computer—but that one took five years and this one was done in three.

The Production of Visual Information

In *Understanding Media* (1964), Marshall McLuhan argues that film changes the temporal and spatial dimensions of our experience. Complex spatial configurations of images replace the linear information of printed texts. Electronic speeds take over from slower mechanical sequences. In *Media Power* (1985), David Altheide argues that the mass media alter our public perceptions of time and space by providing what he calls "formats" for understanding everyday events. Media formats organize our experience of events that are farther away in space but nearer in time than ever before.

But film and television are not made in order to change our concepts of time and space. They are made to be sold to viewers and to sell the products of their sponsors. Movies and television are two of the growing information industries; predictions about their social effects are predictions about the effects of commodity production.

COMPUTERS IN THE MOVIES   Commercial movie production began in America, and U.S. firms still dominate the industry. In the 1920s, four-fifths of all the films shown in the world were made in Hollywood (Smith, 1980:41). Before they were subjected to antimonopoly regulation in the 1950s, eight companies produced 95 percent of America's motion pictures; today they make about 60 percent (Branscomb, 1983:29). Film production is today a diversified and more competitive industry that makes products for television, advertising, and music as well as for movie theaters.

The impact of computers on the motion picture industry has been primarily through the special effects of computer graphics. Combining Disney Studio's development of animated cartoons in the 1920s with Bell Lab's development of computer animation in the 1960s, a number of companies were formed to provide computer graphics for films. Information International's *Star Wars*, Lucasfilm's *Star Trek II*, and Disney Studio's *Tron* are among the best-known products of the computer revolution in movies (Fox and Waite, 1984). Less well known is the extent to which these developments were sponsored by public funding of computer-imaging techniques through the Defense Department and the National Aeronautics and Space Administration. The same special effects that brought us images of the sands of Mars and the moons of Jupiter now give us fantasy images of star fighters and cartoon characters (Fischer, 1985; Rogers and Goldberg, 1986). In the future, old movie scenes—and perhaps even dead movie stars—will appear in electronically animated new films (*Science* May 2, 1986:570).

ART AND ADVERTISING   The future of computer graphics is not limited to special effects in the movies (Myers, 1985b). Just as graphics specialists left the space program for Hollywood, animators are now moving from Hollywood to Madison Avenue (Johnson, 1985). The anticipated merger of computer graphics and videotex will connect the production of images to the catalog sales of traditional goods (Chang, 1985). Retailers are experimenting with illustrated electronic catalogs from which people can shop from home via personal computer. Customers in electronic dressing rooms can "try on" clothes in front of a computerized mirror that shows them how they will look in a new dress (Pauly and Friday, 1985). If you watch television, you have probably noticed the computer revolution in commercials, sports, and news program captions.

The power of the advertising industry has grown considerably in recent years (Fox, 1984). The increasing tie between business and the creators of artistic images is questioned by artists who fear that innovation in the art field will be inhibited (McGuigan et al., 1985). Even more worrisome to some observers is the degree to which cultural symbols are shaped by the advertising industry. Television commercials are often illustrated examples of how we should achieve intimacy and status in our social relationships. The distinction between program and commercial is hard to recognize in the Saturday cartoons or game shows that feature commercial products. It can also be difficult to tell the difference between political campaigns and advertising campaigns. I suspect that an awkward and unattractive individual like Abraham Lincoln would be hard to sell as a modern presidential candidate.

COMPUTERS IN BROADCASTING AND COMMON CARRIER SERVICE   Broadcasting and common carrier services are two industries that distribute cultural information. Broadcasting includes radio and television; common carriers include postal, telegraph, and telephone services. Both industries are being transformed by computer technology. Technological innovations have created regulatory confusion over our categories of broadcasting, publishing, and common carriers. This is because, with the new technologies such as satellite transmissions, it is getting harder and harder to tell television, telephone, and mail service apart (Glatzer, 1983; Pool, 1983). A variety of terms—videotex, teleconferencing, telemarketing, and electronic mail—has been coined to describe what are sometimes simply called the "new communication media."

Computers in broadcasting have contributed to the development of new channel capability by utilizing satellite, microwave relay, and cable technology. As shown in Figure 8, page 83, the electromagnetic spectrum is divided into bands according to wavelength and frequency. The bandwidth assigned to a particular radio or television station is its channel. If two stations (or one station and your vacuum cleaner) broadcast on the same channel, interference results. This is why stations are given a regional monopoly on their channel and why channel capacity is limited. One way to create new broadcasting channels is to use new frequencies like microwave or ultrahigh frequency for broadcasting. Another way is to carry signals together over a television cable, using common carrier technologies as a substitute for broadcasting.

Cable television is a new media challenge to the broadcasting industry, having reached an estimated 50 percent of U.S. homes by 1983. It represents a much wider range of available channels and the possibility of greater programming diversity. Although cable TV has been regulated in the United States as a broadcasting industry, it has the technological capacity to offer voice, data, and video transmission services (Boel and Hauser, 1984). Cable TV's future in computer communication rests on the fate of legislation that would allow it to compete with common carriers (Haber, 1984; Winther, 1984).

Common carriers are being deregulated by the U.S. government, as discussed in Chapter 9. In the context of deregulation, it is difficult to predict the future of telephone and other data-transmission industries beyond an immediate flurry of entrepreneurial activity followed by a "shakeout." Some analysts predict significantly higher rates for individual households and fear that the poor will have more difficulty affording local telephone service (Mosco, 1983). Others fear a deterioration of transmission line quality and service in unprofitable neighborhoods, towns, and regions.

Changes in the U.S. postal system can be expected as new telecommunication technology erases the distinctions between telecommunication and mail service. Federal Express, an overnight shipping service, entered the electronic mail business with Zapmail, which offers facsimile transmission of pictures (Louis, 1984). Among its competitors are MCI Mail, an outgrowth of a long-distance telephone service, and Western Union's EasyLink. With prices falling and the U.S. Post Office dropping out of its electronic mail experiment, other vendors like General Electric's Quik-Comm and ITT's Dialcom are fighting for market shares of an emerging private mail business (Achiron, 1984; Rifkin, 1984; Warner, 1984a).

Computers also facilitate the integration of transmissions, replays, statistics, communication, and graphics. The 1984 Olympic coverage, financed by thirty-five high-tech corporations, represented the most elaborate application of new technology to news coverage to date (Ward and Maremaa, 1984). My local MTV station uses computers more modestly to keep track of the most requested rock video films. At one time I considered programming my computer to call the station a few hundred times a week and play them a tape asking for "We Are the World." Instead, I worked on the problem of who would have the most influence if public opinion were collected directly from home computers via common carriers.

The possibilities for social integration through broadcasting and common carriers extend far beyond the Olympics. The Live Aid Concert on July 13, 1985, brought international musicians, audiences, and technologies together to raise money for African famine relief. Critics deplored the advertisements of Live Aid's corporate sponsors (three of whom were doing business in South Africa), the tight schedule that reduced performers' spontaneity, and the behavior of the Philadelphia audience, which booed the Russian video contribution and left mountains of trash. But even critics reported moments when "one could feel actually involved in something larger, as an active participant in a truly global village" (Corn, 1985:23).

The Microelectronics Industry

The microelectronics industry began in the 1950s, built on earlier developments in wireless transmission, vacuum tubes, and solid state physics. The year that William Shockley invented the transistor at Bell Labs, 1947, is often used to mark the start of what has become a major world industry (Braun and McDonald, 1978). Transistors are made of materials like silicon, which are semiconductors of electricity. They were applied to the infant computer industry in the 1950s, replacing vacuum tubes to create a second generation of computers. By the end of the 1950s, so many new semiconductor firms were located around Palo Alto, California, that Santa Clara County became known as "Silicon Valley."

Transistors were much smaller than vacuum tubes. They also had fewer problems of heat dissipation. The even smaller integrated circuits developed in the 1960s led to a third generation of computers. The invention of semiconductor memories, single chip calculators, and very large-scale integrated (VLSI) circuits produced the fourth generation computer after 1978.

CHIP WARS   Silicon chips are the basic component of computers and a major product of the semiconductor industry. They are also the subject of a complex international industry conflict. As of 1980, the basic raw material for chip production, high-grade polysilicon, was supplied by only ten companies worldwide. Forty percent of the U.S. market for trichlorosilane (a key ingredient in polysilicon) was supplied by a single company—Union Carbide (Gasparello, 1980:66). New materials like gallium arsenide or organic polymers are being investigated as replacements for silicon chips, but in the 1980s, silicon remains the basic raw material for the computer industry (Rifkin, 1986).

Although there has been recent publicity about U.S. decline in world market share of chip production (Marshall, 1985), the ten largest U.S. firms had 39.5 percent of the world market in 1978. U.S. companies increased their share of the world market from 56.5 percent in 1969 to 60.9 percent in 1978 (Braun and Macdonald, 1978:10,151–53). By 1985, although U.S. industry had lost some ground, it still controlled 83 percent of the domestic market, 55 percent of the European market, and 47 percent elsewhere (*Global Electronics*, August, 1985:1). Arguments that the U.S. is losing its share of chip production are usually arguments about U.S. jobs, not U.S. companies. There has been a trend for U.S. firms to locate their manufacturing operations in other countries. As early as 1978, half the employees in U.S. semiconductor manufacturing firms were located overseas (Braun and Macdonald, 1978: 158). This explains how U.S. companies asking Congress for protection from Japanese imports can claim that they have only about 10 percent of the Japanese market while the Japanese claim they have 20 percent. Half of our sales to Japan are of chips made by U.S. companies overseas (*Global Electronics*, August 1985:1; January, 1986:1; Wilder, 1986:28).

The world market shows few signs of settling into a single nation, not even Japan. Other countries, whose labor costs are lower, are trying to attract plants or start their own industries. In 1985, I participated in an Italian government conference in Genoa. Its purpose was to investigate the prospects and problems of bringing American microelectronics technology to the city where Christopher Columbus was born. It reminded me of the historical connections among the world's countries and convinced me that the U.S. microelectronics industry isn't ours any more than the industrial revolution belonged to England.

WAGE WARS   From the viewpoint of American workers, the economic war over chip production is a serious one. But they lose jobs when American companies like Atari move overseas as well as when other nations' manufacturing operations become more competitive in the world market. This situation puts pressure on people's wages all over the world. In each nation, businesses argue that higher worker pay and better benefits would make them less competitive. International companies promise new industry to governments that can guarantee a cheap and disciplined labor force. In El Salvador, the 1980 average wage for assembly workers at Texas Instruments' plant was $4 per day (*Global Electronics*, March, 1983:2). Environmental protections for employees and communities are also inhibited when companies claim they can't afford to locate in areas that require pollution, health, and safety controls (Levenstein and Eller, 1985; Castleman, 1985).

Although it is politically convenient to blame our social problems of industrial change on Japan, no one country can protect itself from the world economy. The private troubles of each nation's economy are part of global issues of economic change. American workers who blame unemployment and falling wages on foreign workers don't realize how often foreign workers blame their low wages and political oppression on American companies.

The Computer Industry

Although the generations of computers are usually defined by their underlying technologies, there are differences in other characteristics as well. First generation machines were large and slow, without high-level languages. In 1957, I saw a first generation UNIVAC machine that filled a huge room in Washington, D.C. Keeping its large vacuum tubes cool (especially in the summer) was a constant struggle. Programming first generation machines was even harder; it involved rewiring components.

Second generation machines (like the IBM 1401 and 7090) were cheaper, used less space, and ran faster and cooler. By today's standards, programming them was difficult. Although some high-level languages like COBOL and FORTRAN were developed, the relatively slow speed, small memory, and scarce access meant that more work was required of programmers. In a university class I took in the mid-1960s, only four batch runs were allowed for each student to get a successfully working program. The only aid to debugging was a printout of the entire contents of the computer's memory in the octal number system. Although some terminals were in use, punched cards were our usual input medium.

Time-sharing appeared in the second generation with Digital Equipment Corporation's PDP-10, as did minicomputers like DEC's PDP-8 and IBM's 1130. Not until the third generation, during the late 1960s, did multiuser systems and minis "take off." But the third generation was over almost as soon as it began. Third generation time-sharing computers such as the IBM 360 and minis like the PDP-11 were quickly overtaken by the fourth generation machines.

INDUSTRIAL BOOM: THE FOURTH GENERATION   In a review of the computers of the 1970s, B. O. Evans (1980) points to two important trends in hardware that made the fourth generation the beginning of the widespread use of computers. First, the cost of processor time and storage dropped precipitously. Today's data manipulations cost only a few percent of their first generation counterparts. Second, the use of terminals rose from less than 30 percent of all computers in 1970 to more than 50 percent in 1980, allowing the costs of service to be widely shared among small users. After 1972, the microprocessor became the basis of the microcomputer, and personal computing, aimed at the small-scale user, became a major trend in fourth generation machines. With the growth of networks and data communication, microcomputers could also challenge larger time-sharing systems for business and scientific customers.

To Evans's analysis of the reasons for the success of fourth generation computers must be added the advantages of fourth generation languages. They are based on procedural queries, rather than on mathematical formulas (like FORTRAN) or on business record systems (like COBOL). It takes about one-tenth the time to write a program in one of the fourth generation languages (Desmond, 1985b). When the Live Aid Concert received one hundred eighty thousand donations in England instead of the expected thirty thousand, a fourth generation language was used to write a pledge-processing program in only three days. Using the program, it took forty volunteer operators only two days to convert the pledges into magnetic tape records for credit card companies. The rapid processing earned Live Aid an estimated \$350,000 in extra interest on the donations (Desmond, 1985c).

DOMESTIC COMPETITION: MINIS AND MICROS   In the IEEE's special "State of Computing" issue of *Computer* (1984), C. Gordon Bell characterizes the minicomputer industry as being in a state of competitive flux. Of the ninety-one U.S. firms producing minicomputers between 1968 and 1972, thirty-eight went out of the business, ten merged with larger companies, and twenty-one stopped building minis. DEC, with its Vax-11 supermini, was one of the only manufacturers to successfully make the transition from the third to the fourth generation.

Figure 14 shows the rapid growth of the personal computer industry in the early 1980s. The first microcomputer produced for personal use was the Kenbak 1 in 1971. Only about forty were sold (*Boston Globe*, April 6, 1986:A20). In 1985 over 2 million PCs were marketed. The PC market is a particularly volatile one. Osborne, with 4 percent of the U.S. market and a 300 percent growth rate in market share during 1982, was bankrupt in 1983. Two years later, Osborne was back in business. IBM and Apple are still the two largest manufacturers, but competition is fierce. The fastest growing share of the market is now "IBM PC clones," inexpensive machines that are compatible with the leading brand (*Wall Street Journal*, June 16, 1986:11D). Although marketed as "home and educational computers," PCs are also used for business and scientific applications. A major reason for this is the rapid growth of networks and data-transmission facilities that can link personal computers to each other or to large data bases and computational facilities. A major problem the industry has yet to solve is the establishment of standards to make it easier for users to connect computers made by different manufacturers (Pfister, 1984).

INTERNATIONAL COMPETITION: THE FIFTH GENERATION   Recent developments in "supercomputers" (like the CRAY) are sometimes called the beginning of a fifth generation of computers. Artificial intelligence, natural lan-

FIGURE 14
GROWTH OF THE PERSONAL COMPUTER MARKET

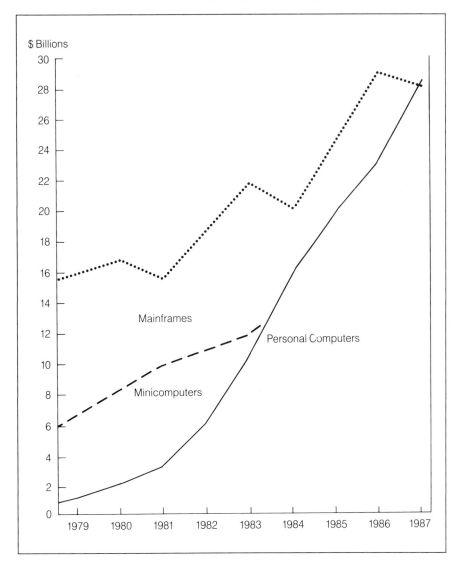

Source: Advertising section prepared by International Data Corporation for the January 23, 1984, issue of *Fortune Magazine.* Used by permission.

guage interfaces, and parallel processing will make fifth generation machines more complicated and more powerful than their fourth generation counterparts. Competition in the computer industry has also grown; in the fifth generation, its focus is international.

In the manufacture of computers, calculators, and data-processing machines, a 1983 U.S. International Trade Commission report noted that U.S. imports have tripled since 1978 while exports have only doubled. Although these figures lead some analysts to argue that we are being overwhelmed by Japan ("America's High-Tech Crisis . . .," 1985), the dollar value of our 1982 exports of computer equipment to Japan was 94.2 percent of the value of our imports from them. As the U.S. balance of computer industry trade (exports minus imports) fell badly during 1983 and 1984, the high value of the U.S. dollar in the world currency market was a large part of the problem. A "strong" dollar makes U.S.-made computers very expensive and makes those made in other countries much cheaper. For example, Asian-made IBM PC clones have become the best-selling personal computers (*Wall Street Journal,* January 10, 1986:1). Other problems more directly caused by the industry itself are its reported low productivity and failure to invest in nonmilitary research and development.

As is the case with electronic components, some of our imports are equipment produced by American firms overseas. For example, the IBM PC costs $860 to manufacture (as of 1985). Of the $465 paid to American firms, about half is spent for parts made overseas. However, despite the automation of domestic computer and calculator production and the trend toward offshore manufacturing, employment in this industrial sector rose slightly in the United States during the early 1980s as the industry expanded. For information on the current status of the computer industry, consult one of its trade publications, such as *Computerworld,* or watch for articles in business publications like the *Wall Street Journal* or *Fortune.*

SOFTWARE   The U.S. software industry, as shown in Figure 15, has grown up with fourth generation hardware. As of 1983, the United States supplied two-thirds of the world market. The industry is characterized by many small companies and rapid growth. Although an assessment of U.S. software's competitiveness finds that "the software industry is virtually the only high-technology area in the U.S. that has not seen its leadership eroded by foreign competition" (Myers, 1985a:81), European and Japanese firms already supply much of their domestic market and are considering plans to increase their world market shares. The future of software is, like the rest of the industry, part of the international economic system.

OCCUPATIONAL CHANGE IN THE INFORMATION SOCIETY

Change in society's occupational structure occurs when jobs are eliminated, when new jobs are created, or when the job tasks, titles, and rewards are being transformed. Historically, industrialization was accomplished by structural differentiation as manual labor was divided into specialized tasks. New occupations developed in all industries for managerial, professional, technical, clerical, and sales employees. Even in declining industries like

FIGURE 15

THE SOFTWARE INDUSTRY

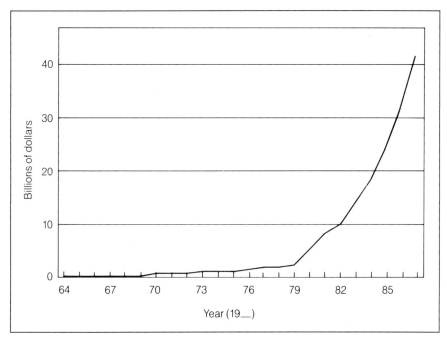

Source: Ware Myers. "An Assessment of the Competitiveness of the United States Software Industry." *Computer* (May 1985): p. 84. © 1985 IEEE. Used by permission.

mining or agriculture, new kinds of white-collar jobs appeared as managing information became an important part of producing goods.

Following World War II, the occupational structure of the United States shifted from a majority of blue-collar to a majority of white-collar jobs. During the process, a phenomenon called **upward social mobility** occurred as people gained status and income in the rapidly expanding managerial, professional, technical, clerical, and sales occupations (Lipset and Bendix, 1966). The social expectation that children should be more successful in their work than their parents was formed as people in industrial societies experienced an unprecedented degree of upward mobility.

Optimistic analyses of the computer revolution focus on the promise of expanded opportunities for interesting, high-status, well-paid jobs in managerial, professional, and technical occupations. The dream of the computer's potential is to eliminate the drudgery of work, thus freeing people to exercise their intellectual and creative skills. Yet John Stuart Mill (a philosopher whose work was influenced by Babbage) argued about the first industrial revolution:

> it is questionable if all the mechanical inventions yet made have lightened the day's toil of any human being. They have enabled a greater population to live

the same life of drudgery and imprisonment, and an increased number of manufacturers and others to make fortunes. They have increased the comforts of the middle classes. But they have not yet begun to effect those great changes in human destiny which it is in their nature and in their futurity to accomplish. (Mill, 1848:332)

As we shift to information-producing occupations, there is no evidence to indicate a new period of upward social mobility in terms of income. Instead, there is some downward mobility as highly paid manufacturing workers in the "sunset industries" lose their jobs and enter the service sector. Computers in the workplace (examined in detail in Chapter 7) will not automatically raise everyone's social status and rewards from work. Their effects depend on the choices made about how to design computers for work and how to reorganize work to facilitate the human/computer interface. These choices, in turn, depend very much on assumptions about what work means and how it is related to human creativity and skill.

The Meaning of Work

Work is **self-actualizing** when individuals have the opportunity to express their sense of self through activity that contributes to the society and gives them a valued social status. Karl Marx argued that people "make themselves" through work. In other words, through cooperative patterns of work, people create culture, which defines what it means to be human. Those who see computerized work as potentially liberating share in Emile Durkheim's vision of organic solidarity, in which new forms of economic activity satisfy individual personalities as well as social and economic needs. Although Marx and Durkheim differ greatly in their assessments of capitalism's effects on labor, both share a vision of a future society in which work is meaningful social activity for all. Some of our worst fears about computerized work are that it will increase the alienation in modern society, making our work and ourselves even more remote from any meaningful social activity.

In the Western cultural tradition, those who work with their minds (thinking, planning, and giving orders) have generally had higher social status than those who work with their hands. It was sometimes even assumed that those who work with their hands were mentally or spiritually deficient. The Greek philosopher Socrates said: "What are called the mechanical arts carry a social stigma and are rightly dishonored in our cities. For those arts damage the bodies of those who work at them. . . . This physical degeneration results also in the deterioration of the soul" (Magdoff, 1982:7). Mental labor has been considered the highest expression of the human spirit. The philosopher Immanuel Kant held that true human work was the seeking of wisdom.

The mental labor of managers and professionals has been rewarded with more income and prestige than the manual labor of common workers. Most people find it natural that talented individuals who have taken the time and effort to develop themselves should be socially valued. Even well-paid skilled workers in manual occupations suffer a certain social stigma because they have little control over their own activities and take orders, implying subservience (Veblen, 1934). Those who have no job suffer even more because, without work, they no longer serve an important social function in a society that places its highest value on economic roles. In capitalist culture, work is more than a job. It is, in the words of sociologists Richard Sennett and Jonathan Cobb (1972:75), a "means toward validation of the self."

Efficiency and Productivity

Whether people's work is defined as mental or manual, computers are predicted to make them more efficient and productive. But what do *efficient* and *productive* mean? These are technical terms to an economist or engineer, but individuals often apply the ideas to ordinary activities. For example, a student might speak of studying efficiently, or a sightseer might refer to a productive day of touring. A practice is efficient if it does not waste money, materials, or time. Higher productivity is achieved when someone can produce more of something in a given period of time.

With the industrial revolution's division of labor, the productivity of manual labor was raised, and the production of goods was made more efficient. Bureaucratic organizations rationalized the mental labor of white-collar workers. However, the productivity of managerial, professional, technical, clerical, and sales workers was difficult to measure. Bureaucratic organizations are often criticized for low efficiency, and the service industries are generally less productive than the industrial sector.

EFFICIENCY   Efficiency can be defined as the maximum amount of one quantity that can be obtained from a fixed amount of another:

$$\text{Efficiency} = \frac{\text{Maximum Output}}{\text{Unit of Input}}$$

An efficient shopper, for example, gets the most groceries per dollar of food budget or else spends the least time at it. An inefficient shopper doesn't bother to check for "best buys," doesn't make a shopping list, and may make frequent trips to the store for forgotten items.

According to the laws of physics, the energy efficiency of a machine or other system will always be less than one. The laws of entropy prevent us from getting more energy or more matter out of a process than we put into it (with the exception of nuclear fission or fusion, during which a small amount of matter is converted into a large amount of energy). Industrial production systems use and waste large amounts of energy. For example, it takes 10 calories of energy to produce 1 calorie of food in the United States, but only .05 calories in many third world countries. However, U.S. agriculture is the most efficient in the world in terms of food production per man-hour of farm labor.

Financial managers typically define efficiency in terms of profit per capital input. They would perform a cost-benefit analysis to see whether the capital costs of new equipment, such as computers, would increase their profits. Although 15 percent would be considered a good annual return on many kinds of investments, it is theoretically possible to make more than 100 percent return on capital inputs to business because money is not a direct measure of the energy or matter in a physical system.

The popular axiom "time is money" expresses another view of efficiency. It assumes that money is a universal medium of exchange with which the cost or value of all desired goods and goals can be measured. Time, in this view, can be assigned a monetary value because it is a means to achieving a desired goal. The social experience of wage labor reinforces this concept of time. Each hour of a worker's time is worth a more or less standard hourly wage.

From a social point of view, however, it is often neither time nor money that we wish to maximize. When we consider efficiency, we must ask "efficient for what?" For example, a new manufacturing process that makes more profit but pollutes the environment may be efficient for the company but not for the society that has to pay the costs of environmental cleanup and health care. When business replaces human labor with machinery, there are sometimes personal and social costs of unemployment as well as more efficient production. From the company's point of view, these social costs are *external* to its financial calculations because the company doesn't have to pay them. Society, however, uses a combination of incentives, laws, regulations, fines, taxes, and credits to help make these costs part of business calculations. In doing so, the society makes economic activity more socially efficient. Economists consider an economy efficient if its pricing structure distributes the greatest good to the most people. Debates about the efficiency of the free market system are about the extent to which it can do this.

PRODUCTIVITY   Productivity is usually measured as worker output within a given period of time. Because providing a worker with more efficient tools generally increases output per hour, we can expect that the computer will raise employee productivity. This seems particularly true in the automation of offices, where the most workers spend most of their time handling paper and other information media. Because the new equipment is expensive, there is no guarantee that higher productivity per worker will lead to higher profits than previously.

Many companies seek new equipment designed for operation by low-skill, low-paid workers. They assume that, for a given annual investment in equipment, lower-wage employees produce more profit than highly paid ones. Yet worker productivity cannot be computed so simply. Employees who consider themselves underpaid or who find their jobs boring tend to be less careful of their work and their tools. Extremely alienated information workers have been known to engage in computer sabotage. Reports one clerical worker: "I found that everywhere I worked somebody knew how to mess them [computers] up" (Goldberg, 1983:91). Also, higher paid, more skilled workers can often make better use of their tools. In surveys of workplaces, the annual output per worker is usually lower for the low-wage employees.

Another way for companies to increase productivity is to use automation to reduce the number of employees without reducing salaries for those remaining, or to expand productivity without hiring new workers. This is why we sometimes find data showing us that worker productivity and unemployment are both going up at the same time. In this case, higher productivity is a form of economic progress for companies because it leads to higher profits, but it may produce costs for society in the form of unemployment. An important issue is whether new jobs are being created at the same rate that old ones are being lost.

In 1983, the U.S. Bureau of Labor Statistics introduced a new multifactor measure of productivity that includes both labor and capital inputs. Figure 16 shows the rise in U.S. private business productivity between 1948 and 1982. Despite a rise in output per hour after 1973, increased capital investments in workers meant that there was almost no growth in multifactor productivity. This means that the computer transformation of work is contributing to higher output per worker but that the new technology has not yet "paid for itself" in terms of higher output when costs are considered.

Two Views of Human Skills

As we saw in Chapter 3, the modern computer originated from the same social conditions that produced factories and industrial machinery. Charles Babbage's design was not only for a machine, but also for a division of labor. In *On the Economy of Machinery and Manufactures* (1832), Babbage analyzed the factory system and recommended a policy for industrialization that treated labor as a factor of production. Babbage emphasized the need for factual information on which to base production and marketing decisions. Much of his argument was a precursor to **scientific management**—the application of scientific principles to the subject of the division of labor in order to make a profit.

Frederick Taylor was an early proponent of assembly line efficiency and is considered a founder of the principles of scientific management. Under Taylorism, the manual laborer was viewed as a component, or manual mechanism, in the production process. Taylor divided work into jobs and tasks that required no thought and little manual movement; even if the worker had skills, Taylor viewed the exercise of them as potentially disruptive of workplace organization. Taylorism assumed that jobs required skills, but that skill resided in the work rather than in the worker.

Although not a direct precursor of Frederick Taylor, Babbage was interested in the same sort of time and motion studies that became the hallmark of scientific management's approach to designing the conditions of work (Gideon, 1982:114). Babbage pointed out that the organization of work into specialized tasks would reduce the cost of labor by reducing the degree of skill required of the laborer. Babbage's analytical engine (the first modern digital computer) was never actually built, but he envisioned its design as contributing to a "new mode of work" that would have a "lasting impulse on manufacturing" (Hyman, 1982:112–34).

FIGURE 16
U.S. MULTIFACTOR PRODUCTIVITY

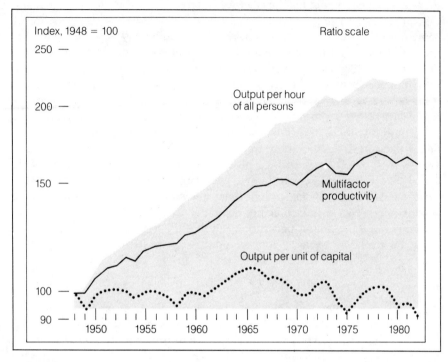

Source: U.S. Department of Labor Bureau of Labor Statistics 1984, Bulletin 2211, "Our Changing Economy: A BLS Centennial Chartbook," p. 19.

The new mode of work established by the industrial revolution used Babbage's ideas about the division of labor but not his analytical engine. Braverman (1974:81–83) says of Babbage:

> Applied first to handicrafts and then to the mechanical crafts, Babbage's principle eventually becomes the underlying force governing all forms of work in capitalist society. . . . This might even be called the general law of the capitalist division of labor.

Not until World War II and the development of cybernetic communication and control technologies did we begin to apply digital computers to industrial work. In doing so, we have tended to make the same assumptions about human skill that were made in designing the factory system. In other words, we designed our computer systems to look like factories. We have extended the industrial revolution by implementing new technologies for rationalizing and mechanizing individual skills and for supervising employees' tasks. But we have only begun to explore the possibilities of a new division of labor based on radically different assumptions about work.

An alternative approach to computerized work applies the logic of the professions rather than the logic of the factory. Human capital theory, the managerial logic most commonly applied to mental work, contrasts sharply with the tenets of Taylorism. In human capital theory, it is assumed that workers bring skills to jobs. One theory suggests that a measure of job skill would have four components: (1) the number of tasks involved, (2) the time required to gain proficiency over tasks, (3) the standards—high or low—required in the completion of tasks, and (4) the extent to which the job requires decision making in an environment of change (Spenner, 1983:826). A high-skill job would call for command over a wide range of tasks. Standards would be high, as would the amount of time required to gain proficiency. Such jobs require a full expression of an employee's training, senses, and decision-making capabilities. The "workplace commitment strategy," shown in Table 8, replaces the control and supervision assumptions of Taylorism with the assumptions that employees are skillful and responsible.

The Deskilling Debate

Analysts tend to agree that computer technology is being used to create a new division of labor; they disagree over what structural form it will take and what types of jobs, working conditions, wages, and social statuses will result. On one side of the debate are analysts like Mike Cooley (1980) and Harley Shaiken (1984) who believe that Taylorism is the dominant ideology of industrial management. Basing their arguments on Harry Braverman's *Labor and Monopoly Capital: The Degradation of Work in the Twentieth Century* (1974), they predict that increasing routinization and automation of computerized work will reduce employee skills and quality of life. On the other side of the debate are analysts like Daniel Bell (1980b) and V. Giuliano (1982) who see the emergence of new management strategies and enhanced working conditions for more skilled employees. As we will see in Chapter 7, empirical research supports both sides of the deskilling debate.

The social impact of the computer in the workplace is not a question of *whether* the technology can enhance employee skills and provide healthier and more interesting jobs or *whether* computerization routinizes work and transfers skills from the person to the machine. Both of these phenomena occur. The issue is whether one of these two technological possibilities predominates or whether we will have a new division of labor *within* computerized work as great as the older distinction between mental and manual labor.

TABLE 8

WORKPLACE COMMITMENT STRATEGY

	Control	Transitional	Commitment
Job design principles	Individual attention limited to performing individual job. Job design deskills and fragments work and separates doing and thinking. Accountability focused on individual. Fixed job definition.	Scope of individual responsibility extended to upgrading system performance, via participative problem-solving groups in QWL, EI, and quality circle programs. No change in traditional job design or accountability.	Individual responsibility extended to upgrading system performance. Job design enhances content of work, emphasizes whole task, and combines doing and thinking. Frequent use of teams as basic accountable unit. Flexible definition of duties, contingent on changing conditions.
Performance expectations	Measured standards define minimum performance. Stability seen as desirable.		Emphasis placed on higher, "stretch objectives," which tend to be dynamic and oriented to the marketplace.
Management organization: structure, systems, and style	Structure tends to be layered, with top-down controls. Coordination and control rely on rules and procedures. More emphasis on prerogatives and positional authority. Status symbols distributed to reinforce hierarchy.	No basic changes in approaches to structure, control, or authority. A few visible symbols change.	Flat organization structure with mutual influence systems. Coordination and control based more on shared goals, values, and traditions. Management emphasis on problem solving and relevant information and expertise. Minimum status differentials to de-emphasize inherent hierarchy.

Compensation policies	Variable pay where feasible to provide individual incentive. Individual pay geared to job evaluation. In downturn, cuts concentrated on hourly payroll.	Typically no basic changes in compensation concepts.	Variable rewards to create equity and to reinforce group achievements: gain sharing, profit sharing. Individual pay linked to skills and mastery. Equality of sacrifice.
Employment assurances	Employees regarded as variable costs.	Equality of sacrifice among employee groups. Assurances that participation will not result in loss of job. Extra effort to avoid layoffs.	Assurances that participation will not result in loss of job. High commitment to avoid or assist in reemployment. Priority for training and retaining existing work force.
Employee voice policies	Employee input allowed on relatively narrow agenda. Attendant risks emphasized. Methods include open-door policy, attitude surveys, grievance procedures, and collective bargaining in some organizations. Business information distributed on strictly defined "need to know" basis.	Addition of limited, ad hoc consultation mechanisms. No change in corporate governance. Additional sharing of information.	Employee participation encouraged on wide range of issues. Attendant benefits emphasized. New concepts of corporate governance. Business data shared widely.
Labor-management relations	Adversarial labor relations; emphasis on interest conflict.	Thawing of adversarial attitudes; joint sponsorship of QWL or EI; emphasis on common fate.	Mutuality in labor relations; joint planning and problem solving on expanded agenda. Unions, management, and workers redefine their respective roles.

7

THE ANALYTICAL ENGINE: WORK IN THE INFORMATION SOCIETY

Did you ever see a film or drawing of the early designs for flying machines? Most resembled birds; many had flapping wings. It was not until we developed theoretical and practical experience with aerodynamics that we designed modern aircraft. Karl Marx, studying the technology of the early industrial revolution, observed:

> To what an extent the old forms of the instruments of production influenced their new forms at first starting, is shown . . . perhaps more strikingly than any other way, by the attempts before the invention of the present locomotive, to construct a locomotive that actually had two feet, which after the fashion of a horse, it raised alternatively from the ground. It is only after considerable development of the science of mechanics, and accumulated practical experience, that the form of a machine becomes settled entirely in accordance with mechanical principles, and emancipated from the traditional form of the tool that gave rise to it. (Marx, 1967:383)

Computers are flexible tools for communication and control. But before we will be able to use them for new purposes, we must free their design from the older systems for coordinating human activity developed during the industrial revolution. In computerizing work, we have tended to make the same assumptions about human skill that were made in designing the factory system.

REDESIGNING WORK

Table 9 shows the transformation of space, time, and control made possible by Babbage's analytical engine. In the process of applying computer technology to work, we tend to think of space, time, and organization in industrial terms: work is done in workplaces in linear sequences of tasks controlled by a human supervisor. However, the computer can be used to organize work spaces rather than places. People can be located anywhere that there are communications links—the idea of workplaces can be replaced by the concept of work spaces defined by computer networks. "Where" people work will mean more than where they are physically located; it will mean what and whom they are connected to.

The time sequences of work can be changed by the design of parallel processors (Silbar, 1985; Tuomenoksa and Siegel, 1985). Instead of work being done one task at a time, it will be possible to perform several activities simultaneously. For a simple example, as I'm editing this, my printer is typing Chapter 6. From my point of view, I'm doing two things at once. My computer, however, is really switching back and forth between two tasks. Parallel processing computers actually perform several tasks simultaneously. The tempo of work need not be paced by regular motions of a mechanical engine; it can be defined by an interactive computer interface designed to accommodate human response times and rhythms.

Telecommuting in the Global Factory:
A New Distribution of Labor

Telecommuting is an arrangement of work in which employees are geographically scattered. Instead of a centralized factory or office with face-to-face supervision of their specialized tasks, coordination and control functions are performed via computer network. The analysis of telecommuting is often restricted to the relatively few people who work in the United States from their homes via personal computer. We have very poor data on how many people actually telecommute. Jack Nilles, who first studied the phenomenon in the 1970s, estimates about twenty thousand (Emmett, 1984:79). However, telecommuters are a small fraction of the more than two million Americans who listed their residence as their main place of work on the 1980 census or the 13 million businesses reported by the U.S. Chamber of Commerce as

TABLE 9
THE POSSIBILITIES FOR COMPUTERIZED WORK

	Computer Applications Designed to:		
Trans-form:	Mechanize Manual and Deskilled Mental Labor	Rationalize and to Some Extent Automate Mental Labor	Coordinate Activities of a Working Community
Space	Workplaces geographically distributed	Work spaces defined by networks instead of geography	Integration of work space and social communications
Time	Machine pacing in interfaces driven by computer response times	Parallel processing and user-driven organizational interfaces	Gradual erosion of work time/social time distinction in community interfaces
Power	Computer takes over the role of supervisor	Direct supervision replaced by control and coordination	Community decision making

being located in homes (Wolfgram, 1984:31). An industry survey of personal computer owners reports that 7 million households do *some* business or office-related work at home (Phillips, 1986:30D), but we cannot tell how many of those people are telecommuters and how many are using computers to do work for their job or business that they used to do at home with typewriter and calculator. Although Nilles predicts that telecommuters will number 10 million by 1990 and 13 million by the end of the century, they are not the most significant part of the new distribution of labor.

THE GLOBAL FACTORY   Most telecommuting arrangements are not between offices and individuals but between companies and their geographically dispersed subsidiaries, suppliers, and subcontractors. In 1970, I worked as a systems engineer in Taiwan, installing a new computer for a Chinese company that supplied keypunch operator services to American firms. The keypunch operators sat at rows of card punch machines. A timeclock kept track of their hours, their keystrokes per hour were recorded, and the keypunch verifier operators reported on error rates. Today on the Caribbean island of Barbados, women earn $1.50 an hour, a wage that represents the bottom of the pay scale for that country, to process data for American companies (Nussbaum, 1983:12). Within the United States, banks and credit card companies have moved their clerical operations to states where wages are low, the demand for work is high, and banking regulations are most favorable. Distributing work to remote sites keeps the division of labor of the factory but scatters the pieces of the factory around the globe. As we saw in Chapter 6, the microelectronics and computer industries distribute their manufacturing operations to countries where wages for manual labor are low. With electronic data communications, clerical work can also be distributed internationally.

THE INDIVIDUAL TELECOMMUTER: ENTREPRENEUR, EMPLOYEE, OR PIECE-WORKER? Alvin Toffler (1980:205) imagines that telecommuting will end worker alienation because:

> If the individual came to own their own electronic terminals and equipment, purchased perhaps on credit, they would become, in effect, independent entrepreneurs rather than classical employees—meaning, as it were, increased ownership of the "means of production" by the worker.

Redefining employees as entrepreneurs can be profitable. Corporations save on office space and equipment, travel expenses, and—in some cases— employee fringe benefits and health provisions. Says Theron Bradley, a personnel executive at Blue Cross/Blue Shield of Massachusetts, "We locate . . . offices in areas of high labor demand so that we don't have to outbid everybody else's wages. . . . Everytime we open an office we are swamped with applications" (Kuttner, 1983:63). Blue Cross/Blue Shield is a leader in the trend toward "suburbanization" of jobs (*In These Times*, May 24–30, 1984). In suburbanization, formerly full-time jobs are retitled and relocated outside the city. The virtually all-female staffs work in two shifts of thirty hours a week each. Because they are technically not full-time, the workers receive no benefits—not even health care benefits (Andrew, 1983:15).

The U.S. Internal Revenue Service disagrees. They have ruled privately (no specific case involved) that home clerical workers are employees for whom Social Security taxes must be paid, saying: "There is no evidence that such computers are not as ubiquitous as typewriters now commonly provided by employers" (*Wall Street Journal*, January 16, 1985:1).

With highly motivated employees, work-at-home arrangements can boost productivity and save corporate overhead (Miller, 1986). For employees, telecommuting is a two-class phenomenon: for the privileged professional, telecommuting offers the chance of working at home under one's own direction and pace. Jack Nilles points out that the "ideal telecommuter has to be autonomous, self-disciplined, and inner-directed." By contrast, the traditional worker "needs extra prodding all the time" (Emmett, 1984:81).

Piecework is an old industrial solution to the problem of worker motivation. Payment by the piece, rather than by the hour, ensures a disciplined, hard-working labor force. The piecework system was used in preindustrial manufacturing—with spinning or weaving put out to the workers' cottages. It also occurred in the early office—where copy work was distributed to clerks who worked at home and were paid by the word—and in sewing by the piece, in which the working-class woman was paid extremely low wages, which nonetheless helped support her family *and* pay for her sewing machine. Under the piecework system, the electronic cottage becomes an "electronic sweatshop" in which a worker can earn as little as $100 per fifty-hour workweek after equipment rental charges and other deductions (Mattera, 1983:390). It can be located at any point in the world where telecommunications facilities are available and the cost of data transfer can be offset by extremely low wages.

THE INDUSTRIALIZATION OF MENTAL WORK

The idea of using computer technology as a means to rationalize intellectual labor dates back at least to Leibnitz's seventeenth-century goal of saving the labor of excellent men. Social theorists like Karl Marx focused on the reorganization of manual labor under capitalism, and the subject of rationalized intellectual labor was taken up by Max Weber and later theorists of bureaucratic organizations. Today, the automation of bureaucratically rationalized mental labor is theoretically possible, based on cybernetics and artificial intelligence. Cybernetics was itself based on the theoretical work of Willard Gibbs, whose research institute became a model for the contemporary division of labor in science.

However, because computers can accommodate multiple tasks occurring at different tempos and sequences, rationalized mental labor does not have to look like factory work. Computers can be used to coordinate work performed by geographically dispersed individuals working at their own pace without direct human supervision. The coordination of mental labor with communications and control technologies integrates individual efforts into larger human projects as easily as it could subordinate their mental activity to alienating working situations. Thus, the way in which computerized work is rationalized depends more upon who is able to define whom as "excellent men" or "anybody else" than upon purely technological possibilities.

As we look at the application of computers to mental work, whether it is the intellectual abilities of skilled blue-collar workers and clerical workers or the technical skills of professionals, we see both Taylorist and human capital theory designs for work. The future conditions for such work depend on the resolution of several issues:

- To what extent will the industrial revolution's processes of rationalization and mechanization be applied to mental work?
- To what extent will the use of computers as technologies of control be shifted to the use of computers as instruments of communication and integration in the labor process?

- How will our evaluations of work be changed to legitimate the shifting configuration of power and control in the work space?
- What will the consequences be for the institutions of stratification and public decision making?

Blue-Collar Robots: Automating the Labor Aristocracy

One of the clearest trends in computerized work has been the automation of the "labor aristocracy." These skilled blue-collar workers, largely through strong unions, had managed to acquire high wages, good benefits, and "middle-class" life-styles despite their status as manual laborers. Now that industrial robots have been designed with enough "intelligence" to perform skilled manual operations, the labor process for unionized industrial workers is changing. Although there were fewer than sixty thousand industrial robots in the world in 1982 (over half in Japan), their numbers are growing rapidly (Asimov and Frenkel, 1985:131).

THE MANAGEMENT PERSPECTIVE   From management's point of view, the advantages of robots are numerous. Robots are fast and dependable; their performance is regular and predictable; unlike people, they do not grow tired, frustrated, or bored. When production requirements change, a robot need not be retrained or even redesigned, but simply reprogrammed. The flexibility of general-purpose communication and control systems means that manufacturing equipment does not have to be designed for specific purposes that will become obsolete with every model change. (The idea that we could avoid changing models in manufacturing seems, to managers, incompatible with marketing goals.)

Robots are more productive—and more profitable—than people because they replace expensive labor with machinery. It is those jobs of the labor aristocracy that cost most to management that are targeted for automation. From a traditional industrial management's perspective, the optimal use of robots as part of a division of labor specifically reduces the power of workers and their unions. Ayres and Miller (1983:31) point out:

> today's robots are usefully employed in highly-structured industrial environments where practically all of the variability and decision-making can be manufactured out of the workplace. Substantial effects on factory performance and costs require the integration of robots and other forms of factory automation into coordinated manufacturing systems.

THE EFFECTS ON LABOR   Unlike skilled union labor, robots pay for themselves in five years and never go on strike. With automation, the skill level required in industrial work is reduced, making workers more easily replaced. This further undermines unions because striking members can be replaced by less skilled nonunion workers. The labor unions acknowledge that robots could be used to a worker's benefit. The most dangerous, dirty, and backbreaking jobs could be performed by the machinery while the workers who oversee and operate them could be given greater control over the labor process. It has, however, been pointed out that "robots are automation, but with a difference. Other machine tools are extensions of human capabilities, while robots are seen mainly as substitutes for human workers" (Ayres and Miller, 1983:28). Harley Shaiken, automation expert at MIT, estimates that every robot introduced in an automobile plant replaces two workers (*Boston Globe*, May 17, 1983:22). Where robots have been installed alongside human laborers, the robots have served to control the laborers (rather than vice versa) through speedups and electronic pacing. For each of these reasons, Shaiken asserts, "for labor to be a beneficiary of the computer age, instead of its victim, labor must help in shaping it" (Shaiken, 1980:76).

The robotics phenomenon could bring about both increased levels of productivity and greater unemployment. Estimates of computer-produced unemployment rates must take into account (1) the growth rate of the economy (Are new jobs being created fast enough to accommodate the displaced workers?), (2) the rate of growth of the labor force (How many new workers are entering the labor market each year?), and (3) the degree of displacement caused by technological change (Sadler, 1981:292). Ayres and Miller (1983:51) predict that if fully exploited, robots could replace about 4 million metalworkers in the next twenty years. They maintain further that in thirty years, "robots will replace almost all operative jobs in manufacturing, about 9% of today's workforce, as well as a number of skilled manufacturing jobs and routine non-manufacturing jobs."

There seem to be no prospects for reversing the robotics trend. Most attention, therefore, is focused on job creation and retraining. Although Shaiken (1983) predicts that "the displaced automobile worker has about as much chance getting a job building robots as the horse did of getting a job building automobiles," some displaced industrial workers view their situation as a private trouble and anticipate a better future for their children. Whether their children's economic futures will be better than their parents' is unclear; what is clear is that few of them will follow their parents into factory jobs.

ROBOTICS IN JAPAN   Japan—a land renowned for its productivity and worker contentment—has been a leader in factory automation. In Japan, although it is next to impossible to fire, or lay off, full-time employees, robots have been used to eliminate a large part-time labor force. Thus, our images of Japanese automation without labor dislocation ignore the fate of the lower strata of its labor force. For full-time employees, research on the changing skills and tasks in automated Japanese factories supports arguments that skill change, rather than deskilling, occurs. Of the ten thousand companies surveyed by the Japanese Ministry of Labor, 24 percent required a higher level of job skills after automation. Only 14 percent reported that less skilled workers could now manage the tasks. But 68 percent reported a shift in skills, generally from simple, repetitive, physically taxing or dangerous activities to more jobs maintaining and overseeing equipment. Only 18 percent reported an increase in simple, repetitive tasks (Bednarzik, 1985:46–47). However, there are psychological costs. A report on Nissan Motors indicates that "the psychological impact of automation is far greater than outside observers imagine" (*Wall Street Journal*, February 28, 1983:21). Nissan's workers are not experiencing the stress of potential job loss, but of the technology itself. The new robots have caused substantial displacement within the plant; workers are transferred out of their old jobs (a strain in itself) and transferred often (even more of a strain). Those who spend an entire day in the company of machines commonly complain of loneliness. The psychological stress is greatest, however, for older workers, who have worked long enough to have earned respect and honor for their skills but who daily face the fact of their obsolescence. In America, where companies do have the power to lay off workers, feelings of worthlessness may become more widespread.

Office Automation: Job Enhancement or Information Factories?

For secretaries and clerical workers in the mostly female "pink-collar" world of office work, computers are both eliminating drudgery and creating factory-like working conditions. Like those jobs occupied by the labor aristocracy, office jobs had escaped many of the rationalizing effects of the first industrial revolution. In the past, the drive toward efficiency and productivity was hindered by sociability in the office. Labor theorist Harry Braverman observes that office automation represents the "squeezing out of the minutes and hours of labor time lost in the personal relations and contacts among secretaries and between secretaries and their 'principals' " (Downing, 1981:283).

Productivity has become an issue of major importance for office managers. Reports William Serrin in the *New York Times* (March 28, 1984:A14): "It has become clear to business that office productivity was lagging significantly and that vast productivity improvements in office work must be achieved if profit levels were to be achieved and office costs, rising at 15% a year, reduced." Moreover, because the machinery is expensive, it will become more important for these corporations to optimize the use of the equipment, even when such optimization threatens a worker's well-being.

The information age office is often arranged like a factory assembly line, with fragmented tasks and increasing distance between the clerical worker and the finished product. Some word processors never see what they have typed except on the VDT screen because the printer is located elsewhere and they do not see the final copy. Although word processor operators now make higher wages than most typists, as the equipment becomes easier to operate and the skill becomes more widespread, wages can be expected to fall. The ease of correcting text with a word processor reduces the demand for accurate typists and generates lower paid jobs for their less skilled replacements.

In its initial stage, automation creates a need for both more jobs and greater skills in those jobs. Once the machinery is in place, however, office (and other) work becomes automated to the point where jobs can be eliminated and deskilled. In one estimation, each word-processing machine is equal to between one and five typists (Reinecke, 1982:142). Studies have reported a 20 to 30 percent decline in the number of clerical jobs in Western European banking and insurance industries (BIFU, 1982; FIET, 1980). It is not surprising that the most routinized of office jobs are characterized by high turnover, that the skills required for the lowest level jobs are so nominal that clerks can be trained in a matter of weeks, or even that routinization has depressed wages.

But office automation can benefit employees. Word processors are a boon in firms where documents are frequently retyped. Reports one legal secretary of word processors: "These are truly marvelous features. In fact, I wouldn't do without them now that I have them; they make my working life so much richer and more fun" (Cassedy and Nussbaum, 1983:91). Although bank clerical tasks have become deskilled, jobs for bank tellers have expanded to include a broader range of financial services and to demand more problem-solving and communication skills (Bosch-Font, 1985). Charles A. Jortberg, an office automation consultant, points out that the automated equipment "makes much more efficient use of the current labor force. It gives more satisfaction to people who work in the electronic office, except for some poor person who has to sit in front of a . . . [video display terminal] all day" (*New York Times*, March 28, 1984:A14). In an office studied by my students, work was rearranged so that all the boring tasks were collected into one job for a word processor operator. Everyone, with one exception, reported that the quality of their working lives had improved. As shown in other studies of office automation (Attewell and Rule, 1984; Turner, 1984), the effects of office automation vary more according to the status of employees and the design of their tasks than by the design of word processor technology. Levels of stress and job satisfaction vary according to these same factors.

RATIONALIZING TECHNICAL, PROFESSIONAL, AND MANAGERIAL WORK

Developments in knowledge engineering offer the technical means to rationalize managerial, professional, and technical occupations by dividing the work in ways that allow part of it to be done or managed by computers. In theory, knowledge engineering subjects mental labor to both the rationalization of its knowledge and the gradual automation of its productive activity. Technical, professional, and managerial work all involve the exercise of expert knowledge. Professional and managerial jobs also involve autonomous professional judgments based upon experience. In addition, managerial activity includes the evaluation and control of others' work. The argument that these mental activities can be routinized requires us to accept claims that computers can perform as technical experts, can acquire a kind of judgment based upon general principles and experience, and can make managerial decisions. These are precisely the claims of knowledge engineers.

Knowledge engineering includes efforts to organize intellectual activity into a set of computer-coordinated tasks by means of data management and decision support systems (Hayes-Roth, 1984). It also includes attempts to mechanize actual decision-making and knowledge production activities using expert systems and other types of artificial intelligence software (Coombs, 1984; Winston and Prendergast, 1984). Although there is too little evidence to judge the effects of knowledge engineering in management in most professions, the computer software industry is a good case in which to observe its effects on technical skill.

The Transformation of Technical Skill: Rationalization and Mechanization in Software Production

In its short history, computer programming has been transformed from a manual labor task of wiring boards (performed by women clerical workers) to a romanticized craft popularly believed to be one of the major sources of future high-tech employment. In reality, software production is being rapidly rationalized into routine work (Kraft, 1977; Kraft and Dubnoff, 1983a, 1983b). When the manual and routine mental work of ENIAC's women "computers" was taken over by machines, the creative component was transferred to male mathematicians who became known as programmers. In this process, both skill enhancement and deskilling occurred as the intellectual work was differentiated into design and execution tasks. The design phase was redefined as creative work; the routinized mental labor was devalued in symbolic and monetary terms and viewed as the appropriate target for automation.

Technological developments in software production, from the compilers of the 1950s to contemporary structured programming, relational data bases, application generators, and expert systems, have all been applied to the routinization of programming, even though most were introduced to spare humans from mental drudgery. In 1958, Commander Grace Murray Hopper reported two consequences of her recently invented compiler. First, U.S. Naval officers found to their satisfaction that the new computer techniques gave project managers better control over programmers' activities. Second, experiments indicated that a new division of labor in programming, with highly skilled systems analysts producing flowcharts and clerically trained high school graduates producing code, was the optimal way to use the new techniques. Although programmers at first opposed the change for fear of losing their jobs, the new division of labor provided upward mobility for the original programmers while creating new low-level jobs for the coders (Hopper, 1959). Analyses of software production in the 1960s and 1970s documented the emergence of a hierarchical division of labor similar to that of blue-collar industries (Kraft, 1977; Kraft and Dubnoff, 1983a, 1983b).

Today, structured programming and its extensions offer new control mechanisms at a time when data security from high-tech crimes is of growing concern to economic institutions. It offers a way to replace temperamental programmer-craftsmen with better disciplined and less expensive technical laborers. It also promises firms a 10 percent to 20 percent increase in program productivity (McClure, 1984), although there was by 1984 no good empirical research supporting these claims (Vessey and Weber, 1984). Structured programming began with a 1967 paper by the Dutch computer scientist Edgar Dijkstra. He offered an elegant mathematical approach to the problem of computer program complexity and thus the hope of "bug-free" software (Olson, 1984). Structured programming rationalizes the process of software design and coding. Easily supervised individual programmers can then be set to making small parts of large software systems. Structured programs are easy to understand, fix, modify, and (most important for routinization purposes) divide up into separate parts.

According to the software engineer Frederick Brooks, Jr. (1982:144), the major impact of structured programming has been to introduce the concept of "control structures" into program design. But such control structures also have the effect of controlling programmers. Relational data base architecture (see p. 6) is an extension of the concept of control structures to data base design. Using it, data can be accessed by people who are not allowed to alter it. This introduces a number of technical improvements in data security and task coordination. But it can also be used to structure the working conditions of programmers in ways that restrict the scope of their activity to well-defined tasks. Structured programming specifications can be so rigid that in some cases computer programs are used to edit the work to remove any nonstandard lines of code. This routinization facilitates the second phase of the deskilling process—mechanization as realized through the use of expert systems.

When combined with research on programmer knowledge (cf. Soloway and Ehrlich, 1984), structured programming techniques can be used in application generators (Horowitz, Kemper, and Narasimhan, 1985). Although application generators are not, strictly speaking, expert systems, they do enough "reasoning" to enable a relatively inexperienced programmer to produce software (Keller and Townsend, 1984). In a survey done by my students of one small company (fifty programmers) that converted to application generators, productivity did increase markedly over a five-year period while real wages fell. Younger programmers were enthusiastic about application generators, reporting that their skills were enhanced. More experienced programmers, however, reported being "deskilled."

Many artificial intelligence experts believe that software production will soon be performed largely by expert systems (Wenger, 1984; Frenkel, 1985). According to Stanford University's Bruce Buchanan (Shurkin, 1983:77), a major problem in software production is caused by the time it takes programmers to convert the acquired knowledge into programs. Implementation of "knowledge acquisition" systems connects the expert directly with the computer and saves all that programmer labor. Programmer labor, however, is a significant part of those expanding high-tech jobs that proponents of the information revolution are promising.

Expert Systems in the Professions

Expert systems are "intelligent programs" that can play chess and analyze the structure of DNA molecules; they can make decisions, learn from their mistakes and experience, and make some adaptations to the environment. Although business analysts report that "most of today's expert systems are limited in scope and quite costly" (Alexander, 1984:118), specialists within the computer industry (Hayes-Roth, 1983; Basden, 1984; d'Agapeyeff, 1984) predict a steady growth in the replacement of humans with expert systems in narrowly defined areas of expertise. In 1985, they made up 10 percent of the artificial intelligence business with less than $100 million in sales (*Boston Globe*, August 8, 1985:45). About a quarter of the "serious" expert systems in use in 1984 were in the professions, as shown in Table 10.

Their creators saw expert systems as a software tool to liberate professionals from the drudgery of routine mental labor. In 1983, Edward Feigenbaum argued: "In the face of large amounts of data we quail: we are unsystematic and forgetful, grow bored, get distracted . . . we should give ourselves credit for having the intelligence to recognize our limitations and for inventing a technology to compensate for them" (Shurkin, 1983:78).

The design of expert systems presupposes that there are human experts to be consulted. But in their implementation, they use expert knowledge so that people with much lower skills can achieve the same results. An emphasis on "user friendliness," understood as the making of increasingly complex computer programs designed for "idiots," may develop expert systems that can replace highly skilled people by adequately trained ones. Even for experienced professionals, the mental labor saved by expert systems might be subjected to heavy pressures for higher productivity rather than freed for more creative intellectual activity.

Because knowledge engineering is a capital intensive effort to relocate knowledge from human experts to machines, some knowledge engineers have begun to identify their potential for automating professional work as a problem. As Feigenbaum said in a 1984 lecture: "Everyone worries about the fate of the blue-collar workers . . . it's the highly paid professionals we ought to start worrying about."

THE CASE OF MEDICINE   At a 1958 international artificial intelligence conference, physician Francois Paycha outlined the logic of medical diagnosis and argued that mechanization could solve some of its difficulties. Although Paycha suggested that we could not anticipate the wider social consequences of mechanized medical diagnosis, another panelist echoed Leibnitz's belief that the labor of excellent men would be saved for devotion "to research proper, to true scientific thought." In the next decades, medical knowledge

TABLE 10

SUCCESSFUL EXPERT SYSTEMS, BY OCCUPATIONAL AREA, 1984

Professional	Medical	15.9%
	Research	7.2%
	Engineering	3.7%
	Professional Services	3.6%
Technical	Computing	19.6%
	Electronics	6.5%
	Oil and Mineral Exploration	7.2%
Managerial	Financial Services	3.6%
Other	Military	10.9%
	Other	21.8%

Note: N = 138.
Source: Based on data from Tim Johnson. *The Commercial Application of Expert Systems Technology.* London: Ovum, 1984.

became the subject of intensive efforts to develop intelligent data bases and software (Magraw and Magraw, 1967). But the various intelligent medical diagnosis programs do not seem as serious a threat to physicians as they would be to a less powerful profession.

Expert systems in the medical profession do seem to be emerging as aids for experts (Goldwasser et al., 1985). Some skills, like using a scalpel, may be lost to laser surgery (Freifeld, 1984). New techniques such as computer-animated X rays will give physicians more skill in diagnosing patients (*Science 86*, March:10). But the serious threats to the status of doctors are the institutional pressures from hospital administrations and health care insurers (Anderson and Jay, 1985). Many government officials and health care professionals would like to rationalize the mental labor of physicians, but no one has seriously suggested automating them in the near future, despite the opinion among knowledge engineers that medical diagnosis is a relatively straightforward process. In the long run, the impacts of computer technology on physicians may be as dramatic as the telephone's and automobile's contributions to shifting health care out of doctor's offices into hospitals (Starr, 1983). But instead of becoming automated, physicians may use computer-based communication networks to move health care back out of the hospitals.

EXPERT SYSTEMS IN ENGINEERING   The entrance of expert systems into less powerful professions such as engineering seems more likely to subject mental labor to rationalization and control. Spokesmen for professional engineering have warned for decades that professional status is reduced by change that threatens expert knowledge: "The engineer who at one time was the educated and elite leader in matching science to society is fast becoming just another member in the industrial labor force" (Forrester, 1967:152). A review of the effects of computers on creativity in chemical engineering education (Drake and Perrolle, 1984) suggests that the employment of less expensive and more narrowly trained technical people may exacerbate the problem of obsolescence for more experienced engineers. In addition, it appears that the mental labor saved by the use of expert systems may be subjected to heavy pressures for higher productivity rather than freed for more interesting types of work. In actual implementations, however, replacing experienced professionals by software and less skilled employees sometimes proves unsatisfactory, even when initially chosen by management (Cass, 1985; Whalley, 1984). Engineering problem solving often calls for broader understandings and more flexible thinking than can be embodied in even an intelligent program. In the hands of experts, expert systems can save the labor of excellent people, as Digital Equipment Corporation found in an experiment using software tools to speed up and improve chip design (Bairstow, 1985). As with clerical work, the effects of computerization on engineering work are mixed. In most case studies that my students base on their full and part-time technical employment, there is evidence of both skill enhancement and deskilling.

THE SOCIAL CONSEQUENCES

If computers can be applied to work in social ways, they are a means of integrating the fragmented structures of the industrial revolution. Instead of mental work becoming more like factory work, factory work could be nearly abolished. Though job dislocations would occur no matter how smooth the transition to the information society, new jobs may be created rapidly enough to absorb displaced laborers and provide them with new skills. If computer interfaces are designed for social relationships of work, the new division of labor would involve creative, decision-making roles for most workers. Yet for this to happen, the people who make decisions about how work is to be organized will have to choose designs that explore the possibilities of the analytical engine—not continue to build and buy computer models of factory work. Whether they will or not is a question of economic power and interests. The social consequences of computer applications to work do not depend so much on the technology itself as on the implementers' assumptions and actions.

Those who believe that even expert systems will enhance mental work assume that what is most creative in mental work is uniquely human and can never be automated. Routine thought processes that are amenable to mechanization are considered part of the drudgery of work—more like the old kinds of manual labor. Indeed, when routine mental work is automated, it can become manual labor the way supermarket checkout has moved away from a computational to a physical task. The optimization of highly skilled human capital is believed to be the appropriate managerial strategy for dealing with creative mental labor. But what about routine thinking? Under assumptions of human capital theory, we would expect to find knowledge engineering applications that did not reduce the incomes, autonomy, or skill of our "best" thinkers. But how will we recognize what creative thinking really is? We could decide that anything a machine can do well (like play chess) isn't that creative. Or we could look around and see who (like teachers) are no longer being well paid to work with their minds. Theorists who believe that our evaluations of one another's statuses tend to follow changes in peoples' economic circumstances would say that the kinds of mental labor that lose out in the economy will lose out in status. In other words, we will devalue some forms of mental labor as we now devalue manual labor. They would also say that the structural consequences of such a devaluation will be to reduce the size, status, and power of the white-collar middle-class occupations (Goldthorpe, 1982; Abercrombie and Urry, 1983). And the immediate consequences for those in factory-style computer interfaces would be alienation, not creativity.

Alienation and Automation

The root of the word *alienation* means "to separate from." In legal terms, a person is alienated from land that he or she sells and alienated from a spouse whom he or she divorces. In its psychological sense, "alienation" implies isolation from other people and from one's surroundings. Marx argued that, under factory conditions, people become alienated from the products of their work because they no longer own what they produce. Because most people are already employees, computerization will not create this sort of alienation. But Marx also argued that workers in a capitalist economy are alienated from the process of their work, from their social relationships with one another, and from their own creative powers. In current usage, *alienation* often refers to the psychological experience of lost control and/or autonomy in one's job.

THE PROCESS OF WORK   Computerization alienates people from the process of their work when the work becomes so fragmented or repetitive that it ceases to have any meaning. In large insurance companies, for example, clerks who once did nothing but process claims all day are now processing a single portion of a claim—a task that requires only the pressing of the same few keys—all day (*Wall Street Journal*, May 6, 1983:15). They were already alienated from the process of providing financial reimbursement to the ill and injured; with factory-style computerization, they even lost sight of the "whole" claim transaction. As more and more tasks are performed on information about the world rather than on objects in the world, people may lose touch with what they are making. People whose job is controlling machines are often providing a service rather than making a product, but even they can be distanced from the physical reality of what they are doing. Automation in the airlines, for example, poses this problem for both pilots and air traffic controllers. The pilot's job now involves more monitoring of machines than actual flying. The danger in this, warns a Delta Airlines executive, is of "physio-psychological atrophy," a machine-induced complacency that dulls a pilot's response in times of emergency (*Newsweek*, Jan. 30, 1984:30). The same holds true for air traffic controllers. According to a study by the Rand Institute (Wesson et al., 1981), the computerized coordination of air traffic can dull attention, degrade skills, and make it difficult for controllers to handle emergencies.

THE SOCIAL RELATIONSHIPS OF WORK   In addition to this removal from the real world, the computerized workplace and its tasks can be structured so that workers are removed from interaction with one another. One automated claims processer for a large insurance firm says that the worst thing about her job is the isolation:

> Virtually all communication is between the clerk and the machine. Since pay is based on output and the job itself requires no human interaction, there is every incentive to keep social conversation to a minimum. . . . Last Christmas they organized a little office party. They had a "Christmas Grab" where everybody picks a name out of a hat. You bring in a little gift for somebody and they bring one in for you. We realized that nobody knew anybody else's name. (Kuttner, 1983:63)

Yet isolation is not something "built into" computerized equipment. Indeed, the exact opposite may be the case in social and organizational interfaces.

ALIENATION FROM ONESELF   One telephone operator, who "likes" his job, describes the work:

> As the voices come into my mind, I just freeze the information in one part of my brain and hold it there. Then I pull it out whenever I need it. This allows me to distance myself from my work and ignore the fact that the callers treat me like a rock. Who I am and what I do don't meet. My identity is separate from my job . . . I'm on automatic. (Singular, 1983:22)

BUT THERE ARE CHOICES   Although it may be argued that telephone operation is hardly creative work, the choices made in implementing computer technology have made it even less so. A survey of the job field finds:

> The computerized system, which has eliminated local phone offices by centralizing work locations, channels calls to the operators, predicts future call flows, computes and catalogs each operator's average time spent per call, and even schedules work breaks. Because the computer schedules virtually no pause between incoming calls—which have doubled or in some locations even tripled in number to between 80 and 120 calls per operator per hour—operators are closely confined to the equipment, causing undue mental and physical fatigue. Considering the fact that operators must now respond to customers with scripted phrases and sentences, technological change has devastated their work. (Straw and Foged, 1983:167)

Yet this need not have been the case, not even within the dictates of productivity. Heidi Gottfried (1982:20) points out that the telephone company could have installed magnetic writing pads instead, but that despite "the comparable performance and the insufficient time allowed to test cost-efficiency of the pads, it seems clear that the computer was adopted for its ability to monitor and control the workday of the operator."

At every job level, from aerospace design engineers (Cooley, 1980) to office clerks, come complaints of alienation. It is unfortunate that a general purpose tool for communication and control should be used so often for control without communication. Still, several business analysts believe that the information revolution will bring about a radically different set of corporate arrangements and values (Hirschhorn, 1984). Norman Macrae, the deputy editor of Britain's business magazine *The Economist*, argues that the new economy will be dominated by "small businesses that are more adaptable to local markets, more attuned to sophisticated consumer needs, and to the growing hunger, among employees, for greater challenge and rewards" (*In Context*, Spring 1983:41). He thinks that many companies will adopt work teams. Workers will have more and better training, and thus more authority and responsibility. The teams would be "semiautonomous," meaning that they would be given all the information, resources, skills, authority, and decision-making power needed to accomplish their function, or tasks.

A CHANGING MEANING OF WORK? One could argue that worker alienation is not a major social problem in the computer revolution. Status, relations with co-workers, a sense of challenge, and having a "nice place to work" can be substitutes, according to some experts, for actual control over work. The status associated with being a professional has been one of the attractions of computerized work. As a result of the computer revolution, more people than before have access to the symbols of professional status. The professional's education, life-style, and income are what our society teaches each of us to strive for—though society also teaches that not all of us have the inherent capacity (the talent) for professionalism. The idea of a career instead of a job implies that the worker is educated, intelligent, dedicated to some ideal of service, and more competent and motivated than the person who just works for money. Unionized garbage collectors and truck drivers earn more money than many information workers but enjoy less status. Thus, although information work itself may be alienating, the social life of those who do it may be enhanced, especially if people think of their social life as occurring separately from their work life and if they seek their satisfaction from leisure.

Stratification and Social Change

As highly paid blue-collar workers lose their jobs, some pink-collar workers are pressed into less desirable forms of work, and even skilled white-collar workers may find themselves downwardly mobile. We are experiencing a massive dislocation in our economic structures. It has been argued that the change will leave us with a smaller middle class than we had before (Kuttner, 1985). Debates about a "declining middle" focus on structural change in the stratification system. Many arguments about the effects of computer technology on the labor force are over issues of unemployment (Attewell and Rule, 1984:1187–88). "Declining middle" analyses are concerned with the changing status and incomes derived from work. The "declining middle" hypothesis predicts that the proportion of jobs at the top and at the bottom of the stratification system will increase, resulting in a two-tier occupational structure.

There is some evidence that the U.S. stratification system is growing at the bottom and that inequality between top and bottom is increasing. But other factors, such as the entrance of the "baby boom" generation into the labor force and increasing participation of women in the labor force, diminish the evidence that introduction of computer technology is solely responsible for the change. Although real incomes (adjusted for inflation) are still rising for American men, an increasing number of men rank in the lowest income category (Dooley and Gottschalk, 1985). The real incomes of families fell slightly between 1973 and 1984. The poorest one-fifth of families with children had 7.4 percent of the total family income in 1968 but only 4.8 percent of total family income in 1985—a loss of one-third of their share (Kuttner, 1985:16). For some sociologists these trends have nothing to do with the computer revolution. Instead, they represent a feminization of poverty and the rise of an "underclass" of disadvantaged Americans.

Using the dynamic input–output analysis that won him the 1973 Nobel Prize in economics, Wassily Leontief and his colleague Faye Duchin (1986) projected the effects of automation on the employment structure. Considering the age composition of the U.S. labor force and projected growth in the economy, Leontief believes fears of technology-induced displacement of workers to be unfounded. One reason is the high capital costs of automation. His data suggest that the upper and lower thirds of the occupational stratification system will grow relative to the middle third, but not so dramatically as extreme predictions of a declining middle class (*Global Electronics*, December 1985:1).

WHERE ARE THE JOBS GOING TO BE? Most new job opportunities will *not* be in the occupations with the most rapid growth (computer service technician, legal assistant, computer systems analyst, computer programmer and operator, office machine repairer, physical therapy assistant, electrical engineer, civil engineering technician, and peripheral EDP equipment operator). These fields are small to start with. Leontief and Duchin's projections indicate that, by the year 2000, there will be only 5.5 million more professional workers as a result of new technology—but up to 15 million fewer clerical workers and 8 million fewer managers (*Science*, May 23, 1986:1022). According to the Bureau of Labor Statistics, high-tech industries will provide only 6 percent of the new jobs in the next decade (Robey and Russell, 1984). Nor will they be in the offices of banks and insurance companies; these are going the way of the automobile assembly line jobs. Most jobs will be in slower growing but much larger occupations, such as custodians, cashiers, sales clerks, registered nurses, waiters, elementary school teachers, truck drivers, nursing aides, and orderlies (Robey and Russell, 1984).

SOCIAL EQUITY IN THE "HIGH-TECH" INDUSTRIES   In Massachusetts, where high tech is a leading new employer, the inequalities between male and female high-tech workers are greater than they are in the state's traditional industries. In 1984, the *Boston Globe* reported that seven out of ten women who work in high tech have low-paying clerical and machine operator jobs; only about one in ten is a manager or professional, and only one in a hundred is in marketing. Their pay, fifty-five cents for every dollar earned in high-tech industries by a man, was less than the fifty-seven cents to the dollar in mature industries like textiles or the sixty-four cents to the dollar national average for women working full-time in all industries.

Among computer scientists and engineers, women and minorities are slowly gaining jobs. In 1976, women made up only 17.3 percent of employed computer specialists, while blacks and Asians accounted for 1.3 percent and 3.3 percent. By 1984, 26.1 percent of computer specialists were female, 2.8 percent were black, and 5.6 percent were Asian (National Science Foundation, 1986). Nationally, figures from the Bureau of Labor Statistics indicate that in 1984, as they had in the previous five years, women in computer professions earned almost 22 percent less than did their male counterparts in the same jobs. This is a better situation for women than the national average; median income for women in all jobs in 1984 was 35 percent less than that for men (*Computerworld*, Feb. 11, 1985:1).

In a 1983 study of the Boston area software industry, sociologists Phil Kraft and Steven Dubnoff were interested in measuring racial, as well as sexual, equality. But there were almost no black programmers to be studied in their sample of over seven hundred professionals. They found that women start at slightly higher salaries than men but run into career dead-ends earlier. Women tend to be applications programmers, documentation specialists, and customer support personnel (the high-tech version of skilled clerical work). Where women were managers, they almost always managed other women. Upper-level programmer management was virtually all male. The highest salaried female manager in the sample earned less than the worst paid male manager. The researchers also found that positions for middle-level managers were being eliminated and that divisions were emerging between analytic and routine work, between work that involves decision-making responsibility and work in which most decisions are made by someone else. A 1984 California study by Myra Strober and Carolyn Arnold found a similar pattern of employment for female computer professionals. Whatever combination of cultural and other factors keep women and minorities from high-status careers in software production, the industry cannot be considered an example of high-tech opportunity for all.

THE DEVALUATION OF MENTAL LABOR   The spread of knowledge engineering seems likely to devalue some kinds of mental labor in both an economic and a cultural sense, regardless of the outcome of the deskilling debate. In the economic sense, professional, technical, and managerial employees who do the kind of thinking that machines do (or that inexpensive workers do with machines) will see a relative reduction in their wages and salaries unless they can acquire new tasks or protect their existing areas of expertise from automation. The implications of this are that the "knowledge elite" predicted by Daniel Bell (1980b) may be much smaller than usually suggested. Also, rather than being composed of our most creative thinkers, it is likely to be composed of those who have most successfully kept their knowledge to themselves.

As knowledge engineering rationalizes and automates some areas of mental labor, those who are less successful at finding creative new activities may turn the focus of job satisfaction from concerns about real control over the labor process to symbolic gestures of social standing. Already the terminology of computer technology defines workers subjected to the control of management systems to be computer "users." Job titles contain the words *manager, designer,* and *analyst* with little correspondence to actual working conditions. Even those who repair computer equipment (who often replace parts with little understanding of how the machinery works) wear business suits and carry their tools in a briefcase. A growing concern among the middle class for what Randall Collins (1979:72) calls a consciousness of formalism "directed away from the material realities of work experience and into the purely relative values of cultural currency" is occurring. In a culture concerned with self and status, the very meaning of work is changing. What one does in an instrumental sense is being replaced by what one displays in terms of symbolic status. So long as the illusion that employees in information factories are managing a system that enhances their intellectual skills is maintained, the symbolic token may be satisfactory. However, the contradiction in this arrangement is that if the computer software devalues labor in economic terms, it will become increasingly difficult to maintain the illusion. In the long run, capitalist culture may teach that intellectual skills are not a source of human satisfaction; in the short run, a crisis of distribution may occur for capitalist culture as downwardly mobile white-collar workers demand the material rewards "due" their middle-class status (Leontief, 1980).

The mechanization of thought processes may also be translated into a cultural devaluation of the rational, logical aspects of human knowledge and intelligence. Turkel (1984) found young children exposed to computerized toys stressing "feelings" rather than "thinking" as the defining criteria of being alive and human. Critics of artificial intelligence and humanist critics of the social injustices of Western technological society tend to agree in condemning instrumental rationality as a form of tyranny over the human spirit. This combination of assertions that the essence of human thought is "what machines can't do" and that feelings rather than logic make us human somewhat paradoxically helps to legitimate turning instrumental decision-making processes over to expert systems programs. The machines are only behaving in coldly instrumental ways that are not true expressions of our humanity. Unfortunately, instrumental decision making is at the heart of democratic political institutions. A devaluation of decision-making logic may render the democratic process even more concerned with emotional symbols of group solidarity and less concerned with rational discussions of issues than it already is.

FURTHER READING FOR PART THREE

Attewell, Paul, and James Rule. 1984. "Computing and Organizations: What We Know and What We Don't Know," *Communications of the ACM* (December):1184–92.

Barcomb, David. 1981. *Office Automation: A Survey of Tools and Techniques.* Maynard, MA: Digital Press.

Baron, Naomi S. 1986. *Computer Languages: An Explorer's Guide.* New York: Doubleday.

Bluestone, Barry, and Bennett Harrison. 1982. *The Deindustrialization of America.* New York: Basic Books.

Braverman, Harry. 1974. *Labor and Monopoly Capitalism: The Degradation of Work in the Twentieth Century.* New York: Monthly Review Press.

Computer and Mathematics-Related Professions. 1984. Bureau of Labor Statistics. #2205-4.

"Computer Software." 1984. Special issue of *Scientific American* (September).

Coser, Lewis A., Charles Kadushin, and Walter W. Powell. 1982. *Books: The Culture and Commerce of Publishing.* Chicago: University of Chicago Press.

Feigenbaum, Edward A., and Pamela McCorduck. 1983. *The Fifth Generation: Artificial Intelligence and Japan's Computer Challenge to the World.* Reading, MA: Addison-Wesley.

Hirschorn, Larry. 1984. *Beyond Mechanization: Work and Technology in a Postindustrial Age.* Cambridge, MA: MIT Press.

Miller, Robert J., ed. 1983. "Robotics: Future Factories, Future Workers," special issue of *Annals of the American Academy of Political and Social Science* (November).

National Science Foundation. 1981. "Computers and Semiconductors," pages 7–37 in *Only One Science, Twelfth Annual Report of the National Science Board.* Washington, DC: U.S. Government Printing Office.

Rada, Juan. 1982. *The Impact of Microelectronics and Information Technology: Case Studies in Latin America.* Paris: United Nations Educational, Scientific, and Cultural Organization.

Reid, T. R. 1985. "The American Revolutions: The Chip," *Science 85* (January/February):32–41.

Shaiken, Harley. 1984. *Work Transformed: Automation and Labor in the Computer Age.* New York: Holt, Rinehart and Winston.

PART FOUR

INFORMATION, PROPERTY, AND POWER IN DEMOCRATIC INSTITUTIONS

CHAPTER

8

PROPERTY, PRIVACY, AND SOCIAL CONTROL: COMPUTERS AND THE LAW

What right do you have to be reading this book? To whom does the information in it belong? What right does anyone else have to keep track of what you read, say, or do? Should people who know the most be able to make decisions for the rest of us? These questions are about information and power. To the individual, they appear to be questions about personal rights to acquire information while protecting their privacy. But they are also questions about power in democratic institutions. There is a tension in democratic societies between individual freedom and social control. In our society, individuals have the right to privacy and to own property; the society has the right to limit individual freedoms in the public interest.

The social concepts of privacy and freedom of information are often in direct conflict with the concept of information as property. The law, which defines and guarantees our rights in a democratic society, is being transformed to recognize and protect information as a form of commodity property.

New laws regulating the ownership, taxation, and liabilities of information products are being proposed, and old ones are being reinterpreted. As lawyers struggle with cases involving computer software and data bases, computer law is emerging as a new specialization within the legal profession.

In law enforcement, the protection of information is of growing concern. Computer-aided crime has emerged as a new form of crime against property. Problems of prevention, detection, and prosecution are challenging computer professionals, auditors, and law enforcement agencies. Such problems also challenge the widespread beliefs that white-collar crime is not very serious and that computer-aided breaking and entering is a clever prank.

Privacy implies the right to be left alone; mechanisms of social control enforce social obligations to the common good. The belief that liberty and social order ought to be balanced is a basic value of democratic institutions. The computer revolution is upsetting the existing balance by shifting information from the public to the corporate domain and by increasing the information available to agencies of social control.

INFORMATION AS PROPERTY:
THE LEGAL TRANSFORMATION

If you bought this book or support a library through tuition or taxes, you used your economic power to acquire an information product. As an author, I receive about $1 for each copy sold and have an economic interest in selling as many as possible. As a teacher, however, I am interested in making information freely available. Thus, I loan my printed copies and make a computerized text file available. My students and colleagues apply normative power by expecting me to give them information in my role as a college professor. The cultural value that production should return a profit to the producer is not the dominant value of nonprofit academic institutions. My personal conflict of interest is reflected in a legal tension between the rights to own and to have access to information.

Information and Change in Legal Institutions

Information has always belonged to people in the sense that those who knew something have used, taught, or traded their knowledge for goods and services. Much of our cultural information, however, is collective property belonging to the whole society and available to anyone who is able to learn it. According to Durkheim (1957:168), all property rights developed out of religious rituals expressing group solidarity. From this perspective, information in the form of communication and shared symbols can be viewed as part of the remaining sacred quality of human group life. To Karl Marx, property rights grow out of a division of labor in which surplus products are unequally exchanged. From both of these perspectives, cultural information that is produced and shared by everyone in society is not private property. The argument that computers accelerate the trend toward information as property focuses on one particular form of property—the commodity. As discussed in Chapter 3, commodities are different from personal or group property in that they are made in order to be sold for a profit rather than for other forms of use or exchange. They are usually the property of the corporations that produce them rather than the personal property of the employees who actually do the work of making them.

THE LEGAL STATUS OF INFORMATION   In order for information products to be sold, law and social custom must recognize them as marketable commodities. A major difficulty with obtaining and enforcing property rights for information products is the traditional social distinction between material objects (which can be owned) and abstract information (which is an intangible personal possession or a part of shared culture). Although several areas of law define some kinds of information as property, people often act according to the belief that reading, using, or copying information is an individual right. Although most people would not break into others' houses or steal their cars, many see nothing wrong with reading their magazines or gossiping about their secrets. Unless social change occurs to make people share a cultural belief in information as property, violations of copyright and other information protection laws will likely continue.

One area of law in which existing statutes seem inadequate is that in which the property involved is information. Electromagnetic impulses transmitting stolen information have been judged not to be property under the Interstate Transportation of Stolen Property Statute (Ribicoff, 1977:131). Yet the electromagnetic coding on a computer tape (and not simply the tape itself) has been found to be property for the purposes of state taxation ("Vt. Software Tapes Taxable," 1983). In the case of tax benefits for software exporters, the requirement that products be "tangible" may cause the U.S. Internal Revenue Service to deny benefits to the software manufacturers (Benoit, 1984). The Library of Congress Copyright Office 1975 regulations requiring that machine-readable copies of computer programs be accompanied by a reproduction or description that could "be perceived visually or read by humans" made the copyright status of software unclear until later legislative amendments.

The question of who owns the information produced by artificial intelligence software has yet to be addressed by the law. Legal institutions respond rather slowly to rapidly changing technologies: "The new technology is asking questions that the 1984 Copyright Act cannot answer. Eventually, either the courts will answer the questions that the act does not, or Congress must produce new forms of protection that are appropriate to new technologies" (Gemignani, 1985:52).

CHANGE IN LEGAL INSTITUTIONS   The legal system is one of the most conservative of social institutions. In his essay on law and social custom, Thorstein Veblen (1969:34) observed that change in legal institutions occurs slowly, especially when it runs counter to established social principles or vested economic interests. Although the vested interests of information producers lie in changing the law in the direction of greater protection for information products, the principles of constitutional law in many ways define information as belonging to individuals or to society. In addition to new legal concepts of property, the social institutions of the legal profession and the administration of justice must adapt to the pressures of the computer revolution. Existing law must be applied to cases involving computers, and new legal concepts must be developed where traditional ones prove inadequate.

COMPUTERS AND THE PRACTICE OF LAW   Law has traditionally been practiced by lawyers who have access to a complex body of information that is relatively inaccessible to individuals without legal training. Although modern law is, according to Max Weber (1978:895), "a rational technical apparatus, which is continually transformable in the light of expediential considerations and devoid of all sacred content," the application of computers in rationalizing the practice of law is likely to be vigorously opposed by lawyers and their professional organizations if that rationalization substitutes information systems management for the activities of lawyers.

In 1958, legal expert Lucien Mehl proposed that "a machine for processing information can be an effective aid in searching for sources of legal information, in preparing the decision of the administrator or judge, and finally in checking the coherence of the solutions arrived at" (1959:757). But he insisted that, although judicial machines would be suited to conduct legal argument, they can never replace human legal experts because they are incapable of formulating precepts.

Although expert systems developers would claim that computers do have the technical capabilities to "replace" many of the functions of lawyers, the trends in computer usage indicate that they are being adopted in ways that facilitate the existing arrangements of legal practice. Although computer programs could be developed to render rational judgments for some sorts of cases, the human quality remains an almost sacred element in the administration of justice; we are thus unlikely to experience computerized judges. Most legal experts would agree with Joseph Weizenbaum (1976) that any conceivable intelligence on the part of a computer would lack the element of human wisdom. Even the use of computers as "informants" or providers of "expert" information is controversial (Jenkins, 1979; Marx and Richman, 1984).

What we can expect is an acceleration of the use of computers to process court cases (now terribly backlogged in most jurisdictions) and to provide legal research services to attorneys. The Lexis and Westlaw systems are examples of specialized data base services for legal research (Bander and Sweetgall, 1983). Their use may lead to the concentration of power in larger law firms, which are able to afford legal data base services. An alternative is to make these services available inexpensively to individual lawyers and small firms at government law libraries. Also, we may expect computer law to become a professional specialization. By 1985, over a thousand lawyers belonged to national and regional computer law organizations (Connolly, 1985:14).

INFORMATION PRODUCT LIABILITY   A new legal concept of information as property seems likely to create new conceptions of product liability law. These are the laws that hold companies responsible for product safety and performance "as advertised." As the law defines information property in order to protect software and data bases, new legal liability problems arise. For example, between 1985 and 1986, an undetected software error in a radiation therapy machine killed one patient and seriously injured two others (*Boston Globe*, June 20, 1986:1). The accidents happened because the interactive program temporarily selected X-ray mode even though the operator had deleted the command and selected the lower power electron beam instead. Because the error occurred only with a fast-typing operator and because the machine's display indicated that it was in the correct mode, the fault was not detected until after the patient's death. Under the Uniform Commercial Code adopted by most U.S. states, people injured by a product may sue the original manufacturer. (In this instance the manufacturer was Atomic Energy of Canada, Ltd., which made the cases an international legal matter.) If computer software is considered "goods" under the law, software suppliers could be held liable for damages caused by program errors. In other words, the company that supplied the software for the therapy machine could be held liable for the patient's death as well as the machine's manufacturer. Also, individual computer professionals have been held liable for malpractice claims similar to those made against doctors and lawyers. In addition, those whose software does not work as claimed can be found guilty of fraud (Mislow, 1984; Beeler, 1985).

The application of liability law to expert systems will be particularly difficult. If the artificial intelligence programs are defined as products, their operation may be legally required to be free from defects—something that expert systems cannot always be designed to do. If the programs are legally defined as services, liability laws are much less strict. Very few court cases have dealt with consumers injured by faulty information. In a review of such cases, attorney Susan Nycum (1986) says that courts have generally held that suppliers of information do not have the same obligations to customers as manufacturers do, that it is the medium (for example, a book or tape) that is sold rather than its informational content, and that to apply strict liability laws to information would interfere with Constitutional guarantees of freedom of speech. However, she warns computer professionals of three cases that may become precedents for information product liability. In one case, the court decided that there was no difference between a power saw manual and its contents, awarding damages to a man injured while using his saw. In the second case, a textbook publisher was found liable for a school chemistry laboratory accident based on erroneous information in the book. In the third case, makers of a faulty aviation chart were held liable for an airplane accident—even though they had accurately compiled incorrect data supplied by the federal government. If information becomes culturally redefined as commodity property, we can expect many more judges and juries to find information products liable for personal injuries.

Older industries use liability insurance to cover the costs of damages their products might do. Liability insurance is now being sought to protect hardware and software manufacturers (Cottrell and Weiss, 1984; Korzeniowski, 1985). Although some computer vendors have tried to avoid liability problems by using contracts in which the purchaser agrees not to hold the supplier at fault, courts generally do not recognize these agreements (Miller, 1984; Kutten, 1985). What this means if you are a software customer is that the company may be responsible for undisclosed defects no matter what you signed to the contrary. Warranties (money-back guarantees) have been recommended as a way to satisfy customers and cut down the risk of lawsuits (Stewart, 1985).

Liability law has been connected to issues of public access to information in the case of computer bulletin boards. Charging that bulletin board operators are responsible for allowing users to exchange pirated programs, some software manufacturers have sought damages. An additional risk of legal action against data base owners comes from libel law. A large financial services corporation was found guilty of libel for incorrectly reporting a firm as being bankrupt (Rifkin, 1985).

The Changing Status of White-Collar Crime

Law is divided into *criminal* and *civil* law. Historically, the distinction arose according to whether the goal was to punish offenders or to compensate victims. Offenses against property can be civil wrongs (called *torts*), as in the case where you damage someone's automobile and must pay compensation. Theft of an auto is an example of a crime that results in punishment rather than compensation. High-status people are more likely to appear in civil court, facing fines; low-status individuals more frequently wind up in criminal court, facing prison sentences.

The term *white-collar crime* was first used by Edwin Sutherland (1949) to describe crimes committed in the course of a person's professional occupation. Most computer crimes fit this description—they are cases of theft or fraud committed during work as a business executive or employee with access to financial data. All sorts of white-collar crime tend to be dealt with in civil rather than in criminal court; even in criminal court the status of the defendants and the nonviolent nature of their offense tends to produce lenient treatment. What underlies the leniency is our apparent failure to consider white-collar crime a serious criminal offense. Fraud and the theft of money or property are illegal. Yet someone who robs a liquor store of a small amount of cash is more severely prosecuted than a bank employee who amasses a fortune by stealing a fraction of a penny from every customer's interest payment.

COMPUTERIZED WHITE-COLLAR CRIME   The growing reports of computer-aided crime are alarming to business and financial institutions because they are beginning to realize how far auditing and financial security procedures have lagged behind data-processing innovations. The "paper trail" used by auditors to track down many white-collar crimes has turned into an "electronic trail" that is difficult for all but the most computer sophisticated accountants to trace, assuming that the electronic trail has not been completely erased from the computer's memory. Although the loss of money due to computer fraud is impossible to measure in the absence of adequate statistics, it is estimated to be our fastest growing criminal problem (Parker, 1983). Only 5.1 percent of the Justice Department's 1977 and 1978 resources were devoted to white-collar crime of any sort, and there are no statistical equivalents of the FBI's Uniform Crime Reports to cover it (Simon and Eitzen, 1982:21). The FBI is now planning a computerized file on suspected white-collar criminals, but civil liberties groups are protesting on the grounds that information on suspects and their "associates" often results in the computerization of vague suspicion and unsubstantiated charges and is likely to lead to abuse by legal authorities (Burnham, 1984).

The Computer Fraud and Abuse Act of 1984 makes it illegal to gain unauthorized access to government data or financial records (such as those of banks) covered by federal laws, though its coverage falls far short of what supporters had sought. Many states now have enacted broader laws governing computer crime (Bloombecker, 1984) and new federal legislation has been proposed to expand the scope of computer crime laws (*Computerworld*, Sept. 23, 1985:15). The problem with prosecuting computer criminals, however, has not been due entirely to the lack of laws against their activities. Instead, it is part of the more basic problem of how white-collar crime is treated by society.

Contrary to the popular image of the computer criminal as an electronic wizard matching wits with sophisticated electronic equipment, most of the crime *so far detected* has been conducted by people with a fairly limited knowledge of computers, using the data-processing systems of their own workplace. A survey of computer-related crimes in government found over 60 percent to be cases of entering fraudulent records into data bases (Whiteside, 1978:143). More recent findings of the U.S. Department of Health and Human Services and the Data Processing Management Association reaffirm the portrait of the computer-aided criminal as an "insider" (Betts, 1985b; Desmond, 1985a). Technically, the problem cannot be solved by sophisticated software to keep out unauthorized users or to examine the incorrect data. Better procedures must be developed for verifying the data that are entered into the system. And these procedures must be developed as patterns for the behavior of individuals within social organizations rather than as computer software. As David Dery (1981:10) says in his study of computers in welfare, "the chief impediment . . . is not technical capabilities, but organization."

The distinction between criminal and civil law may become less significant in the information age. As Steve Blum-West and Timothy J. Carter (1983:549) argue, the handling of federal regulatory law violations (which most white-collar crimes are) as civil or criminal is discretionary and cannot be determined from legal concepts. This means that the distinction between "white-collar" and other crimes against property is based on the offender's social status rather than on formal legal principles. As computerized white-collar crime grows more serious, we may find crimes against information products being treated like electronic breaking and entering and handled in criminal rather than civil courts.

CORPORATE CRIME   In a newer theory of white-collar crime, Simon and Eitzen (1982) define much of it as **elite deviance** (illegal, unethical, or immoral acts committed by the members of the highest strata of society for purposes of personal or organizational gain). Simon and Eitzen point out that elite deviants run little risk of detection or prosecution, although they often create great dangers to the wider society. Examples of this sort of deviance by corporations are illegal disposal of toxic waste products or large-scale fraudulent financial manipulations like the First National Bank of Boston "money laundering" operation (*Business Week*, March 11, 1985:37). A U.S. Government General Accounting Office study of the Defense Department found fraudulent contractors to be the major source of waste (*Common Cause*, 1983:39).

Another example of corporate deviance is welfare fraud. The use of record matching by police and federal agencies has been widely publicized as a way to detect cheating among the relatively powerless welfare recipients ("Are Electronic Foodstamps on the Way?" 1984). However, the majority of financial losses in the welfare system are to socially "respectable" organizations. Investigations of the Medicaid program identified nursing homes, pharmacies, and hospitals as some of the major culprits (*Common Cause*, 1983:47). In the information age, those individuals and corporations with the most power over information resources are in a position to conduct financial manipulations, fraudulent contracts, deceptive advertising, and other illegal business and political activity. Although some large corporations have been fined for defrauding the Pentagon or for illegal banking operations, little of this large-scale organizational crime is prosecuted. As in the old English poem, computer crime legislation is designed to punish those who steal the privately owned information "goose," not the publicly owned information "common."

Protecting Information Products

Despite technical innovations to protect information from employees, from one another, and from outsiders, companies are facing an increase in white-collar crime. The failure of technological solutions to the information law and order problem leads companies to seek legal protection. The U.S. laws protecting information products are state trade secrets laws, federal patent law, and federal copyright law. Abstract ideas are protected only if they are trade secrets; ideas for the design of devices and industrial processes can be protected by patent if they meet a set of stringent criteria; the expression of an idea (but not the idea itself) can be protected by copyright. In the absence of other clearly defined laws to protect information products, leases, purchase agreements, nondisclosure agreements, and other forms of contract among vendors, customers and employees have become a mainstay of software and hardware protection (McEnaney, 1984; Roberts, Paine, and Brownell, 1985). Like other forms of legal guarantee, contracts are based on shared social beliefs in their legitimacy.

THE FAILURE OF TECHNOLOGICAL PROTECTIONS   Although most computer crime is committed by authorized users, existing security arrangements have not usually been very effective at keeping out the minority of unauthorized users. The reasons for this are not those popularly assumed. Most publicized "piracy" or "computer breaking and entering" is performed by people with only moderate technical skill. They are successful because most data are very poorly protected. For example, a software pirate I've met learned to copy all sorts of personal computer diskettes but did not know how to program. He had mastered the techniques without understanding what he was doing; he acquired software he didn't know how to use.

In making the transition from conventional record keeping to computerized data, most organizations relied on the social patterns that keep most strangers from walking into an office and browsing through filing cabinets. They also depend on shared social values that define theft and fraud as "wrong." With computers, however, ordinary forms of social control that depend upon personal surveillance of offices do not apply. In the case of information products, social respect for property rights is not universal.

As owners of data bases and other information products become more concerned over the vulnerability of their property, more elaborate techniques are being adopted to provide security. Some are as simple as realizing that "erased" diskettes and tapes still contain company data (Raimondi, 1985a). Others are protection schemes designed to recognize authorized users. Identification systems include long passwords (which are difficult to determine by experimentation), electronic keys that restrict access to buildings or equipment like Xerox machines, data-encoding schemes based on new developments in mathematical cryptography, and even voice or fingerprint recognition (Albert and Morse, 1984; McEnaney, 1984; Wu and Hwang, 1984).

An interesting variety of measures has been developed to make software copying difficult. In the personal computer software industry, techniques have tended to focus on diskette protections. Variations in recording techniques and software that checks its disk to ensure that it has not been copied to a new one are in use. Read-only memory firmware (programs built into the hardware) are also relatively difficult to duplicate. A software industry organization has proposed an industry-wide standard lock and key system based on a hardware device to monitor data transfers (*Computerworld*, Jan. 13, 1986:1). Also, many companies will sell documentation only to customers who purchase their software. Although these protective measures may discourage the novice, the technically skilled make short work of them. Among both professional programmers and hobbyists, software protection schemes are often considered a form of challenging computer game. This attitude has been reinforced by popular images of home computer pirates as young people engaged in essentially harmless play. It has been estimated that only 10 percent of the home computer software in current use has been legally sold.

The same experts who design computer security measures are able to bypass them. What high school computer science students do as a game, high-tech criminals can do for profit ("Milwaukee Discovers 'WarGamesmanship'," 1983). The most striking example of technical expertise in unauthorized access is the record of the National Security Agency's Tiger Teams at ZARF. ZARF was a government project to investigate computer security arrangements. Operatives claim to have broken into every computer system ever marketed. They also seem to be involved in setting standards for private industry "carefully designed to be just secure enough so that corporate spies outside the government could not break a user's code and just vulnerable enough so that the National Security Agency could break it" ("Computer Encryption . . .," 1977:438). In 1985, the NSA offered to provide banks and companies with secret protection codes—so secret that only NSA would know how they worked (*Science*, October 4, 1985:45–46).

As organizations use these codes to reduce the vulnerability of their computerized records and proprietary information, we may expect a greater share of the assaults on information property originating outside of companies to be conducted by technical experts. Also, as outsiders are discouraged, an even larger share of computer crime will be perpetrated by authorized users. Even well-protected computer systems remain vulnerable to "Trojan horses," authorized programs that contain internal codes to perform unauthorized activity once the computer has been accessed (Boebert, Kain, and Young, 1985). Data bases can be attacked by "viruses," pieces of self-replicating codes that can infect and destroy an entire system, and by "worms" that can be transmitted from system to system over data communications links (*Computerworld*, December 15, 1985:35).

TRADE SECRETS   Secret ideas, processes, designs, or other proprietory information are termed *trade secrets*. Once communicated to the public (by accident or otherwise), they lose their protected status. Companies protect trade secrets with employee and customer contracts prohibiting disclosure of company information. Violators of these contracts may be prosecuted, but anyone else is free to use the information revealed. The advantage of trade secrets for companies is that the information does not have to be filed with the patent or copyright office, so there is no expiration date for the protection.

An example of a trade secret is Kentucky Fried Chicken's recipe of eleven herbs and spices. It can be sold, as it was when Colonel Sanders retired from the fast food business, and can be widely imitated without penalty, so long as the secret was not stolen from the original inventor. Computer programs and hardware often include trade secrets in the form of design features not protected by copyright or patent. These are difficult to conceal from skilled programmers and other technical people. A better legal protection is the use of nondisclosure agreements that users must sign. These contracts are designed to protect the proprietary information being provided by the company to its customers. In practice, however, design features are commonly copied among companies and by customers.

Trade secrets are a modern version of the way medieval guilds and ancient craftsmen protected their knowledge from competitors. As in the cases of ancient Chinese pottery glazes or Egyptian embalming techniques, trade secrets are vulnerable to being forgotten. In the early years of programming, many skilled software developers avoided documenting their programs. In a personal version of trade secrets, programmers protected their work (and occasionally their jobs) by making their programs unintelligible to others. Although the rationalization of the software industry has led to better documentation of software products, many companies try to prevent copying by making it difficult to obtain documentation for their products. Others supply customers with binary object code (data in the form of ones and zeros) rather than source code (a higher-level language version). This protects products by making them difficult to understand. Some individual programmers still try to protect the secrets of their trade by producing programs that are undocumented and difficult to follow the logic of. Understandably, this practice is discouraged by technical management. It can also be a problem for the programmer, who finds it difficult to debug or modify his or her own work.

PATENTS   As provided in the U.S. Constitution, patents are granted to the inventors of innovative processes and machines. Mathematical formulas or "obvious" processes cannot be patented. A patent prohibits others from using the design for seventeen years but is expensive (around $5000), time-consuming to obtain, and requires a full disclosure of the process being patented up to several years in advance of the patent's being granted. Until 1981, software was not generally considered patentable; recently a few software patents have been granted where the software was an integral part of a patentable process. The reason that more software is not patented is that algorithms are considered mathematical formulas and are thus not eligible for patents. Patents protect ideas only when they are implemented in some concrete device. They are not given for abstract intellectual concepts or mental processes.

Senator Robert Dole (*Congressional Record* 131, No. 1, part II, S186, 3 Jan 1985) has introduced legislation that would assign patent rights to technology developed with public funds to corporations. Critics charge that this would be a change from the original intent of patent laws—the reward of individual creativity (Frenzen, 1985). Already many high-tech employees sign contracts giving up claims to patents for anything they invent on company time.

Internationally, patent law has been characterized as inadequate for the microelectronics industry (Braun and Macdonald, 1978:131–32). In a recent case, the Japanese Matsushita Corporation has been sued by Stanford Ovshinsky over the rights to the erasable optical disk (*Fortune*, June 13, 1983). From the perspective of U.S. firms, international patent law needs to be strengthened to protect their property. From the perspectives of developing countries, however, the ownership of patents by the industrial countries and multinational corporations means that their technology remains under foreign control. In a 1964 United Nations study, 89 percent of the patents being used in five developing nations were foreign owned. In Chile in 1967, 95 percent of patents in use were foreign (Barnett and Muller, 1974:140). Some developing countries, such as China, have adopted laws protecting U.S. and other international patents. Their intent is to encourage foreign investment and marketing (Baum, 1985).

Some of the more interesting future patent cases may occur in the field of artificial intelligence. Already patents have been issued for manufactured bacteria, thus eroding the social distinction between manufactured devices and natural organisms. It will be interesting to see if the heuristic programs of artificial intelligence (which are not, mathematically speaking, algorithms) will be considered abstract intellectual processes or ideas embodied in an innovative mechanism. At present, however, patents are mainly used to protect computer hardware. Under the Semiconductor Chip Protection Act of 1984, computer chip design masks receive a ten-year protection under the copyright laws (Wartel, 1985).

COPYRIGHTS   Copyrights do not protect ideas; they protect the original expression of an idea "fixed in any tangible medium." In the case of computer programs, copyrights are registered by submitting a hard copy listing (or tape or disk version that can be made perceivable to the human eye) to the Library of Congress Copyright Office. The Copyright Office has not decided what to do about commercial data bases that are constantly updated (Betts, 1985a). Under the pre-1976 copyright law, protection would be lost if copyrights were not registered or if a permanent copyright notice was not affixed to the work in the proper place. Although under the new law protection begins from the time of authorship (in theory), lawyers advise that it is still important to make copyright notices part of software and documentation. Copyright protection will last the lifetime of the author plus fifty years.

Until the 1980 amendment to the 1976 copyright act in the United States, it was not clear whether binary code was copyrightable because it had been argued that it was not perceivable to humans. Now copyright protection clearly applies to software even when it is in machine-readable object code. The 1983 case of *Apple* v. *Franklin* made copyrights applicable to ROM chips and operating system software. The legality of modified copies of software was not clearly established by the courts. The U.S. International Trade Commission, for example, has been struggling to determine when a foreign copy of an Apple computer chip was a copy and when it was a modified new creation (Wallace, 1984). Some attempts have been made to develop techniques for comparing the designs of original and pirated software that has been rewritten to disguise the theft (Glass, 1985).

At issue here is more than the question of how much "software pirates" would have to rewrite code before they were safe from prosecution. Software compatibility within the industry and customers' rights to modify software to meet their particular needs are also involved. If interface and other compatibility software is found copyrightable, customers will be inconvenienced, and setting industry standards will be more difficult. If modifications to copyrighted software are made completely illegal, it will be difficult for customers to adapt software specifically for their own installations. If a modification such as supporting a nonstandard peripheral device was not legal, smaller equipment manufacturers might suffer. A 1986 Office of Technology Assessment report, "Intellectual Property Rights in an Age of Electronics and Information," suggests that we have given too much protection to copywritten software (*Science*, May 2, 1986:572).

The disadvantage of copyright protection is that it does not cover the algorithm in a program or prevent unauthorized use. It only makes copying illegal. Finally, copyrights have not been very successfully enforced, although several companies (Lotus 1-2-3 and Apple, for example) are vigorously pursuing offenders. Although Lotus has received a substantial out-of-court settlement from one company it sued for making multiple copies of its software (McGeever, 1984), the first jail sentence for a software pirate was not handed down until 1984 (Bartolik, 1984). Piracy remains a major problem in the industry. The statistics of the Canadian Dealers Association report that ˙90 percent of Canada's software programs are illegal (Gunter, 1984).

One problem with enforcing copyright laws is based on the special status of electronic information. In many computer media, one must write the information in order to read it. Because reading information is widely considered an individual's right, copyrights on electronically based information seem to many to be an infringement of the right to use information. Within the copyright law is a "fair use" provision that allows single copies of protected works to be made (under a variety of restrictions) for educational use. Usage is not restricted by copyright law, only the making of copies. However, in the case of many of the new information products, using and copying overlap. This is particularly a problem for networked computer systems. For some network software, each user copies the program (in a technical sense) at every use. It remains to be seen how the courts will resolve this issue. If the case of home audio and video tape recorders is any indicator, we may find the industry abandoning its attempts to prevent copying for personal use and concentrating instead upon preventing copying for resale or by business customers to avoid buying multiple copies.

COMPUTERS AND SOCIAL CONTROL:
THE PRIVACY DEBATE

Because computers facilitate the collection and matching of information about individuals, organizations, and governments, they add a new dimension to the many-sided debate over what sorts of information should be the personal property of individuals and what sorts should be considered business products or shared cultural goods. Computers have enhanced the ability of corporations and law enforcement agencies to monitor the activities of employees, consumers, and citizens. Abuse of such information has created a public debate over the computer's threat to privacy. For example, as more sophisticated mailing lists are made and sold, the volume of junk mail and telephone solicitations increases. Many people fear that their privacy will be invaded by government and credit bureau investigations, with possible abuses of their civil liberties. Businesses are concerned about the privacy of their records and seek protection from corporate espionage and what they view as excessive government interference in their activities. Government concerns include the gathering of enough information to monitor business and individual compliance with tax and other laws. Internationally, governments are also concerned with national security and economic competition. Neither absolute privacy nor totalitarian control are goals sought by participants in the contemporary debate over computers and privacy. Instead, they have serious disagreements about what balance should exist between individual freedom and cultural demands.

Privacy and Social Control

Social historian Barrington Moore defines privacy in two senses. One, a desire for "protection or escape from other human beings, emerges when an individual becomes subject to social obligations that that individual cannot or does not want to meet" (Moore, 1984:268). This concept is found in preindustrial societies and represents a way for individuals to avoid temporarily and in more or less socially accepted ways the demands of their communities. By our own standards, the opportunities for privacy were often limited—all bodily functions, for example, might normally be performed in front of other people. "Being sick" is an example of privacy in this sense. If we are ill, we can stay home and avoid social interaction. However, the urgings of our friends to "get well," the invasion of our body by medical personnel, and organizations' insistence on "a note from your doctor" are social control mechanisms that limit our freedom to be privately sick in the interests of getting us back to our normal social roles (Parsons, 1951:chaps. 7 and 10).

When hospitals and officials interfere with our right to be sick whenever we choose, we experience invasion of privacy in Moore's second sense. This form of privacy involves the individual's rights against external authorities. In modern societies people seek privacy from organizations and institutions as well as from one another. The privacy debate over computer use for government and corporate record keeping is about this second sense of privacy—the right of individuals to be left alone by their government and by the economic organizations of their society. This right of privacy is often in direct conflict with the norms governing our obligations to work and obey society's laws and regulations.

Because no society can exist without patterns of expected behavior, and because information about individuals is essential to the functioning of modern social institutions, the privacy debate is not about *whether* information should be collected. It is about what sorts of data are to be gathered, what they are to be used for, and by whom. The privacy debate is ultimately about information as a source of power for people, corporations, and governments over one another's activities.

THE LEGAL CONCEPT OF PRIVACY   The growth of our legal concept of privacy was based on the idea that the individual, rather than the group, is the basic unit of society. In 1890, attorneys Samuel Warren and Louis Brandeis published a landmark legal opinion in the *Harvard Law Review* defining the right to privacy (reprinted in Johnson and Snapper, 1984). In it they show how the common law rights to life and property are intertwined in the privacy issue. The right to life has been extended to "the right to be let alone" to enjoy life. The right to property has been extended to the right to own "intellectual property"—including information about one's personal life.

Senator Sam Ervin, chairman of the Senate Subcommittee on Constitutional Rights, locates the right to "receive and impart information and ideas" in the First Amendment of the U.S. Constitution. Private telephone conversations are protected by the Fourth Amendment's ban on unreasonable searches and seizures. In 1973, the *Roe* v. *Wade* decision of the Supreme Court extended Fourteenth Amendment protection to the right to give and receive information. To Ervin (1983:160), "privacy is a catchword for the control that the individual exercises over information about himself."

Interpretations of the Constitution that define corporations to be "persons" extend the privacy debate to the issue of how much freedom businesses have to keep information to themselves. Constitutional limits on the privacy of both individuals and corporations exist because of the government's rights to regulate commerce, conduct censuses, tax, and conduct international relations in the public interest.

Who Knows What About You?

In the early 1960s, one of my college roommates was sent a letter stating: "Send us your social security number, and we'll tell you about your sex life." Two decades later that joke on a computer programmer doesn't seem so funny. Despite the provisions of the Privacy Act of 1974, a 1977 report of the government's Privacy Protection Study Commission identified serious abuses of computerized data.

GOVERNMENT DATA COLLECTION   Federal use of computers for data collection grew rapidly in the 1960s and 1970s. By the late 1970s, there were about 4 billion records on individual Americans filed with federal agencies (Bacon and Kelly, 1978). Treasury records (including Internal Revenue Service tax records), Health, Education and Welfare data (including Social Security information), the Department of Commerce files (including census data), and the data bases of the Justice and Defense departments were the largest collections. By 1985, according to a federal Office of Technology Assessment report, the government had records on 114 million Americans. The data banks of the Defense and Justice departments contain information on 109 million of us (*Boston Globe*, Oct. 24, 1985:8).

During the same time, business and nonprofit organizations have gathered extensive records on Americans. These are often made available to the government. Record matching of all this information has become increasingly possible with computerization, especially with the faster search times of new hardware.

CREDIT, INSURANCE, AND PRIVATE INVESTIGATION AGENCIES   The five largest credit bureaus maintain more than 150 million individual credit records. The Fair Credit Reporting Act of 1970 limits access to credit bureau data to those with a court order, permission of the consumer, or a valid business, credit, employment, or insurance request. Yet many abuses are reported. The way credit investigations are done is one source of problems. For instance, one bureau gathered data through such means as sponsoring local welcome wagon ladies, who greet newcomers and report their former residence back to credit bureaus (so that a credit file can be obtained from the previous locale). Another credit bureau, the Retail Credit Company of Atlanta (with 48 million personal records) records "any known connection with a 'peace movement' or any other organization of a subversive type." The errors, to say nothing of the ethics, involved in credit bureau investigating and reporting practices are a major concern. Also, the Supreme Court has consistently upheld federal agencies' rights to access such records ("Computers and Dossiers," 1982:230).

BANKING AND OTHER FINANCIAL INFORMATION   The Electronic Funds Transfer Act of 1980 was designed to modify the Uniform Commercial Code regulation of paper transactions for banks in order to facilitate electronic banking. Although the law requires customer notification of third-party access, it has been clear that bank records are the property of the banks, not their customers. Because financial transactions are among the information that many Americans would most like to keep private, the possibility of record matching by government agencies (like the IRS) has been considered a threat to privacy. Abuses of bank records are inhibited by the Right to Financial Privacy Act of 1978, which specifies the procedures whereby federal agencies can access financial data. However, these laws do not protect people from state and local authorities (Zaki, 1983). Despite privacy safeguards, federal record matching has become routine. Social Security data is used to identify "illegal aliens," child support enforcement officials may search virtually all government and private employment records, and IRS data is used to screen jurors and locate those who fail to register for the draft (Shattuck, 1984). The U.S. Department of Health and Human Services is now matching its welfare roles against state files of interest incomes from banks and other financial institutions. The U.S. Treasury Department has taken money directly from bank accounts of Social Security recipients when it seems to have made overpayments (*USA Today*, Nov. 29, 1983:7A). In contrast to computerized surveillance of low-income and elderly bank customers, the Securities and Exchange Commission does not even record the ownership of stock in U.S. corporations except by people who are empowered to make investments on behalf of others (U.S. Senate, 1980).

MAILING LISTS   In 1975 the average American household received 2.3 pieces of junk mail each week. For most of us today the volume is much higher. The mailing list business produces information by selecting individuals from available commercial or government lists whose characteristics make them likely to respond to specific advertising. Expert systems are now available to select the "best" prospects ("Tool Identifies . . .," 1985). To have your name removed from mailing lists, the Privacy Protection Study Commission recommends that you do *not* write to the company that mailed you its ad. Often they have only paid for a mailing and do not actually have your name until you reply. Instead, you can be "delisted" by the Direct Mail/Marketing Association's Mail Preference Service.

Many of us have experienced an electronic version of direct mail advertising in which a computer dials our phone number and plays a recorded message. Even an unlisted phone number may not help if the computer is trying all the numbers in some exchange. In perhaps the most blatant abuse of this technique, hospital patients in an intensive care ward were called by a computer selling life insurance.

EMPLOYMENT, MEDICAL AND EDUCATIONAL RECORDS   In 1984, the U.S. Department of Housing and Urban Development began a computer matching of low-income tenants with state and federal wage data. The privacy of health records is also threatened by computerization (Olmos, 1985). The federal government, as in the Baby Doe case (over the issue of treating serious birth defects), is making new demands on hospitals to report on the health status of individuals as part of the efforts to regulate treatment. Insurance companies and employers also try to obtain health information about prospective employees. A series of court cases has gradually eroded the privacy of patient records in the interest of institutional "need to know" (Culliton, 1985a). Educational institutions have reported grades, disciplinary actions, and current addresses of students and alumni to government agencies and businesses. In the area of workplace safety, however, "right to know" legislation in several states places the rights of employees and community residents to have information about environmental hazards above the right of companies to keep the chemical composition of its products secret.

Surveillance and Law Enforcement

In a review of the new technologies of surveillance, Gary T. Marx (1985:26) illustrates their scope using the lyrics from "Every Breath You Take," a rock song by The Police:

every breath you take	[breath analyzer]
every move you make	[motion detection]
every bond you break	[polygraph]
every step you take	[electronic anklet]
every single day	[continuous monitoring]
every word you say	[bugs, wiretaps, mikes]
every night you stay . . .	[light amplifier]
every vow you break . . .	[voice stress analysis]
every smile you fake	[brain wave analysis]
every claim you stake . . .	[computer matching]
I'll be watching you	[video surveillance]

Although citizens in a democratic society are inclined to think "It can't happen here," many of these technologies are being applied by businesses and law enforcement agencies to identify people and monitor their behavior.

IDENTIFICATION   Who are you? Can you prove it? Most of us are familiar with showing a driver's license or credit card to prove our identities. Someday you may carry a computer chip on your identification, as "smart cards" replace conventional IDs (McIvor, 1985). According to James Rule and his co-authors (1983), the use of computers is reducing our opportunities to identify ourselves. Instead, our identity is frequently established by matching records in computer data bases.

When two college freshmen with the same name (whose fathers also had the same name) were identified as a single person by my college computer, they were assigned a single dormitory room and sent only one tuition bill. By graduation time they had straightened out the problem and received two diplomas. A New Jersey woman was not so fortunate with the FBI's National Crime Information Center computer. She was mistakenly matched with a Texas welfare fraud case, arrested in front of her co-workers, jailed for over a week, and is now suing the government (Babcock, 1985b). This is the same computer available to your local law enforcement officials. If you are arrested for a traffic violation, you may find your identity being matched against national crime data. One approach to resolving abuses of record matching is to provide many identification codes to each person, one for each agency or company they do business with. Security could be maintained, but the records would be unmatchable (Chaum, 1985). This was actually what identification was like before widespread use of the Social Security number as a national ID number.

Although some people hope for technical solutions to problems of mistaken identity, professionals familiar with large computer systems realize the impossibility of perfect accuracy. Even if computer identifications could be protected from error, many people find them an invasion of everyone's basic right to privacy. Even if we could have computer-based identification systems without record matching or errors, it would still be a social problem if we answer the question of who people are not by interacting with them to find out but by turning to the external authority of technology.

GOVERNMENT SURVEILLANCE   A report by the U.S. Congressional Office of Technology Assessment found that 25 percent of federal agencies (not counting intelligence organizations like the CIA or National Security Agency) currently use electronic surveillance (1985b:14). The report concluded that the two main legal protections against surveillance (contained in the 1968 Omnibus Crime Control and Safe Streets Act and in the 1978 Foreign Intelligence Act) had been overtaken by technological change. For example, under existing law in 1985, cordless telephones are not protected by wiretap legislation—they have no wires. Documenting the need for additional protection, the report argued: "Over time, the cumulative effect of widespread surveillance . . . could change the climate and fabric of society in fundamental ways" (U.S. Congressional Office of Technology Assessment, 1985:11). Just as technological forms of protection fail to protect information products in the absence of social norms respecting property, so technologies of surveillance and law enforcement cannot make those who use them "safe." If anything, they make society ultimately less safe because they reify social relationships of morality and trust into technologies of social control.

COMPUTERS IN LAW ENFORCEMENT   The social institutions that maintain public order are using the capabilities of computers to enhance law enforcement processes, but they are also confronted by a rising tide of computer-assisted white-collar crime. These two opposing trends can be summarized as follows: use of computers is making it increasingly difficult to steal $50 from a gas station but increasingly easy to steal $50,000 from a bank. This is because computerized record systems make it easier for law enforcement officials to track criminals who can be identified or who have previous records (including those of us who neglect to pay our parking tickets), but they make it easier for those with access to computerized information to embezzle money.

Correctional institutions using computerized record systems can respond quickly to events like the Attica prison riot (Rosen, 1983). To provide physical security, a prototype robot security guard will eventually have artificial intelligence and remote sensing capability (Rogers, 1984a). They are planned for use as military sentries, prison guards, and perhaps even night watchmen. A new electronic monitoring technique, the Gosslink, is being tried to keep track of less dangerous criminals. With the Gosslink, prisoners can remain under "house arrest" in their own homes. The computer attached to their bodies reports any violations—including taking off the computer (Nordheimer, 1985). Some law enforcement specialists envision using technologies like the Gosslink to send messages to people as well as to monitor them. Computer surveillance, "if it detects a probability of misbehavior by the parolee, would cause him to desist by delivering an electrical 'zap' to his brain" (Mitford, 1971:248). A similar device was attached to automobiles in Hong Kong for traffic control and road use tax administration (Parks, 1983). It was also designed to keep track of the movements of individual automobile owners as part of a Travel Record and Immigration Control Enforcement System (Pearce, 1985). The resulting public uproar is expected to lead to Hong Kong's first data and privacy protection law (Westin, 1985). These and other innovations, like the Japanese and San Francisco police automatic fingerprint identification system, offer computerized means of more efficient law enforcement but raise the possibility of threats to civil liberties (Batt, 1984a; Serrill, 1985). Abuses have been charged in the form of false arrests due to computer errors in New Orleans (Raimondi, 1985b) and illegal police access to lawyers' confidential files on their clients in San Francisco (Sullivan, 1985).

WORKPLACE SURVEILLANCE   U.S. trucks are being tracked with the same technology that Hong Kong used on automobiles. In this case the surveillance is used to manage drivers' pickup and delivery schedules ("Tracking the Trucks," 1984). According to interviews with taxi operators, the skills and satisfactions of driving transfer rather easily to the human/computer interface (Greenfield, 1983). In theory, better information systems could enhance truckers' skills and increase their productivity and pay. But truckers report that this monitoring system takes discretion away from them. They lose control over choice of routes and delivery times; they feel spied upon by their supervisors. When the technologies of surveillance are applied to work, the result can be loss of employee autonomy.

Yet, when employees have little autonomy, computerized surveillance may be viewed as an improvement. Reports one U.S. postal employee: "If the *foreman's* behind me constantly, I get nervous. I don't care about the machine" (M. Miller, 1985:1, 15). Workplace surveillance by machine depersonalizes relationships of power and authority, reifying them in managerial technologies. It also relocates trust from the employee's personal reports of his or her own behavior to objective measurements of performance. If employees were not trusted in the first place, the machine may be preferred to the human evaluator. In the most extreme case—that of lie detection technology—employees' accounts of even their intentions are no longer trusted by employers. In its most benign form, computerized surveillance replaces the social indignities of being given orders by another person with the impersonal neutrality of the machine. In its worst form, surveillance establishes relationships of oppression as part of the external reality of the workplace.

COMPUTERIZED REPRESSION   There were no computers in George Orwell's novel of political repression, *1984*. Censorship, surveillance, and a Newspeak language from which all subversive words had been removed were effective means of information control for the fictional regime. Yet, had the technology been available, Big Brother would surely have used it. In countries with less privacy protection than our own, computers seem to be contributing to a "Big Brother Is Watching You" climate of surveillance. For example, German law enforcement agencies are considerably freer than our own to gather and use information about citizen activities (Butner, 1982). One result is that political dissidents are denied government and teaching jobs. In South Africa, computers are used to maintain the apartheid registration system limiting the physical movements of the black majority (Conrad, 1982).

Many of the world's military dictatorships are neither wealthy enough nor sufficiently experienced with electronics to monitor their populations by modern means. However, we must expect technologies of repression to be high-priority items in the economic development of nations that maintain social control through force. Despite U.S. laws against exporting computers to be used in the violation of human rights, American technology is in use in South Africa and in countries that claim to be oppressing only communist dissidents (Conrad, 1986; Klare, 1984). But it is easy for the powerfully oppressive to call whomever they choose a communist. For example, among my Filipino acquaintances are a nun and a priest, both anticommunists, who were arrested and tortured for opposing the Marcos government on religious grounds. With computerized repression, we see the worst social consequences of information as power over others. In the next chapter, we will explore the possibilities of computers used to aid groups in agreeing upon and achieving their goals.

CHAPTER
9

INFORMATION AS POWER: COMPUTERS AND SOCIAL DECISIONS

Have you ever had to make a decision when you didn't have enough information to make up your mind? Did you ever have trouble getting the information you needed to make an informed choice? If you work, do you have any say in company policy? Do you turn to the sports or comics section of the newspaper and leave political decisions to politicians?

Decision making requires information. Those who have information, especially when we believe that only they can understand it, have power over society's decisions. Information also contributes to the power of groups and individuals to decide for themselves. As we have seen, computer technology could be the basis for wide networks of social interaction, discussion, and decision making. Organizational and community interfaces could be tools for democratic participation in large, geographically dispersed groups of people. But as we examine the way in which computers have been used in economic and governmental institutions, we realize that computers can also support centralized authoritarian power. It is not the computer itself that influences the distribution of power in society; it is the way the computer system is designed and used.

Most decisions to adopt computer technology are culturally defined as private, economic choices rather than as public, political ones. Yet these choices have consequences throughout our social institutions. If the political process is broadly defined as the way groups arrive at and implement decisions that affect everyone, then the political consequences of the information revolution are not solely a result of government actions. They also result from changes in business decision making, in military goals, and in activities of scientists and other professionals. Those who gain or lose access to computerized information find their power to influence public decisions altered as well.

INFORMATION AND THE PUBLIC INTEREST

"If you knew what I do, you'd understand why we have to do it my way." This sentence is based on one person's claim to have more information than another. There is the additional claim that the decision making ought to be left to the expert. As children or students, we are expected to defer to the authority of those who know more than we do. As we become adults in a democratic society, we learn to arrive at our own informed opinions. But to do so we must have access to information. The idea that citizens should have access to information implies that information is a public good. In order to protect the public interest and ensure widespread participation in the political process, we have laws to regulate the means of information transmission and to promote a free press and scientific inquiry. As information industries grow and legal definitions of information property change, our concept of the public interest in information is also changing.

The Tragedy of the Common

We may find it ridiculous to imagine a world in which most information is private property, but many nonindustrial people could not imagine anyone owning land. Even traditionally free goods like air and sunlight have become issues in legislation for environmental protection and urban zoning. The conservative ecologist Garrett Hardin (1968) argues that unowned resources create a "tragedy of the common" in which the collective property is ruined by the actions of selfish individuals trying to maximize their self-interest. He applies his argument to publicly regulated resources as well on the grounds that people treat government property as "free" and have an interest in ignoring regulation. When Hardin's argument is applied to the information industries, it is assumed that a competitive free market providing information products and services is the most efficient way to serve the public interest. If the means to produce and distribute information are centralized, the goal of meeting public needs is not met. Liberal and radical theorists, in contrast, believe that common property must be protected from the self-interests of those who would like to monopolize it. They do not believe that a free market for information products can protect the public interest in cultural information.

Although Hardin's argument may be applicable to information in the sense that resources like broadcast channels are limited, it does not seem to apply to most cultural information. Unlike natural resources that get "used up," information can be easily shared. Even though there are material costs in maintaining public data and libraries, computer and communications technologies make it possible to provide low-cost "copies." The main kind of information ruined by overuse is the kind that gives one person an advantage over another. Inside information about the stock market won't make you rich if everyone else finds out before you have a chance to buy or sell at the best price. Cultural information, however, must be widely shared if the culture is to integrate people into a single society.

Access to Cultural Records

Some observers fear that a high price for information retrieval will become a barrier to knowledge acquisition. They feel that the future of free libraries is threatened when fees for searches can run over $100 per hour (Turner, 1984). Some cultural records may be lost if public information is converted to for-profit operations because there is little profit to be made from obscure historical documents, even though they are an important source of cultural knowledge. As a result of the Federal Paperwork Reduction Act of 1980, less free public data will be available to libraries (Coughlin, 1985).

HISTORICAL RECORDS   Historians worry that they will have a major problem in the future trying to access computerized text. In general, only material published after 1970 is available from on-line library search services, and many older computerized records are on obsolete tape or disk devices (Burnham, 1985). Perhaps in the future, institutions like Boston's Computer Museum (which maintains working exhibits of vintage computers) will provide services to historians. Literary scholars analyze draft manuscripts made by famous writers of the past. Will they be able to read the floppy disks of today's novelists and poets?

Another problem for historians is more difficult to solve. The accuracy and authenticity of historical documents is a question of grave concern in historical research. Many of the official U.S. computerized records are kept so poorly that "the United States is in danger of losing its memory" (May 1985:9). Among the potential abuses of computerized records is the possibility that history will be rewritten by those with access to historical files and an interest in changing the facts of the past. One step to prevent such problems is the appointment of an FBI historian to oversee its archives (*Chronicle of Higher Education*, May 4, 1984:7).

INTERNATIONAL ACCESS   Computer experts attempting to aid developing countries have argued that computers can provide the remote areas of poor countries with cheap, widely available sources of information and education. Yet some of these programs have failed; one U.S. computer expert resigned from a third world computer education project on the grounds that the project was designed with only the manufacturer's profit in mind (Cooke, 1982). In the world's poorer countries, where computer technology is quite scarce, it is most often used by governments, the military, and large companies (Kling, 1983). No large public market for personal computers exists in countries where the price of a PC is ten times the average per capita income and where less than a tenth of the population has access to electricity.

For most of the less developed nations of the world, the impact of the computer and communications revolution has been to intensify their dependency relationships with the industrial societies and multinational corporations (Rada, 1982b). They have been disadvantaged in the world market by low prices for their products and labor and by high prices for their imports. Although computer technology is being exported to the third world,

> Computers in Africa are no more "African" than the continent's copper, cobalt, uranium, diamonds and cash crops are African; these are all controlled—from investment and marketing to sale and transportation—by companies based elsewhere in the world. Because computers happen to be on "sovereign" African soil is no reason to believe that the functions they are performing so efficiently and speedily are in the interests of Africa. (Carim, 1983:65)

Insofar as the economic interests of industrial societies' governments and multinational corporations remain the exploitation of natural resources, the promotion of politically stable and disciplined labor forces for their subsidiary companies, and the development of markets for their own products, the political impact of the computer revolution on the third world will be to strengthen repressive regimes and to restrict autonomous technological development ("Towards a New Information Order," 1982). Instead of computerized libraries for their villages, many countries are getting electronic surveillance for their police forces and American programs on their televisions. When third world countries try to develop their own computer industry, as in the case of Brazil's minicomputer manufacturing effort, local business relies heavily on government financing and import restrictions to protect their infant enterprise from international competition (Westman, 1985).

Internationally, broadcasting is the focus of a controversy over the United Nations' New World Information and Communication Order, shown in Box 2. On one side of the controversy are governments that wish to control the content of their national broadcasting. They claim that popular entertainment reflecting American cultural values rather than their own is a form of cultural imperialism. For example, between 30 and 85 percent of the programs broadcast over Latin American television are of U.S. origin (Smith, 1980:42–

BOX 2
THE NEW WORLD INFORMATION AND COMMUNICATION ORDER

Resolution 4/19 adopted by the twenty-first session of the UNESCO General Conference, Belgrade 1980. The General Conference considers that

a) this new world information and communication order could be based, among other considerations on:

   i)   elimination of the imbalances and inequalities which characterize the present situation;

   ii)   elimination of the negative effects of certain monopolies, public or private, and excessive concentrations;

   iii) removal of the internal and external obstacles to a free flow and wider and better balanced dissemination of information and ideas;

   iv)   plurality of sources and channels of information;

   v)   freedom of the press and of information;

   vi)   the freedom of journalists and all professionals in the communication media, a freedom inseparable from responsibility;

   vii) the capacity of developing countries to achieve improvement of their own situations, notably by providing their own equipment, by training their personnel, by improving their infrastructures and making their information and communication media suitable to their needs and aspirations;

   viii) the sincere will of developed countries to help them attain these objectives;

   ix)   respect for each people's cultural identity and for the right of each nation to inform the world about its interests, its aspirations and its social and cultural values;

   x)   respect for the right of all peoples to participate in international exchanges of information on the basis of equality, justice and mutual benefit;

   xi)   respect for right of the public, of ethnic and social groups and of individuals to have access to information sources and to participate actively in the communication process;

b) this new world information and communication order should be based on the fundamental principles of international law, as laid down in the Charter of the United Nations;

c) diverse solutions to information and communication problems are required because social, political, cultural and economic problems differ from one country to another and, within a given country, from one group to another.

Source: NACLA Report on the Americas (July/August) 1982, p. 32. By permission of North American Congress on Latin America.

43). On the other side are industry organizations that provide world news and programming service. They charge that "freedom of the press" is endangered by national efforts to restrict the content of news and programs (McPhail, 1981). They also believe that government restrictions on the media are associated with the abuse of human rights.

Regulation and Deregulation

American society has a liberal political tradition of using government regulation for the maintenance of public property and the protection of civil liberties. Speech and written communication were protected as rights. Thus, publishing has not been regulated on the grounds that to do so would violate the First Amendment of the U.S. Constitution. But communication transmission facilities—telegraphs, radio stations, and telephone service—were regulated as scarce resources that had to be protected from overuse. The computer and communications revolution is producing some dilemmas for public policymakers as the technologies for information production and distribution change rapidly.

The broadcasting industry in the United States has been heavily regulated, at first due to a scarcity of available radio and television channels. Later, as FM radio and cable television added to the available channels, regulation continued, based on the importance of its social impact (Branscomb, 1983). TV and radio are licensed and their content is controlled within the limits of the First Amendment. Television, like the motion picture industry, adopted a voluntary censorship code that changed with the changing values of the viewing public and program sponsors (Schumach, 1975). Public broadcasting service is provided through a mixture of government and private funding. The recent U.S. trend has been to reduce public broadcasting support, and eight of the twenty-eight educational television channels were reassigned to pay TV in the early 1980s (Scully, 1983). A large number of broadcasting frequencies are reserved for military use.

Common carriers (mail and phone) were assumed in the United States to be a "natural monopoly for which competition would be disruptive and wasteful" (Branscomb, 1983:43). In most countries they are owned by the government; in the United States they were given to private industries as regulated monopolies. American Telephone and Telegraph (AT&T), General Telephone and Electronics Corporation (GTE), and several smaller, geographically based companies were given exclusive rights to segments of the telecommunications market; the federal government ran the postal service. After a long public debate (Noll, 1980) and a ten-year antitrust suit against AT&T, the federal government moved in 1984 to deregulate telecommunications. AT&T was broken up to meet three goals:

> (1) Promotion of true and fair competition in the telecommunications long distance and equipment markets, (2) preservation of AT&T as a dynamic force, capable of research, manufacturing, and marketing in technologically advanced fields, and (3) protection of the principle of universal telephone service, accessible to all segments of the population, regardless of income. (Greene, 1983:150)

Even with the change in common carrier regulation, U.S. telecommunications policy is widely criticized for failing to keep up with technological innovations and entrepreneurial possibilities (Geller, 1986). Some conservatives (Diamond, Sandler, and Mueller, 1983) argue that regulation of broadcasting should be replaced by a system of private property rights. Ithiel de Sola Pool (1983) envisions the technological merging of publishing, broadcasting, and common carrier service. He believes that the new media are more like speech or print than they are like physically limited resources that must be regulated to prevent overuse. The First Amendment, Pool argues, should be applied to all communications media with minimal regulation to prevent broadcasting interference and support the common carrier principle of universal access. Rather than continue our present regulatory practice of trying to keep telephone, broadcasting, and computer companies separate, Pool thinks that all communications facilities should interconnect and be governed primarily by the principle of free speech.

International Protections for Information

Internationally, the protection of information involves the definition of national security interests and conflicting demands from companies for protection from foreign competition and for aid in export marketing. Although companies are protected internationally by treaties, agreements on patents, and copyrights, government-regulated export control policies are often sought. International regulations to protect information are far from uniform. There is a World Court, but it is unable to enforce its decisions without the consent of the participating parties. Thus, most international regulatory activity occurs through negotiations over treaties and international agreements.

PATENTS AND COPYRIGHTS   From the perspective of U.S. firms, international patent law needs to be strengthened to protect their property (Braun and Macdonald, 1978:131–32). The patent holder for the erasable optical disk, for example, found the Japanese Matsushita Corporation developing it (*Fortune*, June 13, 1983:8). There is also a conflict among the copyright provisions of different nations. An attempt by Japan to replace software copyrights with a fifteen-year protection with required licensing was strongly opposed by the United States (Batt, 1984b; Kirchner, 1984). U.S. software producers claimed that the change would hurt their sales in Japan and reduce their incentives to develop new products. When I lived in Taiwan, pirated copies of American books and records were available cheaply; Taiwan did not recognize U.S. copyrights. For $5 I bought an unabridged English dictionary that had a large blank space between the words *Maori* and *map*. The deletion of Mao Tse-tung from the dictionary illustrates one of the political reasons why countries are concerned about regulating the flow of information over their borders. Some governments want to keep "dangerous" information away from their populations.

INFORMATION AND NATIONAL SECURITY   In the United States, we are protected from dangerous information by the same government security classification that protects our military secrets. When the U.S. Congressional Office of Technology Assessment wrote a report apparently concluding that U.S. military communications and computer equipment would stop working in the event of a nuclear war, officials at the Pentagon classified it as so secret that members of Congress and the person who wrote it aren't allowed to read it (*New York Times*, Feb. 18, 1986:1). One reviewer called it the "most dangerous document I've ever seen." But the question, as in all censorship, is "dangerous for whom?" It is common knowledge among communications specialists that microelectronics equipment fails when reached by a nuclear explosion's shock wave. Experts are skeptical about claims that computers and communications can be shielded. The classification of this report may be a case of protecting the military from unfavorable publicity. It is also part of a strategy to control information used in decision making. How can Congress make sensible decisions about the military budget for new technology if it is not allowed to read reports assessing the effectiveness of current technology?

Academic opposition to strict protection of U.S. technological secrets comes from scientists and researchers who fear an inhibition of international scientific inquiry (Unger, 1982; McDonald, 1984b). Publishers were also alarmed by government plans to restrict the publication of unclassified technical information (Coughlin, 1983). Although the Pentagon has dropped some of its proposals to limit publication of unclassified research at universities (McDonald, 1984a), publishers and international scientific professional associations remain disturbed by the effects of protecting national technological secrets on the free exchange of ideas (Norman, 1984:1295). Internationally, a committee of the Organization for Economic Cooperation and Development is attempting to work out international guidelines for cross-national data flow. By 1985, they had reached a tentative accord (Wilkins, 1985b).

U.S. EXPORT CONTROL POLICY   U.S. export control policy involves the conflicting values and interests of the Defense Department, U.S. companies, and the community of scientists and academics (Goodman, 1982). Defense Department officials are mostly concerned about exports to communist countries. They want export control over software as well as strategic hardware, arguing that even microcomputers and commercial packages have potential military applications (Wilkins, 1984a). Disagreements with Pentagon views on export controls come from businesses, universities, professional associations, and other countries. Although a 1975 Air Force report called the Soviet Union far behind the United States in computer technology and proposed severe export controls, during 1984 Senate hearings, a representative of the Commerce Department questioned the need for export controls, saying that it would be "a gross misstatement to suggest that the Soviets are technologically backward" (cited in Wilkins, 1984b). In a 1985 assessment, the Soviet Union was found still far behind in computers and software. Export controls were not, however, the reason. This is because they are not particularly effective. Scientific journals, public information such as U.S. Patent Office reports, and the ease with which American products can be purchased overseas make copying our technology relatively simple. But, as the president of the Soviet Academy of Sciences said: "Blind copying of a foreign scientific or technical idea is often exactly what leads to falling behind" (Gannes, 1985:116). It becomes a substitute for a nation's own capacity for technical innovation.

American companies wish to sell small computers and software abroad without the expense and red tape of export licensing. Small companies find it especially difficult to complete the necessary paperwork. Many also question whether their products are really vital military secrets. Even if they are, the widespread commercial availability of small systems and the fact that their multinational competitors are supplying similar products make export licensing ineffective. It is estimated that small U.S. firms are losing about $1 billion a month in lost overseas sales (Wilkins, 1985c). Some 1985 regulations exempt business data and text-handling software, but export licenses must be obtained for system software, high-level languages, assemblers, compilers, and interpreters. Unrestricted hardware exports are limited to small memory computers and low transmission speed equipment (Wilkins, 1985a). The U.S. Customs Service's "Operation Exodus" works with European governments to identify technology transfers to forbidden customers (Wilkins, 1984d). As the $1.5 million fine of Digital Equipment Corporation indicates, a company can be penalized for selling equipment to a "legal" customer who then resells it to a restricted country (Adams, 1984).

The CIA has been active in identifying U.S. firms supplying high-tech products to communist countries. Its 1984 director, William Casey, defines U.S. national security interests to include commercial competition from Japan as well (Wilkins, 1984a). The recent FBI "sting" operations that caught representatives of Japan's Hitachi Ltd. and Mitsubishi Electric Corp. engaged in industrial espionage in Silicon Valley are an example of U.S. domestic intelligence agency response to industrial demands for protection from foreign information industry products. But not all high-tech firms view international competition as a threat. In a survey of 275 New England companies, 39 percent thought that competition encourages technological innovation; only 36 percent see international competitors as a threat (Dougherty and Janowsky, 1984:3). Because many computer companies are actively engaged in exporting their products, protectionist policies can hurt their sales and market shares.

Federal law also requires a license before allowing the export of *technical data*, defined as:

> Information of any kind that can be used or adapted for use in the design, production, utilization or construction of an article of material. The data may take a tangible form such as a model, prototype, blueprint or an operating manual; or it may take intangible form such as technical services. (Kutten, 1984b:ID4)

To many information specialists, this definition is so vague that it might be used to inhibit the international flow of almost any kind of technological information. Protectionism is by no means a policy with universal support within the information industries. Some industry observers are disturbed to see federal law enforcement and intelligence agencies working to protect information products at the cost of discouraging international sales.

COMPUTERS AND DECISION MAKING

Computers, by nature of their ability to support communication and coordinate activity among widely separated individuals, are an ideal means for exerting power through large social structures. Questions of who has access to what sorts of information are basic to the political process. Decision making in business and government organizations is based on information often not equally available to all participants. Those who own or control information can become the experts whose advice is heavily weighed in public policy-making. Computerization, by changing information access, may enhance the power of some decision makers to the disadvantage of others. Because information is itself a means of exercising power, struggles to acquire and maintain control over its proliferation can occur. In these conflicts, the position of those who depend on their knowledge and technical skills will be strengthened if the new technology provides them with a more powerful means of influencing group behavior. But our ability to participate in politics is reduced if decisions are left to human and computer "experts" who have information that we don't.

Computers provide the potential means to centralize decision making into the hands of fewer government, business, and military authorities. Centralized decision making in political institutions violates a basic value of democracy—that people should be able to participate in the decisions affecting them. In economic institutions, computers provide high-level managers with the potential to directly supervise many corporate activities formerly delegated to middle managers and technicians. Large corporations, especially the multinationals, may use the computer to dominate markets at the expense of their smaller, localized competitors. If the means to manage information concentrate in the hands of relatively few managers and corporations, there will be a corresponding concentration of economic power. This could shrink the middle classes in industrial societies, thus creating an even more powerful elite and a larger and less powerful lower class. Military use of computers is very hierarchical, and the growing economic power of the military has channeled technological and social resources into centralized defense activities. Critics claim that the institutional success of the military threatens the social system (or even the species) with destruction.

The Nobel prize–winning economist Herbert Simon (1985) has pointed out that, although both centralized and decentralized computer systems are technically possible, it is the decision-making processes with which we implement technological change that determines any changes in the distribution of power. Computer-based decision making will not favor centralized power unless decisions about which designs to use are made by those who want their own power increased and centralized. Power will not become centralized if computer and communication technologies are built to distribute information widely. Some analysts believe that if everyone has a personal computer and if a lively market in small-scale computer-based services develops, information technology will not become centralized. They see the spread of new communication media facilitating democratic decision-making processes.

Management Decision Making

A central characteristic of the first industrial revolution was the development of rational bureaucratic and economic organizations in which information management became increasingly important for decision making (Weber, 1978: Chaps. 2 and 11). Today new styles of management are emerging, based upon more effective business information. Kenneth Arrow (1980) argues that computerized information will have an enormous positive effect on the abilities of both small and large businesses to produce effectively by means of improved decision making. Within organizations, better decision making is arrived at by more efficient division of the work of managing information. In the larger business community, better decision making translates into competitive advantage for well-managed firms. Thus, computer use in business organizations can increase cooperation within companies and increase competition in the economy.

COMPUTERIZED DECISION MAKING   In the 1950s, the application of computers to management decision making was believed to be limited to the performance of routine clerical tasks and objective decisions based solely on economic criteria. Although admitting that management decisions ought to be objective wherever possible (and thus should be subject to automation), Merriman and Wass (1959) viewed managerial decisions as part of the spiritual nature of man. Like doctors and lawyers, managers claimed for themselves a special and creative role in human decision making. In the next decades' debates over the possibility and desirability of mechanized thought processes, it was widely believed that what managers do simply could not be done by machine.

Today the capacities of expert systems include such domains as financial services currently performed by highly paid managerial employees (Sullivan, 1984). As Gio Wiederhold (1984:73) argues, the use of knowledge-based systems can "move well-understood decision-making processes to the computer system." This includes a wide range of middle-managerial tasks. Even more important are developments in management information systems that allow a concentration of decision making in the hands of fewer managers. Although Herbert Simon (1985), Kenneth Arrow (1980), and other economists who have examined the impact of information systems on business decision making are rather optimistic that centralization will not occur, they recognize the possibilities. In modern petrochemical plants and in the military, some of the new technological possibilities for centralized decision making are being realized. Examples of this, embedded systems, are combinations of hardware and software designed to function in integrated environments of military or production technology. In chemical processing plants, integrated management information systems permit centralized control of everything from purchasing decisions on feedstocks to projected markets, pricing, process design, and overall system optimization ("The New Cockpits of Industry," 1983; Drake and Perrolle, 1984). This industrial trend extends the workplace routinization process to financial and other middle-level managers who formerly made independent evaluations and decisions in their own areas of expertise.

Evidence that managerial jobs are being eliminated by new technologies is mixed. There was a managerial recession in the early 1980s. U.S. Bureau of Labor Statistics data showed that unemployment for managers has been high. *Fortune* magazine reported that this was at least partly because "computerized systems lessen the need for information-gathering, a principal task of corporate bureaucrats" (Feb. 6, 1984:113). But an analysis of the labor force in Silicon Valley indicates that there are more jobs called "manager" (11 percent) in the computer and microelectronics industries than in older manufacturing in the region (9 percent). What there are less of is professional and technical jobs—28 percent of high-tech but 34 percent of other manufacturing (Eisenscher, 1984:7). Yet throughout 1985 came reports of large management reductions in both manufacturing and information industries (Babcock, 1985a; Green, 1985; Nielsen, 1985). Business analysts like Peter Drucker (1985) believe we are moving toward a "flatter" management structure, with fewer levels of managers and more direct communication between upper management and lower levels of organizational structure.

INFORMATION IN CORPORATE CULTURE   The term **corporate culture** refers to the shared values and norms of a particular company or industry. It includes ethical standards and the criteria by which managers will be judged successful. One negative aspect of a corporate culture is the possibility that business managers begin to be judged more by their social interactions, their appearances, and their abilities to manipulate information for presentations than for their abilities to influence corporate production. As more of the actual production work is done by computerized machines, and as much of the technical "knowledge work" is routinized, there has been a shift in business management interests from the actual production of goods to the command over information systems.

> Factory managers are perceived as greasy-fingernail types, hardly suitable for the polished executive suite. Sharp engineers go into production design rather than production technology. . . . Even our engineering and management educational programs give short shrift to real production technology. Most courses concentrate on PERT charts, organizational factors, and other "professional" aspects of running a factory rather than the nitty gritty of real machines and real parts. (Haavind, 1983:2)

Even in the area of agricultural production, a preference for managing information is appearing:

> While his neighbors spend their time worrying about agricultural techniques, Jesse Griffith of Blackfoot, Idaho, is using a personal computer as a management tool to farm a little smarter. . . . "I never had any formal agricultural training," Griffith says, "but I spend a lot more time on bookkeeping than my neighbors do." (Rubin, 1983:96)

This trend is part of what Randall Collins (1979:72) sees as a consciousness "directed away from the material realities of work experience and into the purely relative values of the cultural currency." What he means is that business decision makers are often less concerned about actual productivity than they are about the symbols of management status.

The positive aspect of a corporate cultural emphasis on information is the potential for improvements in business decision making. In *The Change Masters* (1983), Rosabeth Moss Kanter identifies open access to information and communication networks as characteristics of the most innovative U.S. companies. She also finds them committed to decentralized resources and information, rather than centralized and hierarchically controlled. For example, Andrew Grove (1983), president of Intel Corporation, tries to foster a corporate culture that eliminates status symbols that interfere with the flow of ideas, facts, and points of view. He believes that, if his company is to survive, employees with technical knowledge must participate in decision making along with managers in positions of authority. This new style of management interested in the power to accomplish group goals rather than power over subordinates seems to be more effective in new product development.

Ezra Vogel (1985:2), a specialist on Japanese culture and factory organization, points out, "The Japanese try to win an arrangement rather than an argument. They're not as interested in beating down the opposition as they are in winning an agreement that everybody can stick by." This represents the idea that the power to achieve cooperation can be more effective than the ability to win or have power over people. Japanese management also has a long view of business planning. The founder of the Matsushita Corporation laid out a two-hundred-fifty-year plan for what became one of the most successful Japanese firms. The present chief executive officer of the NEC Corporation has a vision of computers and communication as a major force in the eventual achievement of world cooperation (Kobayashi, 1986). In contrast, many U.S. managers adopt extremely short planning times (Jaques, 1985). They are often in conflict with their own scientists and technical employees who take a longer view of innovations and products (Dubinskas, 1985).

BUSINESS INFORMATION AND ECONOMIC RESPONSE TIME   Better business information can produce longer-range plans and shorter times between the occurrence of economic changes and the managers' knowledge of those changes. In other words, with computer-based data and models, managers can find out what is happening sooner and can make plans on the basis of more comprehensive information. Shorter response times can lead to faster billing and ordering, better cash flow, and smaller inventories to be stored. More rapid response time in financial markets, however, can be a problem. Adam Smith's "invisible hand" works as a regulating mechanism in the stock market when brokers use information about price fluctuations to buy or sell. A phenomenon known as "program trading" creates sudden, sharp drops in the stock market as the computers of many brokerage firms simultaneously "decide" it's time to sell. For example, if many brokers' computers are programmed to sell for profit when the Dow Jones Industrial Average reaches 1900, then the market will begin to drop as soon as it passes the line. The sudden surge of selling will inhibit the market from rising above 1900. Also, sudden drops in the market set off different computers, programmed to sell out if things start going downhill. So a short period of program trading can set off a small landslide.

An international version of this effect could be seen in the collapse of Continental Illinois, one of the largest U.S. banks. It began when Japanese currency traders decided not to transfer funds to the already troubled bank. By the time markets opened for business in the United States and Europe, information that Continental Illinois was in trouble had spread through the system, leading to more fund transfer decisions that brought the bank to near collapse. The lag time between the Continental Illinois disaster and the intervention of the U.S. Federal Reserve Board indicates a major problem with computerized markets. Institutions that regulate financial transactions, as the Federal Reserve does, have not computerized their operations to the point where they can keep up with the faster market. As we computerize our business operations, we make our financial transactions more "real-time." In other words, our data gets closer in time to actual events. In the short run, this destabilizes our economy, because some parts of the system respond to change much more rapidly than others.

Computers in Government

In an assessment of the impact of the information revolution on political institutions, Theodore J. Lowi (1981) argues that an increase in power over the environment and an increase in susceptibility to manipulation are coexisting tendencies of the information revolution to which societies must adjust by adapting their institutions. As in economic organizations, better information can lead to more effective functioning by government agencies and political groups. But the ability of individuals and groups to manipulate information media creates new problems for the political process. Centralization and decentralization occur in politics as well as in business. Extreme centralization is characteristic of totalitarian regimes and military dictatorships. Democracies are more decentralized. The U.S. political system has been characterized by pluralism—the distribution of power among a large number of competing interest groups that seek their own goals in a democratic framework. The ability of businesses, labor unions, citizens groups, and other interests to organize support is essential to their success in influencing political decisions. Analysts using a pluralist model are interested in the effects of computers on communication and organization within interest groups and their relative access to information. Analysts who believe that an economically powerful elite plays the largest role in American politics tend to focus on the consequences of computers for redistributing economic power, arguing that political influence is exerted by those with the most economic resources.

Political scientist Hazel Henderson (1974) predicts greater pluralism as new information-system-based interest groups are able to form. For example, the U.S. political left was advised that computer technology can help "overcome many of the organizational deficiencies that have bedeviled our efforts to build and control our own institutions. . . . they can streamline fundraising and political organizing" (Roper, 1983:142). Established interest groups are also using computers to increase their organizational effectiveness. The Republican Party used computers to manage logistics and communications among delegates at its 1984 presidential convention (Hughes, 1983). But Lowi (1981:463) fears that:

> The primary sources of politics in such a society could be conflicts between the old and the new groups rather than orderly competition between political parties or between established groups. . . . This kind of process, where new groups must fight for a place, is almost certain to be defined as disorder, and this gives established elites additional incentive to use information as a means of social control.

The separation of power among the legislative, executive, and judicial branches of government and among federal, state, and local institutions helps maintain decentralized political power. However, this can also create complex bureaucratic organizations that make it difficult to arrive at and implement political decisions. One of the effects of the computer revolution predicted by Lowi is a trend away from bureaucratic hierarchy in favor of other information-based management processes that may even convert the processes of government itself into a type of management. This would also be a trend away from direct political participation in decision making toward more expertly controlled political structures. In support of Lowi's argument is the evidence at the federal level of an enormous growth in the power of the executive branch of government in the United States in recent decades. A study by Stephen Frantzich (1982:242) shows a traditional political group, Congress, struggling to halt the trend.

> One of the primary motivations of computer promoters in Congress stemmed from the desire to regain some of the power lost to the executive branch and outside interest groups due to an imbalance of relevant information. The experience on the state level clearly indicated that when legislatures improved

their information-handling capabilities, they were able to venture successfully
into new policy areas . . . and generally improved their competitive advantage
over the executive branch.

At the state level, governors and legislators have clashed over access to
computerized financial information, viewing it as a change in the existing
balance of power (Raimondi, 1985c). In a study of computers in American
local governments, Danziger, Dutton, Kling, and Kraemer (1982) show them
to be used more by city managers than by elected officials. But they found
very little evidence that computers are being used to shift power from elected
local government officials to bureaucratic administrators.

Despite claims that the information revolution is leading to a utopian
higher political consciousness based upon a widespread distribution of political power and participation (Toffler, 1980:416–43; Capra, 1982:398), the
resolution of contemporary political conflicts in ways that strengthen decentralized democratic institutions is problematic. If, as in business information networks, the length of time between public opinion change and new
legislation is shortened, we may find the political process more concerned
with popular, short-term issues rather than with long-term policy solutions.
The expression of public sentiment as law is not the same as political
participation if public information is manipulated or if the public does not
understand the issues facing it. Although U.S. use of computers in voting and
political campaigns certainly provides the technical capacity for widespread
participation by informed citizens, computer system vulnerability to fraud is
equally applicable to voter registration systems and election return tallying
programs (Waskell, 1986). In one growing political use of computerized
information, politicians and special interest groups develop private data banks
as an aid to influencing voters and legislation (*Fortune*, March 19, 1984:102–
3). The computer-aided efforts of government agencies and social scientists
(Campaigns and Computers, 1982–83; Alexander, 1983) to monitor such
activities reflect the sort of struggle described by Lowi rather than a de-
mocratizing trend. Lowi believes it is possible for societies to head off the
centralization of information as the secret property of the powerful, offering
the Pentagon Papers and Watergate as evidence that information can still be
wrested from established power holders and used by citizens. However, he
sees this as possible only if cultural and educational institutions produce "a
true citizen, a person who demands knowledge of the world around him"
(Lowi, 1981:472).

The experiments of Sweden, Austria, and the Netherlands in gathering
informed public opinion before setting national technological development
policies show that decentralized decision making is possible (Nelkin, 1977).
However, in many countries computer use has heightened the tension between
centralized information and individual rights, as in Germany (Butner, 1982),
or created factional political disputes over policies for computerizing the
economy, as in the Soviet Union (Turn and Nimitz, 1975:21). The overall
pattern in international relations seems to be one of political conflict over

economic issues. Some observers think multinational corporations will be in the best position to utilize the information revolution. The United States, as it finds its economic power in the world system being threatened by the multinationals and the more centrally planned economies of Japan and Europe, has increasingly emphasized its military power in the international arena.

The Military Influence on Computer Development

Although most of the wars of history have been fought without computers, beginning with guided missile work in World War II and continuing through the development of the "electronic battlefield" in Vietnam, computers have become one of the major research and development items in the huge U.S. military weapons budget.

> We have seen that the military has funded, overseen and guided virtually every significant electronic invention since World War II. In both the pace of development and the direction taken by new technologies, the military has asserted an active role. We have seen examples so recent that there can be little doubt that the Defense Department plans to continue as the most important American institution responsible for technological development. (Atwater, 1982:5)

During the 1980s, growing defense expenditures have increased the military's influence on the entire computer industry—from semiconductors to software. Because businesses and academic scientists view defense contracts as a large source of revenue, they are often willing to modify their products and their research programs to meet military goals. This means that the needs of the military, rather than those of other types of planning groups of business or public leaders, are likely to go on shaping the future of computers.

ADA   The U.S. Defense Department's Ada project is part of a major effort to rationalize military decision making. The Ada project is intended to produce a huge standardized language for large-scale intelligent software applications (Barnes, 1982). The language is named for Lady Lovelace, a friend of Babbage who first suggested the idea of computer software for his analytical engine. By requiring military software to be programmed in the Ada language, the project represents a step toward promoting industry software standards. Because military decision making is hierarchical, these standards are likely to promote centralized power. Technical criticisms of the Ada project (Hoare, 1981; Ledgard and Singer, 1982; Skelly, 1982; and Winchman, 1984) include arguments that it is too big and too expensive for any but large organizations to implement. Also, some critics believe that the size and complexity of Ada programs guarantee that they will contain errors. They fear that the belief that such systems can be made bug-free and reliable enhances the probability that military decision making (especially in the area of nuclear defenses) will be embedded in them. Social critics argue that it represents a stifling by military interests of other new programming ideas (Begley, 1983; Rosenberg, 1983). To them, the new Ada language and advances in structured programming seem more useful as tools for rationalizing worker's tasks in ordinary computer applications than as reliable safeguards against Defense Department errors. Proponents see Ada as a major step forward in structured programming and software compatibility standards (Stallings, 1986).

THE STRATEGIC COMPUTING INITIATIVE   The Strategic Computing Initiative is supporting computer science research to produce pilot's assistants, autonomous tanks, and battlefield management systems. Although there are nonmilitary spin-offs, some observers fear that we are losing ground in the international market for commercial software by investing too heavily in military applications. However, most conflicts over the Strategic Computing Initiative are about the wisdom of "Star Wars" software. Critics believe that the risk of an accidental computerized triggering of nuclear war is being significantly increased by the Pentagon's chosen directions in computer technology development (Barnaby, 1982). This is partly because computers, by vastly increasing the speed and accuracy of weapons, have actually reduced the time available for human beings to make decisions or to try negotiations in the face of imminent danger. This threat is inherent in the size and complexity of military computer systems. At that scale, some hardware and software failures must be expected, as have already occurred in the U.S. satellite nuclear sensor system (Thaxton, 1980).

Box 3 is an assessment of the Ballistic Missile Defense (BMD) system by a Defense Department study panel. Critics of the program (CPSR, 1984; Lin, 1985; Parnas, 1985) do not believe that a computer software system estimated to contain 10 million lines of code that cannot be tested fully, but which must work correctly the first time it is used, can be made. With the speed and complexity of computer-based decisions, they argue, comes a degree of unreliability that cannot be tolerated in life-or-death decisions involving the fate of the entire species. Although the personal interests of many computer scientists lie in getting a share of Pentagon resources in order to pursue scientifically interesting projects, many of them feel a professional obligation to speak out when they do not believe their work can really produce reliable defensive weapons. One Defense Department software consultant resigned from the Strategic Defense Initiative Panel. Although he believes that people with a strong sense of social responsibility should continue to work for national defense (something not all SDI critics are willing to do), he did not believe the software could be made reliable:

> Like President Reagan, I consider the use of nuclear weapons as a deterrent to be dangerous and immoral. If there is a way to make nuclear weapons impotent and obsolete and end the fear of nuclear weapons, there is nothing I would rather work on. . . . I could not convince myself that it would be useful to build a system that we did not trust. And if SDI is not trustworthy, the U.S. will not abandon the arms race. Similarly, the U.S.S.R. could not assume that SDI

would be completely ineffective; seeing both a "shield" and missiles, it would feel impelled to improve its offensive forces to compensate for the defense. . . . Instead of the safer world that President Reagan envisions, we would have a far more dangerous situation. Thus, the issue of our trust in the system is critical; it is important that Americans understand why responsible leaders would never trust a "Star Wars" shield. (Parnas, 1986:32–34)

VIDEO GAMES AND MILITARY FANTASIES   The U.S. military has more than 350 war games, simulations, and interactive training systems in use (Martin, 1985:3). Its proposed new weapons more and more resemble video games. Real issues of complexity and reliability tend to be ignored. The extreme vulnerability of electronic weapons systems cannot be denied when a few Wisconsin youngsters can penetrate a Defense Department system ("Milwaukee Discovers . . .," 1983; Bertoni, 1983). Psychiatrist Eric Chivian, whose organization International Physicians for the Prevention of Nuclear War won the 1985 Nobel Peace Prize, says: "We have come to rely on weapons we can't use, but we can't admit publicly that these weapons can't be used because of the psychology of deterrence" (*Boston Globe*, November 11, 1985:56). We are caught in the fantasy that we are faced by an implacable enemy and can only be safe if we build more weapons. Just as surveillance technologies can reify microlevel social relationships of mutual trust, so international relations can be reified in military technology.

In the long evolutionary interaction between tools and humans who gather in groups to throw them at one another, the computer has provided greater action at a distance than ever before. In both war and playing at war, face-to-face contact with a human opponent has been replaced by remote sensors and electronic acts of aggression. In the process, the speed of the thrown rock, ball, or bullet has become the speed of the electron. In magical thinking, in play, and in dreams, the wish to have power over others is the deed. Computer-aided military thinking is turning fantasies of power into designs for communications and control technology. The next extension in conventional warfare appears to be a voice- and eye-movement-guided "super-plane" of which the U.S. Air Force's AFTI/F-16 is a prototype. As in the fantasy movie *Foxfire*, these weapons will almost respond to the intentions of the "warrior." American social institutions, by investing enormous resources in the military and by accepting their guidance in technological development, are actively engaged in supporting the fantasy of international relations as a military contest. But, as political scientist Karl Deutsch reminds us, "game theory usually assumes that most games have an end, but international politics resembles rather an unending game in which no great power can pick up its marbles and go home" (1966:69).

Computer Models and Policy-Making

Appropriate uses of computer modeling can be an invaluable aid to human understanding of complex problems of the physical environment or the in-

BOX 3

THE STRATEGIC COMPUTING INITIATIVE:
CONCLUSIONS OF THE FLETCHER PANEL

MAJOR CONCLUSIONS—ENGINEERING COMPLEXITY, SOFTWARE

Any BMD system will deal with tens of thousands of objects and probably several tiers of defense. The problem of achieving the computational speed and capacity needed to make decisions and to manage a complex and rapidly evolving battle has been emphasized in almost every study of antiballistic missile (ABM) technology. The Panel sees this as a challenging and difficult problem and has recognized in its proposed technical program the need to develop computing devices and processors of greatly increased speed and capacity, as well as algorithms to make choices quickly and flexibly. However, in the end, it is a complex of broader engineering issues that dominates the Panel's concerns and recommendations. These issues relate to the difficulties of specifying and designing a system that will be of unprecedented complexity and to the reliability and safety of any resulting system that may finally be deployed.

A BMD system will be made up of many elements—sensors, weapons, computers, data links, all controlled by complex software. Most of these will be replicated many times. Each by itself will be highly complex and will serve as one link in a figurative chain. All hardware and software links of this chain must function if the chain is to do its job. The software of the battle management system governs the coordinated activity of many chains, functioning side by side, and makes the whole aggregate of hardware behave as a purposeful entity. The engineering design of these elements and chains is a task that may be comparable in challenge and complexity to the Apollo program. To design and create the software that ties this system together and makes it both effective and safe is probably the dominant problem for battle management.

The problem is greater than just writing good software code, important as good code is. It is first a problem of systems design, bearing on the effectiveness, safety, and economy of the BMD system as a whole, and then a problem of realizing that design, exactly, in reliable software.

Conclusion 1

Specifying, generating, testing, and maintaining the software for a battle management system will be a task that far exceeds in complexity and difficulty any that has yet been accomplished in the production of civil or military software systems.

The battle management system will, through its software, define and control the functioning of the entire defense and, thereby, define its effectiveness and establish performance requirements for weapons and sensors. Accordingly, the Panel reached the following conclusions.

Conclusion 2

The battle management system and its software must be designed as an integral part of the BMD system as a whole, not as an applique.

Conclusion 3

Although a strong concern for the development of software prevails throughout the civil and military data-processing community, more emphasis needs to be placed on the specific problem of BMD.

— Expanded efforts to generate software development tools are needed.

— Further emphasis is needed on simulation as a means to assist the design of battle management systems and software.

— Specific work is needed on algorithms related to critical battle management functions.

MAJOR CONCLUSIONS—SAFETY AND CREDIBILITY

No BMD system will be acceptable to the leaders and the voters of the United States unless it is widely believed that the system will be safe in peacetime and will operate effectively when needed. There will be no way, short of conducting a war, to test fully a deployed BMD system.

Conclusion 6

The problem of realistically testing an entire system, end-to-end, has no complete technical solution. The credibility of a deployed system must be established by credible testing of subsystems and partial functions and by continuous monitoring of its operations and health during peacetime.

There are, of course, weapons systems on which this country already depends that are not subject to end-to-end testing in peacetime. The Panel raises the issue here both because of the unprecedented complexity of the BMD system and because the issues of safety and credibility bear strongly on features of the battle management system itself.

Specifically, there are two battle management functions that are absolutely critical to the safety, credibility, and effectiveness of a BMD system:

— Authorized release of weapons and

— Ordnance safety during peacetime and testing

These two issues are critical in themselves and are made more so because many elements of a BMD system will be highly automated and will be operating unattended in space.

Weapons certainly should not be released when not authorized, and weapons must be released in a timely manner when they are needed and authorized.

Conclusion 7

There is no technical way to design absolute safety, security, or survivability into the functions of weapons release and ordnance safety. Standards of adequacy must, in the end, be established by fiat, based upon an informed consensus and judgment of risks.

Weapons release also has a human side. Statute requires explicit authorization by the President for the use of nuclear weapons, and common prudence requires that other warlike acts be properly considered and authorized. Nevertheless, the time constraints of an ABM battle, particularly if joined in the boost phase, do not allow for elaborate human decision processes or consultative activities.

Conclusion 8

The battle management system must provide for a high degree of automation to support the accomplishment of the weapons release function.

The Panel has recommended a program to evaluate the feasibility of various command doctrines and their supporting automated aids in situations that realistically represent possible battle scenarios within an ABM system.

Source: Battle Management, Communications, and Data Processing, B. McMillan, Panel Chairman, Vol. V. of *Report of the Study on Eliminating the Threat Posed by Nuclear Ballistic Missiles*, J. C. Fletcher, Study Chairman (Washington, D.C.: Department of Defense Technologies Study Team, February 1984): 4–9.

tricacies of international relations. They can have an enormous impact on public policy by raising long-range planning issues. One of the earliest models, described below, projected what the world's population and resource situation would be like in the future if we did not make major changes.

THE LIMITS TO GROWTH MODEL   The development of the Limits to Growth Model was sponsored during the 1970s by an international group of industrialists, the Club of Rome. In the decade of commentary and criticism the model provoked, many of the assumptions and techniques used by the modeling group have been shown to be flawed. However, the model remains important for two reasons. First, it was a pioneering attempt to model global environmental and economic conditions and led to enormous advances in computer-modeling techniques. Second, the controversy it generated placed issues of world food shortages, population growth, pollution, and natural resource depletion on the policy agenda of many national and international bodies (Humphrey and Buttel, 1982; Oltmans, 1974; Tinbergen, Dolman, and van Ettinger, 1976). The projections, two of which are shown in Figure 18, did not "come true," nor were they intended to. A model like this one tells us "what if," when the ifs are our assumptions about the way the world system works and our best measurements of amounts, rates, and changes. In retrospect, the Limits to Growth Model was oversimplified—it left out a factor for technological or political change, for example. However, although its shortcomings are a warning to all future computer modelers, Limits to Growth created a useful public debate.

THE NUCLEAR WINTER MODEL   The Nuclear Winter Model's projections of what the earth would be like following a nuclear war seems to be having an impact on public policy debates similar to that of the Limits to Growth Model by raising the issue of war as a risk to species survival (Revkin, 1985). It models the atmospheric and biological effects of a thermonuclear war and suggests that winter conditions would prevail all over the earth following even

FIGURE 18

PROJECTIONS OF THE LIMITS TO GROWTH MODEL

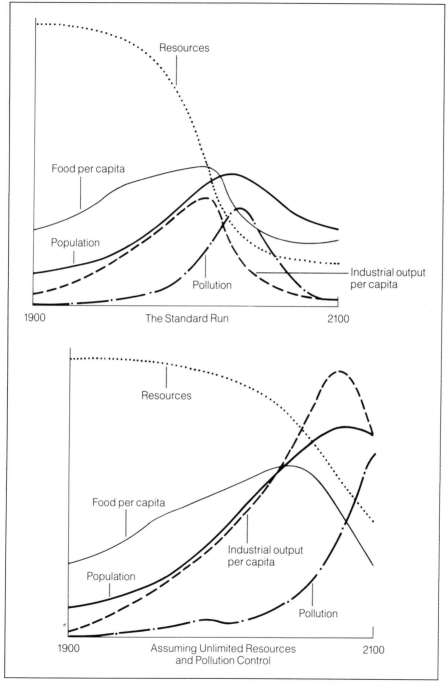

Source: Donella H. Meadows, Dennis L. Meadows, Jørgen Randers, William W. Behrens III, *The Limits to Growth: A Report for the Club of Rome's Project on the Predicament of Mankind.* A Potomac Associates book published by Universe Books, New York, 1972. Graphics by Potomac Associates.

a limited nuclear exchange. Like the Limits to Growth model, the original Nuclear Winter model (in 1983) oversimplified the complexities of the earth's atmosphere. Its projected temperature declines depend on assumptions about how much smoke would be generated in nuclear firestorms and how long the particles would remain in the air, reflecting sunlight back into space. The Pentagon, which bases some of its strategic planning on "winning" a limited nuclear conflict, has sponsored research designed to show that there would be less smoke and more rapid dissipation of particles than assumed in the Nuclear Winter model. A report issued in 1986 projects less drastic winter conditions but repeated warnings of catastrophic biological effects on food crops and other organisms. For most participants in the nuclear weapons debate, the Nuclear Winter Model has added to the seriousness of the issues. Proponents of a nuclear freeze argue that the model supports their view that a nuclear war must be avoided at all costs; the Pentagon now argues that the model's results make U.S. military strength more important than ever before.

MODELS AND SOCIAL PLANNING   In 1985, a U.S. district court awarded damages to families of three fishermen who died because the National Weather Service failed to repair equipment that could have forecast a severe storm (*New York Times*, August 13, 1985:1). It was the first time the courts had held the Weather Service responsible for accurate predictions. After twenty-five years of weather satellite operations (Smith et al., 1986), we have come to rely on computer models of the weather and to hold modelers responsible for their accuracy. In Institute, West Virginia, a Union Carbide modeling program was given incorrect data and erroneously predicted that a cloud of leaking toxic gas would remain stable over the plant. When it drifted over a residential area instead, plant officials belatedly sounded an alarm (Desmond, 1985d). Unlike projective models that tell us "what if" under a wide variety of approximate conditions, predictive models are intended to tell us what will happen. When decisions are based on the results of computer models, it is extremely important that we can trust the model's hardware, software, and input data.

Projective models are more often used in the policy-making process. As in the case of earthquake modeling (Raugh, 1985), we do not yet expect accurate reports of where and when. But we do use the models to anticipate environmental events and plan steps to avoid the worst consequences. By giving policy-makers a better idea of the consequences of natural and social processes, computers can be applied to a wide range of policy issues from city transportation planning to the economic effects of acid rain on buildings and crops. Computers also affect the process of negotiating policies. Delegates to the Law of the Sea Conference disagreed among themselves over how to distribute the costs and proceeds from seabed mining in international waters. A computer model designed to show the consequences of various countries' proposals had the unanticipated effect of making it easier for delegates to abandon their national position in favor of a compromise (Koh, 1984). The same psychological effects found in decision-making via computer network were observed. Emotional commitments to national pride were reduced; rational discussion was facilitated. Delegates who changed their minds were not in the position of feeling they had lost to another person; they could attribute their new position to the objective "facts" presented by the computer. The use of computer-based information to facilitate cooperative political processes is an attractive alternative to computerized conflict.

THE SOCIAL FUTURE OF INFORMATION

What will the social future of information be? It is always tempting to reach beyond the analysis of historical and contemporary phenomena and predict a definite future. In doing so, it is much easier to predict developments in technology than in society. In 1931, the editors of *Fortune* magazine quite accurately predicted technological developments in energy sources, plastics, air transport, communications, and television. Of the social consequences of these, they said:

> It is not possible to transpose oneself spiritually from one environment to another. Even had the Victorians predicted what we have accomplished with the steam engine, they would never have conceived the corporate economics derived from it, nor the modern woman derived from the corporate economics. (*Fortune*, June, 1931:150)

But we can be certain that the social future of information will be determined by social processes, not by technology alone.

Distance, Time, and Social Interactions

Computers are distancing people from direct physical information about the world and each other. This can lead to alienation and the reification of social relationships. Yet at the same time, computers provide us with more information about the world than we have ever had; this can increase our capacity to anticipate change and adapt ourselves or our environments. As the world changes, information about it can be obtained more and more rapidly, bringing our perceptions of change closer in time to actual events. This transformation of time and distance threatens to destabilize our conversational norms, our workplaces, our economy, and our international relations. Yet it also offers us new possibilities for communication, work, and decision-making. One of the challenges of the information revolution is to develop new concepts of our interactions with the world and with each other. Although computers can be used for both conflict and cooperation, the technology magnifies the consequences of conflict and increases the need for cooperation. Thus, if we are to have a future, it will be one in which computer technology is an instrument of social integration.

Property and Privacy

From a sociological point of view, the problem of protecting information property is similar to that of protecting other forms of property in that no amount of protection is really effective unless there are shared social beliefs in the "rightness" of ownership. Society operates to a large extent upon trust and mutual agreement to respect the property of others. The problem of protecting information property is not primarily a technological one. It is a problem of changing social conceptions of property.

A social attempt to solve the problem of computer piracy has been initiated by the Association of Data Processing Service Organizations, Inc. ("Firms Take Different Routes . . .," 1985). By publicizing the need for corporate policies to promote respect for information property rights as part of "corporate culture," advocates of a social solution hope that a sense of corporate responsibility, expressed through concrete management policies and business practices, will provide the sorts of social controls needed to make formal legal protections effective. A new book on computer crime prevention recommends measures to keep employees happy, arguing that disgruntled employees are responsible for many information product abuses (Van Duyn, 1985).

From a broader social perspective, the prevention of crimes against information property becomes ultimately confounded with the issue of individual privacy. Attempts to deter this sort of crime will also create struggles between governments and corporations over control of sensitive information. The interests of individuals are represented by the laws protecting individual rights and by the public administration of those laws. A computerized version of the classical political tension between the maintenance of social order and the freedom of individuals is taking shape. In our quest for the security of information property, it is important to keep in mind that the majority of the computer crime from which we want protection is committed by people with a legitimate right to access the data involved. Increasing government surveillance or a fortresslike mentality for property protection has not been successful in the past as a solution to the law and order problem. The protection of computerized information requires a society that respects the information rights of individuals and organizations.

Ethics and Politics

The ethical issues of computer use involve responsible decision making by individuals, professional organizations, corporations, and political institutions. Computers do not automatically cause information to become property or to be controlled by a few decision makers. If used for different purposes, they can be the basis of public information systems and provide communication networks helpful for democratic discussion and debate. Predictions about the social future of information range from fears of widespread repression to visions of more individual freedom within democratic in-stitutions. What actually occurs will depend on how we solve the political issues now facing us.

Ethical standards adopted by associations of computer professionals (Box 4) are part of efforts to provide new social norms and roles to regulate the use of information and protect both property and individual privacy. To these we must add a concern that the work of computer professionals does not undermine the social interactions, institutions, and processes that they them-selves value. Ethical uses of information involve far more than the protection of property and privacy; they include socially responsible uses of the comput-er's power.

Artificial Intelligence and Human Decisions

Artificial intelligence, besides being a challenge to the self-esteem of those who define themselves as thinking beings superior to the rest of creation, raises a practical question: how much do we want computers to think for us? Within the narrow range of thinking where computer programs can be current-ly designed to perform lie the possibilities for decision-making industrial robots that could outperform skilled human workers, medical diagnosis pro-grams to identify and prescribe treatment for human illness, and "smart" weapons that take some military decisions out of the hands of strategists. How much are we willing to share our decision-making capabilities with comput-ers? Technological determinists assume that we will use computers for what-ever they are capable of doing. Yet philosophers and theologians like Harvey Cox (1984:189) believe that the world is becoming "one in which the exagger-ated claims made for science and technology will be modulated. We already see an impressive element of self-criticism in recent scientific thought, a growing unwillingness to claim that science is either the best or the only mode of knowing. The advent of nuclear weapons and the recognition of the finitude and precariousness of the planet have also given some scientists pause. It is no longer obvious that *if* one can do something then one *should.*"

Of the many analysts of the computer's impact on society, Joseph Weizenbaum is perhaps the most adamant about what machines should not be designed to do. Although he is a leading artificial intelligence expert, he writes:

> I have argued that the individual human being, like any other organism, is defined by the problems he confronts. The human is unique by virtue of the fact that he must necessarily confront problems that arise from his unique biological and emotional needs. . . . No other organism, and certainly no computer, can be made to confront genuine human problems in human terms. . . . Computers can make judicial decisions, computers can make psychiatric judgments. They can flip coins in much more sophisticated ways than can the most patient human being. The point is that they *ought* not be given such tasks. They may even be

BOX 4
PROFESSIONAL ETHICAL STANDARDS

Excerpt from the Data Processing Management Association Code of Ethics:

In recognition of My Obligation to Society I shall:

Protect the privacy and confidentiality of all information entrusted to me.

Use my skill and knowledge to inform the public in all areas of my expertise.

To the best of my ability, ensure that the products of my work are used in a socially responsible way.

Support, respect, and abide by the appropriate local, state, provincial, and federal laws.

Never misrepresent or withhold information that is germane to a problem or situation of public concern nor will I allow any such known information to remain unchallenged.

Not use knowledge of a confidential or personal nature in any unauthorized manner or to achieve personal gain.

Excerpt from the Association for Computing Machinery Code of Professional Conduct:

An ACM member should use his special knowledge and skills for the advancement of human welfare.

Ethical considerations.

An ACM member should consider the health, privacy, and general welfare of the public in the performance of his work.

An ACM member, whenever dealing with data concerning individuals, shall always consider the principle of the individual's privacy and seek the following:

To minimize the data collected.

To limit authorized access of the data.

To provide proper security for the data.

To determine the required retention period of the data.

To ensure proper disposal of the data.

Excerpt from the Institute of Electrical and Electronics Engineers Code of Ethics:

Article IV

Members shall, in fulfilling their responsibilities to the community:

1. Protect the safety, health, and welfare of the public and speak out against abuses in these areas affecting the public interest.
2. Contribute professional advice, as appropriate, to civic, charitable, or other non-profit organizations.
3. Seek to extend public knowledge and appreciation of the profession and its achievements.

Excerpt from the Code of Ethics for Certified Computer Professionals:

2.2 Social Responsibility

One is expected to combat ignorance about information processing technology in those public areas where one's application can be expected to have an adverse social impact.

Source: Deborah G. Johnson and John W. Snapper, *Ethical Issues in the Use of Computers.* Belmont, CA: Wadsworth, 1985: 23–40. Excerpts reprinted by permission of the ACM, the IEEE, and ICCP.

able to arrive at "correct" decisions in some cases—but always and necessarily on bases no human being should be willing to accept. (Weizenbaum, 1976: 223–25)

For many people, the areas in which computers "ought" to make decisions lie in those applications for which man/machine interactions extend the human's ability to manipulate large and complex assemblages of information about the environment, especially for regions, like outer space or the subatomic universe, into which the human senses cannot go unaided. The computer's speed in calculations can be used to answer questions previously unanswerable because of time limitations, or it can be used to perform necessary but boring operations quickly. Intelligent machines may prove to be valuable sources of advice upon which to base human decisions for human purposes, if the power of the computer is seen as a tool for decision makers. If, however, the power of computers is viewed as outside the political process, we will lose the opportunity to make group decisions about the direction of technological development. In other words, if we allow ourselves to build our decision-making expertise into machines and then begin to think of decisions as technical questions rather than political issues, we will lose control over public policy to technical experts. Instead of politics, we will have administration.

Communications and Social Movements

In a summary of the impact of microelectronics on the third world, UN technology transfer specialist Dieter Ernst (1983:11) predicted the emergence of new forms of political resistance to the imposition of a new international division of labor. But it is not clear what forms these conflicts will take and what means will be at the disposal of the dissidents. The United Nations adopted the resolution calling for a new world information and communication order based upon principles of economic equality and political democracy (UNESCO, 1980). But the UN is far from being a world government, and it has been historically ineffectual at implementing its resolutions. It is a fundamental problem of the information age that nation-states have not developed effective international political institutions to deal with the growing political power of international economic institutions. Although a worldwide system of computer-based political democracies is technologically possible, there are no formal political institutions with which to implement it.

The revolutionary transformations of the modern world have been based on changes in economic power during the industrial revolution and on the coercive power of military revolution. Social theorists argue that the social movements of the future will use information as a source of power. Those groups who own and control information will be able to define the nature of social reality and will influence social norms and values. Alvin Gouldner (1979) believes that a new international class of intellectuals is forming, though it is far from being a ruling elite. William Evan (1981:14–16) sees the emergence of a global community based on the ethical values of international professional and scientific associations. Koji Kobayashi (1986) echoes the theme from an international business perspective. But shared cultural values among the world's knowledge elite will not necessarily make them powerful in the economic or political realm. Repressive military or religious movements (as in Iran) may instead dominate the means of communication.

Computers and communications are affecting the politics of the world's people in both repressive and liberating ways. In some places, the U.S. military supplies the computer technology for population surveillance and totalitarian control (Klare, 1984; Conrad, 1982). The same information specialists who advise U.S. political candidates have advised governments on how to run elections in El Salvador and the Philippines (Dowie, 1983). But, more optimistically, communications media have become a powerful force for social movements in countries like South Africa and the Philippines. In the case of the Philippines, the revolution was televised. During the Marcos-Aquino election, television viewers around the world saw powerful images of people struggling to keep their ballot boxes from being carried away by government soldiers. In the United States, a major backer of the Marcos government, the public and the Congress saw election fraud as it happened. As the democratically elected Aquino government ousted the Marcos regime, television viewers around the world were shown a crowd of people preventing one faction of the military from attacking the other by standing between them, a demonstration of the strength of normative power. Computers and communications technologies, by bringing the citizens of the world into one another's living rooms and by facilitating shared cultural symbols, may be a powerful force for movements based on democratic ethical values.

Individuals, Computers, and Social Change

Our individual experiences with computers and communications technologies intersect the larger processes of social change. We are participants in social change, not mere observers or recipients of it. We can become more conscious of how our actions contribute to social change by becoming reflexive computer users. If we anticipate the consequences of our small technological choices, learn to see our private experiences as part of public issues, and do not let computer interfaces become a substitute for social relationships, we will preserve our power to decide where we want the information revolution to go. Though we may not always have the power to reach our goals, at least we will not be giving up the power we do have.

If you design or purchase computers and communications equipment, ask yourself: Would I want to use this product? Would I want people I care about to use it? Do I want to live in a world where it is used? If the answers are "no," then ask yourself why you are choosing that particular design, or indeed any computer technology at all. If you can decide which way you want the information revolution to go, you will be in a position to act on your beliefs— often in minor ways, but nevertheless contributing to the social construction of a reality you desire.

Because the social world involves conflict and the exercise of power, you should be prepared for political struggles over the future of computers. In communities, workplaces, states, nations, and international relations, there will be disagreements over information policy. If you leave policy decisions to the politicians, to the technical experts, or to the expert systems, you will have chosen to let other people decide the social future of information. If you do nothing to preserve your right to produce and exchange information freely, you may forfeit any possibility of doing so.

FURTHER READING FOR PART FOUR

Burnham, David. 1983. *The Rise of the Computer State.* New York: Random House.

Clinard, Marshall B., and Peter C. Yeager. 1980. *Corporate Crime.* New York: Free Press.

Dahl, Robert A. 1985. *A Preface to Economic Democracy.* Berkeley: University of California Press.

Deutsch, Karl W. 1966. *The Nerves of Government: Models of Political Communication and Control.* New York: Free Press.

Domhoff, G. William. 1983. *Who Rules America Now? A View for the Eighties.* Englewood Cliffs, NJ: Prentice-Hall.

Erlich, Paul R., Carl Sagan, Donald Kennedy, and Walter Orr. 1984. *The Cold and the Dark: The World After Nuclear War.* New York: Norton.

Johnson, Deborah G., and John W. Snapper, eds. 1985. *Ethical Issues in the Use of Computers.* Belmont, CA: Wadsworth.

Keyworth, George A. 1985. "Ballistic Missile Defense: The Case For," *Issues in Science and Technology* (Fall):30–44.

Kutten, L. J. 1984. *The Law and Software.* Englewood Cliffs, NJ: Prentice-Hall.

Office of Technology Assessment. 1986. *Strategic Defenses.* Princeton, NJ: Princeton University Press.

Pool, Ithiel de Sola. 1983. *Technologies of Freedom.* Cambridge, MA: MIT Press.

Rockart, John F., and Christine V. Bullen, eds. 1986. *The Rise of Managerial Computing.* Homewood, IL: Dow Jones-Irwin.

Smith, Merritt Roe, ed. 1985. *Military Enterprise and Technological Change.* Cambridge, MA: MIT Press.

"Toward a New Information Order." 1982. Special issue of *NACLA (North American Congress on Latin America) Report on the Americas* 16, 4 (July/August).

Union of Concerned Scientists. 1984. *The Fallacy of Star Wars.* New York: Vintage.

Westin, Alan. 1967. *Privacy and Freedom.* New York: Atheneum.

REFERENCES

Abelson, Philip H. 1985. "Corporate Classrooms," *Science* 229,4718 (September 13):1043.

Abercrombie, Nicholas, and John Urry. 1983. *Capital, Labor, and the Middle Classes*. London: George Allen and Unwin.

Abrahamson, David. 1985. "Tamarins in the Amazon," *Science 85* (September):59–63.

Achebe, Chinua. 1959. *Things Fall Apart*. Greenwich, CT: Fawcett.

Achiron, Marilyn. 1984. "Zapping the Mailman," *Newsweek* (August 20):64.

Adams, Jane Meredith. 1984. "U.S. Fines Digital $1.5 Million for Export Violations," *Boston Globe* (September 5):33.

Aeppel, Timothy. 1983. "Tech Invaders: School Survival Shifts Center Screen," *Christian Science Monitor* (April 15):B1–B2.

Agee, James, and Walker Evans. 1960. *Let Us Now Praise Famous Men*. New York: Houghton Mifflin.

Albert, Douglas J., and Stephen P. Morse. 1984. "Combatting Software Piracy by Encryption and Key Management," *Computer* (April):68–73.

Alexander, Herbert E. 1983. *Financing the 1980 Election*. Lexington, MA: D. C. Heath.

Alexander, Tom. 1984. "Why Computers Can't Outthink the Experts," *Fortune* 20 (August):105–18.

Altheide, David L. 1985. *Media Power*. Beverly Hills, CA: Sage.

" 'America's Competitive Challenge': Excerpts from the Report." 1983. *Chronicle of Higher Education* (May 18):10–13.

"America's High-Tech Crisis: Why Silicon Valley is Losing its Edge." 1985. *Business Week* (March 11):56–67, 128.

Amsden, Alice H. 1980. *The Economics of Women and Work*. London: Penguin.

Anderson, James G., and Stephen J. Jay. 1985. "The Impact of Computers on the Practice of Medicine," presentation to the American Sociological Association (August). Washington, DC.

Anderson, Niels-Bjorn. 1983. "The Changing Roles of Secretaries and Clerks," in Harry Otway and Malcolm Peltu. *New Office Technology: Human and Organizational Aspects*. Brussels: Ablex.

Andreski, Stanislav. 1969. "Description and Theory," in *The Uses of Comparative Sociology*. Berkeley: University of California Press.

Andrew, John. 1983. "Terminal Tedium," *Wall Street Journal* (May 6):15.

"Are Electronic Foodstamps on the Way?" 1984. *Newsweek* (July 23):13.

Aries, Philippe. 1977. "The Family and the City," in Alice Rossi et al., eds. *The Family*. New York: Norton.

———. 1962. *Centuries of Childhood: A Social History of Family Life*. New York: Vintage.

Arnold, Carolyn, and Myra Strober. 1984. "Integrated Circuits/Segregated Labor: Women in Three Computer–Related Occupations," Institute for Research on Education, Finance and Governance Report No. 84–A27. Palo Alto, CA: Stanford University School of Education.

Arrow, Kenneth. 1980. "The Economics of Information," in Michael Dertouzos and Joel Moses, eds. *The Computer Age: A Twenty-Year View*. Cambridge, MA: MIT Press.

"Art and Animation." 1985. Special issue of *Computer Graphics and Applications* 5,7 (July).

Asimov, Isaac, and Karen A. Frenkel. 1985. *Robots*. New York: Harmony Books.

Attewell, Paul, and James Rule. 1984. "Computing and Organizations: What We Know and What We Don't Know," *Communications of the ACM* 27,12 (December):1184–92.

Atwater, Harry. 1982. "Electronics and Computer Development: A Military History," *Technology and Responsibility* 1, 2 (Fall):1–5.

Aubert, Vilhelm, ed. 1969. *The Sociology of Law*. London: Penguin.

Axelrod, Robert. 1984. *The Evolution of Cooperation*. New York: Basic Books.

References

Ayres, Robert, and Steven Miller. 1983. "Robotic Realities: Near-Term Prospects and Problems," *Annals of the American Academy of Political and Social Science* 470 (November):28–55.

Baaklini, A. I., and J. J. Heaphey, eds. 1977. *Comparative Legislative Reform and Innovations*. Albany, NY: Comparative Development Studies Center. Cited in Frantzich, 1982.

Babbage, Charles. 1982. Cited in Philip Kraft, Butler-Cox Foundation Lecture. Davos, Switzerland.

———. 1832. *On the Economy of Machinery and Manufactures*. London: Charles Knight.

Babcock, Charles. 1985a. "DP Personnel New Victims of Corporate Cuts," *Computerworld* (November 18):1.

———. 1985b. "On-Line Crime Suspect System Implicated in False Arrest," *Computerworld* (August 19):12.

Bacon, Donald C., and Orr Kelly. 1978. "Uncle Sam's Computer Has Got You," *U.S. News and World Report* (April 10):44–48.

Bairstow, Jeffrey N. 1985. "Chip Design Made Easy: A New Generation of Tools Enables Nonexperts to Design Custom Integrated Circuits Cheaply and Easily," *High Technology* 5,6 (June):18–25.

Bander, Edward, and Susan Sweetgall. 1983. "Westlaw and Lexis: A Comparison," in *New Technology and Law*, spring issue of *The Advocate* 14,2:9–12.

Barash, David. 1979. *The Whisperings Within: Evolution and the Origin of Human Nature*. New York: Penguin.

Barcomb, David. 1981. *Office Automation: A Survey of Tools and Techniques*. Maynard, MA: Digital Press.

Barnaby, Frank. 1982. "Microelectronics in War," in Gunter Friedrichs and Adam Schaff, eds. *Microelectronics and Society: For Better or for Worse*. New York: Pergamon Press.

Barnes, J. G. P. 1982. *Programming in Ada*. Reading, MA: Addison-Wesley.

Barnett, Richard, and Ronald E. Muller. 1974. *Global Reach*. New York: Simon and Schuster.

Baron, Naomi S. 1986. *Computer Languages: An Explorer's Guide*. New York: Doubleday.

Barr, Avron, and Edward A. Feigenbaum. 1982. *The Handbook of Artificial Intelligence*. Stanford: Heuris Tech Press.

Bartolik, Peter. 1984. "First Conviction, Jail Term Given for Copyright Violations," *Computerworld* (August 6):14.

Basden, A. 1984. "Application of Expert Systems," in M. J. Coombs, ed. *Developments in Expert Systems*. New York: Academic Press.

Bateson, Gregory. 1972. *Steps to an Ecology of Mind*. New York: Chandler.

Batt, Robert. 1984a. "Fingerprint ID System Quick to Solve Criminal Cases," *Computerworld* (March 19):25–26.

———. 1984b. "U.S. Officials Decry Japanese Copyright Plan," *Computerworld* (March 19):100.

Baum, Julian. 1985. "New Law in China to Protect Patents," *Boston Sunday Globe* (March 24):A97, A99.

Becker, George. 1978. *The Mad Genius Controversy*. Beverly Hills, CA: Sage.

Bednarzik, Robert W. 1985. "The Impact of Microelectronics on Employment: Japan's Experience," *Monthly Labor Review* 108,9 (September):45–48.

Beeler, Jeffry. 1985. "NCR User Wins $5.8 Million Suit," *Computerworld* (June 3):1.

Begley, Sharon, with Robb A. Allan. 1983. "Can Ada Run the Pentagon?" *Newsweek* (January 10):71.

Belkin, Gary S., and Norman Goodman. 1980. *Marriage, Family, and Intimate Relationships*. Chicago: Rand McNally.

Bell, C. Gordon. 1984. "The Mini and Micro Industries," *Computer* (October):14–34.

Bell, Daniel. 1980a. "The Return of the Sacred?" in *The Winding Passage*. New York: Basic Books.

———. 1980b. "The Social Framework of the Information Society," in Michael Dertouzos and Joel Moses, eds. *The Computer Age: A Twenty-Year View*. Cambridge, MA: MIT Press.

———. 1973. *The Coming of Post-Industrial Society*. New York: Basic Books.

Bendix, Reinhard. 1977. "Legal Domination: The Emergence of Legal Rationality," in *Max Weber: An Intellectual Portrait*. Berkeley: University of California Press.

―――, and Seymour Martin Lipset, eds. 1966. *Class, Status, and Power*. New York: Free Press.

Benedict, Ruth. 1934. *Patterns of Culture*. Boston: Houghton Mifflin.

Bennett, William J. 1985. "Why We Should Cut Federal Aid," *Newsweek on Campus* (April):21.

Benoit, Ellen. 1984. "Black Box Taxation," *Forbes* (August 27):66.

Berg, Ivar. 1970. *Education and Jobs: The Great Training Robbery*. New York: Praeger.

Berger, Peter. 1969. *A Rumor of Angels*. New York: Doubleday.

―――, Brigette Berger, and Hansfried Kellner. 1973. *The Homeless Mind*. New York: Random House.

Berglas, Steven. 1984. Interview in *Boston Globe* (February 6):34.

Bernal, J. D. 1939. *The Social Function of Science*. London: Routledge and Kegan Paul.

Bertoni, Phil. 1983. "Can Defense Computers be Tricked?" *Boston Globe* (July 11):37.

Betts, Mitch. 1985a. "Copyright Office Inquiry Targets Electronic Data Bases," *Computerworld* (June 24):24.

―――. 1985b. "Federal DP Crooks Profiled," *Computerworld* (July 1):2.

―――. 1985c. "Focus of NIOSH VDT Study Under Fire," *Computerworld* 14 (January):2.

―――. 1985d. "House Report Recommends No Federal VDT Regulation," *Computerworld* (September 6):26.

―――. 1985e. "VDT Shield Introduced," *Computerworld* (March 11):9.

Bic, Lubomir, and Jonathan P. Gilbert. 1986. "Learning from AI: New Trends in Database Technology," *IEEE Computer* (March):44–53.

BIFU (Banking, Insurance and Finance Union). 1982. *New Technology in Banking, Insurance and Finance*. London: BIFU.

Binford, Lewis R. 1984. *Faunal Remains from Klasies River Mouth*. Orlando, FL: Academic Press.

Binning, Gerd, and Heinrich Rohrer. 1985. "The Scanning Tunneling Microscope," *Scientific American* 253,2(August):50–56.

"Biochips: Can Molecules Compute?" 1984. *High Technology* (February 4):36.

Birren, Faber. 1978. *Color and Human Response*. New York: Van Nostrand.

Blauberg, I. V., V. N. Sadovsky, and E. G. Yudin. 1977. *Systems Theory: Philosophical and Methodological Problems*. New York: Progress Publishers.

Blauner, Robert. 1964. *Alienation and Freedom: The Factory Worker and His Industry*. Chicago: University of Chicago Press.

"Blind 'See' Tactile Screen." 1983. *Science Digest* (November):37.

Bloombecker, Jay, ed. 1984. *The Computer Crime Law Reporter*. Los Angeles: California State University.

BLS Handbook of Methods, Vol. I. 1982. U.S. Dept. of Labor, Bureau of Labor Statistics (December). Bulletin 2134–1.

Bluestone, Barry, and Bennett Harrison. 1982. *The Deindustrialization of America*. New York: Basic Books.

Blum, Harold F. 1968. "Order, Negentropy, and Evolution," in *Time's Arrow and Evolution*. Princeton, NJ: Princeton University Press.

Blum-West, Steve, and Timothy J. Carter. 1983. "Bringing White-Collar Crime Back In: An Examination of Crimes and Torts." *Social Problems* 30,5:543–54.

Blumenthal, Marjory, and Jim Dray. 1985. "The Automated Factory: Vision and Reality," *Technology Review* (January):23–37.

Boden, Margaret. 1977. *Artificial Intelligence and Natural Man*. New York: Basic Books.

Boebert, Earl, Richard Kain, and Bill Young. 1985. "Trojan Horse Rolls Up to DP Gate," *Computerworld* (December 2):65–69.

Boel, Harold, and Gustave M. Hauser. 1984. "Pro and Con: Should CATV Move Data Down the Pipes," *Computerworld on Communications* 18, 36A (September 5):7–9.

Bok, Derek. 1985. "The President's Report" (March). Cambridge, MA: Harvard University.

References

Bolt, Richard A. 1985. "Conversing With Computers," *Technology Review* (February/March):34–43.

———. 1984. *The Human Interface: Where People and Computers Meet.* Belmont, CA: Lifetime Learning Publications.

Bombeck, Erma. 1982. "Keeping Women at Home," *Boston Globe* (August 19):66.

Bonham, George W. 1983. "Computer Mania: Academe's Inadequate Response to the Implications of the New Technology," *Chronicle of Higher Education* (March 30):72.

Bosch-Font, Francisco. 1985. "Retail Banking and Technology: An Analysis of Skill Mix Transformation," Institute for Research on Educational Finance and Governance Report 85–B3. Palo Alto, CA: Stanford University School of Education.

Boserup, Ester. 1965. *The Conditions of Agricultural Growth.* Chicago: Aldine.

Bottomore, T. B. 1966. *Classes in Modern Society.* New York: Pantheon.

———, ed. 1964. *Karl Marx: Selected Readings in Sociology and Social Philosophy.* New York: McGraw-Hill.

———. 1963. *Karl Marx: Early Writings.* New York: McGraw-Hill.

Boulding, Kenneth E. 1981. "Commodities as an Evolutionary System," in *Evolutionary Economics.* Beverly Hills, CA: Sage.

Bourne, Charles P. 1977. "Computer-Based Reference Service as an Alternative Means to Improve Resource Poor Local Libraries in Developing Countries," *International Library Review* 9:43–50.

Bowles, Samuel, and Herbert Gintis. 1976. *Schooling in Capitalist America: Educational Reforms and the Contradictions of Economic Life.* New York: Basic Books.

Boyd, Robert, and Peter J. Richerson. 1985. *Culture and the Evolutionary Process.* Chicago: University of Chicago Press.

Brady, James T. 1986. "A Theory of Productivity in the Creative Process," *IEEE Computer Graphics* (May):25–34.

Braidwood, Robert J. "The Agricultural Revolution," *Scientific American* 203, 3 (September 1960):130–48.

Brand, Stewart, Kevin Kelly, and Jay Kinney. 1985. "Digital Retouching: The End of Photography as Evidence of Anything," *Whole Earth Review* 47 (July):42–50.

Branscomb, Anne W. 1983. "Communication Policy in the United States: Diversity and Pluralism in a Competitive Marketplace," in Patricia Edgar and Syed A. Rahim, eds. *Communication Policy in Developed Societies.* Boston: Kegan Paul International.

Braudel, Fernand. 1981. *The Structures of Everyday Life: Civilization and Capitalism, 15th–18th Century.* New York: Harper and Row.

Braun, Ernest, and Stuart Mcdonald. 1978. *Revolution in Miniature: The History and Impact of Semiconductor Electronics.* London: Cambridge University Press.

Braverman, Harry. 1974. *Labor and Monopoly Capital: The Degradation of Work in the Twentieth Century.* New York: Monthly Review Press.

Brod, Craig. 1984. *Technostress.* Reading, MA: Addison-Wesley.

Brooks, Frederick P., Jr. 1982. *The Mythical Man-Month: Essays on Software Engineering.* Reading, MA: Addison-Wesley.

Brownstein, Henry H. 1984. "How I Contacted a Human Form Through My Computer," *The Humanist Sociologist* 9,4 (December):5–7.

Bruner, Jerome S. 1966. *Toward a Theory of Instruction.* Cambridge, MA: Harvard University Press.

———. 1962. *On Knowing: Essays for the Left Hand.* Cambridge, MA: Harvard University Press.

Brutzkus, E. 1980. "The Technological Advance Beyond the Optimum," *Ekistics* 47 (September):384–89.

Buckley, Walter. 1967. *Sociology and Modern Systems Theory.* Englewood Cliffs, NJ: Prentice-Hall.

Bulkeley, William M. 1984. "Software Firms Urge Big Buyers to Curb Illegal Copying of Programs by Employees," *Wall Street Journal* (October 23):31.

"Bulletin Boards Target of Crime Legislation?" 1985. *Computerworld* (July 1):23.

Burch, John L., ed. 1984. *Computers: The Non-Technological (Human) Factors: Recommended Reading List on Computer Ergonomics and User-Friendly Design.* Lawrence, KS: The Report Store.

Burgan, John U. 1985. "Cyclical Behavior of High Tech Industries," *Monthly Labor Review* 108,5 (May):9–15.

Burke, J. G., ed. 1966. *The New Technology and Human Values.* Belmont, CA: Wadsworth.

Burnham, David. 1985. "Computer Called Peril to U.S. Record Keeping," *New York Times* (March 6):A11.

————. 1984. "FBI May Test Computer Index for White-Collar Crime Inquiries," *New York Times* (October 25):A1,B17.

————. 1983. *The Rise of the Computer State.* New York: Random House.

Burton, K. 1985. "Studies Relate Birth Defects to High-Tech Toxins in Water," *Computerworld* (January 28):84.

Bushnell, Davis. 1985. "Texext's Technology Aimed at Publishing," *Boston Globe* (August 19):34–36.

Butner, Marion. 1982. "Computerized Big Brother: From a German Perspective," *Science for the People* 15,2 (March/April):6–13.

Cakir, A., D. J. Hart, and T. F. M. Stewart. 1980. *Video Display Terminals: A Manual Covering Ergonomics, Workplace Design, Health and Safety, Task Organization.* New York: Interscience.

Calder, Nigel. 1970. *Technopolis: Social Control of the Uses of Science.* New York: Clarion Books.

California Newsreel. 1981. *New Technology: Whose Progress?* (Color, 40 minutes, 16mm). San Francisco.

Calvin, William H. 1983. *The Throwing Madonna: Essays on the Brain.* New York: McGraw-Hill.

"Campaigns and Computers." 1982–83. Special section of articles in *Campaigns and Elections* beginning with 3,3 (Fall).

Campbell, Patricia, and George McCabe. 1984. "Predicting the Success of Freshmen in a Computer Science Major," *Communications of the ACM* 27,11 (November):1108–13.

Capra, Fritjof. 1982. *The Turning Point.* New York: Bantam Books.

Carim, D. Enver. 1983. "Coming to Grips with the New Technology," in *Africa's Computer Revolution*, special issue of *African Business* 58 (June):9.

Carlson, Sune. 1974. "International Transmission of Information and the Business Firm," in *The Information Revolution*, special issue of *The Annals of the American Academy of Political and Social Science* (March):55–63.

Carroll, John M., and Caroline Carrithers. 1984. "Training Wheels in a User Interface," *Communications of the ACM* (August):800–806.

Cass, Christopher. 1985. "Linking Computer Technology with Plastic Modelling to Produce Quality-Assured Piping Drawings," paper presented to the American Engineering Model Society, Boston (May).

Cassedy, Ellen, and Karen Nussbaum. 1983. *Nine To Five: The Working Woman's Guide to Office Survival.* New York: Penguin.

Castleman, Barry I. 1985. "The Double Standard in Industrial Hazards," in Jane H. Ives, ed. *The Export of Hazards.* Boston: Routledge and Kegan Paul.

CBEMA (Computer and Business Equipment Manufacturers Association). 1985. "Guide to the Draft American National Standard for Human Factors Engineering of Visual Display Terminals." CBEMA, 311 First St., NW, Washington, DC 20001.

Chamberlain, Tony. 1983. "Computers at Sea," *Technology Review* (October):70–77.

Chandler, David L. 1985. "Tools of Science Now 'Artists' Brushes,' " *Boston Globe* (March 25):37–39.

Chang, Keith Y. 1985. "Microcomputer Graphics and Applications with NAPLPS Videotex," *IEEE Computer Graphics and Applications* 5,6 (June):21–33.

Chaum, David. 1985. "Security Without Identification: Transaction Systems to Make Big Brother Obsolete," *Communications of the ACM* 28,10:1030–44.

References

Cherry, Colin. 1977. "The Telephone System: Creator of Mobility and Social Change," in Ithiel de Sola Pool, ed. *The Social Impact of the Telephone*. Cambridge, MA: MIT Press.
———. 1966. *On Human Communication*. Cambridge, MA: MIT Press.
"Chinese/Kanji Text and Data Processing." 1985. Special issue of *IEEE Computer* 18,1 (January).
Chinlund, C. 1984. "High-Tech: New Products, New Hazards," *Boston Globe* (July 23):35–37.
Chirot, Daniel. 1977. *Social Change in the Twentieth Century*. New York: Harcourt Brace Jovanovich.
Chizeck, Howard Jay. 1985. "Helping Paraplegics Walk: Looking Beyond the Media Blitz," *Technology Review* 88,5 (July):54–63.
Chodorow, Nancy. 1978. *The Reproduction of Mothering: Psychoanalysis and the Sociology of Gender*. Berkeley: University of California Press.
Chorover, Stephan L. 1980. *From Genesis to Genocide*. Cambridge, MA: MIT Press.
Chronicle of Higher Education. 1983. (June 8):9, 25.
"Churches Move into the Computer Age." 1984. *Boston Globe* (August 6):5.
Cleveland, William S., and Robert McGill. 1985. "Graphical Perception and Graphical Methods for Analyzing Scientific Data," *Science* 229 (August 30):828–33.
Clinard, Marshall B., and Peter C. Yeager. 1980. *Corporate Crime*. New York: Free Press.
Clubb, Oliver. 1985. *KAL Flight 007: The Hidden Story*. New York: Permanent Press.
Codd, E. F. 1982. "Relational Database: A Practical Foundation for Productivity," *Communications of the ACM* 25, 2(February):109–17.
Cohen, I. Bernard. 1985. *Revolution in Science*. Cambridge, MA: Harvard University Press.
Collier, William L., Gunawan Wiradi, and Soentoro. 1973. "Recent Changes in Rice Harvesting Methods," *Bulletin of Indonesian Economic Studies* 9(2):36–45.
Collins, Randall. 1985. *Three Sociological Traditions*. New York: Oxford University Press.
———. 1979. *The Credential Society*. New York: Academic Press.
Common Cause. 1983. Special issue, "Are Americans Getting the Government They Want?" 9,3(May/June).
Computer and Mathematics-Related Professions. 1984. Bureau of Labor Statistics, #2205–4.
"Computer Encryption and the National Security Connection." 1977. *Science* 29 (July):438–40.
"Computer Password Is a Well-Kept Secret." 1986. *New York Times* (February 13):A14.
"Computer Software." 1984. Special issue of *Scientific American* (September).
"A Computer-Aided Robotic Arm/Worktable System for the Higher-Level Quadriplegic." 1981. *IEEE Spectrum* (January):41–47.
"Computers and Dossiers." 1982. *Texas Law Review*. Reprinted in Dennie Van Tassel and Cynthia Van Tassel, eds. *The Compleat Computer*. Chicago: Science Research Associates, 1983.
"The Computers of Summer." 1983. *Newsweek* (May 23):55.
Congressional Record. 1985. 131 (No. 1, part II), S186 (January 3).
Connolly, James. 1985. "Patent Disputes, Hacking Major DP Law Issues in '85," *Computerworld* (January 21):14.
Conrad, Thomas. 1986. "Computing Apartheid," *CPSR (Computer Professionals for Social Responsibility) Newsletter* (Spring):5–8.
———. 1982. "U.S. Data Processing Corporations Are Supplying South Africa with the Brains of its Military and Police Services," *Multinational Monitor* 3,4:1–14.
Cooke, Robert. 1982. "A Brouhaha at Paris Research Center," *Boston Globe* (December 3):3.
Cooley, Mike. 1980. *Architect or Bee? The Human/Technology Relationship*. Boston: South End Press.
Coombs, M. J., ed. 1984. *Developments in Expert Systems*. New York: Academic Press.
Coons, Phyllis. 1983. "Hub Teachers Prepare to Enter Computer Era," *Boston Globe* (April 17):B72.
Corn, David. 1985. "Media Cool Aid," *In These Times* (July 24–August 6):23,24.
Coser, Lewis. 1956. *The Functions of Social Conflict*. New York: Free Press.
Coser, Lewis, Charles Kadushin, and Walter W. Powell. 1982. *Books: The Culture and Commerce of Publishing*. Chicago: University of Chicago Press.

Cottrell, Paul, and Barry D. Weiss. 1984. "Third Party Liability Insurance Protection in Case of Computer Error," *Computerworld* (April 2):ID/1–ID/7.

Couger, J. Daniel. 1985. "Motivating Maintenance Personnel," *Computerworld* (August 12):ID/5–14.

Coughlin, Ellen K. 1985. "Proposed Rules on Government Data Worry Librarians and Scholars," *Chronicle of Higher Education* (June 12):11.

———. 1983. "Publishers Alarmed by Government Plan to Review Manuscripts for Possible Leaks," *Chronicle of Higher Education* (June 8):25.

Cowan, Ruth Schwartz. 1976. " 'The Industrial Revolution' in the Home: Household Technology and Social Change in the Twentieth Century," *Technology and Culture* 17,1 (January):1–23.

Cox, Archibald. 1981. *Freedom of Expression*. Cambridge, MA: Harvard University Press.

Cox, Harvey. 1984. *Religion in the Secular City*. New York: Simon and Schuster.

CPSR (Computer Professionals for Social Responsibility). 1984. "The Strategic Computing Initiative: An Assessment," *The CPSR Newsletter* (June):1–4.

Csikszentmihalyi, Mihaly, and Reed Larson. 1984. *Being Adolescent: Conflict and Growth in the Teenage Years*. New York: Basic Books.

Culliton, Barbara. 1985a. "Court Rules in Patient Privacy Case," *Science* (July 26):360–61.

———. 1985b. "New Curriculum at Harvard Medical School," *Science* (January 11):153.

d'Agapeyeff, Alex. 1984. Quoted in *Computer* 17, 12 (December):106.

Dahl, Robert A. 1985. *A Preface to Economic Democracy*. Berkeley: University of California Press.

Danziger, James N., William H. Dutton, Rob Kling, and Kenneth L. Kraemer. 1982. *Computers and Politics: High Technology in Local Government*. New York: Columbia University Press.

Darwin, Charles. 1859. *The Origin of Species by Means of Natural Selection*. London: J. Murray.

Davies, D. W., and W. L. Price. 1984. *Security for Computer Networks*. New York: Wiley.

Davis, David B. 1985. *Slavery and Human Progress*. New York: Oxford University Press.

Davis, Kingsley. 1949. *Human Society*. New York: Macmillan.

Deken, Joseph. 1983. *Computer Images*. New York: Stewart, Tabori, and Chang.

———. 1981. *The Electronic Cottage*. New York: Bantam.

Dery, David. 1981. *Computers in Welfare*. Beverly Hills, CA: Sage.

Desmond, John. 1985a. "Crime Survey Indicts 'Insiders,' " *Computerworld* (June 10):2.

———. 1985b. "Language Barrier: The Fourth Generation at Work," *Computerworld* (November 11):1,55,61–62.

———. 1985c. "Live Aid Hunger Fund Profits from Donated System's Speed," *Computerworld* (July 29):10.

———. 1985d. "Union Carbide Modeling Program Given Wrong Data," *Computerworld* (August 19):6.

Desruisseaux, Paul. 1984. "Growth is Explosive in Corporations' Gifts of Equipment," *Chronicle of Higher Education* (November 21):1,11.

Deutsch, Karl W. 1966. *The Nerves of Government: Models of Political Communication and Control*. New York: Free Press.

Diamond, Edwin, Norman Sandler, and Milton Mueller. 1983. *Telecommunications in Crisis: The First Amendment, Technology, and Deregulation*. Washington, DC: Cato Institute.

Diebold, John. 1984. Findings reported at the World Conference on Ergonomics in Computer Systems, New York (September 27).

The Diebold Group. 1984. Findings reported in *Proceedings of the World Conference on Ergonomics in Computer Systems*. Garden Grove, CA: Ericsson Communications.

Dince, Robert. 1983. "How to Diddle," *Fortune* (September 5):155.

Dixon, Marlene, Susanne Jones, and Ed McCaughan. 1982. "Reindustrialization and the Transnational Labor Force in the United States Today," *Contemporary Marxism* 5:101–15.

Dolnick, Edward. 1985. "Study Links Cancer, Microwave Radiation," *Boston Globe* (March 15):1.

References

————. 1984. "We Won't All Be in High-Tech," *Boston Globe* (August 20):41–42.

Domhoff, G. William. 1983. *Who Rules America Now? A View for the Eighties.* Englewood Cliffs, NJ: Prentice-Hall.

Dooley, Martin, and Peter Gottschalk. 1985. "The Increasing Proportion of Men with Low Earnings in the United States," *Demography* 22,1(February):25–34.

Dougherty, Linda, and Melanie Janowsky. 1984. "High-Tech Houses Divided on Foreign Threat," *Boston Business Journal* (March 26–April 1):3.

Douglas, John H. 1983. "Electronic Publishing Takes Off," *High Technology* (June):24–26.

Douglas, M., and A. Wildavsky. 1982. *Risk and Culture.* Berkeley: University of California Press.

Dowie, Mark. 1983. "Coca-Cola Democracy," *Mother Jones* (June):9.

Downing, Hazel. 1981. "Word Processors and the Oppression of Women," in Tom Forester, ed. *The Microelectronics Revolution.* Cambridge, MA: MIT Press.

Doyle, James A. 1985. *Sex and Gender.* Dubuque, IA: William C. Brown.

Dozier, David M., Susana A. Hellweg, and John A. Ledingham. 1983. "Implications of Interactive Cable Systems: Reduced Consumer Contact," in Robert N. Bostrom, ed. *Communication Yearbook 7.* Beverly Hills, CA: Sage.

Drake, Elisabeth, and Judith A. Perrolle. 1984. "Computer-Aided Creativity." Presentation to the American Society of Chemical Engineers, Atlanta (March).

Dreyfus, Hubert L. 1972. *What Computers Can't Do.* New York: Harper and Row.

————, and Stuart Dreyfus. 1986. *Mind Over Machine: The Power of Human Intuition and Expertise in the Era of the Computer.* New York: Free Press.

Drucker, Peter F. 1985. "Playing in the Information-Based 'Orchestra'," *The Wall Street Journal* (June 4):32–33.

Dubinskas, Frank A. 1985. "The Cultural Chasm: Scientists and Managers in Genetic–Engineering Firms," *Technology Review* 88,4 (May/June):24–30,74.

Durkheim, Emile. 1965. *The Elementary Forms of Religious Life.* New York: Free Press.

————. 1957. *Professional Ethics and Civic Morals.* London: Routledge and Kegan Paul.

————. 1933. *The Division of Labor in Society.* New York: Free Press.

"Ears to Technology!" 1986. *Electronic Education* (April):10–11.

Edel, Matthew. 1973. "Economics and Ecology," in *Economies and the Environment.* Englewood Cliffs, NJ: Prentice-Hall.

Ehrbar, A. F. 1983. "Grasping the New Unemployment," *Fortune* (May 16):106.

Eimbinder, Jerry, and Eric Eimbinder. 1982. "Videogame History," *Radio-Electronics* (July):50–4.

Eisenscher, Michael. 1984. *Silicon Valley: A Digest of Electronics Data.* San Jose, CA: Michael Eisenscher.

Eisenstadt, S. N. 1971. *Social Differentiation and Stratification.* Glenview, IL: Scott Foresman.

"Electrical Engineers Not Happy." 1984. *Boston Globe* (May 15):**pp. no.**

Elkin, Frederick, and Gerald Handel. 1978. *The Child and Society,* 3rd ed. New York: Random House.

Ellul, Jacques. 1964. *The Technological Society.* New York: Knopf.

Emmett, Arnelle. 1984. "Telecommuting: The Home to Office Link," *Personal Computing* (April):77–87,162.

Engels, Frederich. 1942. *The Origin of the Family, Private Property and the State.* New York: International Publishers.

Environmental Protection Agency. 1985. *Risk Assessment and Risk Management: Framework for Decisionmaking.* Washington, DC: U.S. Government Printing Office.

Ericsson Information Systems. 1984. *Proceedings of the World Conference on Ergonomics in Computer Systems.* (September.) Garden Grove, CA: Ericsson Communications.

Erikson, Erik. 1964. *Childhood and Society.* New York: Norton.

Erikson, Kai T. 1976. *Everything in Its Path.* New York: Simon and Schuster.

Erlich, Paul R., Carl Sagan, Donald Kennedy, and Walter Orr. 1984. *The Cold and the Dark: The World After Nuclear War.* New York: Norton.

Ernst, Dieter. 1983. "The Impact of Microelectronics on the Worldwide Restructuring of the Electronics Industry: Implications for the Third World," *IDOC Bulletin* 3–4:5–11.

Ervin, Sam, Jr. 1983. "Justice, the Constitution, and Privacy," in Dennie Van Tassel and Cynthia L. Van Tassel, eds. *The Compleat Computer.* Chicago: Science Research Associates.

Evan, William M. 1981. *Knowledge and Power in a Global Society.* Beverly Hills, CA: Sage.

Evans, B. O. 1980. "Computers and Communications," in Michael Dertouzos and Joel Moses, eds. *The Computer Age: A Twenty-Year View.* Cambridge, MA: MIT Press.

Everett, Melissa. 1983. "Education: Stemming the Math Science Brain Drain," *Cambridge Express* (Massachusetts) 14(May):9,15.

Everhart, Robert B. 1984. *The Public School Monopoly: A Critical Analysis of Education and the State in American Society.* San Francisco: Pacific Institute for Public Policy Research.

Ewen, S. 1976. *Captains of Industry: Advertising and the Social Roots of Consumer Culture.* New York: McGraw-Hill.

"The FBI Goes High Tech." 1982. *Newsweek* 15(November):56.

Feigenbaum, Edward. 1984. Lecture at the Massachusetts Institute of Technology, October 31.

Feigenbaum, Edward, and Pamela McCorduck. 1983. *The Fifth Generation: Artificial Intelligence and Japan's Computer Challenge to the World.* Reading, MA: Addison-Wesley.

Feiner, Steven. 1985. "APEX: An Experiment in the Automated Creation of Pictorial Images," *Computer Graphics and Applications* (November):29–37.

Fersko–Weiss, Henry. 1985. "The Side Effects of Electronic Mail," *Personal Computing* (January):72.

FIET (International Federation of Commercial, Clerical, Professional and Technical Employees). 1980. *Bank Workers and New Technology.* Geneva: FIRT.

"The Fight Against Paralysis." 1982. *Newsweek* (October 18):102–6.

"Firms Take Different Routes to Curtail Software Piracy." 1985. *Computerworld* (February 4):6.

Fischer, Dennis K. 1985. "The Last Starfighter: A Computer Revolution in Special Effects," *Cinefantastique* 15,1(January):24–36.

Fisher, Arthur. 1985. "New Languages for Old," *Mosaic* 16,3:18–25.

Fisher, Sarah, and Steven Pulos. 1985. "Adolescent Interests in Computers: The Role of Self-Concept, Attitude, and Socio-Economic Status," *Global Electronics* 59:4.

"Footnotes." 1983. *Chronicle of Higher Education* (August 3):21.

Forester, Tom, ed. 1981. *The Microelectronics Revolution.* Cambridge, MA: MIT Press.

Forrester, Jay. 1967. Speech at the NAE fall meeting, Washington, DC. Cited in Nigel Calder. *Technopolis: Social Control of the Uses of Science.* New York: Clarion Books, 1970.

Foster, Kenneth R. 1986. "The VDT Debate," *American Scientist* (March–April):163–68.

Foucault, Michael. 1984. "What Is an Author?" in Paul Rabinow, ed. *The Foucault Reader.* New York: Pantheon.

Fox, David, and Mitchell Waite. 1984. *Computer Animation Primer.* New York: McGraw-Hill.

Fox, L. 1977. "The Effects of Sex-Role Socialization on Mathematics Participation and Achievement," in L. Fox, E. Fennema, and J. Sherman, eds. *Women in Mathematics: Research Perspectives for Change.* Washington, DC: NIE.

Fox, M., M. Greenberg, A. Sathi, J. Mattis, and M. Rychener. 1983. "Callisto: An Intelligent Project Management System," technical report, Intelligent Systems Laboratory, Robotics Institute, Carnegie Mellon University, Pittsburgh (November).

Fox, Stephen. 1984. *The Mirror Makers: A History of American Advertising and Its Creators.* New York: Vintage.

Frank, Ronald E. 1985. "Coexisting with Corporate Classrooms," *Chronicle of Higher Education* (August 14):31.

Frantzich, Stephen E. 1982. *Computers in Congress: The Politics of Information.* Beverly Hills, CA: Sage.

Frederick, Sharon. 1983. "More Older Engineers: Stuck in the Rut of Mid-career," *Boston Globe* (May 23):B21.

Freiberg, J. W. 1981. *The French Press: Class, State, and Ideology.* New York: Praeger.

Freifeld, Karen. 1984. "Obsoleting the Scalpel," *Fortune* (August 27):130.

Frenkel, Karen A. 1985. "Toward Automating the Software-Development Cycle," *Communications of the ACM* 28,6 (June):578–89.

Frenzen, Donald. 1985. "Letter to the Editor," *Science* (August 9):512.

Freud, Sigmund (James Strathey, tr.). 1922. *Civilization and Its Discontents*. London: Hogarth Press.

Freyer, Felice. 1983. "Overdue Process: The Evolution of Computer Law," *Boston Phoenix* (May 10): section 4, 18.

Friedmann, G. 1961. *The Anatomy of Work*. London: Heinemann.

Fromkin, Victoria, and Roberta Rodman. 1983. *An Introduction to Language*. New York: Holt, Rinehart and Winston.

Fruchter, Norm. 1983. "Quality of Education Reports Attack the Wrong Problems," *In These Times* (July 27–August 9):17.

Gallant, John. 1984. "Supreme Court May OK New Way to Fight Pirates," *Computerworld* (April 30):4.

Galyean, Beverley-Colleene. 1983. "The Use of Guided Imagery in Elementary and Secondary Schools," *Imagination, Cognition, and Personality* 2,2:145–51.

Gannes, Stuart. 1986. "Marketing Is the Message at McGraw-Hill," *Fortune* (February 17):34–37.

———. 1985. "The Soviet Lag in High-Tech Defense," *Fortune* (November 25):107–20.

Gasparello, Linda. 1980. "Drought in Silicon Valley?" *Forbes* (November 10):66–67.

Gaus, Andy. 1984. "Program Notes: Software Systems for Writing Music," *Boston Globe* (January 30):23.

Geller, Henry. 1986. "Telecommunications Policy," *Issues in Science and Technology* (Winter):30–37.

Gemignani, Michael. 1985. "Who Owns What Software Produces?" *IEEE Software* (September):48–52.

"The Gender Gap: High-Tech Is No Different." 1984. *Boston Globe* (June 19):4.

"A Generation Meets Computers on the Playing Fields of Atari." 1981. *Smithsonian* 12 (September):50–61.

Gerbner, George, and Marsha Seifert, eds. 1984. *World Communications: A Handbook*. New York: Longman.

Ghiglieri, Michael P. 1985. "The Social Ecology of Chimpanzees," *Scientific American* (June):102–14.

Ghiselin, Brewster, ed. 1952. *The Creative Process*. New York: Mentor.

Giddens, Anthony. 1971. *Capitalism and Modern Social Theory*. Cambridge: Cambridge University Press.

Gideon, Siegfried. 1982. *Mechanization Takes Command*. New York: Norton.

Giuliano, V. 1982. "The Mechanization of Office Work," *Scientific American* 247,3 (September):148–65.

Glass, Robert L. 1985. "Software Theft," *IEEE Software* (July):82–85.

Glatzer, Hal. 1983. *The Birds of Babel: Satellites for the Human World*. Indianapolis: Howard W. Sams.

Glossbrenner, Alfred. 1984. *The Complete Handbook of Personal Computer Communications*. New York: St. Martin's Press.

Goldberg, Roberta. 1983. *Organizing Women Office Workers: Dissatisfaction, Consciousness, and Action*. New York: Praeger.

Goldstine, Herman H. 1972. *The Computer: From Pascal to Von Neumann*. Princeton, NJ: Princeton University Press.

Goldstone, Jack A., ed. 1986. *Revolutions: Theoretical, Comparative, and Historical Studies*. New York: Harcourt Brace Jovanovich.

Goldthorpe, John. 1982. "On the Service Class, Its Formation and Future," in Anthony Giddens and Gavin Mackensie, eds. *Social Class and the Division of Labor*. New York: Cambridge University Press.

Goldwasser, Samuel M., R. Anthony Reynolds, Ted Bapty, David Baraff, John Summers, David A. Talton, and Ed Walsh. 1985. "Physician's Workstation sith Real-Time Performance," *Computer Graphics and Applications* (December):41–57.

Good, Michael D., John A. Whiteside, Dennis R. Wixon, and Sandra J. Jones. 1984.

"Building a User-Derived Interface," *Communications of the ACM* 27,10 (October):1032–43.

Goode, William J. 1970. *World Revolution and Family Patterns*. New York: Free Press.

Goodman, S. E. 1982. "U.S. Computer Export Control Policy: Value Conflicts and Policy Choices," *Communications of the ACM* 25,9 (September):613–24.

Goody, J., and I. Watt. 1962–1963. "The Consequences of Literacy," *Comparative Studies in Society and History* 5:304–45.

Gorstein, Daniel. 1985. "The Enormous Theorem," *Scientific American* 253,6 (December):104–15.

Goslin, David A., ed. 1969. *Handbook of Socialization Theory and Research*. Chicago: Rand McNally.

Gottfried, Heidi. 1982. "Keeping the Workers in Line," *Science for the People* 14,4 (July, August):19–24.

Gough, Kathleen. 1980. "The Origin of the Family," in Arlene Skolnick and Jerome Skolnick, eds. *Family in Transition*. Boston: Little, Brown.

Gould, Steven Jay. 1980. "Our Greatest Evolutionary Step," in Steven Jay Gould. *The Panda's Thumb*. New York: Norton.

Gouldner, Alvin W. 1979. *The Future of Intellectuals and the Rise of the New Class*. New York: Seabury Press.

————. 1976. *The Dialectic of Ideology and Technology*. New York: Oxford University Press.

Gourlay, John S. 1986. "A Language for Music Printing," *Communications of the ACM* (May):388–401.

Graber, Doris A. 1984. *Processing the News: How People Tame the Information Tide*. New York: Longman.

Graham, Robert L., and A. A. J. Hoffman. 1984. "The Legal Protection of Computer Software," *Communications of the ACM* 27:5 (May):422–26.

Green, Cynthia. 1985. "Middle Managers are Still Sitting Ducks," *Business Week* (September 16):34.

Greenberg, Clement. 1961. *Art and Culture*. Boston: Beacon Press.

Greene, U.S. District Judge Harold H. 1983. "Opinion of July 8," *United States v. AT&T: Court Documents, 1974–1984*. Frederick, MD: University Publications of America, Inc. 35mm microfilm (30 reels).

Greenfield, Patricia. 1983. "Video Games and Cognitive Skills," *Video Games and Human Development: Research Agenda for the 80's*. Papers and proceedings of a symposium held at the Harvard Graduate School of Education, May 22–24. Cambridge, MA: 19–24.

Gregory, R. L. 1981. "Eye and Brain Machines," in *Eve and Brain*, 3rd ed. New York: McGraw-Hill.

Grove, Andrew. 1983. "Breaking the Chains of Command," *Newsweek* (October 3):23.

Grundy, Richard D. 1978. "Radiation Exposures from Consumer Electronic Products," in Samuel S. Epstein and Richard D. Grundy, eds. *Consumer Health and Product Hazards, Volume 1 of the Legislation of Product Safety*. Cambridge, MA: MIT Press.

Gunter, Laura Jo. 1984. "CCDA Statistics Show 90% of Canada's Programs Illegal," *Computerworld* (December 17):18.

Guster, Dennis. 1985. Study reported in *Computerworld* (February 25):35.

Haavind, Robert. 1983. "Fast Action Needed in Upgrading Factories," *High Technology* (July):2.

Haber, Lynn. 1984. "CATV Future as Communications Service Seen Dim," *Computerworld* (May 14):33.

Habermas, Jurgen. 1979. *Communication and the Evolution of Society*. Boston: Beacon Press.

Hales, Michael. 1980. *Living Thinkwork*. London: CSE Books.

Hall, Edward T. 1983. *The Dance of Life: The Other Dimension of Time*. New York: Doubleday.

————. 1977. *Beyond Culture*. New York: Doubleday Anchor.

Hampden-Turner, Charles. 1982. *Maps of the Mind*. New York: Collier.

Hampson, Norman. 1968. *The Enlightenment*. Harmondsworth, Middlesex, England: Penguin Books.

Hardin, Garrett. 1968. "The Tragedy of the Common," *Science* (December 13):1243–48.

Harlan, Jack R. 1976. "The Plants and Animals That Nourish Man." *Scientific American* 235,3(September):89–97.

Harvey, S. M. 1984. "Electric-Field Exposure of Persons Using Video Display Units," *Bioelectromagnetics* 5:1–12.

Haugeland, John, ed. 1981. *Mind Design*. Cambridge, MA: MIT Press.

Hawkins, L. H. 1984. "The Possible Benefits of Negative-Ion Generators," in Brian Pearce, ed. *Health Hazards of VDT's?* New York: Wiley.

Hawkinson, Suzanne. 1980. "Computer Poetry," in *Likenesses*. Lexington, MA: Solo Press.

Hayes-Roth, Frederick. 1984. "The Knowledge-Based Expert System: A Tutorial," *IEEE Computer* 17,9 (September):11–28.

———. 1983. Roundtable discussion at Carnegie-Mellon (June 3) reported in *IEEE Spectrum* (November):114–15.

Hayes-Roth, Frederick, Donald A. Waterman, and Douglas B. Lenat, eds. 1983. *Building Expert Systems*. Reading, MA: Addison-Wesley.

Heaton, Thomas H. 1985. "A Model for a Seismic Computerized Alert Network," *Science* (May 24):987–90.

Heise, David R., and Roberta G. Simmons. 1985. "Some Computer-Based Developments in Sociology," *Science* 228,4698 (April 26):428–33.

Helander, Martin G., Patricia A. Billingsey, and Jayne M. Schurick. 1984. "An Evaluation of Human Factors Research on Video Display Terminals in the Workplace," in *Human Factors Review: 1984*. Santa Monica, CA: Human Factors Society.

Henderson, Hazel. 1974. "Information and the New Movements for Citizen Participation," *The Information Revolution*, special issue of *Annals of the American Academy of Political and Social Science* (March):34–43.

Higgins, Richard. 1985a. "A New Window into Living Cells: Video-Enhanced Microscope Allows Study of Chemical Movement Inside Neurons," *Boston Globe* (August 12):37.

———. 1985b. "Soviets Plan to Usher Students into Computer Age," *Boston Globe* (August 18):3.

"High Tech and the Schools." 1983. *Dollars and Sense* 87 (May/June):6–7, 18.

"High Tech Hatred." 1984. *Newsweek* (December 24):19.

The High-Tech Research Group. 1984. *Massachusetts High-Tech: The Promise and the Reality*. Somerville, MA: The High-Tech Research Group.

Hiltz, Starr Roxanne. 1984. *On Line Communities: A Case Study of the Office of the Future*. Norwood, NJ: Ablex.

Hiltz, Starr Roxanne, and Murray Turnoff. 1985. "Structuring Computer-Mediated Communication Systems to Avoid Information Overload," *Communications of the ACM* 28,7(July):680–89.

Hirota, Patty. 1983. "New Police Technologies," *Science for the People* (March/April):25–29.

Hirschhorn, Larry. 1984. *Beyond Mechanization: Work and Technology in a Postindustrial Age*. Cambridge, MA: MIT Press.

Hoare, C. A. R. 1981. "The Emperor's Old Clothes," *Communications of the ACM* 24, 2 (February):75–83.

Hobsbawn, E. J. 1968. "The Origins of the Industrial Revolution," in *Industry and Empire*. London: Pelican.

Holden, Constance. 1985. "Surveillance Laws Need Overhaul," *Science* (November 8):645.

Hollands, Jean. 1984. *The Silicon Syndrome: A Survival Handbook for Couples*. Palo Alto, CA: Coastlight Press.

Hopper, Grace. 1959. "Automatic Programming: Present Status and Future Trends," in National Physical Laboratory, 1959:155–94. London: Her Majesty's Stationery Office.

Hornig, Lilli S., et al. 1985. "Women in Technology," *Technology Review* 87,8:29–52.

Horowitz, Ellis, Alfons Kemper, and Balaji Narasimhan. 1985. "A Survey of Application Generators," *IEEE Software* (January):40–54.

Howard, Robert. 1985. "Utopia: Where Workers Craft New Technology," *Technology Review* (April):42–49.

Hughes, T. Lee. 1983. "GOP to Use Computers at Dallas Convention," *Boston Globe* (August 16):10.

Huizinga, Jehan. 1980. *Homo Ludens: A Study of the Play Element in Culture*. London: Routledge and Kegan Paul.

Human Factors Society. 1985. "American National Standard for Human Factors Engineering of Visual Display Terminal Workstations," Review draft available from Human Factors Society, P.O. Box 1369, Santa Monica, CA 90406.

Humphrey, C., and F. Buttel. 1982. "The Sociology of the 'Limits to Growth Debate,' " in *Environment, Energy, and Society*. Belmont, CA: Wadsworth.

"Hunan Research Institute of Electronics has Announced an English–Chinese–Japanese Dot Matrix Printer." 1985. *Computerworld* (February 4):24.

Hutchins, Edwin. 1983. "Understanding Micronesian Navigation," in Dedre Getner and Albert L. Stevens, *Mental Models*. Hillsdale, NY: Lawrence Erlbaum Associates, Publishers.

Hydebrand, Wolf V. 1983. "Technocratic Corporatism: Toward a Theory of Occupational and Organizational Transformation," in Richard H. Hall and Robert E. Quinn, eds. *Organizational Theory and Public Policy*. Beverly Hills, CA: Sage.

Hyman, Anthony. 1982. *Charles Babbage: Pioneer of the Computer*. Princeton, NJ: Princeton University Press.

Hyman, A. 1980. *The Coming of the Chip*. New York: New English Library.

IBM. 1982. "The Economic Value of Rapid Response Time," document GE 20 0752-0 (November).

"IBM, Digital to give MIT $50-Million to Develop Computerized Curriculum." 1983. *Chronicle of Higher Education* 8 (June):1,8.

"Impact of Microcomputer on Devices to Aid the Handicapped." 1981. *IEEE Spectrum* (January):35.

"Industry Suffers with Salary Gap." 1985. *Computerworld* (February 18):40.

"INS to Use Social Security Rolls to Find Illegal Aliens." 1983. *Philippine News* (March 1): 1–2.

International Data Corporation. 1984a. "Personal Computing: Productivity Tool for Business," *Fortune* (January 23):97–150.

———. 1984b. "Trends in Computing: Systems and Services for the 80's," *Fortune* (July 9):129–30.

Jacobs, Jane. 1961. *The Death and Life of the Great American Cities*. New York: Vintage.

Jaques, Elliott. 1985. Work reported in *Fortune* (February 4):127–28.

Jencks, Christopher, et al. 1972. *Inequality: A Reassessment of the Effect of Family and Schooling in America*. New York: Basic Books.

Jenkins, Martha M. 1979. "Computer-Generated Evidence Specially Prepared for Use at Trial," in William E. Cwiklo, ed. *Computers in Litigation Support*. New York: Petrocelli.

Jensh, R. P., I. Weinberg, and R. L. Brent. 1982. "Teratologic Studies of Prenatal Exposure of Rats to 915-MHz Microwave Radiation," *Radiation Research* 92:160–71.

Jervis, Simon. 1984. "Introduction," in *Dictionary of Design and Designers*. Harmondsworth, Middlesex, England: Penguin.

Johnson, Deborah G., and John W. Snapper, eds. 1984. *Ethical Issues in the Use of Computers*. Belmont, CA: Wadsworth.

Johnson, Gib. 1985. "Forsaking Film for Advertising," *Boston Globe* (November 3):B1, B5.

Johnson, Tim. 1984. *The Commercial Application of Expert Systems Technology*. London: Ovum.

Jones, Barry. 1982. *Sleepers Wake! Technology and the Future of Work*. London: Oxford University Press.

Jones, Ernest. 1961. *The Life and Work of Sigmund Freud*. New York: Basic Books.

Kalaghan, Paul M. 1983. Quoted in "College Aims to Educate Leaders of Computer Technology, Not Train Computer Technicians," *Northeastern Alumni Magazine* (July/August):12.

Kanter, Rosabeth Moss. 1983. *The Change Masters: Innovation and Entrepreneurship in the American Corporation*. New York: Simon and Schuster.

Karasek, R. A., et al. 1981. "Job Decision Latitude, Job Demands, and Cardiovascular Disease," *American Journal of Public Health* 71:694–705.

Kasschau, R., R. A. Lachman, and K. R. Laughery, eds. 1982. *Information Technology and Psychology.* New York: Praeger.

Katz, James Everett, ed. 1986. *The Implications of Third World Military Industrialization.* Lexington, MA: Lexington Books.

Kedzierski, B. 1982. "Communication and Management Support in System Development and Environments," in *Proceedings, Conference on Human Factors in Computer Systems.* Gaithersburg, MD (March).

Kegan, Robert. 1982. *The Evolving Self.* Cambridge, MA: Harvard University Press.

Keller, Evelyn Fox. 1985. *Reflections on Gender and Science.* New Haven: Yale University Press.

———. 1983. *A Feeling for the Organism: The Life and Work of Barbara McClintock.* New York: Freeman.

Keller, Robert, and Peter Townsend. 1984. "Knowledge-Based System," *Computerworld Office Automation*:32.

Kerr, Richard A. 1985. "Pity the Poor Weatherman," *Science* 228 (May 10):704–706.

Kevles, Daniel J. 1985. *In the Name of Eugenics: Genetics and the Uses of Human Heredity.* New York: Knopf.

———. 1978. *The Physicists: The History of a Scientific Community in Modern America.* New York: Knopf.

Keyworth, George A. 1985. "Ballistic Missile Defense: The Case For," *Issues in Science and Technology* (Fall):30–44.

Kidder, Tracy. 1982. *The Soul of a New Machine.* New York: Avon.

Kiesler, Sara, Lee Sproull, and Jacquelynne Eccles. 1983. "Second-Class Citizens?" *Psychology Today* (March):41–48.

Kikuchi, Masao, Anwar Hafid, Chaerul Saleh, Sri Hartoyo, and Yujiro Hayami. 1979. "Class Differentiation, Labor Employment and Income Distribution in a West Java Village," *Rural Dynamics Series* No. 7, Bogor, Indonesia: Agro-Economic Survey.

King, Wayne. 1985. "Link by Computer Used by Rightists," *New York Times* (February 15):11.

Kinnucan, Paul. 1983. "Flexible Systems Invade the Factory," *High Technology* (July):32–67.

Kirchner, Jake. 1984. "Japan Buries Copyright Bill; U.S. Fears It May Resurface," *Computerworld* (April 23):92.

Klare, Michael T. 1984. *American Arms Supermarket.* Austin: University of Texas Press.

Kling, Rob. 1985. "The Impacts of Computing on the Work of Managers, Data Analysts, and Clerks," working paper 78–64. Irvine, CA: Department of Information and Computer Science, University of California, Irvine.

———. 1983. "Value Conflicts in Computing Developments: Developed and Developing Countries," *Telecommunications Policy* (March):12–34.

———. 1980. "Social Analyses of Computing: Theoretical Perspectives in Recent Empirical Research," *Computing Surveys* 12,1 (March):61–110.

Kobayashi, Koji. 1986. *Computers and Communications.* Cambridge, MA: MIT Press.

Koh, T. T. B. 1984. "Computer-Assisted Negotiations: A Case History from the Law of the Sea Negotiations and Speculation Regarding Future Uses," in H. Pagels, ed. *Computer Culture: The Scientific, Intellectual, and Social Impact of the Computer.* New York: New York Academy of Sciences.

Kollock, Peter, Philip Blumstein, and Pepper Schwartz. 1985. "Sex and Power in Interaction: Conversational Privileges and Duties," *American Sociological Review* 50,1 (February):34–46.

Korzeniowski, Paul. 1985. "Firms Run into Obstacles to Insure MIS Data," *Computerworld* (December 23):4.

———. 1984. "Site Licensing Suggested as Software Piracy Deterrent," *Computerworld* (April 30):5.

Kraft, Philip. 1977. *The Sociology of Computer Programmers.* New York: Springer Verlag.

Kraft, Philip, and Steven Dubnoff. 1983a. *The Division of Labor, Fragmentation, and Hierarchy in Computer Software Work.* Detroit, MI: Society for the Study of Social Problems.

————. 1983b. "Software Workers Survey," *Computerworld* (November):5–13.

Kroeber, A. L., and Clyde Kluckhohn. 1952. *Culture: A Critical Review of Concepts and Definitions.* New York: Random House.

Kuhn, Thomas S. 1970. *The Structure of Scientific Revolutions,* 2d ed. Chicago: University of Chicago Press.

Kusserow, Richard. 1984. "The Government Needs Computer Matching to Root Out Waste and Fraud," *Communications of the ACM* 27,6(June):542–45.

Kuttẹn, L. J. 1985. "Disclaimers May Not Protect Vendors from Suffering Liability," *Computerworld* (November 18):151.

————. 1984a. *The Law and Software.* Englewood Cliffs, NJ: Prentice-Hall.

————. 1984b. "What Can Be Exported Where," *Computerworld* (March 5):ID/3–ID/12.

Kuttner, Robert. 1985. "A Shrinking Middle Class is a Call for Action," *Business Week* (September 16):16.

————. 1983. "The Declining Middle," *Atlantic Monthly* (July):60–71.

"Lab Course for the Blind." 1985. *Chronicle of Higher Education* (February 27):31.

LaDou, J. 1984. "The Not So Clean Business of Making Chips," *Technology Review* (May/June):23–36.

Landes, David S. 1983. *Revolution and Time: Clocks and the Making of the Modern World.* Cambridge, MA: Harvard University Press.

————. 1972. *The Unbound Prometheus.* Cambridge: Cambridge University Press.

Landsbergis, Paul A. 1985. "The Uses and Abuses of Stress Research: The Case of Air Traffic Controllers," Society for the Study of Social Problems (August 23–26), Washington, DC.

Langlois, Richard N. 1983. "System Theory, Knowledge, and the Social Sciences," in Fritz Machlup and Una Mansfield, eds. *The Study of Information.* New York: Wiley.

Lasch, Christopher. 1980. "The Family as a Haven in a Heartless World," in Arlene Skolnick and Jerome Skolnick, eds. *Family in Transition.* Boston: Little, Brown.

Laws, Kenneth. 1984. *The Physics of Dance.* New York: Schirmer.

Ledgard, Henry F., and Andrew Singer. 1982. "Scaling Down Ada (Or Towards a Standard Ada)," *Communications of the ACM* 25,2(February):121–25.

Leibnitz. 1959. In D. E. Smith, ed. *A Sourcebook of Mathematics,* Vol. 1. New York: Dover.

Leibowitz, Lila. 1983. "Origins of the Sexual Division of Labor," in Marion Lowe and Ruth Hubbard, eds. *Women's Nature.* New York: Pergamon.

Leontief, W. 1980. "The Distribution of Work and Income," in *The Mechanization of Work.* San Francisco: W. H. Freeman.

Leontief, Wassily, and Faye Duchin. 1986. *The Future Impact of Automation on Workers.* New York: Oxford University Press.

Lessem, Don. 1985. "Video-Imaging Was Key in Identifying Mengele," *Boston Globe* (August 5):37.

Levenstein, Charles, and Stanley W. Eller. 1985. "Exporting Hazardous Industries: 'For Example' is not Proof," in Jane H. Ives, ed. *The Export of Hazards.* Boston: Routledge and Kegan Paul.

Levy, Steven. 1984. *Hackers.* New York: Doubleday.

Lewontin, R. C., Steven Rose, and Leon J. Kamin. 1985. *Not in Our Genes.* New York: Pantheon.

Library of Congress. 1975. Circular 61 (March).

"The Library of Congress." 1983. *Chronicle of Higher Education* (November 2):5.

Lin, Herbert. 1985. "The Development of Software for the Ballistic-Missile Defense," *Scientific American* (December):46–53.

"Lip Reading Glasses." 1985. *Science 85* (March):6.

Lipset, Seymour Martin, and Reinhard Bendix. 1966. *Social Mobility in Industrial Society.* Berkeley: University of California Press.

"Lotus Files Infringement Suit." 1984. *Computerworld* (August 6):14.

References

Louis, Arthur M. 1984. "The Great Electronic Mail Shootout," *Fortune* (August 20):167–72.

"Love, Computer Style." 1983. *Boston Globe* (February 3):12–13.

Lowe, Marian. 1983. "Sex Differences, Science, and Society," in Jan Zimmerman, ed. *The Technological Woman: Interfacing with Tomorrow.* New York: Praeger.

Lowi, Theodore J. 1981. "The Political Impact of Information Technology," in Tom Forester, ed. *The Microelectronics Revolution.* Cambridge, MA: 453–72.

Lukes, Steven. 1973. *Emile Durkheim: His Life and Work.* London: Penguin.

Lyman, H. Thaine, James Anderson, and Jeffrey Plewa. 1985. "Are You Rushing too Fast to Subsecond Response Time?" *Computerworld* (September 9):ID5–14.

Machlup, Fritz. 1983. "Cultural Diversity in Studies of Information," in Fritz Machlup and Una Mansfield, eds. *The Study of Information.* New York: Wiley.

———. 1962. *The Production and Distribution of Knowledge in the United States.* Princeton, NJ: Princeton University Press.

MacLeish, Archibald. 1962. "Ars Poetica," in *The Collected Poems of Archibald MacLeish.* Cambridge, MA: Riverside Press.

Magdoff, Harry. 1982. "The Meaning of Work," *Monthly Review* 34,5 (October):1–15.

Magraw, Richard M., and Daniel B. Magraw. 1967. "Automating Medicine," *Saturday Review* (October 7):66–67.

Main, Jeremy. 1984. "The Recovery Skips Middle Managers," *Fortune* (February 6):112–20.

Malone, Thomas W. 1985. "Designing Organizational Interfaces," in *Proceedings, Human Factors in Computing Systems.* San Francisco: ACM Special Interest Group on Computer and Human Interaction (April 14–18).

———. 1983. "How Do People Organize their Desks? Implications for the Design of Office Automation Systems," *ACM Transactions on Office Automation Systems* 1,1(January):99–112.

Malthus, Thomas. 1798. *Essay on the Principle of Population.* London: J. Johnson.

Mandrou, Robert. 1973. *From Humanism to Science: 1480–1700.* Harmondsworth, Middlesex, England: Penguin.

Mann, Horace. 1976. Fifth Annual Report of the Secretary of the State Board of Education (Massachusetts, 1842). Quoted in Samuel Bowles and Herbert Gintis, *Schooling in Capitalist America.* New York: Basic Books:164.

Marbach, William D. 1985. "The Revolution in Digitech," *Newsweek* (March 18):48–49.

Marbach, William D., with William J. Cook, Kim Willenson, Richard Sandza, Frank Gibney, Jr., and Kim Foltz. 1983. "The Race to Build a Supercomputer," *Newsweek* (July 4):58–64.

Marcuse, Herbert. 1962. *Eros and Civilization.* New York: Vintage Books.

Marshall, Eliot. 1985. "Fallout from the Trade War in Chips," *Science* (November 22):917–19.

Martin, James. 1984. *An Information Systems Manifesto.* Englewood Cliffs, NJ: Prentice-Hall.

———. 1978. *The Wired Society.* Englewood Cliffs, NJ: Prentice-Hall.

Martin, Josh. 1985. "Wargames," *Multinational Monitor* (December/January):3–5.

Marx, Gary. 1985. "I'll Be Watching You: The New Surveillance," *Dissent* (Winter):26–34.

Marx, Gary T., and Nancy Richman. 1984. "Routinizing the Discovery of Secrets: Computers as Informants," *American Behavioral Scientist* 27,4(March/April):423–52.

Marx, Karl. 1973. *The Poverty of Philosophy.* Moscow: Progress Publishers.

———. 1967. *Capital,* vol. 1. New York: International Publishers.

———. 1964. *The Economic and Philosophic Manuscripts of 1844.* New York: International Publishers.

Maslow, A. H. 1954. *Motivation and Personality.* New York: Harper and Row.

Mattera, Philip. 1983. "Home Computer Sweatshop," *Nation* (April):390–92.

May, Ernest R. 1985. Cited in "Independent Panel Urges Federal Officials to Give Priority to Preservation of Records," *Chronicle of Higher Education* (February 27):9.

Mayer, Martin. 1983. "Here Comes the Smart Card," *Fortune* (August 8):74–81.

Maynard, Douglas. 1985. "On the Functions of Social Conflict Among Children," *American Sociological Review* 50,2(April):207–23.

McClintock, Charles. 1984. "Expanding the Boundaries of Work: Research on Telecommuting," presentation to the American Association for the Advancement of Science. New York (May).

McClure, Carma. 1984. Computer Applications Seminar in Structured Techniques for Fourth Generation Languages. Washington, DC (April 2–4).

McCorduck, Pamela. 1979. *Machines Who Think*. San Francisco: W. H. Freeman.

McDonald, Kim. 1984a. "Pentagon Drops Proposal to Limit Publication of Some Unclassified Research at Universities," *Chronicle of Higher Education* (May 30):17.

———. 1984b. "Scientists Fear Effects of Government Security Rules," *Chronicle of Higher Education* (February 29):1,12.

McDonell, Donald J. 1984. "Teaching Psychology by Telephone," *Social Science in Canada* 12,1(May):7,11–12.

McEnaney, Maura. 1985. "Balanced Contract Best Defense," *Computerworld* (February 25):61,70.

———. 1984. "Handprints Tested as ID on Army ATMs," *Computerworld* (September 10): 36.

McGeever, Christine. 1984. "Lotus Consents to Settlement in 1-2-3 Copying Suit," *Computerworld* (October 22):118.

McGuigan, Cathleen, with Maggie Malone, Janet Huck, and Shawn Doherty. 1985. "A Word from our Sponsor," *Newsweek* (November 25):96–98.

McIvor, Robert. 1985. "Smart Cards," *Scientific American* 253,5 (November):152–59.

McLaughlin, Jeff. 1984. "The Information Revolution Hits Music," *Boston Globe* (January 30):23.

McLuhan, Marshall. 1962. *The Gutenberg Galaxy*. Toronto: University of Toronto Press.

———. 1964. *Understanding the Media*. New York: McGraw–Hill.

McPhail, Thomas L. 1981. *Electronic Colonialism: The Future of International Broadcasting and Communication*. Beverly Hills, CA: Sage.

Meadows, D. H., D. L. Meadows, J. Randers, and W. Behrens, III. 1972. *The Limits to Growth*. New York: Universe Books.

The Mechanization of Work. 1982. San Francisco: W. H. Freeman.

Megarry, Jacquetta, David R. F. Walker, Stanley Nisbet, and Eric Hoyle, eds. 1983. *World Yearbook of Education 1982/83: Computers and Education*. New York: Nichols.

Mehl, L. 1959. "Automation in the Legal World," in *Mechanisation of Thought Processes* National Physical Laboratory 2:755–80.

Menninger, Karl W. 1969. *Number Words and Number Symbols: A Cultural History of Numbers*. Cambridge, MA: MIT Press.

Merriman, J. H. H., and D. W. G. Wass. 1958. "To What Extent Can Administration Be Mechanized?" *National Physical Laboratory* 2:809–18.

Merton, Robert K. 1968. *Social Theory and Social Structure*. New York: Free Press.

Meszaros, Istvan. 1970. "Aspects of Alienation," in *Marx's Theory of Alienation*. London: Merlin Press.

Meyer, Thomas J. 1985. "Freshmen Are Materialistic but not Conservative, Study Finds," *Chronicle of Higher Education* 29,18(January 16):1–15.

Middleton, Russell. 1962. "Brother–Sister and Father–Daughter Marriage in Ancient Egypt," *American Sociological Review* 27,5 (October):603–11.

Miles, Dana E. 1984. "Copyrighting Software After Apple v. Franklin," *IEEE Software* 1:2(April 1984):84–87.

Milgram, Stanley. 1969. *Obedience to Authority*. New York: Harper and Row.

Mill, John S. 1848. *The Principles of Political Economy*. London: Longmans Green.

Miller, Jeffrey A. 1984. "How Strong a Shield Are Vendors' Form Contracts?" *Computerworld* (August 13):53.

Miller, Michael W. 1985. "Computers Keep Eye on Workers and See if They Perform Well," *The Wall Street Journal* (June 3):1,15.

Miller, Robert J., ed. 1983. "Robotics: Future Factories, Future Workers," special issue of *Annals of the American Academy of Political and Social Science* (November).

Miller, Russell. 1985. "Bugs and Hugs," *In These Times* (April 10–16):24,22. (This article begins on page 24 and continues on page 22.)

Miller, Thomas. 1986. "Telecommuting Benefits Business with DP's Help," *Computerworld* (February 17):51–55.

Mills, C. Wright. 1967. *The Sociological Imagination.* New York: Oxford University Press.

———. 1956. *The Power Elite.* New York: Oxford University Press.

"Milwaukee Discovers WarGamesmanship." 1983. *Newsweek* (August 22):83.

Minsky, Marvin. 1985. "Our Roboticized Future," in Marvin Minsky, ed. *Robotics.* Garden City, NY: Anchor Press/Doubleday.

Mislow, Christopher M. 1984. "Imposing Legal Liability on DP Vendors: Two Theories," *Computerworld* (June 25):90.

Mitchell, Peter W. 1985. "Computers for the Handicapped," *Boston Phoenix* (January 8):9,15.

Mitford, Jessica. 1971. *Kind and Usual Punishment.* New York: Random House.

Molm, Linda D. 1986. "Gender, Power, and Legitimation," *American Journal of Sociology* 91,6 (May):1356–86.

Molotch, Harvey L., and Deirdre Boden. 1985. "Talking Social Structure: Discourse, Domination, and the Watergate Hearings," *American Sociological Review* (June):273–88.

Moore, Barrington, Jr. 1984. *Privacy: Studies in Social and Cultural History.* New York: M.E. Sharpe.

Moore, Wilbert E., ed. 1972. *Technology and Social Change.* Chicago: Quadrangle.

———. 1963. *Social Change.* Englewood Cliffs, NJ: Prentice-Hall.

"More Older Engineers: Stuck in the Rut of Mid-Career." 1982. *Boston Globe* (May 23):B-21.

Mosco, Vincent. 1983. "Research Pressure Points of the Information Age," presentation to the Conference on Communications, Mass Media, and Development. Chicago: Northwestern University.

Moses, Joel. 1980. "The Computer in the Home," in Michael Dertouzos and Joel Moses, eds. *The Computer Age: A Twenty-Year View.* Cambridge, MA: MIT Press.

Mozeico, Howard. 1982. "A Human/Computer Interface to Accommodate User Learning Stages," *Communications of the ACM* 25,2 (February):100–104.

Mukerji, Chandra. 1983. *From Graven Images: Patterns of Modern Materialism.* New York: Columbia University Press.

"Multimedia Communications." 1985. Special issue of *IEEE Computer* (October).

Mumford, Lewis. 1963. *Technics and Civilization.* New York: Harcourt Brace and World.

Murch, Gerald M. 1984. "Physiological Principles for the Effective Use of Color," *IEEE Computer Graphics* 4,11 (November):49–54.

"Murdoch Jolts Fleet Street." 1986. *Fortune* (March 3):8.

Muro, Mark. 1984. "Charting Children's Fantasies," *Boston Globe* (November 7):77–78.

Murray, Linda. 1983. "Computer Sex Therapists," *Science Digest* (November):96–98.

Murray, W. 1984. "Video Display Terminals: Radiation Issues," *IEEE Computer Graphics and Applications* 4,4(April):41–44.

Myers, Ware. 1985a. "An Assessment of the Competitiveness of the United States Software Industry," *IEEE Computer* 18,3(March):81–92.

———. 1985b. "Computer Graphics: The Next Twenty Years," *Computer Graphics and Applications* 5,8(August):69–76.

Nardone, Thomas J. 1986. "Part-time Workers: Who are They?" *Monthly Labor Review* (February):13–19.

Nash, Manning. 1966. *Primitive and Peasant Economic Systems.* San Francisco: Chandler.

National Academy of Engineering. 1985. *Information Technologies and Social Transformation.* Washington, DC: National Academy Press.

National Commission on Excellence in Education. 1983. "A Nation at Risk: The Imperative for Educational Reform," *Chronicle of Higher Education* (May 4):11–16.

National Physical Laboratory. 1959. *Mechanisation of Thought Processes, Proceedings of a Symposium November 24–27, 1958.* London: Her Majesty's Stationery Office.

National Science Foundation. 1986. *Women and Minorities in Science and Engineering.* Washington, DC: U.S. Government Printing Office.

————. 1981. "Computers and Semiconductors," in *Only One Science, Twelfth Annual Report of the National Science Board.* Washington, DC: U.S. Government Printing Office.

Needham, Joseph. 1956. *Science and Civilization in China.* Cambridge: Cambridge University Press.

Negroponte, Nicholas. 1980. "The Return of the Sunday Painter," in Michael Dertouzos and Joel Moses, eds. *The Computer Age: A Twenty-Year View.* Cambridge, MA: MIT Press.

Nelkin, Dorothy. 1977. *Technological Decisions and Democracy: European Experiments in Public Participation.* Beverly Hills, CA: Sage.

Nelson, Benjamin. 1969. *The Idea of Usury: From Tribal Brotherhood to Universal Otherhood.* Chicago: University of Chicago Press.

Nessbaum, Karen. 1983. "Office High-Tech Is Not Here For Good," *In These Times* (May 24–30).20.

"The New Cockpits of Industry." 1983. *Fortune* (November 28):108–17.

Nielsen, John. 1985. "Management Layoffs Won't Quit," *Fortune* (October 28):46–56.

Nilles, Jack. 1984. "Telecommuting: The Home-to-Office Link," *Personal Computing* (April):77–162.

Nilles, J., S. Carlson, P. Gray, and G. Hanneman. 1976. *The Telecommunications–Transportation Tradeoff.* New York: Wiley.

"Nine To Five in Barbados." 1984. *In These Times* (April 4–10):24.

Nisbet, Robert A., ed. 1972. *Social Change.* New York: Harper and Row.

————. 1969. *Social Change and History.* London: Oxford University Press.

Noble, David F. 1984. *Forces of Production: A Social History of Industrial Automation.* New York: Knopf.

————. 1980. "Preface," in Mike Cooley. *Architect or Bee?* Boston: South End Press.

————. 1977. *America By Design.* New York: Knopf.

Noll, Roger G. 1980. "Regulation and Computer Services," in Michael Dertouzos and Joel Moses, eds. *The Computer Age: A Twenty-Year View.* Cambridge, MA: MIT Press.

"Non-ionizing Radiation—Current Issues and Controversies: A Mini-Symposium." 1983. *Journal of Occupational Medicine* 25,2 (February):95–110.

Nordheimer, Jon. 1985. "Jail Moves into Probationer's Home," *New York Times* (February 15):9.

Nordstrom, S., E. Birke, and L. Gustavsson. 1983. "Reproductive Hazards Among Workers at High Voltage Substations," *Bioelectromagnetics* 4:91–101.

Norman, Colin. 1984. "Mixed Signals on Export Controls," *Science* 226 (December 14):1295.

"NSA to Provide Secret Codes." 1985. *Science* (October 4):45–56.

Nussbaum, Karen. 1983. "Office High Tech is Not Here for Good," *In These Times* (May 24–30):12.

Nycum, Susan H. 1986. "Legal Liability for Expert Systems," *CPSR (Computer Professionals for Social Responsibility) Newsletter* 4,2 (Spring):12–14.

Nyhart, J. D., James D. Sebenius, Elliot L. Richardson, and Tommy Kou. 1983. "The Development and Use of MIT Deep Ocean Mining Model in Law of the Sea Negotiations; Critique of Development and Use of Model for these Negotiations." Presentations and panel discussion at New York Academy.

Ogburn, William F. 1932. *Social Change.* New York: Viking Press.

Ollman, Bertell. 1979. *Social and Sexual Revolution: Essays on Marx and Reich.* Boston: South End Press.

————. 1971. *Alienation: Marx's Conception of Man in Capitalist Society.* New York: Cambridge University Press.

Olmos, David. 1985. "Suit to Affect All Computer Users," *Computerworld* (February 18):15.

Olmstead, Michael, and A. Paul Hare. 1978. *The Small Group.* New York: Random House.

Olson, Margrethe. 1983. "Remote Office Work: Changing Work Patterns in Space and Time," *Communications of the ACM* 26,3 (March):182–87.

Olson, Steve. 1984. "Sage of Software," *Science 84* (January/February):74–80.

Oltmans, Willem L., ed. 1974. *On Growth.* New York: G. P. Putnam's Sons.

Palyka, Duane M. 1985. "Computer/Art—Depolarization and Unification," *Computer Graphics and Applications* 5,7 (July):46–56.

Papert, Seymour. 1980. *Mindstorms: Children, Computers, and Powerful Ideas.* New York: Basic Books.

Parker, Donn B. 1983. *Fighting Computer Crime.* New York: Scribners.

Parker, Stanley. 1983. *Leisure and Work.* London: George Allen and Unwin.

Parks, Michael. 1983. "Hong Kong to Charge for 'Road Use,' " *Boston Globe* (October 9):17.

Parnas, David. 1986. "Why I Quit Star Wars," *Common Cause Magazine* (May/June):32–35.

———. 1985. "Software Aspects of Strategic Defense Systems," *American Scientist* (September–October):432–40.

Parsons, Talcott. 1971. *The System of Modern Societies.* Englewood Cliffs, NJ: Prentice-Hall.

———. 1966. *Societies: Evolutionary and Comparative Perspectives.* Englewood Cliffs, NJ: Prentice-Hall.

———. 1951. *The Social System.* New York: Free Press.

Parsons, Talcott, and Edward A. Shils, with the assistance of James Olds. 1951. "Categories of the Orientation and Organization of the Actor," in Talcott Parsons and Edward A. Shils, eds. *Towards a General Theory of Action.* New York: Harper and Row.

Pauly, David, and Carolyn Friday. 1985. "Computers Make the Sale," *Newsweek* (September 23):46–47.

Paycha, F. 1959. "Medical Diagnosis and Cybernetics," in *Mechanization of Thought Processes. National Physical Laboratory* 2:635–60.

Pearce, Brian, ed. 1984. *Health Hazards of VDT's?* New York: Wiley.

Pearce, Francis. 1985. "Tender for Biggest Gov't Project Closes," *Asian Computerworld* 2,19 (September 16):2.

Pearson, Judy Cornelia. 1985. *Gender and Communication.* Dubuque, IA: William C. Brown.

Peden, Joseph R., and Fred R. Glahe, eds. 1986. *The American Family and the State.* San Francisco: Pacific Institute for Policy Research.

Perrolle, Judith A. 1985a. "Computers and Capitalism," in John Williamson, Linda Evans, and Michael Rustad, eds. *Social Problems: The Contemporary Debates.* Boston: Little, Brown.

———. 1985b. "Computers Encourage Systems Thinking," *Society for the Study of Social Problems Newsletter* 16,3 (Summer):9–10.

———. 1984a. "The Computer: An Environmental Impact Assessment," *Society for the Study of Social Problems* (August).

———. 1984b. "The Electronic Mill," *Directions* 1,2 (May):1–3.

———. 1983. "Computer Technology and Class Formation in the World System," *Proceedings, Communications, Mass Media, and Development Conference.* Chicago:1950–91.

Perrow, Charles. 1984. *Normal Accidents: Living with High-Risk Technologies.* New York: Basic Books.

Peterson, Franklynn, and Judi K. Turkel. 1983. "Those Computer-School Come-Ons, *Boston Globe* (June 20):12.

Pfister, George M. 1984. "A Call for Standards," *Computerworld Office Automation* (August 15):47–49.

Phillips, Amy Friedman. 1983. "Computer Conferences: Success or Failure," in Robert N. Bostrom, ed. *Communication Yearbook 7.* Beverly Hills, CA: Sage.

Phillips, Carolyn. 1986. "Who Needs It? In Some Homes the Computer is a Vital Workhorse; in Others It's an Expensive Piece of Furniture," *The Wall Street Journal* (June 16):30D.

Piaget, Jean. 1948. *The Moral Judgement of the Child.* Glencoe, IL: Free Press.

Pieper, Josef. 1952. *Leisure, the Basis of Culture.* New York: Pantheon.

Pinsky, M., M. Zybko, and L. Slesin. 1984. "Video Display Terminals: 1983 Health and Safety Update," *Microwave News.*

Plumb, J. H. 1950. *England in the Eighteenth Century.* Harmondsworth, Middlesex, England: Penguin.

Pogrow, Stanley. 1983. *Education in the Computer Age.* Beverly Hills, CA: Sage.

Polanyi, Karl. 1944. *The Great Transformation.* Boston: Beacon Press.

Pool, Ithiel de Sola. 1983. *Technologies of Freedom.* Cambridge, MA: MIT Press.

Popper, Karl R. 1968. *The Logic of Scientific Discovery*. New York: Harper and Row.

Population Reference Bureau. 1983. "The Changing American Family," *Population Bulletin* 38,4 (October).

Porat, Marc U. 1978. "Communication Policy in an Information Society," in Glen O. Robinson, ed. *Communications for Tomorrow*. New York: Praeger.

Postan, M. M. 1975. *The Medieval Economy and Society*. Harmondsworth, Middlesex, England: Penguin.

Powell, Lawrence Alfred. 1985. "Telecommunications and the Elderly: Autonomy or Social Control?" Society for the Study of Social Problems, Washington, DC (August).

Prigogine, Ilya, and Isabelle Stengers. 1984. *Order Out of Chaos: Man's New Dialogue with Nature*. New York: Bantam.

"Psycho-Computing: Software for Troubled Minds and Lonely Hearts. 1985". *TWA Ambassador* (March):70

Puryear, Jeffrey M. 1982. "Higher Education, Development Assistance, and Repressive Regimes," *Studies in Comparative International Development* 18, 2:3–35.

Pylyshyn, Zenon W. 1980. "Artificial Intelligence," in Bruce Arden, ed. *What Can Be Automated: The Computer Science and Engineering Research Study*. Cambridge, MA: MIT Press.

Rada, Juan F. 1982a. *The Impact of Microelectronics and Information Technology: Case Studies in Latin America*. Paris: United Nations Educational, Scientific, and Cultural Organization.

————. 1982b. "A Third World Perspective," in Gunter Friedrichs and Adam Schaff, eds. *Microelectronics and Society: For Better or for Worse*. New York: Pergamon Press.

Radl, Gerald W. 1985. *Ergonomic Principles Applied to Work Place Design*. Waltham, MA: Nixdorf Computer, Inc.

————. 1984. "Optimal Presentation Mode and Colours of Symbols on VDU's," in Brian Pearce, ed. *Health Hazards of VDT's?* New York: Wiley.

Raimondi, Donna. 1985a. " 'Erased' Tapes Present Potential Security Threat," *Computerworld* (September 16):73.

————. 1985b. "False Arrests Require Police to Monitor System Closely," *Computerworld* (February 25):23.

————. 1985c. "New Hampshire Leaders Wrestle with Data Access Issue," *Computerworld* (June 10):28.

Rainey, Froelich. 1974. "Technology Is Forcing History to Change," *New York Times* (August 25):E-20.

Raugh, Michael R. 1985. "Modeling California Earthquakes and Earth Structures," *Communications of the ACM* (November):1130–50.

"Reagan's Revised Information Act Under Scrutiny." 1984. *Boston Globe* (January 27):16.

Reid, A. A. L. 1977. "Comparing Telephone with Face-to-Face Contact," in Ithiel de Sola Pool, ed. *The Social Impact of the Telephone*. Cambridge, MA: MIT Press.

Reid, T. R. 1985. "The American Revolutions: The Chip," *Science 85* (January/February):32–41.

Reinecke, Ian. 1982. *Electronic Illusions*. New York: Penguin.

Renfew, Colin. 1983. "The Social Archaeology of Megalithic Monuments," *Scientific American* 249,5:152–63.

"Report on Excellence in Education Acclaimed: Panelists Criticize Reagan's Interpretation." 1983. *Chronicle of Higher Education* (May 11):1.

Revkin, Andrew C. 1985. "Hard Facts About Nuclear Winter," *Science Digest* (March):62–81.

Reynolds, Terry S. 1984. "Medieval Roots of the Industrial Revolution," *Scientific American* (July):123–30.

Ribicoff, Abraham. 1977. "Statement to the U.S. Senate on June 27." Reprinted in Whiteside, 1978:129–40.

Rice, Faye. 1986. "Electronic Self–Improvement," *Fortune* (February 17):137–40.

Rice, Ronald E., et al. 1984. *The New Media: Communication, Research, and Technology*. Beverly Hills, CA: Sage.

Richardson, Jacques, ed. 1984. *Models of Reality: Shaping Thought and Action*. Mt. Airy, MD: Lomond Publications.

References

Rifkin, Glenn. 1986. "On Beyond Silicon: A Look at New Semiconductor Technologies," *Computerworld* (April 14):49–62.

———. 1985. "Data Base Libel Decision Termed 'Blow to Info Industry,' " *Computerworld* (July 8):60.

———. 1984. "Electronic Mail," *Computerworld Office Automation* 18,33A (August 15):35–38.

Roberts, Jerome J., Marianne D. Paine, and Michael P. Brownell. 1985. "Contracts Key for Clarifying Software Owner's Rights,' " *Computerworld* (September 23):84.

Roberts, Martin B. 1983. *EDP Controls: A Guide for Auditors and Accountants*. New York: Wiley.

Roberts, Wayne. 1983. "Corporate Decentralization," *In Context* (Spring):41–43.

Robey, Bryant, and Cheryl Russell. 1984. "A Portrait of the American Worker," *American Demographics* 6,3 (March):16–21.

Robins, Kevin, and Frank Webster. 1985. "Luddism: New Technology and the Critique of Political Economy," in Les Levidow and Bob Young, eds. *Science, Technology, and the Labor Process*. Atlantic Highlands, NJ: Humanities Press.

Rockart, John F., and Christine V. Bullen, eds. 1986. *The Rise of Managerial Computing*. Homewood, IL: Dow Jones–Irwin.

Rogers, Michael. 1984a. "Birth of the Killer Robots," *Newsweek* (June 25):25.

———. 1984b. "Selling Psych-out Software," *Newsweek* (January 16):52.

Rogers, Michael, with Lee Goldberg. 1986. "Of Pixels and Flicks: Special Effects Grow Up," *Newsweek* (February 17):76–78.

Roper, Christopher. 1983. "Microcomputers and the Left," *Nation* (February 5):141–42.

Rosen, M. Daniel. 1983. "In the Computer Age, Corrections are Still Chasing Paper," *Corrections Magazine* (April):18–29.

Rosenberg, Ronald. 1983. "The Military Goes Great Guns for Ada," *Boston Globe* (January 23):A1–A5.

Rubin, Charles. 1984. "High-Powered Presentation Graphics," *Personal Computing* (April):65–74.

Rubin, Charles, with Dick Landis. 1983. "Farming Smarter with a Computer," *Personal Computing* (June):96–101.

Rule, James B., Douglas McAdam, Linda Stearns, and David Uglow. 1983. "Documentary Identification and Mass Surveillance in the United States," *Social Problems* 31,2 (December):222–34.

Russell, David O. 1985. "Synthesized Keys Stir Real Fears," *In These Times* (April 24–30):20–21.

Ryan, William T. 1971. *Blaming the Victim*. New York: Pantheon.

Sabel, Charles. 1982. *Work and Politics: The Division of Labor in Industry*. Cambridge: Cambridge University Press.

Sahlins, Marshall D. 1960. "The Origins of Society," *Scientific American* (September)203,3:88–96.

Salaman, Graeme. 1982. "Managing the Frontier of Control," in Anthony Giddens and Gavin Mackenzie, eds. *Social Class and the Division of Labor*. Cambridge: Cambridge University Press.

"Salary Gap Pervades DP." 1985. *Computerworld* 19(February 11):1.

Salholtz, Eloise. 1985. "Help Wanted: Teachers," *Newsweek* (September 9):99.

Salvendy, G., and M. J. Smith, eds. 1981. *Machine Pacing and Occupational Stress*. Philadelphia: Taylor and Francis.

Samuelson, Paul A. 1976. *Economics*. New York: McGraw-Hill.

Santillana, Giorgio de, and Hertha von Dechend. 1969. *Hamlet's Mill: An Essay Investigating the Origin of Human Knowledge and Its Transmission Through Myth*. Boston: Godine.

Saunders, Robert J., Jeremy J. Warford, and Bjorn Wellenius. 1983. *Telecommunications and Economic Development*. Baltimore, MD: Johns Hopkins and the World Bank.

Saxe, Leonard. 1985. "Umpiring Controversy: Liars and Lie Detection," *Society* (September/October):39–43.

References

Schumach, Murray. 1975. *The Face on the Cutting Room Floor: The Story of Movie and Television Censorship*. New York: Da Capo Press.

Schweinitz, Karl de, Jr. 1964. *Industrialization and Democracy*. Glencoe, IL: Free Press.

Scimecca, Joseph A. 1980. *Education and Society*. New York: Holt, Rinehart and Winston.

Scragg, Greg W. 1985. "Some Thoughts on Paper Notes and Electronic Messages," *SIGCHI Bulletin* 16,3 (January):41–44.

Scully, Malcolm G. 1983. "8 Channels Reserved for Education to Be Reassigned to Pay Television," *Chronicle of Higher Education* (June 8):9.

"The Search for Copyproof Software." 1984. *Fortune* (September 3):83.

Secord, Paul F., ed. 1982. *Explaining Human Behavior: Consciousness, Human Action, and Behavior*. Beverly Hills, CA: Sage.

"The Semiconductor Industry: A Chip of the Pentagon's Block." 1983. *Dollars and Sense* (October):12–15.

Sennett, Richard. 1977. *The Psychology of Society: An Anthology*. New York: Vintage.

———. 1974. *The Fall of Public Man: On the Social Psychology of Capitalism*. New York: Vintage.

Sennett, Richard, and Jonathan Cobb. 1972. *The Hidden Injuries of Class*. New York: Random House.

Serrill, Michael S. 1985. "The No Man's Land of High Tech: New Devices Aid Police but Threaten the Right of Privacy," *Time* (January 14):58.

Serrin, William. 1984. "Automated Offices," *New York Times* (March 28):A14.

———. 1983. "Up to a Fifth of U.S. Workers Now Rely on Part-Time Jobs," *New York Times* (August 14):1.

Shaiken, Harley. 1985. "The Automated Factory: The View from the Shop Floor," *Technology Review* (January):16–27.

———. 1984. *Work Transformed: Automation and Labor in the Computer Age*. New York: Holt, Rinehart and Winston.

———. 1983. Lecture at Northeastern University. Boston: March 9.

———. 1980. "Computer Power to the People," *Technology Review* (February):76.

Shannon, Claude. 1948. "A Mathematical Theory of Communication," *Bell System Technical Journal* 27(July and October):379–423,623–56.

Shattuck, John. 1984a. "Computer Record Matching Is a Serious Threat to Individual Rights," *Communications of the ACM* 27,6(June):538–41.

———. 1984b. "In the Shadow of 1984: National Identification Systems, Computer–Matching, and Privacy in the United States," *Hastings Law Journal* (July):991–1005.

Short, James F. 1984. "The Social Fabric of Risk: Toward the Social Transformation of Risk Analysis," *American Sociological Review* 49,6 (December):711–25.

Shorter, Edward. 1975. *The Making of the Modern Family*. New York: Basic Books.

Shurkin, Joel N. 1984. *Engines of the Mind: A History of the Computer*. New York: Norton.

———. 1983. "Expert Systems: The Practical Face of Artificial Intelligence," *Technology Review* (November/December):72–78.

SIGCHI Bulletin. Publication of the ACM Special Interest Group on Computers and Human Interaction.

Silbar, Margaret L. 1985. "The Pursuit of Parallelism," *Mosaic* 16,3:8–17.

Silverstein, Michael. 1983. "Beyond the Nuclear Stalemate: The Hope of High-Tech Weapons," *Boston Phoenix* (February 8):1.

Simon, David R., and D. Stanley Eitzen. 1982. *Elite Deviance*. Boston: Allyn and Bacon.

Simon, Herbert. 1985. "The Consequences of Computers for Centralization and Decentralization," in John B. Williamson, Linda Evans, and Michael Rustad, eds. *Social Problems: The Contemporary Debates*. Boston: Little, Brown.

Singular, Stephen. 1983. "A Robot and Liking It, Thanks," *Psychology Today* (March): 22.

Sirbu, Marvin A. 1982. "Understanding the Social and Economic Impacts of Office Automation," paper prepared for the Japan-U.S. Office Automation Forum.

Skelly, Patrick G. (for the ACM Standards Committee). 1982. "The ACM Position on Standardization of the Ada Language," *Communications of the ACM* 25, 2 (February):118–20.

Skocpol, Theda. 1983. "Methods of Comparative Historical Sociology." Presentation to the American Sociological Association. Detroit: September.

Skocpol, Theda, and Ellen Kay Trimberger. 1986. "A Structural Approach to Revolutions," in Jack A. Goldstone, ed. *Revolutions: Theoretical, Comparative, and Historical Studies*. New York: Harcourt Brace Jovanovich.

Skolnick, Arlene. 1978. *The Intimate Environment: Exploring Marriage and the Family*. Boston: Little, Brown.

Skolnick, Arlene, and Jerome Skolnick, eds. 1980. *Family in Transition*. Boston: Little, Brown.

Sliney, D. H. 1985. "Eye Hazards of Environmental Lighting," *The Medical and Biological Effects of Light, Annals of the New York Academy of Sciences* 453 (September 20):114–20.

Sluizer, S., and P. Cashman. 1985. "XCP: An Experimental Tool for Managing Cooperative Activity," *Proceedings. ACM Computer Science Conference*. New Orleans (March).

Smelser, Neil J., ed. 1973. *Karl Marx on Society and Social Change*. Chicago: University of Chicago Press.

Smith, Adam. 1966. *The Theory of Moral Sentiments*. New York: Augustus M. Kelley.

———. 1937. *The Wealth of Nations*. Edwin Cannon, ed. New York: Modern Library.

Smith, Anthony. 1980. *The Geopolitics of Information: How Western Culture Dominates the World*. New York: Oxford University Press.

Smith, D. E. 1959. *A Sourcebook of Mathematics*, vol. 1. New York: Dover.

Smith, Merritt Roe, ed. 1985. *Military Enterprise and Technological Change*. Cambridge, MA: MIT Press.

Smith, Ruth Bayard. 1983. "Apples for the Teachers," *Boston Globe Magazine* (March 13):13–32.

Smith, W. L., W. P. Bishop, V. F. Dvorak, C. M. Hayden, J. H. McElroy, F. R. Mosher, V. J. Oliver, J. F. Purdom, and D. Q. Wark. 1986. "The Meteorological Satellite: Overview of 25 Years of Operation," *Science* (January 31):455–70.

Snow, C. P. 1963. *The Two Cultures and a Second Look: An Expanded Version of the Two Cultures and the Scientific Revolution*. New York: New American Library.

Soloway, Elliot, and Kate Ehrlich. 1984. "Empirical Studies of Programming Knowledge," *IEEE Transactions on Software Engineering* SE-10,5(September):596–609.

Sorel, George. 1969. *The Illusion of Progress*. Berkeley: University of California Press.

Spencer, Herbert. 1898. *First Principles*. New York: Appleton.

Spenner, Kenneth I. 1983. "Temporal Change in the Skill Level of Work," *American Sociological Review* 48,6 (December):824–37.

Stallings, William. 1986. "Department of Defense Fights for Own Uniform Standards," *Computerworld* (January 13):19–23.

Starr, Paul. 1983. *The Social Transformation of American Medicine*. New York: Basic Books.

Stellman, Jeanne, and Mary Sue Henifin. 1983. *Office Work Can Be Dangerous to Your Health*. New York: Pantheon Books.

Stevens, Chandler Harrison. 1981. "Many-to-Many Communication," Center for Information Systems Research, Working Paper 72. Cambridge, MA: MIT Press.

Stewart, Leon F. 1985. "Software Warranties Ease Glitches for Users, Vendor," *Computerworld* (May 13):52.

Stone, Jack. 1984. "Electronic Data Systems: Public Service or Federal Crime?" *Computerworld* (December 10):61.

Strassmann, Paul. 1985. "Information Payoff," *Computerworld* (February 11): ID/15–ID/32.

Straw, Ronnie, and Lorel Foged. 1983. "Technology and Employment in Telecommunications," *Annals of the American Academy of Scientific Research* 470(November):163–70.

Sullivan, Kathleen. 1985. "Police Face Allegations of Accessing Confidential Files," *Computerworld* (February 25):8.

———. 1984. "Financial Industry Fertile Ground for Expert Systems," *Computerworld* (October 22):29–31.

Sun, Marjorie. 1986. "Federal VDT Study Finally Wins Approval," *Science* (June 27):1594–95.

Sutherland, Edwin H. 1949. *White Collar Crime.* New York: Dryden Press.

Task Force on Legal Aspects of Computer-Based Technology. 1984. "Protection of Computer Ideawork—Today and Tomorrow," *IEEE Software* 1:2 (April):74–82.

Taylor, Charles. 1982. "Consciousness," in Paul F. Secord, ed. *Explaining Human Behavior: Consciousness, Human Action, and Behavior.* Beverly Hills, CA: Sage.

Taylor, Frederick. 1911. *The Principles of Scientific Management.* New York: Harper and Row.

Teicholtz, Eric, ed. 1985. *CAD/CAM Handbook.* New York: McGraw-Hill.

Teicholtz, E., and B. Berry. 1983. *Computer Graphics and Environmental Planning.* Englewood Cliffs, NJ: Prentice-Hall.

"Telecommuting: The Home-to-Office Link." 1984. *Personal Computing* (April):77–85.

"Terminal Tedium." 1983. *Wall Street Journal* (May 6):1.

Teune, Henry, and Z. Linar. 1978. *The Developmental Logic of Social Systems.* Beverly Hills, CA: Sage.

Text of the College Board's outline of the basic subjects for study in high school. 1983. *Chronicle of Higher Education* (May 18):14–15.

Text of statement on computer literacy. 1983. *Chronicle of Higher Education* (May 18):15.

Thaxton, Richard. 1980. "Nuclear War by Computer Chip: How America Almost 'Launched on Warning,' " *The Progressive* (August):29–30.

Thomas, Robert H., et al. 1985. "Diamond: A Multimedia Message System Built on a Distributed Architecture," *IEEE Computer* (December):65–77.

Thompson, E. P. 1968. *The Making of the English Working Class.* London: Penguin.

Thompson, Ken. 1984. "Reflections on Trusting Trust: Should We Trust the Program or Its Creator?" *Communications of the ACM* (August): 758–60.

Thornton, Arland, Duane F. Alwin, and Donald Camburn. 1983. "Causes and Consequences of Sex–Role Attitudes and Attitude Change," *American Sociological Review* (April):211–27.

Thurow, Lester. 1986. "The Economic Case Against Star Wars," *Technology Review* (February/March):11–15.

Tierney, Brian. 1983. "Constitutionalism in England," in *The Middle Ages, vol 1: Sources of Medieval History*, 4th ed. New York: Knopf.

Tinbergen, Jan, Antony J. Dolman, and Jan van Ettinger, eds. 1976. *Reshaping the International Order: A Report to the Club of Rome.* New York: E. P. Dutton and Company.

Tjønn, H. H. 1984. "Report of Facial Rashes among VDU Operators in Norway," in Brian Pearce, ed. *Health Hazards of VDT's.* New York: Wiley.

Toffler, Alvin. 1980. *The Third Wave.* New York: Bantam.

Tomkins, Silvan S. 1965. "The Biopsychosociality of the Family," in Ansley J. Coale, Lloyd A. Fallers, David M. Schneider, and Silvan S. Tomkins. *Aspects of the Analysis of Family Structure.* Princeton, NJ: Princeton University Press.

"Tool Identifies Potential Buyers from Mailing List." 1985. *Computerworld* (July 22):39.

Tornatzky, L., J. Eveland, M. Boylan, W. Hertzner, E. Johnson, D. Roitman, and J. Schneider. 1983. *The Process of Technological Innovation: Reviewing the Literature.* Washington, DC: National Science Foundation, Productivity Improvement Research Section, Division of Industrial Science and Technological Innovation.

"Towards a New Information Order." 1982. Special issue of *NACLA (North American Congress on Latin America) Report on the Americas* 16,4(July/August).

"Toxic World." 1984. *Global Electronic News* 43(June):3.

"Tracking the Trucks." 1984. *Computerworld on Communications* 18,36A (September 5):55–58.

Tsipis, Kosta. 1983. *Arsenal: Understanding Weapons in the Nuclear Age.* New York: Simon and Schuster.

Tufte, Edward F. 1984. *The Visual Display of Quantitative Information.* Cheshire, CT: Graphics Press.

Tulin, Roger. 1984. *A Machinist's Semi-Automated Life.* San Pedro, CA: Singlejack Books.

Tuomenoksa, David Lee, and Howard Jay Siegel. 1985. "Task Scheduling on the PASM

Parallel Processing System," *IEEE Transactions on Software Engineering* SE–11,2 (February):145–57.

Turkle, Sherry. 1984. *The Second Self: Computers and the Human Spirit.* New York: Simon and Schuster.

————. 1983. "The Psychological Machine: Computers and the Culture of Self-Reflection," lecture at the New York Academy of Sciences Science Week Symposium (April 8).

Turn, Reid, ed. 1979. *Transborder Data Flows: Concerns in Privacy Protection and Free Flow of Information.* Washington, DC: American Federation of Information Processing Societies.

Turn, R., and A. E. Nimitz. 1975. "Computers and Strategic Advantage: I. Computer Technology in the United States and the Soviet Union." R-1642-PR (May). Santa Monica, CA: Rand.

Turner, Jon A. 1984. "Computer-Mediated Work: The Interplay Between Technology and Structured Jobs," *Communications of the ACM* 27,12 (December):1210–17.

Turner, Jonathan H., and Alexandra Maryanski. 1979. *Functionalism.* Reading, MA: Benjamin/Cummings.

Turner, Judith Axler. 1986. "Computers Are Said to be Little Used on Many of the World's Campuses," *The Chronicle of Higher Education* (June 4):31.

————. 1984a. "Computerized Data Base Services Bringing Era of 'Free' Library Service to End," *Chronicle of Higher Education* (September 19):23,26–27.

————. 1984b. "Dealing with the Computer-Publications Glut: Reading, Stacking, Throwing Away," *Chronicle of Higher Education* (October 10):25–27.

"Unemployment: The Failure of Private Enterprise." 1983. *Monthly Review* 35,2 (June):1.

UNESCO. 1980. "The New World Information and Communication Order," resolution 4/19 adopted by the twenty-first session of the UNESCO General Conference, Belgrade. Reprinted in *NACLA Report on the Americas* 16,4 (July/August):32.

Unger, Stephen H. 1982. "The Growing Threat of Government Secrecy," *Technology Review* (February/March):30–39.

Union of Concerned Scientists. 1984. *The Fallacy of Star Wars.* New York: Vintage.

"U.S. Army Adopts the Games." 1982. *Multinational Monitor* (December):7.

U.S. Congressional Office of Technology Assessment. 1985a. *Automation of America's Offices.* Washington, DC: U.S. Government Printing Office.

————. 1985b. *Federal Government Information Technology: Electronic Surveillance and Civil Liberties.* Washington, DC: U.S. Government Printing Office.

————. 1985c. *Reproductive Health Hazards in the Workplace.* Washington, DC: U.S. Government Printing Office.

U.S. Department of Labor, Bureau of Labor Statistics. 1984. "Our Changing Economy: A BLS Centennial Chartbook," Bulletin 2211. Washington, DC: U.S. Government Printing Office.

U.S. Privacy Protection Study Commission. 1977. *Personal Privacy in an Information Society.* Washington, DC: U.S. Government Printing Office.

U.S. Senate Committee on Governmental Affairs. 1980. *Structure of Corporate Concentration.* Washington, DC: U.S. Government Printing Office.

"U.S. To Study Pollution in High-Tech Area." 1983. *New York Times* (October 30):33.

Useem, Elizabeth L. 1986. *Low Tech Education in a High Tech World: Corporations and Classrooms in the New Information Society.* New York: Free Press.

Uttal, Bro. 1983. The Lab That Ran Away from Xerox, *Fortune* (September 5):97–102.

Van Duyn, Julia. 1985. *The Human Factor in Computer Crime.* Princeton, NJ: Petrocelli.

Van Gelder, Lindsay. 1984. "Lighting up Broadway," *Enter* (February):30–34.

Van Horn, Richard L. 1984. Quoted in " 'Psychological Access' to Computers," *Chronicle of Higher Education* (August 29):22.

VDT News: The VDT Health and Safety Report. Bimonthly. New York.

Veblen, Thorstein. 1969. *The Vested Interests and the Common Man.* New York: Capricorn.

————. 1934. *The Theory of the Leisure Class.* New York: Random House.

Vessey, Iris, and Ron Weber. 1984. "Research on Structured Programming: An Empiricist's Evaluation," *IEEE Transactions on Software Engineering* 10,4(July):397–407.

Vickers, Brian, ed. 1984. *Occult and Scientific Mentalities in the Renaissance.* New York: Cambridge University Press.

"Video Games Under Fire: Malaysia Bans Arcade Games." 1982. *Multinational Monitor* (December):6.

Vitalari, Nicholas P., Alladi Venkatesch, and Kjell Gronhaug. 1985. "Computing in the Home: Shifts in the Time Allocation Patterns of Households," *Communications of the ACM* 28,5(May):512–22.

Vogel, Ezra. 1985. Interview in the *Boston Globe Magazine* (December 1):2.

von Bertalanffy, Ludwig. 1968. *General Systems Theory.* New York: George Braziller.

Vonnegut, Kurt, Jr. 1952. *Player Piano.* New York: Dell.

Voy, Robert O. 1984. "Technology, Health, and Human Performance," *Technology Review* (August/September):29–37.

"Vt. Software Tapes Taxable." 1983. *Boston Globe* (August 16):58.

Vyssotsky, Victor A. 1980. "The Use of Computers for Business Functions," in Michael Dertouzos and Joel Moses, eds. *The Computer Age: A Twenty-Year View.* Cambridge, MA: MIT Press.

Wagreich, J. 1982. "Electronic Mail for the Hearing Impaired and Its Potential for Other Disabilities," *IEEE Transactions on Communications* COM-30,1(January):58–65.

Wallace, Jonathan D. 1984. "Import Ban of Micros Adding to Copyright Security," *Computerworld* (April 30):114.

Wallace, Michael. 1985. "Technological Change in Printing: Union Response in Three Countries," *Monthly Labor Review* (July):4–43.

Wallace, Walter, ed. 1969. *Sociological Theory.* Chicago: Aldine.

Wallach, Hans. 1985. "Perceiving a Stable Environment," *Scientific American* 252,5 (May):118–25.

Wallerstein, Immanuel. 1974. *The Modern World-System.* New York: Academic.

Ward, Bernie, and Thomas Maremaa. 1984. "The Computerizing of the Olympics," *Popular Computing* 3,10(August):96–109.

Warner, Edward. 1984a. "House Panel Recommends Killing Postal Service's Intelpost," *Computerworld* (April 23):6.

———. 1984b. "Office Politics Blocks OA Implementation," *Computerworld* (October 22):25.

———. 1984c. "Psychological Stumbling Block Mires Micro Revolution," *Computerworld* (October 15):22.

Warren, Samuel D., and Louis D. Brandeis. 1985. "The Right to Privacy," in Deborah G. Johnson and John W. Snapper, eds. *Ethical Issues in the Use of Computers.* Belmont, CA: Wadsworth.

Warrick, Patricia. 1980. *The Cybernetic Imagination in Science Fiction.* Cambridge, MA: MIT Press.

Wartel, Sidney J. 1985. "Federal Protection Act Benefits Designers of Chip Masks," *Computerworld* (February 11):82.

Wartella, Ellen, and D. Charles Whitney. 1983. *Mass Communication Yearbook, part 8: American Telecommunications Policy.* Beverly Hills, CA: Sage.

Washburn, Sherwood L. 1960. "Tools and Human Evolution," *Scientific American* 203,3 (September):3–15.

Waskell, Eva. 1986. "Computerized Voting—No Standards and a Lot of Questions," lecture to the Computer Professionals for Social Responsibility, (March 19). Cambridge, MA.

Watt, Dan. 1983a. "LOGO: What Makes It Exciting?" *Popular Computing* (August):106–13.

———. 1983b. "Teaching in the Computer Age: These Days It's a Struggle Just to Stay One Step Ahead of the Class," *Popular Computing* (August):65–67.

Weber, Max. 1978. *Economy and Society.* Berkeley: University of California Press.

———. 1958. *The Protestant Ethic and the Spirit of Capitalism.* New York: Scribner's.

Weizenbaum, Joseph. 1983a. "The Computer in Your Future," *New York Review of Books* (October 27):58–62.

———. 1983b. Lecture at Framingham State College (May 3).

———. 1976. *Computer Power and Human Reason: From Judgement to Calculation.* San Francisco: W. H. Freeman.

References

Wenger, Peter. 1984. "Capital-Intensive Software Technology," *IEEE Software* 1,3(July):7–43.

Werner, Carol M., and Lois Haggard. 1985. "Temporal Qualities of Interpersonal Relationships," in Mark L. Knapp and Gerald R. Miller, eds. *Handbook of Interpersonal Communication.* Beverly Hills, CA: Sage.

Wesson, Robert, Kenneth Solomon, Randall Steeb, Perry Thorndike, and Keith Wescourt. 1981. *Scenarios for Evolution of Air Traffic Control.* Santa Monica, CA: The Rand Corporation. Report number R–2698–FAA.

Westin, Alan. 1985. Lecture reported in *Computerworld* (November 18):137.

———. 1967. *Privacy and Freedom.* New York: Atheneum.

Westman, John. 1985. "Modern Dependency: A Crucial Case Study of Brazilian Government Policy in the Minicomputer Industry," *Studies in Comparative International Development* 20,2(Summer):25–47.

Westrum, Ron. 1985. "Blinded by the Light," *The Sciences* (May/June):48–52.

Wexler, Philip. 1983. *Critical Social Psychology.* Boston: Routledge and Kegan Paul.

Whalley, Peter. 1984. "Deskilling Engineers? The Labor Process, Labor Markets, and Labor Segmentation," *Social Problems* (December):117–32.

"When the TV Is on, Who's Watching?" 1982. *Newsweek* (October 18):108.

Whiteside, Thomas. 1978. *Computer Capers.* New York: New American Library.

Wicklein, John. 1981. *Electronic Nightmare: The Home Communications Set and Your Freedom.* Boston: Beacon Press.

Wiederhold, Gio. 1984. "Knowledge and Database Management," *IEEE Software* 1,1(January):63–73.

Wiener, Norbert. 1967. *The Human Use of Human Beings.* New York: Avon.

———. 1948. *Cybernetics: Or Control and Communication in the Animal and the Machine.* Cambridge, MA: MIT Press.

Wilder, Clinton. 1986. "Japanese Chipmakers Refute SIA Claims," *Asian Computerworld* (September 16):28.

Wilkins, Bryan. 1985a. "Export Rules Relaxed for Low End Only," *Computerworld* (January 14):89,97.

———. 1985b. "U.S. Negotiators Win Accord on Transborder Data Flow," *Computerworld* (April 8):15.

———. 1985c. "Will Export Review Work," *Computerworld* (January 28):75,89.

———. 1984a. "CIA Chief Says 300 Firms Diverting Military Tech to Eastern Bloc," *Computerworld* (June 25):38.

———. 1984b. "DOD Now Wants Export Controls over Software too," *Computerworld* (April 23):7.

———. 1984c. "OECD Subcommittee to Attempt Accord on Transborder Data Flow," *Computerworld* (June 25):38.

———. 1984d. "Systems Firm Caught up in High-Tech Transfer Furor," *Computerworld* (August 20):9.

Williams, Bernard O., and John L. Burch. 1985. *Human Foundations of Advanced Computing Technology: A Guide to the Select Literature.* Lawrence, KS: The Report Store.

Williams, Dennis A., and Robb A. Allan. 1982. "The Computerization of CMU," *Newsweek* (November 1):91.

Williams, Dennis A., with Vern E. Smith. 1982. "Making Mississippi Smarter," *Newsweek* (December 13):94.

Williams, Dennis A., with Jacob Young. 1983. "Oberlin Keeps the Faith," *Newsweek* (April 4):79.

Winchman, Brian A. 1984. "Is Ada Too Big? A Designer Answers the Critics," *Communications of the ACM* 27,2(February):98–103.

Winston, Patrick H. 1977. *Artificial Intelligence.* Reading, MA: Addison-Wesley.

Winston, Patrick H., and Karen A. Prendergast, eds. 1984. *The AI Business: The Commercial Uses of Artificial Intelligence.* Cambridge, MA: MIT Press.

Winther, Mark. 1984. "CATV: The Legal Implications," *Computerworld* 18,36A(September 5):41–46.

Wittfogel, Karl A. 1957. *Oriental Despotism*. New Haven, CT: Yale University Press.

Wolfgram, T. H. 1984. "Working at Home: The Growth of Cottage Industry," *Futurist* 18(June):31–34.

Wolleat, P., J. Pedro, A. Becker, and E. Fennema. 1980. "Sex Differences in High School Students," *Journal for Research in Mathematical Education*. 11,4(November):356–66.

Work in the 21st Century. 1983. Alexandria, VA: American Society of Personnel Administration.

Working Women. 1981. "Workers Face Office Automation," *Science for the People* (May–June):5–9.

World Health Organization. 1986. "Provisional Statements of the WHO Working Group on Occupational Health Aspects in the Use of Visual Display Units," *VDT News* (January/February):13.

Worthley, J. A. 1977. *Legislatures and Information Systems: Challenges and Responses in the States*. Albany, NY: Comparative Development Studies Center.

Wright, Erik Olin, and Joachim Singlemann. 1982. "Proletarianization in the Changing American Class Structure," *American Journal of Sociology* 88 Supplement:S176–S209.

Wright, Patricia. 1984. "Creating Good User Documentation," Ericsson Information Systems. *Proceedings of the World Conference on Ergonomics in Computer Systems*. Garden Grove, CA: Ericsson Communications. (September).

Wrigley, Julia. 1982. "The Division between Mental and Manual Labor: Artisan Education in Science in Nineteenth-Century Britain," in Michael Burawoy and Theda Skocpol, eds., *Marxist Perspectives*. Supplement to the *American Journal of Sociology*, vol. 88. Chicago: University of Chicago Press:S31–S51.

Wu, Meng-Lih, and Tai-Yang Hwang. 1984. "Access Control with a Single-Key Lock," *IEEE Transactions on Software Engineering* (May):185–90.

Xerox Corporation. 1984. "The Myth of the Paperless Office," *High Technology* (May):43.

Yankelovich, Nicole, Norman Meyrowitz, and Andries van Dam. 1985. "Reading and Writing the Electronic Book," *IEEE Computer* (October):15–30.

Yarbrough, J. Paul. 1984. "The Diffusion of Computers Among Farmers: A Case Study in the Expansion of Information Inequities," American Association for the Advancement of Science. New York: (May).

Zaki, Ahmed S. 1983. "Regulation of Electronics Fund Transfer: Impact and Legal Issues," *Communications of the ACM* 26,3(February):112–18.

Zelby, Leon W. 1983. Letter in reply to Bonham, 1983. *Chronicle of Higher Education* (ca March 9):34.

Zimmerman, Don, and Candace West. 1975. "Sex Roles, Interruptions, and Silences in Conversation," in Barrie Thorne and Nancy Henley, eds. *Language and Sex: Difference and Dominance*. Rowley, MA: Newbury House Publishers.

Zoler, Mitchel L. 1983. "The Bionic Ear," *Boston Globe* (October 17):44.

Zue, Victor. 1985. "His Master's (Digital) Voice," *Time* (April 1):83.

Zurcher, Louis A. 1977. *The Mutable Self: A Self-Concept for Social Change*. Beverly Hills, CA: Sage.

GLOSSARY

ABM   AntiBallistic Missile

Ada   a fifth-generation computer language named for Lady Ada Lovelace, who first proposed the idea of software

adaptive capacity   the ability of a system to deal with change by modifying its structure and function

AI   Artificial Intelligence

algorithm   a mathematical formula specifying the solution to a problem; a set of instructions for solving a problem using a computer program

alienation   Marx's theory that workers in capitalist society are separated from ownership and control over their work, the commodities they produce, one another, and their own creative capabilities

analog computer   a computer that processes continuous signals rather than binary data

analysis   the interpretation of systematic observations of natural or social phenomena

analytical engine   Charles Babbage's 1832 design for the first modern digital computer

anomie   Durkheim's concept of when people have no norms to govern their behavior, indicating a failure of social solidarity and control

application   the system, such as banking or medical diagnosis, for which a computer program is written

application generators   computer programs that accept high-level specifications as input and produce programs suited to a particular application as output

architecture   *see* **data base architecture**

artificial intelligence   computer systems capable of making decisions and solving problems based on rules that do not guarantee a solution and that can be modified through experience

ASCII   American Standard Code for Information Interchange; a standard seven-bit code (usually transmitted with an eighth-parity bit)

assemblers   software that translates a low-level computer language program into one readable by a machine

authorized release of weapons   an attack made according to military rules of authority

automatic teller machine   computer terminal used to process customer bank transactions automatically

automation replacing human labor with machines

bandwidth *see* **frequency band**

BASIC Beginner's All-purpose Symbolic Instruction Code; a common user-friendly computer language

batch run the noninteractive processing of a single computer program

binary number system the base two number system, consisting of the digits 0 and 1

bit a 1 or a 0 in the binary number system; a binary digit; the smallest unit of data in a computer system

BMD Ballistic Missile Defense technologies

broadcasting transmitting information through the air in the form of electromagnetic waves

bug an error caused by a hardware or software malfunction

bulletin board a data base that can be accessed and updated by many users

cable a collection of conductors insulated from one another and enclosed in a single sheath

cable television television signal sent through a cable instead of being broadcast

CAD Computer-Aided Design

catastrophic change change in which the structure and function of a system are destroyed

cathode ray tube a vacuum tube similar to that found in a television set

central processing unit the main part of a computer, which controls all of its functions

channel a specific frequency band or particular path used in transmitting information

character a letter, number, or special symbol that can be manipulated by a computer

character font a complete set of letters, numbers, and special symbols of a particular size and style

chip an integrated circuit on a small wafer usually made of silicon

circuit a system through which electricity can flow

class *see* **social class**

COBOL Common Business Oriented Language; the earliest high-level language still widely used in business applications

code the meaning assigned to characters; to assign characters to represent larger items of data; to write a computer program; lines in a written computer program; the sequence of bits representing numbers, letters, and special symbols; a set of ethical rules

coercive power the use of force or the threat of force

cognitive factors how people perceive, interpret, and learn

command language a set of words (and rules for using them) to issue instructions (commands) to a computer system

commodity product made for profit (rather than for social reasons) using rationally organized wage labor

common carrier a communications medium such as mail, telephone, and telegraph that was organized as a regulated monopoly and required to carry messages for everyone

communications network a network used for telecommunications

community a group with a common territory, shared interests, communications, and a sense of belonging to one another

community interface an electronic network that connects members of a community to each other; a computer-based communication system that supports a geographically dispersed community

compatibility the ability of two systems to be joined by a common interface, permitting the exchange of information or parts; *see* **interchangeable parts**

compilers software that translates a high-level computer language program into one readable by a machine

compulsive programmer a person who is obsessed with the process of programming a computer and motivated by a desire to master the machine; *see* **hacker**

computer a general-purpose tool for communication and control as well as computation

computer-aided design the use of computer systems in the work of designing

computer-based depending on computer programs and data

computer code *see* **code, machine-readable code,** and **object code**

computer competency understanding how computers work, what to use them for, and what their consequences are—as well as the technique for using them

computer crime the illegal use of a computer to acquire information, money, or other resources

computer graphics the production of visual images using computers

computer-imaging *see* **computer graphics**

computer language a set of pre-defined words and the rules for using them to write computer programs

computer literacy knowing the technique for using a computer

computer memory *see* **memory**

computer model a model implemented as a computer program

computer networks *see* **networks**

computer phobia the irrational fear of using a computer; often misused to describe people reluctant to use computers for other reasons

computer revolution a rapid structural change in society brought about through the use of computers and communications technologies

computer tape *see* **tape**

conductor a material through which electricity will flow easily

conflict theory any theory that views the exercise of economic or coercive power as the major cause of social change

control structures the part of structured programs that determines how communication will take place among different parts of the program and how functions will be performed

copyright legal protection for the expression of an idea

corporate crime crime committed by companies for profit

corporate culture the shared norms and values of a particular company

crime an offense that requires punishment under criminal law

CRT Cathode Ray Tube

cryptography the making of secret codes

cultural imperialism the imposition of a foreign culture on people through the use of coercive or economic power

cultural values *see* **values**

culture the entire way of life shared by a people, including information, material objects, and behaviors

cybernetic impact the way the informational content of culture affects the physical world

cybernetics the study of communication and control in biological organisms and machines

data specific numerical or other symbolic representations of facts

data base a collection of data organized so that items can be stored into it or retrieved from it

data base architecture the design of data structures

data base capacity the amount of data that can be stored in a data base

data base inquiries commands to cause a computer to retrieve data or display relationships among data

data entry putting data into a medium that can be input to a computer, such as cards, magnetic tape, or directly from a keyboard or optical character reader

data processing moving or making calculations from data without creating any new information

data retrieval system system to get data out of a computer storage medium

data structures the relationships among data elements; the information available from a set of data

debugging finding and correcting the bugs in a computer program or hardware system

declining middle theoretical argument that more jobs are being created at the top and at the bottom of the stratification system, resulting in a shrinking middle class

demonstration effect in the diffusion model of technological change, the assumption that those seeing a successful demonstration of new technology will consider adopting it

deskilling reducing the level of intelligence, creativity, and skill required to perform a task

devaluation of mental labor theoretical argument that the kinds of mental work computers can do will decline as a source of status, income, and satisfaction

diffusion model of technological change the theory that technology spreads from innovators to adopters

digit the numerals 0–9 in the decimal number system; 0 and 1 in the binary number system; 0–F in the hexadecimal number system

digital computer a computer that processes digits

disk a computer storage medium similar in shape and recording technique to a phonograph record

disk file a collection of related data treated as a single unit and stored magnetically or optically on a round, flat device

diskette *see* **floppy diskette**

display the visual output of a computer, usually on a television-like screen

division of labor the structural differentiation of work into specialized jobs

documentation written material explaining how to use a computer system and how it works

downward social mobility falling in social status in the course of one's life

dynamic stability change in which the structure and function of a system are not altered

economic power power based on ownership or control of resources, property, and other socially valued goods

efficiency producing the maximum amount of one quantity using a fixed amount of another

elective affinity Weber's term for two interrelated variables for which we cannot specify which is the cause and which is the effect

electromagnetic field a region of space affected by electromagnetic radiation

electromagnetic radiation a form of propagated energy, arising from electric charges in motion, that produces a wavelike variation in electric and magnetic fields in space

electronic cottage the concept that social life and work will be reintegrated in the home

electronic funds transfer financial transactions via computer network

electronic mail written messages sent and received via computer network

electronic sweatshop an electronic cottage with low-wage piecework

electronic trail the record of computer transactions that takes the place of paper records used by auditors and accountants

electronics the study, design, and production of devices based on the flow of electricity through vacuum, gas, or semiconductors

electrostatic produced by electrically charged particles that are not accelerating

embedded systems computer systems integrated into an industrial process or military weapons system

emissions the output of electromagnetic radiation

empirical generalizations general statements about the world arrived at by inductive reasoning from systematic observations

entrainment a process in which interacting people adopt the same rhythm

entropy a measure of the degree of

disorder in a system; its central characteristic is to increase; systems using information and energy inputs can counteract this tendency

ergonomics   the study of the human/technology interface; human factors research

error message   the message a computer displays when something went wrong

expert system   an artificial intelligence designed to function as a human expert for some specific kind of problem solving

external costs   the cost of producing something that is paid by society rather than by the producer

facsimile transmission   sending an image over a communications line, which is then reproduced on paper

feedback   information about the outcome of an action used to modify that action

fifth generation   computers with VLSI microprocessors, parallel processing, natural language interfaces, and artificial intelligence capabilities; in the design stage at present

file   a collection of logically organized lines of data or a program

firmware   a combination of hardware and software in which programs are built into the hardware

first generation   computers built with vacuum tubes

five-bit code   the code used in terminals for the deaf; each character is represented by a sequence of five 1's and 0's

floppy diskette   a small, flexible disk used in personal computers (usually 5¼ or 8 inches in diameter)

font   *see* **character font**

FORTRAN   **FOR**mula **TRAN**slator; one of the oldest high-level languages; designed for problems involving mathematical formulas

fourth generation   computers built with semiconductor chips and very large-scale integrated circuits

frequency and wavelength   at a beach, frequency is how often waves come in; wavelength is the distance between the crest of one wave and the crest of the next; in electromagnetic radiation, the greater the frequency, the shorter the wavelength

frequency band   a specific range of frequencies allocated to some particular use

function   what a system does

functionalism   a paradigm for society that emphasizes its systems characteristics and focuses on stability and normative social controls

gender   the social roles associated with being biologically male or female; masculine or feminine

global factory   a production process with parts scattered around the world but centrally controlled

graphics   *see* **computer graphics**

hacker   a highly skilled person who is fascinated by the process of computer programming and motivated by the belief that system resources ought to be available to anyone who can find clever ways to acquire, use, and redistribute them; *see* **compulsive programmer** and **computer crime**

hard copy computer output on paper

hard disk a disk made of rigid material coated by magnetic material

hardware the physical part of a computer system

heuristic a problem-solving method that uses trial and error and cannot guarantee a solution; see **algorithm**

high-level language a computer language with words that are in a natural language, like English, rather than in a special code

high-tech a popular term for industries and occupations involving computers and other new technologies

higher-level information relationships among items of information forming more abstract concepts

human capital the concept that employee knowledge and skill is a valuable resource for organizations and societies

hypotheses well-specified predictive statements about the world, arrived at by deduction from theory and tested with systematic empirical observations

ideal type Weber's concept that the general features of a social process or structure can be used as a model when analyzing variation in real cases; for example, the ideal type corporation is rationally organized for the purposes of making a profit, so actual companies can be compared in terms of their organizational effectiveness and profitability

ideology paradigms, social facts, or other concepts that explain and justify relationships of status, property, and power; believed to be true with no scientific testing of their validity

IEEE Institute of Electrical and Electronics Engineers

induction reasoning from specific cases to a general principle; discovering a general principle by systematically observing events; *see* **pattern recognition**

industry a work role classified according to the product or service supplied by the employer

information relationships among facts; a useful selection and organization of data

information processing creating new relationships among data items; moving information from one medium to another or from place to place

information society Daniel Bell's term describing society after the computer revolution

input what goes into a system

input/output characteristics the way a system exchanges information, energy, and material with its environment

insulator a material that resists the flow of electricity

integrated circuit an electronic circuit manufactured in a single operation

intellectual labor *see* **mental labor**

interactive having a conversation-like interface

interchangeable parts data, software, or hardware produced by one computer system that can be used by another; in manufacturing, standard components

interface the shared boundary between two systems

internalization during socialization, the process of making the norms, values, and roles that we have learned into part of our own personalities

interpreters programs that translate source code and act on it one line at a time

ionizing radiation high-frequency radiation that produces electrically charged ions

ions atoms, molecules, or groups of atoms and molecules that have a positive or negative electrical charge

keyboard typewriter-like keys connected to a computer terminal

keypunch machine a device to put the holes in cards used as computer input

keypunch verifier a person who repunches data to check its accuracy

keystrokes the individual actions of pressing a key on a keyboard

keyword dictionary a data base structured so that information is associated with predefined words

knowledge an evaluation and understanding of information in terms of human purposes

knowledge elite Daniel Bell's term for an elite whose status is based on their knowledge

knowledge engineering the construction of software and data bases containing the information of human experts and the procedures they use in problem solving

labor force all of the people in a society who engage in paid economic activity

laser a device that produces a narrow beam of radiation

legitimate believed to be legal or right

leisure activity with a minimum of social or economic restraint; activity done for its own sake; freely chosen activity without time constraints

liability insurance insurance against the possibility that a product or service will cause harm to clients, customers, or the community

life chances Weber's term for an individual's class position based on property, wealth, and occupational opportunities

LISP LISt Processing; a high-level computer language used in artificial intelligence

listing a hard-copy printout of a computer program

LOGO a conversational language designed to introduce beginners to high-level, symbol-manipulating languages

Luddite member of an early industrial revolution protest movement that destroyed the machinery putting laborers out of work; a term now applied to someone who opposes industrial automation

machine instructions codes (usually composed of 1's and 0's) that cause a computer to perform some operation, such as adding two numbers

machine-readable code code in the binary number system that can be used by a computer

macro large-scale

macroergonomics the study of the technology/society interface; the study of the consequences of technology for social relationships, processes, and institutions

macrotheory theory about large-scale social institutions and processes, often stressing economic or coercive power as sources of change

mainframe a large computer (as distinguished from a minicomputer or microcomputer)

manual labor working with one's hands

means of production raw materials, capital, and technology needed in order to produce goods

mechanical solidarity the social bonding among members of pre-industrial society, where all share the same activities

media the physical means for expressing and transmitting information; for example, paper, broadcasting, film, or oil paint on canvas

memory area in a computer where data can be stored and retrieved

mental labor working with one's mind

micro small scale; a microcomputer; one millionth

microchip a small computer chip

microcomputer *see* **personal computer**

microelectronics extremely small electronic circuits, such as computer chips

microergonomics the small-scale, immediate effects of the human/technology interface

microprocessor a chip containing

the entire central processing unit of a personal computer

microtheory theory about small group interactions, structures, and processes, often stressing normative power as a mechanism of change

microwave electromagnetic waves with wavelengths between 3 millimeters and 1.3 meters

microwave relay a device to receive and retransmit a microwave signal

minicomputer an intermediate-sized computer

minis *see* **minicomputer**

MTV Music TeleVision; a station broadcasting video versions of popular music

multifactor productivity a measure of productivity combining output per worker and output per unit of capital

multimedia interfaces interfaces employing more than one information transmission media; for example, print and sound

multinational corporation a corporation with branches in many countries; *see* **global factory**

myth a symbolic explanation of the universe in the form of a story

natural language interface interface in which communication between user and computer is in a human language, such as English

network a system consisting of one or more computers and interconnected terminals and input/output devices

noise unwanted interference with a signal

non-ionizing radiation radiation in

the lower frequencies that does not produce electrically charged atoms

normative power the ability to influence another's behavior based on status, respect, and shared norms

norms the unwritten rules for how to behave in particular situations

object code binary code produced by translating a high-level computer language into a form readable by a machine

occupation a work role classified according to the task that the person performs

oceanic self concept of self as being part of or having power over the whole universe

octal number system the base 8 number system consisting of the digits 0 through 7

operationalize to specify how we will go about measuring and systematically observing phenomena

optical character reader a computer input device that visually identifies characters or coded symbols

optical disk a disk made of heat-sensitive material on which data is recorded using a laser

organic solidarity the social bonding among members of industrial society, where each is dependent on the specialized roles of others

organization a group of individuals or roles joined together to pursue a common goal in a formally structured way

organizational interface the parts of an organization's computer system that connect human users to each other

output what comes out of a system

paradigm a general model of the way the world works; differs from a theory in that it is less well formulated and is often thought not to require testing; differs from ideology in that it is not used to justify existing political and economic arrangements

parallel processing a computer actually performing multiple tasks at the same time

particularistic social relationship one in which people are treated differently depending on their sex, race, ethnicity, or other characteristics given at birth

password a sequence of characters that must be known and used in order to access a computer system or data base

patches new lines of computer code added to an existing program to fix a bug

patent legal protection for hardware and industrial processes

pattern recognition the inductive process by which a computer discovers a common characteristic in the observed cases

PC personal computer; a microcomputer used by a single person

peripheral equipment devices like printers and disks that are operated by a computer for input, output, and storage

personal computer a small computer used by one person

physical self self-concept based on biological experience

piecework getting paid by the num

ber of products made rather than by the hour or month

piracy illegal copying of computer software or hardware

pluralism the widespread distribution of political power among competing interest groups

political institutions institutions like town meetings, congresses, and political parties that make and enforce collective decisions

political socialization learning the process of group decision-making and the role of citizen

politics the process by which human groups arrive at collective decisions and go about implementing them

predictive models models that predict what will actually happen

printout *see* **hard copy**

productivity output per worker per hour

product liability law the area of civil law establishing penalties for those whose products do harm

program a logically organized set of instructions in a computer language designed so that the computer will perform the desired result; to write a program

program trading buying and selling stocks using expert systems

projective models models that tell us what would happen under a variety of assumed conditions

rationalization the process of making something logically organized for the purpose of accomplishing a goal according to universalistic rules

read-only data that can be read but not modified or erased

real-time the time as measured by an ordinary clock; computer systems that work rapidly enough to interact with or control events as they happen

real wages a measure of wages over time that controls for inflation

record matching combining information about individuals from several different data bases to produce a more comprehensive record of their characteristics and activities

reflexive self self-concept based upon reflection on one's thoughts and experiences

reflexive user a person who develops habits of computer use without losing the ability to think about what it means

reification treating an abstract concept or social relationship as if it were an object

relational data base a data base structured so that the user does not have to keep track of how data is stored and can retrieve relationships among data

relationship the connection between components in a system; repeated social interaction between two individuals

repression Freud's theory of the social subjugation of immediate gratification for the sake of socially useful goals

resolution the distinction between a displayed character and its background

response time the time it takes a computer or a person to respond to a message

revolutionary change change in

which the existing structure and function of a system are replaced

rituals group activities in which people act out symbolic meanings

robotics a field of artificial intelligence dealing with the design and production of robots

Route 128 a region around Boston, Massachusetts, where "high-tech" industry has grown rapidly

routinization making something regular, repetitive, and routine

sacred inspiring reverence

scientific management the application of scientific principles to the subject of the division of labor in order to make a profit; *see* **Taylorism**

scrolling the movement of a displayed page of computer output up or down the screen

SDI Strategic Defense Initiative; Reagan administration plan to use computer technology for defense against nuclear missiles

second generation computers built with transistors

secular part of the ordinary world; not religious

self-actualization behaving in ways that contribute to self-esteem; the ability to act in ways that reinforce one's self-concept

self-esteem a feeling of satisfaction or pride

semiconductor a material through which electricity flows only moderately well; the basis of most microelectronics devices

sensors instruments that can detect radiation or signals from objects at a distance

sex role socialization the process of learning masculine and feminine gender roles

sex role stereotype a rigid mental concept that men and women always behave in ideally masculine and feminine ways

sexual division of labor assigning occupational roles according to sex

shield material arranged to block the emission of electromagnetic radiation

signal the information-bearing part of a transmission

silicon a semiconductor material; the raw material of the microelectronics industry

Silicon Valley a region in Santa Clara County, California, where the microelectronics and computer industries are highly developed

simulation a computer program that simulates some process or system; in the ballistic missile defense system, the art of making a decoy look like a real target

social class group of people with the same economic position in society; for Weber, those having the same life chances; for Durkheim, those with the same position in the division of labor; for Marx, those with the same relationship to the means of production

social control the use of normative, economic, or coercive power to enforce the rules of social behavior

social fact a cultural belief with consequences for human behavior

social institutions fairly durable

arrangements of interrelated social roles

social integration   a type of structural change in which new relationships are created among roles, linking them more closely to each other

social interaction   a situation in which two or more people communicate and modify each other's behavior; the basic process in a social system that establishes social relationships

social interface   interface through which humans communicate with one another

social mobility   the process by which people rise or fall from the status they receive at birth

social network   an interrelated set of individuals who communicate regularly with one another

social roles   positions in society, along with their associated norms of expected behavior

social self   self-concept defined in terms of roles and relationships

social structure   relatively stable patterns of social interaction; the relationships, roles, groups, and institutions of society

socialization   the process that teaches people their roles, norms, values, and statuses, producing a new generation of social components

software   the information part of computer systems, especially computer programs

software tools   programs used to produce other software

sort   to arrange in sequence, such as alphabetically or chronologically

source code   computer programs written in a computer language that a programmer can read

Star Wars   popular name for the Strategic Defense Initiative; a movie with elaborate computerized special effects

state   *in society*, territorially based institution with a monopoly on the legitimate use of force; *of a system*, one particular arrangement of components, with each component in a well-defined condition, out of all the possible ways they could be arranged

status   the rank of an individual or a social role in society; one's evaluation by others

store   to put data into a computer's memory, disks, tape, or other physical devices designed to record data

Strategic Computing Initiative   the software part of the strategic defense initiative

stratification   the institution based on inheritance of unequally distributed property, power, and status

structural change   when new roles are being added to the social system, when existing roles are being redefined, or when the relationships among roles are changing

structural differentiation   a type of structural change in which two or more new specialized roles are replacing a single old one

structure   the relationships among components in a system; *see* **data structures** and **social structure**

structured programming   a rational organization of computer programs into logical units with standard interconnections among them

symbols meaningful representations of objects or abstract concepts

system a model of specific components connected by well-defined relationships, having a boundary and input/output characteristics

tape magnetic recording tape used for data storage and retrieval; formerly, paper tape used for computer input and output

Taylorism Frederick Taylor's concept that the manual laborer is only a component in the production process

technical support an occupational role providing technical information and assistance to customers or clients

technique a method for performing a task; does not necessarily require any understanding of what is being accomplished

telecommunications the transmission of data over telephone lines to and from remote locations

telecommuter a person who goes to work via computer network without leaving home

telecommuting working via telecommunications at a remote location

teleconferencing holding a conference via computer network

telemarketing selling products via telecommunications

terminal a device, usually with keyboard input and video display output, connected to a remote computer

theories logically interconnected statements about the world that describe, explain, and predict the occurrence of physical and social phenomena

third generation computers built with integrated circuits

time-sharing a computer switching rapidly enough among several users to give the impression that each is using the machine at the same time

tool an object or agent through which human activity is directed toward some goal

tort a civil wrong requiring compensation for damages according to civil law

track part of a disk similar to one band on a long-playing phonograph record

trade secret information protected by law so long as it is not disclosed

tragedy of the common the abuse of collective resources by individuals acting in their own self-interest

training simulator computer system that imitates a working environment for the purposes of teaching, for example, how to fly an airplane or operate a weapons system

transistor an early semiconductor electronic device

transmission transferring data, information, or electromagnetic pulses from one point to another, as in broadcasting or over phone lines

transmission line quality the capacity of a wire or cable to transmit clear, undistorted signals

universalistic social relationship one in which the same norms apply to everyone, regardless of race, ethnicity, sex, or other characteristics acquired at birth

upward social mobility rising in social status in the course of one's life

user   the person who uses a computer system

user friendly   an interface that is easy to understand and use; by implication, one that meets the needs of the human user

vacuum tube   an electronic device using a hollow glass tube

validity   the degree to which data correspond to the reality they represent

values   shared cultural concepts of what is desirable, good, or obligatory

VDT   video display terminal; a computer output device resembling a television screen

video display terminal   a terminal whose output is on a television-like screen

Videotex   a multimedia interface offering graphics and text

VLSI   Very Large Scale Integrated circuits

voice-operated computers   computer systems that can accept spoken input from people

voice recognition   a field of artificial intelligence dealing with computer systems that can accept voice input and identify individual speakers

voice synthesizer   computer system to produce voice output

wavelength   *see* **frequency**

white-collar crime   crime commited by a professional individual in the course of his or her occupation

wireless transmission   an early term for broadcast signals

word processor   a computer system designed to be used for the production of written documents; also used to mean the person who operates such a system

world-system   economically and politically integrated social system spanning the globe

work   activity constrained by the economic power of employers and the worker's sense of obligation to meet social expectations; activity directed toward a goal rather than done for its own sake; necessary but undesirable activity

work space   geographically scattered work organized and integrated by computer technology

workstation   where a person works at a small computer or terminal

INDEX

3.25
3.65
3.95